Author's Note

Everything in this book is true and documented. Some conversations have been re-created from memory. Certain names have been changed.

STORMS

My Life with Lindsey Buckingham and Fleetwood Mac

Carol Ann Harris

CHICAGO REVIEW PRESS

An A Cappella Book

Library of Congress Cataloging-in-Publication Data
Harris, Carol Ann.
  Storms : my life with Lindsey Buckingham and Fleetwood Mac / Carol Ann
Harris. — 1st ed.
     p. cm.
  ISBN-13: 978-1-55652-660-2
  ISBN-10: 1-55652-660-1
  1. Buckingham, Lindsey. 2. Rock musicians—Biography. 3. Harris, Carol
Ann. 4. Fleetwood Mac (Musical group) I. Title.

  ML419.B84H37 2007
  782.42166092'2—dc22
  [B]

                              2006100149

Cover and interior design: Emily Brackett / Visible Logic
Cover images: Bettmann/CORBIS (band); MedioImages/Getty (clouds)
All photos courtesy of the collection of Carol Ann Harris unless otherwise
noted.

Published by Chicago Review Press, Incorporated
814 North Franklin Street
Chicago, Illinois 60610
ISBN 978-1-55652-790-6
Printed in the United States of America
10 9 8 7 6 5

This book is dedicated to the memory of my parents, Ruth and Tom Harris. I miss you more than words can say.

A special recognition to my husband, Swiss rock drummer Martin Ehrsam, for his endless patience, love, guidance, and support that has never wavered from the moment we met . . . thank you for not only believing in me, but giving me the courage to follow my dreams.

Acknowledgments

I would like to thank Yuval Taylor and Chicago Review Press for their support, encouragement, and hard work on my book. Special thanks to Michelle Schoob for her editing input. I gratefully acknowledge the dedication and friendship of my agent B. J. Robbins. Thanks again to one of the best photographers on the planet, Ed Roach, for the generous use of his fabulous photographs in this book. And many thanks to my friend, the brilliant Charles Bush, for his amazing photographs.

I also want to acknowledge and give my loving and heartfelt thanks to the people who offered me their love, friendship, and shoulders to lean upon during the years when I needed it the most: John Courage, Sara Fleetwood, Julie McVie, Bjorn Sailor, Sheri Morgan, Bruce Derr, Lori Lazenby, Garry B., and my six sisters, Margaret, Tommie, Patsy, Sue, Dana, and Jeannie. To Dennis Wilson, thanks for all the laughter and the memories. I will never forget you.

Last but not least, I'd like to give a special thank you to my extended family in Switzerland who are too numerous to name. A special, special thanks to Erika and Heinz Ehrsam, Roland and Janet Leibundgut, Urs and Adrian Buser, Andy and Claudia Strub, Antonia and Markus Stauffenegger, and Rolf Wirz. And to wonderful Salva Di Gregorio—I love you, and many thanks for letting me use your laptop computer during my many visits to my home away from home! I love you all.

CONTENTS

INTRODUCTION

"Do you think we're gonna make it?" Lindsey kept asking me, with all the insecurity and persistence of a little boy.

Lindsey wasn't asking about our relationship because—with the naive optimism of youth—we both *knew* that it could only blossom, and that we would be together forever. No—he was asking about the band.

If the new album did well, the band could stay together, and perhaps survive another tour—feuding, angry, but solvent. Christine, John, and Mick could get their green cards, which was important if the band, in whatever form, wanted to stay in the United States.

So, we just hung around Producer's Workshop, where I worked as studio manager, dodging the rain between the dirty concrete buildings that were Studio A and Studio B, drinking machine coffee and vodka, smoking anything that came to hand, listening to the constant dripping from the leaky roof . . . and hoping. Sometimes, someone would sing Stevie's words, "Thunder only happens when it's raining," and we'd all burst into frantic laughter, verging on tearful hysteria.

It rained all winter. In 1977 Los Angeles had the coldest, stormiest winter in living memory. As we drove down Hollywood Boulevard, windshield wipers playing backup to Lindsey's songs, just starting to break on every radio station, we'd see the Warner Bros. vans surfing through drowned streets with new deliveries to the record stores. People paddled from the stores, bent double, protecting their album from the downpour, jumping puddles in the car lots, driving home to shelter, to listen. Was it *his* album, *Rumours*? We wondered every time.

The eventual success of *Rumours* far surpassed our wildest hopes. Within twelve months, that album would sell more than any Beatles album has ever sold. And if the Beatles had been "phenomenal," what word was unique enough to encompass this Fleetwood Mac shockwave? In the first month after release, a million copies were sold—as good as it gets for the lifetime of most record albums. Selling a million—"going platinum"—

that's the aim of every good rock band, but this album did it even *before* its official release date. *Rumours* reached number one on the charts in four weeks, and stayed there unchallenged for thirty-one weeks, longer than any album since *West Side Story* back in the early 1960s. Today, almost thirty years later, it remains in the top five rock albums of all time, ahead of such classics as *Hotel California, Born in the U.S.A.,* and *Bat out of Hell.* After thirty million sales, Warner Bros. is still counting.

Recording the album in the first place had been an act of faith and desire to hold on to a winning formula. The *Fleetwood Mac* album, with the new lineup that included Lindsey Buckingham and Stevie Nicks, had produced three top-ten hits and sold an impressive but hardly legendary four million copies. Mick Fleetwood, perpetually on the brink of bankruptcy, desperately needed another hit.

But the band was falling apart. As the music gossip columns announced, John and Christine McVie's seven-year marriage had ended, and the Cathy and Heathcliff of the band—wispy, otherworldly Stevie Nicks and enigmatic, gifted Lindsey Buckingham—had parted with extreme prejudice. Mick Fleetwood had chased after the wife he'd divorced and had remarried her, but the graft hadn't taken. I'd read the stories myself and saw, when I met the band, that they were painfully true: Fleetwood Mac was a band at war with itself.

I came in as the battle raged, and stayed at the front line for eight years, collecting my own scars along the way. I met Lindsey—who, with Richard Dashut, the sound engineer, was putting the finishing touches to the final mix at Producer's Workshop—and tried to resist the lightning romance that drew us together and brought me into the Fleetwood Mac inner circle. I just wanted to build my career as a sound engineer, not fall in love and enter the fray.

In all the years that I lived with Fleetwood Mac, I saw exactly how musical genius works its magic, and how the music industry claims its dues from monsters or heroes: it really doesn't matter to the money men which you are. I was access-all-areas, public and private, privy to the infighting. Like the others, I was shielded from reality. But unlike the other insiders, I recorded what I saw and felt—secretly, on tape—as a sort of diary that helped me think things through. But these tapes came close to destroying Fleetwood Mac, and they almost destroyed me, too.

INTRODUCTION

It's quite a story. Back in 1976, facing the disintegration of his brain-child band, Mick Fleetwood had an idea. "Hey guys, why don't we chill out here and do some *transcending* [his favorite word] and just write music about all this hassle?" It was the 1970s equivalent of that old Hollywood chestnut "Let's do the show right here!" Using personal heartbreak as the core of their album caught the mood of the moment—our backs are to the wall, so let's use it to our advantage and make it through, slugging it out, taking it on the chin.

Lindsey took to Mick's songs-as-therapy idea like a piranha to blood, channeling his anger at his ex-lover, Stevie, into "Go Your Own Way": "Packing up, shacking up, is all you wanna do!" he wrote. She never forgave him for making her sing, at every gig, the lyrics that he'd dismissed her with. Her "Dreams" and "I Don't Want to Know" had been so much kinder about him, just leaving him with the hope that rain would wash him clean. And Christine poured her emotions into poignant and upbeat songs about hope and love that bore the message "Don't stop thinking about tomorrow, 'cause yesterday's gone."

But the song that captures the spirit of Fleetwood Mac in those endless rainy days before we all started thinking too hopefully about tomorrow was "The Chain," the only composition by all five band members. The magical creed of our binding organization and blood brotherhood was just this—"Never break the chain."

That song was an incantation. All along the years, if tempers reached flash point during rehearsals, Mick would start to beat insistently and rhythmically on the bass drum, Lindsey would riff, and the band would move as one toward the mikes:

> And if you don't love me now
> You will never love me again
> I can still hear you saying
> You would never break the chain

Everyone in the drafty rehearsal hall would be chilled into silence, even Stevie's constantly giggling band of girl fans. And after the last shudder had died away, someone would ask, as the band members gave each other knowing smiles and got back on course, "What was that all about?"

I'd shrug and say, "It's our anthem."

The truth was that "The Chain" was really our alma mater song. Mick had been educated at a British boarding school. He left at fifteen to join a band, but he was eternally the boy from that exclusive, privileged-yet-deprived background, from a school with high-arched Victorian Gothic stained glass windows, stories of heroism, sadistic beatings, incomprehensible traditions, loneliness, and banding together against the odds. His plea to us to "hang on in there" came from the depths of his bitterest memories, which he shared with John Courage, who was, as he told us, one of the Courage brewing family in the United Kingdom. J.C.'s family, like the American Vanderbilts, were business aristocrats. It meant little to the U.S. contingent but a great deal to Mick, and to John and Christine, who hadn't shared the education but appreciated it. The four of them understood the unwritten rules of class and hierarchy and took it upon themselves sometimes to explain them to those of us from the U.S.

John McVie was the straight-faced, badly dressed joker, with a brilliantly dry wit, never sober, the big, crazy brother you never had, while Christine could out-drink any man but had never learned to do girly things or dress up like a homecoming queen. Once, driving to a band photo shoot with Richard Avedon, one of the world's most famous photographers, she was pulled over by the NYPD, who suspected they'd seen her snorting coke as she drove. Fortunately she'd snorted the entire stash, so there was no proof. But to her humiliation and fury she'd been strip-searched while wearing the large graying pair of knickers we all keep in the bottom of our lingerie drawer. "I was saving my new pink silk ones for the shoot!" she screamed at us all, still raging, when she arrived. "I was wearing my usuals!"

"Oh my God, Chris, not the cotton English granny knickers?" Stevie gasped. Big knickers weren't Stevie's style. From a wealthy family, she'd grown up in silk.

Christine nodded and burst into tears.

John Courage leapt to his feet, shaking his fist. "I'll have their badges!" he promised.

Christine was a guys' girl, a good sport—think Katherine Hepburn's elegance and boyish charm, or Hilary Swank in *Million Dollar Baby*. She was earthy and tough, despite the pure voice and the poignant love songs she wrote. She was the band mother, as Stevie was the wayward band child.

There were sixteen of us, including the band, in the family. We were part religious cult, part sex surrogates, part battle partners or sworn enemies, but always drifting as one. The original band had toured, recorded, toured again, leaving their roots in the UK. We were all the family each other needed, Mick used to say, and I remember wondering if that's what he'd been told by his classmates when, as a scared little boy, he was first sent to boarding school.

We were an incestuous, intense, self-sufficient group crowding around, and protecting, the five band members at its hub. Nothing was allowed to hurt the band, except the band itself. So when Lindsey ruined a live broadcast concert and shocked the entire audience, Christine was allowed to slap him across the face. That was in the rules.

Another rule was that if any band members played silly games, we could all join in. With her mystical naivete, Stevie was an easy target for jokes as the males in the band bonded and wept and swore brotherhood in maudlin drunkenness. At the start of the *Rumours* tour, Stevie had left her hard contact lenses in while she partied for two days to celebrate the band's success, and had worn off her cornea. After being carried piggyback onto the stage by the famed promoter Bill Graham, she struggled through the rain-swept gig, wincing every time the spotlight hit her, and was immediately ordered by the doctor to keep her eyes bandaged for a few days. It was too much of a temptation for the jokers, even for her regular band of adoring girlfriends who traveled everywhere with her. For the entire four days that she was blinded, they dressed her in outrageous outfits—"You look really pretty today," we'd all grin—they put food and drink just out of her reach, and set booby traps for her to fall into. Very childish, of course, but we laughed like idiots. There was a touch of cruelty about it, but there was that boarding school undertone in much of the joshing that Mick and the two Johns initiated. They'd experienced bullying in their school days. Gently, and with a flourish, they passed it on down the chain.

Just outside this charmed inviolate circle of sixteen were the partners, male and female. None of them traveled relentlessly, as I did, with the tours all over the world, so mostly we met up in breaks. Julie Ruebens, John's girlfriend and later his wife, preferred to stay home. So did Jenny Fleetwood, who had two small daughters to care for. But when Mick's marriage failed, and his affair with Stevie faltered, I was joined on tour by the wonderful

Sara Recor, his girlfriend whom he eventually married. She was my confidante, and together we made our "road diary tapes" for our ears only.

The outer circle—the secretaries, engineers, makeup, wardrobe, technicians, and regular road crew—was headed and directed by the impeccable John Courage, known universally as J.C. He was Big Daddy with a cut-glass accent, efficient, wonderfully funny. Tall, with longish blond hair and a full mustache, he looked every inch the handsome, cavalier Englishman that he was. Sometimes he played butler, sometimes doctor, doling out illicit nonprescription dosages; sometimes he was a shoulder to cry on, always a rock. He would invariably know what to do. Among his crew was the handsome and debonair Curry Grant, the band's lighting director and resident playboy. During *Rumours* Christine was his conquest, and it was for him that she wrote the breathtaking "Songbird," then—when she discovered his infidelities—"Oh Daddy," not, as fans mistakenly speculate, for John. Years later, after both songs were beloved by millions, she would say that "Songbird" was written for and dedicated to "everyone" and that "Oh Daddy" was about Mick.

Curry never could keep it in his pants. At one band meeting he came in, leaned back surveying us all, then told me in front of Christine, "You know, you're the only chick in here I haven't screwed!" He never did, either. No one would have dared try it with Lindsey's old lady. Lindsey could terrify.

Unlike the gentle giant Mick. What the press and fans didn't understand is that the band was held together by "The Chain." It had no real manager, just Mick Fleetwood, playing at doing the job. He performed the task with a bumbling amateurism that was again the legacy of his upbringing. There's a particularly British upper-middle-class characteristic of almost willing yourself *not* to succeed. Everything has to appear effortless, and money is vulgar. It's the total opposite of the American Dream. So Mick's greatest pleasure was "transcending," a word he'd claimed for himself from old hippie meditation jargon, but downgraded from its religious context. To him it meant hanging out, getting stoned. Mick's ritual chant, paraphrasing Robert Frost, "the woods are lovely, dark and deep / and we have miles to go before we sleep," would always herald the mirror filled with lines of cocaine in the recording studio.

We used to say that he lived under a little black cloud—nobody, surely, could be *that* unlucky with money? *He* was, because he'd been brought up not to care about it. Despite the band's successes he later went bankrupt three times. And *he* was managing *our* affairs? How insane was that?

Yet Mick's influence was subliminal. We didn't realize at the time how pervasive it was, and how we'd all been drawn into his childhood world of medieval myth and magic, reinterpreted by Victorians, which we represented, Hollywood-style. Fleetwood Mac's stage clothes were romantic costumes. Mick's black velvet knickerbockers minstrel outfit with hanging wooden balls, Stevie's black chiffon, sequined scarves, and top hat—they were from the pages of British children's books, stained glass, the shadows of the past, intriguing but also darkly menacing.

Many writers have speculated about the origins of the mythology and imagery that underpins the Fleetwood Mac phenomenon. In fact, there is only one legitimate way to understand why this imagery resonated so strongly with the audience. Each band member was specifically an archetype, immediately recognizable to a world waiting for the legendary. Mick was the six-and-a-half-foot Wandering Minstrel announcing his arrival in the next town, the next performance, with pelvic thrusts that made his "wooden balls" click like a metronome. Stevie was the White Witch of your darkest perversions. Christine was the Warrior Queen—regal, inviting challenge, suddenly tender in defeat. John was the Court Jester in garish outfits, staggering drunkenly with a wry smile, while Lindsey, lurking in the shadows, was the Demon King.

These are all intense and archetypal figures straight out of our collective unconscious, and they connected powerfully with audiences the world over.

And me? Well, I became the Lady of Shallott. I read that Tennyson poem in high school and never remembered it until I started to live it. It tells of a woman imprisoned on an island, forced to look at the reflections of life through a mirror and weave tapestries to tell the stories of what she sees. She must never look out of the window. She must never confront, or be a part of, real life.

"It's so Fleetwood Mac!" I said, the first time I saw the home in Hancock Park that I chose for Lindsey and me to share. It was a perfect storybook setting for "The Chain." The living room ceiling was covered in murals of knights and ladies, dragons and princesses. The windows were stained glass, depicting knives dripping with blood and heraldic devices. Yet it was built in 1920. It was swashbuckling old Hollywood, a tower for a lady.

We threw a housewarming party there on Halloween, appropriately, during our first break from the *Rumours* tour. It was, of course, the hottest party ticket in town. There was a rich gourmet spread of expertly arranged food and drink, with vials of coke and bags of weed amid this mock baronial splendor. But after two hours of meeting and greeting the Warner Bros. executives, the Dodgers baseball team, the Beach Boys, and members of Eric Clapton's band, we did what the Fleetwood Mac sixteen always did—we left them to it. The Chain locked together, crept upstairs, hid in a suite of rooms with our own stash, and partied among ourselves. We felt safer that way. We were more in control with our own self-generated magic than any that could be created by the rock press.

They were usually wrong, anyway. They were certainly wrong about Lindsey, the soft-spoken brilliant guitarist who apparently hung back from the mythmaking and the dressing up, darkly mysterious. He always preferred to remain in the background, so it seemed, in those early days when rain fell incessantly and we both waited in Producer's Workshop for whatever the future would bring. Hoping to run from our own separate shadows, hand in hand, we raced into the darkness.

My reasons for writing this book are twofold. First, as an eyewitness, I want to share with you the highs, the lows, the truth behind the lies, the loving, and the hating that all went to make up an extraordinary band. Fleetwood Mac wrote the soundtrack to the lives of a whole generation—the band will always be part of my life, just as their music will probably always be part of yours, too.

Then there is a second, more personal reason for this book. In the years since I escaped from the Inner Circle—and I had to escape, as you will see, or perish—I have exorcized some demons, and made some sense of the beautiful insanity that was Fleetwood Mac at its most transcendent during the years from 1976 to 1984. But with one minor exception, I have never given any interviews or sought publicity: I prefer not being quoted to being quoted inaccurately. Here in this book, I want to go on the record—testify, if you will—about a time in my life that was happy, tragic, historic, and resonant with the music of its era. There is something profoundly and essentially human about the music of Fleetwood Mac, and it is that essence that I must attempt to crystallize in these pages.

So, without further ado . . .

Ladies and gentlemen . . .

Prepare to embrace the band that rocked a generation . . .

Ladies and gentlemen . . .

This is how it really happened . . .

Please give a warm welcome to . . .

Fleetwood Mac!

NEVER BREAK THE CHAIN

"Hi," he said, "I'm Lindsey Buckingham."

He turned silently out of the shadows in Studio B and just stared at me. I think I stared back. But there was a time lapse. What is it with some memories? They etch themselves indelibly on your mind afterward, yet at the time there's just confusion and resistance and a flood of emotion to fight through.

But now I remember so clearly that first time I saw him. I remember in exact and overwhelming detail the light on the angles of his face, the slow, sensuous smile, the dark, dark halo of hair, the satanic goatee and mustache. I was face to face with my nemesis, staring into eyes of a blue that was never Californian. This blue was misty, like those English skies I'd seen on my travels.

I shuffled my studio schedules, turned my gaze away.

"I'm . . . I'm Carol Ann. Nice to meet you. I've, uh, gotta get back to work," I stammered, trying to sound bright and efficient. But I could see he wasn't fooled, and neither was I. I raced toward the office, almost stumbling in my haste to get away, slamming my papers down on the desk once I'd reached my sanctuary.

Oh listen, I'd seen beautiful men before. Out here, in Los Angeles, and in the recording industry, they were regular fixtures and fittings. I'd seen hundreds of one-hit wonders, each with a different come-on theme song, different lyrics.

Lindsey Buckingham, 1977.

This one was different. This one was unlike anything or anyone I'd ever seen before. This one had magnetism so intense that I felt a shock go through me the minute I saw him.

But who was Lindsey Buckingham? I had no idea, amazing as that might sound. I scanned the sheaf of papers for clues. Was he an engineer? Was he a technician? Was he just a delivery boy with a tape recorder? Whoever he was, he was scary. Well, he had me scared, at any rate, and despite my small-town background and my waiflike appearance, I didn't scare easily. I'd run my own music business since I was nineteen, and here I was, three years later, just trying to settle into the studio manager job, with a sound engineering internship on the side. I was going places. I needed to. I was in a dead-end relationship with a man who had hardly spoken to me for years and had forced me to part with the only person who ever mattered to me. I had to get out. I wanted independence. I was being smothered alive, and twenty-two was too young to die.

But now I'd just bumped into someone who felt dangerous. And danger wasn't what I was looking for. I told myself that I'd probably never meet him again and I forced my attention back on the scheduling book in front of me. Yes, this was it. Studio B. Richard Dashut and Lindsey Buckingham, it said. Post Production. *Fleetwood Mac/Rumours*. I checked that out again, and for want of anything better to do, with a shaky hand corrected the spelling. *Rumors*.

Over the next few days I avoided going into Studio B, just in case. I was trying to be absolutely professional, against my instinctive urge to see and speak to the guy again, if he was still around. For all I knew he could have driven off into the huge metro of L.A. and would have been just one of those random images that haunts your dreams for years.

But he ended up coming to me, just appearing out of nowhere two days later, asking for a coffee, explaining who he was. He said that he and Richard were putting the finishing touches on the *Rumours* album, so he'd be a fixture for a while. The rest of the band, Fleetwood Mac, would be coming in a few days to add extra vocal tracks for dubbing.

Fixture indeed—within minutes of each afternoon arrival he would appear at the doorway of my office and ask for a cup of coffee. I'd point him to the machine and hide my smile as he struggled to make small talk.

"A lot of rain. Don't you think we've had a lot of rain this week?"

"Well, yeah, Lindsey, we really have."

Both of us felt the fusion every time we came within four feet of each other. Neither of us knew how to handle it. We stammered and fidgeted and smiled at each other to fill in the gaps where words should have been, drank bad coffee, and then one of us would have to leave the unspoken longing hanging in the air and get back to work.

"You know I broke up with my girlfriend?" he asked me one day, when he'd popped in to ask about the next day's schedules.

"Oh yeah?"

"Stevie Nicks. You know?"

"No," I said. "Really?"

I knew. That first week I'd checked it out. I'd found out exactly who he was. I knew that he was the new guitar player for a band that had been around for over ten years. A band that I'd listened to and admired in high school. A band that just happened to be in my studio putting the finishing touches on their next album.

He didn't seem sad about his lost relationship. If anything, he seemed resigned, even relieved. There was a sense of sweetness and vulnerability about him. When I looked into his eyes I could see a longing that made me want to reach out and touch his face. Each day it got a little bit harder to go home to my boyfriend, John. But then I'd been finding it hard to go back to John for ages. So I'd get in my car, drive out of Producer's Workshop and through the garish decay of Hollywood Boulevard, past the sex shops and the pimps, the slouched addicts, the broken flashing neon signs over the greasy diners, my head still buzzing with whatever it was that was happening to me with this complex and mesmerizing stranger.

I really didn't want to get involved with another dream angel.

John and I had been living together for over four years. He was the cousin of my best friend, Lori Lazenby. Lori and I left Tulsa together three days after high school graduation and drove the legendary Route 66, both of us singing along to the car radio, all the way to the City of Angels.

I met John on my first day in Los Angeles. I was eighteen and a virgin. He was my first angel, or so I thought. Anyway, he was a nice guy, pretty interesting, and within three weeks I slept with him. It just seemed like that's what you did in cities like L.A. The point of getting out there in the first place had been to say, "Look, I'm cool! I'm independent! I'm sophisticated!"

Within five weeks I was pregnant. He asked me to live with him, but didn't ask me to marry him. As the months passed, John would reduce me to hysterical tears as he began to tell me over and over that he didn't want a child after all. When our baby, Claire, was five months old, I realized with horror that he'd never even picked up his own daughter. His disinterest in her was terrifying to me.

I spent sleepless nights agonizing over my daughter's future. I wanted her to have the best that life could offer and I knew that being alone and just a child myself, I couldn't give it to her. I'd grown up in Tulsa, Oklahoma, surrounded by my six sisters in a loving, stable home with *two* parents who loved me. We didn't have a lot of money, but we were secure and I always, always felt safe. I desperately wanted that for Claire. I realized after crying many, many tears that by giving her up for adoption, I could give that to my little girl. I chose an agency and poured out my heart to them.

Because it was a private adoption agency, I was able to choose her new family from among four that were presented to me. I chose a wealthy family who already had two adopted sons. The parents were highly educated and loved books, music, and children. They wrote a letter to me asking me to allow them to raise my daughter. They promised that when she was old enough, they would tell her all about me. They swore that they would tell her that her birth mother loved her enough to give her up so that she would never, ever have to worry or want for anything.

On the day I signed the adoption papers John thanked me and said he wanted to take me out to the movies to a double feature to make me feel better. He took me to see *Kotch*, a movie starring Walter Matthau about an unmarried pregnant teenage girl who struggles to decide whether she should keep her baby or give her up for adoption. The second feature was *The Other*, a bloody horror movie about a child who kills an infant and then puts it in a large jar. I will never forget the shock, pain, and sheer horror I felt on that afternoon as I watched the flickering images in a dark theater as the father of my child sat silently beside me. After that, Claire was something we never talked about. I never discussed her with anyone.

From that moment we lived life on John's terms. And I'd clung to it because I thought that was what love was, and that it was my duty to work in the record business we'd set up as a kind of replacement for what had brought us together. I know that whenever I looked at him a part of me felt close to my lost daughter, although I never mentioned her again to him. For on the day I signed the adoption papers, a part of me died, and was still dead.

So that's why I knew that hoping for a miracle love affair was as mad as the drug-crazed visions shared by teenage hookers on Hollywood Boulevard. In real life, like in the gritty films shown to battered men in dirty overcoats, there are no angels. Are there?

But if I had some obligations and ties, however frayed at the edges, the man I was trying not to fall in love with was bound in chains. He had family responsibilities on a scale I'd never seen before. His family was Fleetwood Mac, and over the next few days I would be introduced to each larger-than-life relative.

2

DON'T LOOK BACK

The day after Lindsey told me about breaking up with Stevie, I was sitting on the floor in the reception room of Studio B when a tiny hummingbird of a woman brushed past me in a blaze of color, on a cloud of patchouli and ylang-ylang. I stared. I'd never seen anything so bright and dynamic before, so compelling, so intensely certain of the vibe she created.

I watched as she jumped up onto a scuffed, low table in the center of that dingy gray room with its shabby carpets and grubby open shelving, creating a stage, inviting an audience. She moved and spoke at lightning speed, sniffing, pushing stray locks of long, blonde hair out of her eyes, smoothing her peasant blouse, swishing her silken skirts to create a backing track as she started to describe her Acapulco holiday.

"Like . . . mystical . . . and the moonlight . . . and so translucent, and kinda deep dark, dancing under the stars, and the ocean, there, black and pounding—"

Words just poured out of her, words and sniffs, then, after pausing, "It was life changing. Life changing!" She sniffed again.

I'd just met Stevie Nicks. She was without a doubt the most mesmerizing woman I'd ever encountered. I didn't need to be told that she was a star. Her light was blinding. People gathered around. I sat transfixed, still on the floor, looking up at this five-foot-nothing exquisite firebrand.

And then Lindsey came into the room. There was a moment's hesitation, then he barked at her and she bit back, and I knew instantly that the two were familiar old sparring partners, with a history of love and loathing, and a sharp professional jealousy that would spark up and wound for as long as they lived.

"Hey," Lindsey whispered suddenly, as Stevie's voice sang on in the background. I looked up and he was right next to me, crouched beside me. "See what I have to put up with?" he said.

"We should compare notes," I replied, sighing as I thought of John and the aching spaces between us.

"Tonight?" he asked.

His breath was warm on my cheek. His eyes were too blue. He was too close. All this was too much.

"I live with this guy—" I started to explain, but I couldn't go on. Not then. This was all too raw and painful.

"OK," he whispered.

Above us, loudly, Stevie was announcing, "And next year I'm going to Cozumel . . . Pyramids! You know what they say about pyramids?" Then she laughed. And everyone in the room laughed with her. Except me. I just watched Lindsey as he loped away, and didn't blame him for one minute. I didn't understand the joke about pyramids either, and wouldn't have even if I'd been thinking about it. I was thinking instead about the touch of Lindsey's breath on my cheek. I could still feel it. I couldn't wash it off, not even after getting home later to spend another silent evening with John. It was as if Lindsey had already claimed me, and I'd already cheated. In my mind, I had.

When I arrived at work the next day I found a drawing of a wizened old man's face on my desk calendar with a note that read, "Richard and I are going to see *King Kong* after work. Wanna go?"

Hell, yes, I wanted to go! As excitement turned my cheeks pink, I immediately called John and told him I had to work late. I felt a twinge of guilt about lying, but none at all about going out with Lindsey. I was too excited about seeing Lindsey to even take note of the fact that my lack of guilt spoke volumes about my feelings for John. It was over at last. I couldn't pretend any longer. Funny, isn't it? A night at the movies ended my first love affair. A night at the movies would start the next.

I waited impatiently for 6 P.M. and saw little of Lindsey during the course of the day. The remaining three members of Fleetwood Mac were due in the studio the next day, so he and Richard were working feverishly to finish the mixes before they arrived.

I kept telling myself there was no harm in going to a movie with Lindsey. Richard was coming with us. Richard was a lady-killer. Standing at five foot nine, he had curly black hair just past his collar and a full mustache that would make a pirate proud. With his handsome face and wit, women loved him. He was also Lindsey's roommate and best friend.

Lindsey had been sensitive and careful over his choice of date and the arrangements he'd made for it. A movie—with a chaperone. I felt respected and as nervous as a high school girl on her first big girl-boy thing. Oh, and there was Uncle Richard, of course, to make sure that the girl-boy thing didn't get out of hand!

Lindsey drove us. Richard sat in the back. I trembled in the front seat, overcome with excitement and apprehension. As he helped me out of the car, Lindsey put one arm pro-tectively around my shoulders.

"You have the most fragile shoul-ders I've ever felt," he murmured.

"Fragile?" I asked.

"Fragile feel. That's what I meant," he explained. "You have a fragile *feel* to your shoulders. I love them." He seemed unembarrassed by this declaration.

Lindsey.

I looked at Richard, who rolled his eyes, and I started to laugh. "I think that's the first time in my life that anyone's complimented my shoulders!" Since I was five foot five and weighed 101 pounds soaking wet, I was not too surprised that he thought my shoulders felt fragile.

Halfway through the movie we both stopped pretending to watch the gorilla. We clasped each other's hands tightly as I laid my head on his shoulder and closed my eyes. A feeling of utter contentment came over me and I listened to his breathing and felt his heart beating under my hand on his chest. Finally there was a dead gorilla, the world was saved, the fragile woman had stolen the hero's heart, and the three of us walked back to our car and drove to the studio.

Richard climbed out first and held the door open for me. Lindsey shook his head. "She's not going anywhere. We're going to take a drive."

"God, Lindsey," Richard yelled. "'Mick and the others arrive tomorrow! You can't—" His words were lost in the squeal of Lindsey's tires as we sped out of the parking lot. As we drove down streets shaded with palm trees, Lindsey began to talk to me. "I have to tell you something, Carol."

He pulled over to the side of the street and turned off the ignition. My palms started to sweat as I waited for whatever horrible blow he was about to deliver.

"I've been seeing a girl. We've been going out almost three months, and I spent the night at her house two days ago."

My world was crashing around me as I listened to his words. All I could do was nod for him to go on.

"What I need to tell you is this. I spent the night at her house and I didn't touch her. We slept in the same bed, and I couldn't bring myself to touch her. All I did was lie there and think about you. I want you. I know you're living with someone, Carol Ann, but you can't deny that there's something amazing happening between us. Will you see me? Do I have a chance?"

I threw myself into his arms and kissed him hard. I was shocked, flattered, breathless, and incredibly relieved. Words started spilling out as I told him about my relationship with John. I told him about my daughter. I saw a reflection of the sorrow I was feeling on his face as I poured my heart out to him. As he stroked my hair and whispered that I did right by my child, I felt as though he was taking part of my pain onto his own shoulders. I chose her family, I told him in a low voice. She has two brothers and a beautiful home and will go to college. It's in the contract I signed. And one day, I sighed, maybe we'll find each other. Blinking back tears, I looked into his eyes.

I told him that I wanted to be with him too; that all I did was think about him, first thing in the morning and last thing at night. I promised him that I would see him, but as long as I lived under the same roof as John, I couldn't and wouldn't take what we had together to the next level. I couldn't do that to John. Instead I'd start the painful process of breaking up with him so that I could move out.

As I listened to myself saying all of these things to Lindsey, I realized how ready I was to start a totally new life. It was time to move on. With or without Lindsey, I wanted to be free of my past and the everyday reminders of what I'd lost with Claire's adoption.

It took us ten minutes to drive to West Hollywood. It took us an hour to drive back to the studio, for at every stop sign and every red light Lindsey and I leaned toward each other and kissed passionately. When we arrived at

Producer's Workshop we sat in the parking lot and kissed some more. A yellow glow of light spilled out from the opening door of Studio B as Richard pushed the heavy door open and screamed Lindsey's name into the quiet night. "*Lindsey!* Lindsey, I need you! Goddammit, *please, please* come back inside!"

Lindsey and I looked at each other, then with a sigh we said goodbye and I got out and climbed into my car. After one last wave I drove home.

I walked into a dark house, quietly removed my clothes, and climbed into bed beside John. As I closed my eyes I felt Lindsey's kiss again, and fell fast asleep with a smile on my face.

The next morning, as I struggled into the building through the pelting rain, he was waiting for me with a matching smile. He wiped the rain from my face tenderly. "Do you think you'll have time to come over and listen to a few of our songs today?" he asked. "You'll be one of the first outside of the circle to hear the finished mixes and Richard and I really need an outside opinion. If you hate it, you have to promise to tell us." The words rushed out as Lindsey's fingers danced up and down my arm nervously. I looked down at his hands and for the first time noticed how long his fingers were. His hands looked incredibly strong, yet graceful somehow. The hands of an artist.

"Bob Ezrin's down for Studio A. I have to see him first. Then I'll come across," I promised, checking the day's schedules.

"Make it soon!" Lindsey said, kissing the tip of my nose before he left me to it.

Bob Ezrin was the young, hip producer of Pink Floyd. He arrived and began to talk up a storm about his new band, the Babies, that was recording that day, and at the same time started asking a lot of probing questions about me. Not too personal; more professional than anything. With my mind entirely on Lindsey waiting for me in Studio B, I breezily answered his questions, cutting him off in mid-sentence more than once, then finally excused myself and ran to Studio B, cursing the driving rain that seemed to be trying to pummel Los Angeles clean during that torrential winter.

There were five people sitting around the console: Lindsey, Richard, and three total strangers. One of the strangers was hunched over a large hand mirror chopping up white powder. He looked up at me and smiled.

"Just in time for a white Christmas! Hi, you must be Carol Ann, you're just as Lindsey described you! I'm Mick, Mick Fleetwood." His voice was soft, elegantly British. I liked him immediately.

STORMS

He rose, carefully set the mirror down on the edge of the mixing board and took a few steps toward me. My eyes widened as he stretched both arms over his head before extending his hand to me. He was one of the tallest men I'd ever seen. His head seemed to almost brush the ceiling as he looked down, smiling. He wore his brown hair pulled back in a sleek ponytail and was dressed like a character from an Agatha Christie novel, in an elegant tweed suit complete with a watch fob dangling from his pocket.

I blushed, murmured hello, and looked over at the man and woman still seated in front of me. The woman, striking, statuesque almost, had a disheveled blonde pageboy cut and held a large vodka tonic in one hand (with a half-full bottle of vodka sitting on the floor beside her) and a Marlboro Red in the other. She jumped up and I heard Christine McVie's laugh for the first time. Loud and raucous, it rang out with enough passion and vitality to make all of us start laughing with her. She gestured to me to sit down, just like an old friend. Lindsey grabbed a chair from against the wall and moved it next to him. I sank onto it.

The final stranger approached. John McVie, Christine's ex-husband. Wearing a red Hawaiian shirt and baggy surfer shorts (belying the 50-degree temperature and rain) he came over with drink in hand, leaned down, and kissed me on the cheek. "So you're to be our first critic! Be kind to us," he said. "If you hate our songs, tell us in a nice, flowery way. It's too early for us to get completely smashed, which we will if we're subjected to ridicule." British humor—it went with the British weather outside.

And then the music began to wash the room, like rain. I closed my eyes, wishing I were next door, back in Studio A, where I wouldn't be in the position of judge and jury to people I barely knew; warm, kindly people who looked as if they'd stepped out of a costume party.

After the first thirty seconds of Christine's song "You Make Loving Fun," I sat up straighter in my chair. This was unbelievable. There was a sharpness in the backing track that I'd never heard before, each instrument distinctly picked up, faded out, the vocals enriched by three contrasting harmonies.

"Dreams" came next and I heard Stevie Nicks's voice, low, haunting, and sensual. I was lost. As each song came and went I realized that I was listening to an absolutely unique sound. There was so much love and pain; so clear, so agonized, so raw, and yet so precisely directed and produced. I stared wide-eyed at Lindsey, who threw his arms around me and whispered into my ear, "You like it, don't you?" Richard pushed the stop button on the twenty-four-track tape machine and the room fell deathly quiet.

"Lindsey, I don't know what to say. It's incredible. I love it. Oh my God," I said, swallowing back the lump in my throat, "this is the most amazing album! It's going to be huge!"

Christine's delighted laughter rang out as Mick jumped up with the mirror in his hand and, with a bow, ceremoniously handed it to me. So that's what Mick meant when he said it was a white Christmas? That mound of snow? I looked at the mirror, looked at Lindsey, and said in a hesitant voice, "Umm . . . no thanks. I'll take a rain check. Have to work!" I hoped I'd passed whatever test it was meant to be.

Lindsey eased the mirror out of my hands and took a rolled-up twenty-dollar bill from Christine. I hadn't fooled him. He'd realized I'd never done a line in my life and wouldn't know where to start. "Make a line, inhale it. It wakes you up—it, well, it just keeps you going. You don't have to do any if you don't want to." He offered it to me again and I shook my head. I wasn't sure why he was pleased that I didn't want any, but I could tell that he was. I was as embarrassed as hell that I was so unsophisticated. I watched in fascination as the five of them made huge, messy lines and inhaled them through the rolled-up bill, straight up their noses. Almost immediately the room was filled with frenzied voices and nervous laughter. John and Christine quickly lit their Marlboros, while Richard and Lindsey shared a joint.

"'Gold Dust Woman' needs something," Lindsey announced through the smoke. "It's not atmospheric enough. So . . . we brought some sheets of glass and set up microphones in the parking lot. We want to record the sound of splintering glass and work it into the song."

Mick's eyes fired up with a devilish gleam. He rubbed his hands together fiendishly. "I want to be the one who gets to crash the glass! Me, me! I'm the tallest! I'm the best glass-breaker in the friggin' world! *Let's do it!*"

He scampered into the rain with Richard by his side. I stayed in the control room with Lindsey and listened to the hysteria from the parking lot booming through the huge speakers in the room. It took Richard five minutes to stop Mick from laughing, but once he did, the sound of breaking, shattering glass was recorded. The finished version of "Gold Dust Woman" begins with an unearthly tinkling that sounds dark and ominous.

It changed the whole vibe of the song. This was the first of many times that I'd see Lindsey's genius at work.

I looked at my watch and with a start realized that I'd been in Studio B for almost two hours. "My God! I have to go! I've completely abandoned poor Bob Ezrin and his new band!" A shadow crossed Lindsey's face and he seemed about to say something. I knew he didn't want me to go, but I had to. I leaned over, kissed him on the cheek, yelled goodbye to John and Christine, and flew out the door. Lindsey called after me, "Leave your number on your desk! I need to talk to you about something special—"

"OK!" I shouted back and returned to my abandoned work, the songs I'd just heard resonating in my head.

I left my home phone number propped up against my desk calendar. I hadn't figured out yet how I was going to end my relationship with John. I didn't want anyone to get hurt. But what could you do when you've already heard the glass break?

The phone at home rang around 8 P.M. John was locked in his studio working on the latest bootleg release from his label.

"I miss you," Lindsey's voice whispered. I shivered head to foot.

"Me too," I whispered. I didn't want to break the spell of intimacy by speaking out loud. It was better that way. He felt so close. If I reached out, I could almost touch . . .

"What are you doing tomorrow night?" I could hear Stevie's voice in the background and realized that Lindsey was trying to keep from being overheard. "The band's having a private dinner to celebrate the finish of the album. It's at a French restaurant on Melrose. Please come. Be with me, huh?"

"I'll—" I struggled to work out an excuse for John as Lindsey waited silently. "I'll tell him I'm with a client!"

"I hope to be much more than that, little girl. I'll see you tomorrow, OK?"

"OK," I murmured, and put the phone down just before John emerged from the studio.

Oh, I was scared. I really was. Terrified. Playing around had never been my style, and I didn't know whether I could carry this off, but the next night I knew I had no option. Lindsey had claimed me. I was his girl. And it was my choice to accept the claim.

I parked up on Melrose that next night, just behind Lindsey's car, as arranged, and he raced out and held me until I thought I'd break into tiny pieces. Dressed head to toe in black velvet, wearing spike heels, and with a heart on fire, I drifted into the restaurant on his arm, into a private, exclusive dining room, lit with the flicker of candles reflected in gilt-framed mirrors. Two chairs at the long, linen-draped table stood conspicuously empty, obviously reserved for us. I sat down on Lindsey's right and looked up and down the table. Christine was opposite, beaming. John and Mick took places of honor at each end, and among the guests were technicians and roadies I'd already seen in the studio.

Lindsey began pointing everyone out to me. In the center of the table was a man whose presence was almost palpable. Blond and thickset, he held court while offering attention to all. His eyes were never still. I sensed that he was at the hub of this turning wheel.

"J.C.," Lindsey whispered in my ear. "John Courage. Our road manager." And then he said out loud, "This is Carol Ann. Say hello, John."

"Well," John drawled in an impeccable English voice, "who is this little flower?" He raised his eyebrows and his glass to me. I blushed. He winked. I was going to get on with J.C. He was an instant friend. He would remain a friend at all times.

"And," Lindsey continued, his hand gripping mine under the table, his voice low, "there's Judy Wong, the band secretary"—tiny, Asian, black hair to her waist, and strikingly beautiful, she spoke animatedly, faster than anyone I'd ever seen, to the strong-boned, handsome woman beside her, a woman with a serene smile—"talking to Julie Ruebens, John's lady." *John, I thought, should think himself lucky.* Julie oozed class and calm, warmth and wisdom. "And you know Richard." Richard winked at me. "And next to him, that's Ken, our other engineer . . ." Ken was a nerdy kind of guy. Nice enough, though. ". . . and Ray, who looks after my guitars." Ray seemed to want the table to open up and swallow him. He looked uncomfortable, as shy as I was. "And the heartbreaker over there is Curry Grant. Crazy name, huh?"

I could see what he meant. If I hadn't been hand-held and spellbound by Lindsey's breath on my neck, I may have succumbed. But he was a tad obvious despite his chestnut curls and his marron-glacé eyes. Not for me.

"He's Christine's—for now," Lindsey laughed. I looked into his eyes. Mist blue did it for me, every time, over sickly nut browns. My glance told him I was not really impressed with the opposition.

"Where's Stevie?" I asked.

"Don't ask," Lindsey murmured with his lopsided grin. "She kinda decided not to come."

What exactly was he trying to say here?

"She's just going to have to get used to it. I haven't really seen anyone seriously since we broke up a year ago and, well, I guess she knows that I'm pretty serious about you."

My breath stopped. Stevie Nicks was jealous of me? This was going to make things interesting. I held on to his hand and tried to concentrate on answering Christine's probing questions about my background, which were coming fast and furious. She wanted to know just about everything about me, and I answered her as best I could. I told her about Elbereth Enterprises, my record company, and the many bootleg records that I'd released with John, my "roommate." I explained that we went to concerts—the Stones, David Bowie, Bob Dylan, the Faces, and others—and we recorded the show using a shotgun microphone and a tiny reel-to-reel Nagra recorder. We then mixed the tapes, designed the album covers, made "mother" acetates, and took them to a pressing plant. Our records were made from colored vinyl and we sold them via mail-order all over the world. And now I was training to be a recording engineer while working as studio manager. She nodded her head with each answer and looked meaningfully at Mick and John as Lindsey hung on my every word. What was she doing? Interviewing me? Had I got the job or not? And what exactly was the job?

"So . . ." Christine stared at me, piercingly. Everyone fell silent. "Have you bootlegged *Rumours*, Carol Ann?"

I flushed hideously. "No!" I managed to stammer. "Why . . . ?"

"Now that we know what your little sideline is, we wondered how safe we are from the bootleggers." Without taking her eyes off me, she downed another large vodka in one swallow. John looked embarrassed but nodded. Lindsey was hanging on to my every word. I glanced at him. Yes, there was even doubt in *his* eyes.

I found myself boxed in, explaining that our music business wasn't that kind of bootlegging—we weren't "counterfeiters." What we did wasn't illegal! And I would never, ever, copy tapes from work. My voice was fogging with tears, but Lindsey squeezed my hand.

"S'OK, Carol Ann," Christine said, suddenly laughing uproariously. "Just testing! We all thought the air ought to be cleared over a couple of nagging doubts before we gave you the seal of approval."

"Approval?" I asked, disbelieving what I'd just heard.

"We needed to know, see, if you're going to be one of us. I was voted Woman Most Likely to Uncover Hidden Motives. But you really don't have any, do you? OK, Lindsey, back to you now. I'm just going to the little girls' room!"

"You did great!" Lindsey whispered to me as she staggered away.

"But . . ."

"It's OK, forget it. This is Fleetwood Mac, you know, and we have to be careful. Christine volunteered to sound you out. And you passed the test. Now just relax and try to enjoy yourself."

I was speechless. I'd been subjected to an interrogation there, and everyone, even the guy I was falling for, had ganged up on me. It felt like I'd just taken an entrance exam for La Cosa Nostra.

What was this I was getting into? Out of the corner of my eye I noticed the restlessness in the room as the gourmet food was presented—and ignored. People moved in and out of the bathrooms at frightening speed, even as I was talking to them. I was completely unaware, in my innocence, that everyone but Judy was taking cocaine breaks.

There were toasts to the album and war stories about the past year they had spent creating it. The noise level and pitch at our table was getting louder and higher with each trip to the bathroom, and the jokes cruder. I felt like an outsider and an intruder more than a participating member of this exclusive, crazed group of people. When Mick got out of his chair for the fourth or fifth time and almost fell over his own feet, Lindsey asked me if I was ready to leave. I smiled with relief and grabbed my purse and coat as Lindsey made our goodbyes. My first Fleetwood Mac party was over— and my first fears had surfaced.

We left clinging to each other like the drowning to driftwood, sheltering in his car from the rain, curling into each other's warm spaces. I belonged in this world I'd found in Lindsey's arms and nothing else mattered. It was 3:30 A.M. when reality came crashing back.

"My God, Lindsey, I have to go! He'll think I've been in a car accident!" Lindsey scowled at my reference to John, and pulled me back down to the depths.

"Carol Ann, I think I'm falling in love with you."

I was stunned. I never knew it was possible to feel as happy as I did that moment. At the same time, a voice in my head whispered *Is he telling me this now because I passed some secret rite of passage during dinner?* As I stared into his eyes, gazing into the clear blue, I knew that the band had given me their seal of approval and Lindsey was now free to tell me how he felt about me. Thrill, then terror. I couldn't. But I would. I knew I would.

"I'm so happy, Lindsey," I murmured into the cloud of his soft, damp hair.

And then I got into my car to drive home through the deserted streets, as he stood cast adrift, waving me goodbye. I turned the radio on for company, pushed a button blindly on the console, and the guitar riff from "Go Your Own Way" blasted out from my small speakers. I'd only heard it in the studio, never, ever on the radio. I hit the brakes hard, almost fishtailing on the wet pavement. I sat in the middle of the street, rain still falling, and listened to Lindsey's voice, a man committed. One phrase repeated itself in my mind as I listened: *The man who's singing this song is the man who just told me he's falling in love with me.*

The rest of the drive home was a blur.

I walked through the front door of my condo at 4:30 A.M. The house was dark, a tomb. I saw a flashing red light coming from the answering machine and, thinking that Lindsey had called me while I was driving home, I rushed to it and pushed the play button.

"Carol Ann, Carol, dear, where are you?"

My mother. My mother had never before left a message for me on an answering machine, and had rarely called at night. With a true mother's instinct she must have sensed that I was entering an unknown world, a sleeping child's world of giants and monsters with a handsome prince to save me, if he could. To this day I don't know how she knew—but she did. She told me how much she missed me, how much she hated the fact that I was so far away from her, and she talked for ten minutes about all the things that millions of mothers tell their children.

He'll be good to me, Mama, you'll see, I told her in my heart, hoping, almost certain, that it was true.

My mother was wonderful. In my eyes, she was the best mother in the entire world. She'd devoted her life to my six sisters and me. She was a brilliant woman with gorgeous red hair who was always laughing, always busy, and always taking care of her girls. She didn't know how to drive a car, but she wrote poetry and short stories, was a gifted artist, and instilled a love of books in all of her daughters. In the Harris family, the public library was like a second home and at any given time you could find one or all us curled up with a book, lost in yet another story.

My father was a Tulsa city engineer who had a second career as a substitute math teacher—raising a family of seven girls was an expensive proposition. He was a gentle man who bore a striking resemblance to Clark Gable and I adored him. My parents had their family in stages. My oldest sisters, Margaret, Tommie, and Patsy, were all born more than ten years before me. Sue came next, and Dana, Jeannie, and I followed more than four years later.

It was nonstop chaos in a home that was ruled by two parents who used humor and love as their tools of discipline. We were never yelled at, never spanked, and while I'm sure we were a handful, none of us gave them much grief. My older sisters had all gone to college and had their degrees, but I had chosen to move to L.A. with Lori instead. I'd always felt that remaining in Tulsa was not my destiny, always felt that there was a different future meant for me. As I sat in the dark replaying my mother's message, I suddenly felt as though I was racing toward it.

I'd been tearing myself apart with guilt over John, but when the end came it was almost comic relief. At least that's how it feels when I look back on the morning of slammed doors and shrieking curses. He was on the rampage downstairs. I was still in bed, reliving every snatched moment with Lindsey, every whispered phone call, every opportunity to ask each other "How was your day?"

This day didn't sound too good from John's perspective.

I slipped quietly out of bed and into my ripped blue jeans and a man's red corduroy shirt. *You can do this, Carol,* I told myself. *Just stop living a lie, will you, girl?* I squared my shoulders, took a deep breath, and walked slowly down the staircase. John was perched on a bar stool next to our answering machine, red-faced, ready for nuclear war.

"Sit down, Carol! Sit and listen to what I have to play for you."

He pushed the button residentially, smirking already at the prospect of fallout. On the answering machine I heard myself talking to Lindsey. It was the conversation we'd had when he invited me to the Fleetwood Mac dinner. As soon as I heard his voice, I smiled involuntarily. John caught the smile. It pushed him over the edge.

"You're seeing him! Don't deny it! I caught you! I can smell him on your clothes when you come home from work!"

I froze. Taping my calls was bad enough, but smelling my clothes? So gross! *Well, that does it,* I thought, as I took two steps away from him. "First of all, that's really freaky, John, but whatever." And then I told him. I told him about Lindsey, told him I'd fallen in love, told him that I was leaving, and I told him calmly and clearly. It was such a relief. I felt strong—strong enough to use all the words I'd been running through my head for weeks now. It was easy.

"Look, you don't love me. You're just used to me. You didn't want our baby, and you didn't want to marry me when I needed you the most. I haven't slept with Lindsey. And you didn't have to go through that stupid detective act. You know what you could have done? You could have asked. But we never talked about anything, did we? We didn't even care enough to talk."

And then I left, went upstairs, and phoned Lindsey.

"He's been doing *what?* Is he completely *nuts?* Do you want me to come get you? I want you out of that house and here with me. Now!" he yelled.

"Lindsey, John would never hurt me and besides, I'm leaving right now. But if there's any trouble, I'll call you again. I'll see you in about forty-five minutes. If I'm not there in an hour, here's my address." I hung up the phone and with my purse, a change of clothes, toothbrush, and car keys in hand, I walked out of the life I'd been living for the past five years.

Lindsey was sitting on his front stairs waiting for me and sprinted toward my car as I pulled into his driveway. He swept me into his arms and swung me off my feet, kissing me over and over again. Neither one of us said a word. We stood and looked at each other, sharing the wonder of the first blue sky of winter, and he led me by the hand into his small one-story house. I was washed clean of the past.

My first day as Lindsey's girlfriend was about to begin. I was free. I was in love. I had a job that fascinated me and pushed me hard. I'd never felt so alive, ever. Alive and in control for the first time.

Lindsey and I went to a deli for breakfast and sat just looking at each other in giggling amazement.

"Shit!" he said suddenly. "I'm flying to Aspen tomorrow on a ski trip with Mick and Richard. I'll get out of it. I won't go."

I reached over and touched his cheek. "Hey, I'm a big girl, you know! I'm going to find an apartment just for me! It's an adventure—it's been years since I had one of those!"

My mind went back to those wild summer days almost five years before, driving in from Tulsa with Lori, the wind in our hair, down Route 66. That was the last time I had a new beginning. And this tickling inner excitement felt exactly as it did that day. Lindsey and love had given me back the hope I had then. I had been eighteen and the world was waiting for me. Just as it was now. I wasn't at all afraid.

So we went shopping for Lindsey's ski boots. I invaded the silent home I'd left to pick up some of my clothes and I moved in with Lindsey, just for one crazy night together when all that longing, all that holding back, all that slow, easy slide into love, exploded into the passion that it had tried to deny.

We didn't sleep at all. Lindsey's flight to Aspen was at 8 A.M. and at 7:00 he sat up in bed and pulled me close. He told me he loved me. It was a huge moment, that confession, but he didn't need to say it. He'd shown me. Every surface of my body, heart, and mind had been touched by his tenderness, by the artistry in those long, long fingers that now wound themselves in my tousled hair.

"I love you, too," I whispered, exhausted and deliriously happy. "Always."

We'd arranged that I'd stay in his house while he was away, so that I could go looking for my dream apartment. Something told me that I'd find exactly what I was looking for. Fairy-tale happy endings were being written into this story on every page. There was just no point accepting second best or making do, ever again. So, when the first ten apartments I'd looked at weren't perfect, I continued the search, knowing that any day now another miracle would happen.

And it did. Just as I was driving to work down Hollywood Boulevard, a building caught my eye and I pulled over on the spur of the moment. There was a beautiful, shady courtyard surrounded by stuccoed, Spanish-style pueblo apartments. How many times had I driven past and never noticed it? A "No Vacancy" sign hung over the entrance but, despite that, I rang the manager's buzzer.

"Do you have an apartment available, by any chance?" I asked.

She was taken aback. "How did you know? The girl just moved out yesterday—we haven't even had a chance to sweep the floors! Would you like to see it? It's $200 a month, furnished, with utilities paid."

A magnolia tree, heavy with pink blossom, scented the air as we climbed the stairs to a first-floor apartment, and I discovered my home at last. It reminded me of my grandmother's house, with heavy, old, dark-wood furniture, but bathed in light from the floor-to-ceiling windows overlooking the courtyard and that magnificent magnolia tree. Within hours I collected the keys.

Lindsey had been calling me every single night and each time we talked for at least two hours. I couldn't wait to tell him that night about my apartment.

"I'm really glad for you, Carol Ann. I'd kinda hoped you'd still be at my place when I got back," he murmured.

"Well, maybe you can come round to mine?" I laughed.

By the time Lindsey returned from Aspen, I was all moved in. I'd decided to leave my furniture and keepsakes from my relationship with John at the house I had shared with him. I wanted nothing from my old life intruding into my new one. I took Claire's baby book and antique cradle, my clothes, family pictures, and a few pots and pans. That's all. It was the beginning of February 1977 and I was turning the page.

3

GOLD DUST

Since his return from Aspen, Lindsey and I had fallen into a routine. He picked me up every night at 6 P.M. and after a quick dinner we'd return to the privacy of my new apartment. We spent every night together—happy, relaxed, and in love. All of our nights were passionate, and our lovemaking this night had been no exception. I was exhausted and content as I fell asleep in his arms.

In the dead of night, I awoke with a start. The room was bathed in shadows, soft moonlight seeping through the cheap Venetian blinds that covered the large bedroom window. Sensing that something was wrong, my heart started pounding as I sat up quickly in bed, reaching for Lindsey. With a shock, I saw that he was sitting with his knees drawn tightly up against his chest. He had his head lowered and was rocking back and forth.

"Are you all right, baby?" I whispered.

"I guess," he answered in a low voice.

I put my hand softly on his shoulder. "Do you want to talk about it?"

Lindsey pushed his tousled curls out of his face and took a deep breath. He tried to laugh, but it sounded more like a moan as he answered, "I have a lot on my mind."

The tension coming from Lindsey felt like a dark presence in the room. Again he started to rock back and forth and I could sense that he was close to tears. "It's the tour . . . I'm worried about the tour and the rehearsals we have coming up. It was so hard making the album. So many damn fights! John's breakup with Christine and mine with Stevie was a total nightmare. Can we get past all that ugliness and do a tour?"

As I sat and listened to him talk I involuntarily bit my lip at the mention of Stevie. Lindsey had never really talked to me about what happened during the recording of *Rumours*. He'd told me briefly about John and Christine's divorce and that he and Stevie had been broken up for a year before we met. I'd never asked him about the details of his relationship with her. Like everyone else, I'd heard the songs on the album. The rage, pain, and blatant accusations of infidelities spoke volumes. Listening to him in the dark, I knew that tonight was not the time to ask him to reveal intimate truths.

"I know that all of us are on our best behavior now," he continued in a shaky voice. "We've called a truce. I only hope that it'll last. The band has to be tight on stage, Carol. If we're not, the tour will suck."

"Shhh, baby. It's going to be OK. From what I can see, each and every one of you wants this to work. You guys will be ready . . . if you don't feel that you are, then you can fix that in rehearsals, right?"

He nodded and stared quietly into the darkness.

As I struggled for words to soothe him, I knew that what was happening to the five members of Fleetwood Mac must be as frightening as it was phenomenal, for it was as obvious as it was invisible. Lindsey was about to be crowned a rock 'n' roll superstar. It was a crown that was heavy with expectations. Superstardom and all of its trappings were what he'd been working toward for years but had never expected to possess. And now that it was happening, I knew that he was both aware and afraid that the weight of it might, in a very short time, crush him. My heart ached for him. I swore to myself that I would do everything within my power to help him through whatever might lie ahead for him—and us.

Rumours was due to be released in a month's time. If the radio airplay was any indication, then the album could be very, very successful. But as every artist knows, even when you have a huge album, you have to prove yourself on stage, again and again. The bigger the band, the more the public expects and wants. Maybe for some musicians, having an amazing record and a so-so live show was good enough—but it wasn't good enough for Fleetwood Mac. They wanted to have it all: the best record of the year *and* the best show. Anything less would be failure. And Lindsey wasn't a man to accept failure—either from himself or anyone else in the band.

I pulled Lindsey into my arms, feeling fear for us both. As I stroked his hair and lulled him back to sleep, I knew it was I, not Lindsey, who was going to be sleepless for the rest of the night. Rehearsals were beginning. I now knew that it wasn't going to be a party—it was going to be hard work for Lindsey and tension for us all. I realized that not only did I have Lindsey to bolster, but also I would, for the first time, be spending a lot of "quality time" with Stevie Nicks. She had avoided me at the celebration dinner, but she had to go to rehearsals—as did I. Lindsey and I were determined that nothing could keep us from spending our evenings together—not even an upcoming world tour. Since his attendance was mandatory at rehearsals, so was mine.

This, of course, would be a very intense situation for me. I was very aware that so far, Stevie had done little to make me feel welcome. I didn't blame her. I wouldn't be keen on having the new girlfriend of my ex-lover hanging around either. There was nothing for it, however. She and I would have to find a middle ground where we both could live with each other. And it would start at rehearsals. Lindsey was quickly becoming the most important person in my life, and I had no intention of going anywhere.

The band had already had some raw rehearsals in a small studio in the San Fernando Valley called, of all things, Rat. Beginning the next evening, the real rehearsals for the *Rumours* tour would be held on a large sound-stage at the famed SIR Studios on Sunset Boulevard. Lindsey gave me specific directions before I left him in the morning and made me promise to be there as soon as I could after work. I looked at his pale face and tangled brown curls and told him that nothing could keep me away. He smiled and kissed me gently before I went out the front door into another day of drizzling rain.

I spent the whole day just going through the motions at Producer's Workshop. I kept thinking of Lindsey and his midnight confession of anxiety about the upcoming tour. Would I be strong enough, smart enough, to help him cope? I had to be. He needed me. No matter how hard it might be for me, I was going to be there for him, I vowed to myself. I counted the minutes until I could see him again.

As soon as the clock struck six, I dashed out of Producer's Workshop, trying desperately to keep my hair from becoming wet in the ever-present drizzle, and jumped into my car for a mad shopping spree at Century City shopping center. This would be the first night I'd spend any length of time around Lindsey's ex-girlfriend, Stevie Nicks. And as every woman knows, a dress and a new pair of shoes can become a suit of armor when facing such a challenge. Let's face it, walking into Fleetwood Mac's first big rehearsal for their tour would be a huge deal for anyone. Walking in as the new girl-friend of the guitar player whose ex is a rock 'n' roll goddess and one of the lead singers in his band would constitute a challenge for any female in the world.

Running into Country Club Fashions, I grabbed a sexy little black dress and platform shoes that laced up around my ankles. I got dressed in the store's dressing room and stuffed my blue jeans and T-shirt into a shopping bag as I ran out of the shop's door to my car. Already late, I touched up my makeup under the red glare of stoplights and chain-smoked the entire way to SIR. I pulled into the large multiplex of soundstages and entertainment offices and drove up to the window of the small guard station. Giving my name, I watched as the guard checked it off the short guest list in his hand. I parked just outside Soundstage B, and shivered in the darkness and cold as I climbed out of my car. My dress and small jacket did little to ward off the chill that I was feeling both from the cold of February and the butter-flies in my stomach. Taking a deep breath, I headed toward the big doors that opened onto Soundstage B.

It was huge. I stood quietly at the back of the rehearsal hall to get my bearings. There was a brightly lit area straight ahead of me in the arena-size room. In the center of the light, I could see Mick's drums, Lindsey's guitars on their stands, huge amps, and microphones with snakes of cables extending off into the darkness behind. As I took baby steps toward the light, rows of metal chairs came into view, grouped in front of the stage area.

The first person I saw was Stevie Nicks, sitting on the edge of a wooden crate with an acoustic guitar strapped around her neck. Lindsey was lean-ing over her with his hands on his head in a classic pose of frustration. As I approached, unseen, Lindsey let out a loud wail of frustration.

"Jesus, Stevie! You said you wanted to play guitar on 'Go Your Own Way'! This sounds like shit! It's easy to play, so what's the problem? Try it again. Now!"

Stevie bent her head over the guitar and slowly, painstakingly tried to make it through the opening guitar riff of "Go Your Own Way." She sound-ed like a child playing her big brother's Gibson acoustic. John, Mick, and Christine were all lounging in the front row of metal chairs, not even trying to muffle their snickers and laughter.

Lord help me, I said to myself, *could I have picked a worse time to arrive?*

Lindsey let out another "Arrghh!" at full volume and began to stomp away from Stevie toward the cheap folding chairs. He stopped dead in his tracks when he saw me standing just outside the circle of light. His angry expression left his face, replaced with a glow of pleasure as he walked quickly toward me. Cringing inside, I felt all eyes upon me as I unwillingly became the center of attention. The band swiveled in their chairs, vodka tonics in hand, to become spectators to the play that was unfolding before them. As Lindsey reached me, he picked me up and swung me around in his arms. Looking over his shoulder, I could see Stevie standing up—anger and disgust etched on her face. With a toss of her hair, she took the guitar from around her neck and threw it on the floor. She then stalked off into the gloom behind the stage.

"I was about to lose it! Man, you probably saved her life by coming in just now! Where have you been? I was worried about you! You look good, angel. Come take a walk with me." Lindsey pulled me by the hand into the shadows and began to kiss me. I heard a loud guffaw from Christine, and then John and Mick started applauding. "Well done, Lindsey! Make her feel welcome, my boy!"

Even though I was completely embarrassed, I couldn't help but laugh between kisses at the comments coming from John and Mick—comments about male virility and lust. To my relief Lindsey finally let me up for air and then took me by the arm, steering me toward the row of seats. As I got closer, I could see that John's girlfriend Julie was sitting directly behind him and that J.C. had appeared from out of nowhere.

"Welcome, m'dear!" J.C. proclaimed as he pulled out a chair for me. "Need a drink?"

"No, thanks." I murmured, looking shyly at Julie, and the rest of the Mac.

"Everyone, dinner is ready. Where's Stevie?" J.C. innocently asked. A fresh round of laughter broke out among the seated group and a small frown crossed his face. "What happened?"

"Nothing, J.C.," Stevie declared loudly as she came storming out from behind the drum riser. Holding her head high, she glared at Lindsey and me as she swept past regally with an entourage of three girlfriends in tow. All of them took turns shooting daggers at me as they passed me by. *So much for making friends tonight,* I thought.

"She's had a rough night, don't mind her," Lindsey murmured with a smirk on his face. I nodded quickly in response and followed him to the buffet.

After everyone had eaten, Lindsey walked me over to Julie Ruebens and pulled out the chair next to her. "Julie will watch over you while we rehearse, won't you, Julie?"

With a bright smile, Julie nodded as Lindsey kissed me quickly and then headed toward his guitar stands. I smiled at Julie, noticing once again how pretty she was with her brown hair falling in waves to her shoulders. The kindness that I had noticed about her at the band's celebration dinner was shining from her eyes.

All of the band were congregating on "stage" and after ten minutes of warming up, they launched into "You Make Lovin' Fun," and then continued playing their new songs from *Rumours*. To my ears, it sounded great, although it was obvious that in some of the songs, the band was struggling to get in sync with each other.

But there was magic there.

I could feel it as it echoed throughout the large, oppressive soundstage. Lindsey, seemingly content to stand at the back of the stage, was focusing on his intricate guitar licks as he watched John and Mick out of the corner of his eye. On the other side of the stage, John McVie stood in yet another garish Hawaiian shirt. Solid, loud, in the tradition of most bass players, he was an anchor to Mick Fleetwood's clowning behind the drums. Christine was pounding on her keyboards with a wry smile on her face in between her vocals, making it apparent to everyone that she was having a blast.

I watched Stevie sing and realized again just how beautiful she was. As the band started into "Rhiannon," she took on a bewitching, hex-like quality as she spun in front of the microphone. Wearing a long black skirt that shimmered as she moved, with a simple top and a silk scarf around her neck, she was drop-dead gorgeous. Watching her, I realized that she was a combination of little girl and erotic fantasy. With a smoky voice and an aura of mysticism that promised great pleasures and even greater dangers, she was a force to be reckoned with.

I knew then and there that she was going to be one hell of a match for me. As I slumped down into my chair, I told myself that even though I would never, ever have her musical ability, I'd do everything within my power to match her in other areas—even if it killed me.

I know that this sounds overly dramatic, but when you're twenty-two years old and your new boyfriend's ex-lover is a rock goddess, you tend to take things very seriously.

I sighed and looked over at Julie. As though she could read my mind, Julie smiled at me sympathetically and grabbed my hand. "Come on. I have something you might like. Let's go to the bathroom," she whispered.

We stood up, passing the row of chairs occupied by Stevie's girlfriends. I hadn't been introduced to them, but as far as I could tell, they looked as though they'd all been dressed from Stevie's closet. Long skirts, velvet scarves, and varying shades of blonde hair marked them as Stevie's girls. I would soon discover that Stevie never went anywhere without her entourage of "girlfans."

Walking by Julie's side dressed in my black knee-length cocktail dress, I heard their whispers following us down the aisle. With a dismissive sniff, Julie said quietly, "Don't mind them. They're Stevie's little replicas. You'll get used to it. Believe me, I have." I looked at her gratefully and started to relax.

Crossing the huge soundstage, we entered a large dingy tiled bathroom. To my surprise, but apparently not Julie's, Curry Grant, the band's lighting director, was leaning nonchalantly against the wall. "Hello ladies. I wondered how long it would take for you to get in here."

Julie laughed as she walked quickly toward him. "How nice that you just 'happened' to be here, Curry. I was just about to offer Carol Ann a little bit of a pick-me-up. Would you care to join us?"

With a bright smile he nodded his head and watched as Julie pulled a small bottle out of her pocket, unscrewed the top, and poured some of the powder out onto her wrist and inhaled it. A look of utter satisfaction crossed her face and she motioned for me to come to her.

"Julie," I stammered, "I don't know if I should. I've never had any . . ."

Curry laughed as he put his arm around me. "Hey, little girl. We're here to corrupt you. Come on, now, give it a go."

Julie shot a warning glance toward him, saying, "Curry, if you know what's good for you, you'll get your hands off of her. Lindsey wouldn't be pleased."

He dropped his hand from my shoulder as though I were on fire.

Julie turned to me. "You've got to try blow sooner or later, Carol. All of us do it. It's no big deal. It'll make you feel great, I promise!"

Not wanting to look stupid in front of my new friends, I eyed the bottle warily and then shrugged my shoulders. "Sure. OK. Uh, how do I do it?"

"Just inhale. That's it. The blow will do the rest."

So I did just that. And I waited for something to happen. Nothing did. I didn't feel any different. With Julie and Curry watching me expectantly, I smiled and said, "Hey, great. Thanks." They seemed to be satisfied with my response and started talking and giggling as they poured more out onto their wrists and inhaled again. They dumped another pile on my wrist and I sniffed it again. Nope. I didn't feel any different.

Julie looked at me searchingly, apparently no longer fooled by the smile I kept plastered on my face. "Carol, it's no big deal if you don't feel anything the first time. That happens a lot. We'll do some more later. You're gonna love it, I promise."

Yeah, right, I thought to myself.

Hearing a break in the music, Julie and I looked guiltily at each other. We were supposed to be watching! We rushed out the door and headed back to our seats. Lindsey wasn't anywhere in sight, but Stevie was. She was waiting for me. Standing next to the chair that I'd been sitting in. With a feeling of trepidation, I sat down.

"Carol, I just wanted to tell you something. I don't know if you're aware of this, but you and I have the same birthday, May 26," Stevie said as she sank down into the chair next to mine.

"Gee, Stevie. That's weird," I answered hesitantly.

"Do you wear black clothes a lot?" she asked in a husky whisper.

"Yes, I do. Blondes look good in black, I think." I tried to keep the bewilderment out of my voice as I spoke to her. Where in the hell was this going?

"Don't you see?" She beamed. "That explains everything! Black has always been my color and we were born on the same day! You know, Carol, you must be so much like me that it's beyond coincidence. It's almost mystical." She was smiling now in triumph. "No wonder Lindsey would go for you!"

Sitting in stunned silence, I didn't know if I should laugh or scream. Looking at Stevie's deadly serious face, I realized with a sinking feeling that I was embarking on my first real conversation with her and I felt as though I were entering the Twilight Zone.

Why does it have to be so weird? I thought miserably to myself. *Is she seeing how far she can push me? For cripes sake, does she really believe that Lindsey's with me because my horoscope is the same as hers?*

"Well, gee, Stevie, I think it's really cool that we have the same birthday. Really. Did you know that John Wayne was born on May 26, too?"

Stevie's eyes began to narrow as I continued. "Anyway, the black clothes thing is just, well, blondes look great in black! I wear a lot of white and turquoise as well. Lindsey's seen me in a lot of different colors. Trust me, Stevie, it's not my birthday or the color of my clothes that attracts Lindsey. You'll just have to take my word for it."

Seeing Stevie's now-red face and narrowed eyes, it was obvious that I hadn't given her the response she expected. If it were possible to cast a bad spell over another person, she was giving it her all. I could feel her anger washing over me in waves. With a toss of her hair and a last furious glare, she growled, "I see. Well, I just wanted to tell you. I thought you'd like to know, that's all."

With that, she rose quickly to her feet, almost knocking the chair over in her haste. Making a beeline for her girlfriends, she whispered something to them and they all turned and stared at me. Once again, I slumped down into my chair and watched as they walked out of the circle of light and into the shadows at the back of the soundstage.

That went well. Now she really hates me, I thought wearily as I chewed my fingernail. Suddenly, I felt a wave of exhaustion and leaned my head against the back of the metal chair, closing my eyes. My mind was reeling. I wanted to go home. Back to a world where reality ruled instead of astrology and mystic signs and, by the look on Stevie's face, black spells.

As though reading my thoughts, Lindsey appeared by my side and slid into the chair where Stevie had been sitting moments before. "Let's get outta here, angel. Want to go home?" Lindsey asked as he reached for my hand. I nodded my head and he pulled me to my feet. "I have plans for you tonight, darlin'. Hope you're not too tired!" My spirits lifted as I looked into his blue eyes and we walked arm in arm out of the soundstage into the cold night.

As soon as I closed the door of my apartment, Lindsey pulled me into the bedroom and broke the strap of my dress as he pulled it off. I laughed and kicked it to a corner of the room. After Stevie's remarks, I never wanted to wear it (or black) again.

As the deluge of winter storms continued to besiege L.A., Fleetwood Mac was cut off from the rain and wind howling outside the soundstage, the members gathering each night in the warmth of the spotlights. Days swept by and each night the band became tighter. Gone were the hesitant vocals and jagged harmonies. Lindsey's playing and singing was hard and assertive. John's bass was a solid, thundering backdrop to Mick's pounding drums.

Stevie, now dressed each night in her black chiffon stage skirt and five-inch platform boots, with tambourine in hand, was mesmerizing at center stage. Her throaty vocals sent chills down the spines of the handful of us privileged to be sitting in the audience. The backdrop of a withered tree and Gothic moon against a black background looked not only like an illustration from a Brothers Grimm fairy tale, but also a window into the forest in which Rhiannon lived. Richard Dashut and Ken Caillet were sound-engineering magicians at the mixing board set up behind us at the very edge of the circle of light in the soundstage.

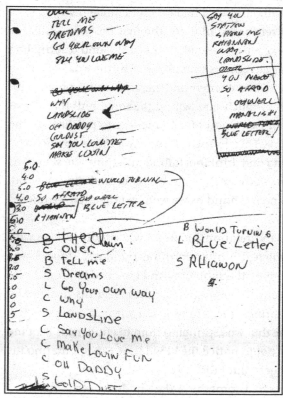

Lindsey's ideas for the set list for the Rumours *tour.*

All that was left to do was to finalize the set. A band's set is critical: the order and choice of songs in a concert should flow and keep the audience enthralled. After trying out endless variations, which provoked more than a few fights among the members, Fleetwood Mac finally hit on a set order that was a masterpiece of musicianship. Today I have absolutely no doubt that anyone who was lucky enough to see the shows of the 1977–78 *Rumours* tour will agree with me.

By the end of rehearsals Stevie and I had settled into an uneasy truce. Even though I could feel her resentment like a dark mist washing over me each time I was near her, I kept a smile on my face and tried to never let her see how much I was bothered by it. What I truly hoped was that one day Stevie and I would be friends. But if that day never came, then so be it. I knew that I would rise above everything she might try to throw at me to break up my relationship with Lindsey. I had to. I had made a vow.

It was the last night of rehearsals and, for the first time, an audience had been invited. Warner executives, friends of the band, and a sprinkling of family members filled the cavernous soundstage. The air was humming with anticipation. The band was excited and nervous to be playing for an audience, but there was so much goodwill in the large hall that it was easy for the five members of Fleetwood Mac to move into position on the stage area and start the show. They launched into "You Make Loving Fun" and people stopped laughing and drinking, falling into complete silence as they sat in awe of the power of the music that was coming from the band. I stood by Julie's side, holding her hand as we watched the men we adored dazzle the crowd.

It was four months into our relationship and I was madly in love with Lindsey. As I stood and watched him perform on the dusty stage, I was struck by his vulnerability under the spotlights and I wanted to protect him with all of my heart and soul. The way that Lindsey held his head as he looked down at his guitar strings, playing as usual without a guitar pick, completely lost in the music that was springing from his fingertips kept me frozen in place. He seemed not to notice the blood that was splattering his guitar from his savaged fingers. But I did.

For the first time I perceived something that hadn't been obvious to me before that night's dress rehearsal. Dressed in his stage clothes, guitar strapped around his neck, Lindsey had a power and a purity that shone in its brightness. And I knew that I would do everything within my power to protect him. Suddenly words rang out in my mind with the clarity of a church bell: *I'll never do anything that will come between Lindsey and his music.*

At once it was clear to me what Lindsey essentially was: half man and half pure music—savage, unformed, and fundamentally dangerous. I knew, as I stood and watched him play, that if I wanted the first half I'd have to nurture and protect the second, inner half of Lindsey, the part that was sheer musical genius. No matter what it might cost me personally.

But as those words kept ringing through my head—*I'll never do anything that will come between Lindsey and his music*—I made a vow to live by this commandment. The alternative, I realized, would be a life without Lindsey—something I couldn't even begin to think about. The love I felt for him was such that life without him would no longer be worth living.

Rehearsals had ended and *Rumours* was due to be released in three days. All of us were nervous and excited. Even though the radio had been playing the album nonstop for the past month, it was the reviews and sales figures that initially would spell out the record's success and, following that, the *Rumours* tour ticket sales would be the further measure of it. Without good reviews and sales, the tour would be an uphill battle to prove that Fleetwood Mac had what it took to be a success story in the music industry.

The band took a two-week break before the start of the tour to promote *Rumours,* and everyone was heading off to Hawaii or Mexico to rest up, party, and try to forget about the pressure that was building like a hurricane with each passing day. But Lindsey, instead of flying to a vacation spot, wanted to go home. He called me at Producer's Workshop and asked me to drive up to northern California with him to meet his family that weekend. My palms turned sweaty as I gulped and answered, "Sure, baby, I'd love to go." I could feel the blood draining out of my face as I hung up.

What am I going to wear? What will I do if his family decides I'm not right for him? What if they just flat-out hate me? I thought, as I laid my head down on my desk and tried to will away the nerves that were threatening to make me nauseous. *You can do this, Carol. You'll love them and Lindsey will be proud of you. I mean, he wants me to meet his family, so that's a big deal. I'll try so hard to be perfect and I'll make them like me. Even if it kills me.*

Two days later I climbed into Lindsey's blue and somewhat battered BMW 328i and we began the long drive up to Palo Alto. During the nine-hour trip Lindsey smoked joint after joint and told me about his childhood and his family. His brother Jeff was responsible for his learning to play guitar, he told me. Apparently Jeff would rush out and buy rock 'n' roll 45s the minute they were released and play them for Lindsey when they were still in elementary school. Lindsey begged his parents for a guitar and they bought him a $35 Harmony. He taught himself how to play by listening to Elvis and Kingston Trio records.

As approaching headlights swept the interior of the car, Lindsey had a smile and a faraway look on his face as he went on with his tales of childhood highlights. He told me he won his first singing contest playing "Black Slacks" at the age of seven while on vacation with his family in Arizona. A star was born.

Lindsey took another long drag of his joint and kept talking. "I went to Menlo-Atherton High School. I'll drive you by it. Anyway, Stevie went there too and she was a year ahead of me. I joined a high school rock band named the Fritz Rabyne Memorial Band. In 1967 we regroup, shorten the name to just Fritz, Stevie joins as the lead singer, Bob Aguirre is on drums, a guy called Brian is on lead guitar, and I played bass and sang."

"You played bass? Why?" I couldn't imagine Lindsey not having a lead guitar in his hands.

He looked sheepishly at me and told me that because the music was pretty psychedelic, he didn't feel he could play it that well. "Then, later on," he said, "the band breaks up and Stevie and I form Buckingham Nicks. We had an album out on Polydor. The fuckers dropped us from the label while we were playing a small club tour in the South. I'll tell you all about it later. We have plenty of time for all that," he added meaningfully as he reached for my hand.

"Hey Lindsey," I said, "I have someone in my family who is pretty damn famous!" As Lindsey looked at me with a surprised expression, I continued. "My great-uncle is Frank Hamer. He's probably the most famous Texas Ranger in the world! He was the Ranger who tracked down Bonnie and Clyde in the 1930s! He actually received a citation medal from Congress for doing it. He also captured the Dalton Gang and the Newton Boys—some of the worst gangs of bank robbers in the old West!

Oh, and he was also famous for his sarcasm. When a small town in Texas called in the Rangers to put down a riot, my uncle came to the rescue. When he stepped off of the train—alone—the townspeople said to him, 'We have a riot down here! Where are the rest of the Rangers?' And he answered, 'One riot, one Ranger' . . . *and* he stopped the rioting single-handed! Isn't that cool?"

"I've heard that quote, but I didn't have a clue who said it! That's totally amazing, Carol. That makes what I do seem like a cakewalk," Lindsey answered.

"Well, I wouldn't say that necessarily, but at least you're not being shot at. He was my grandmother's brother and she told me that he was in over fifty gunfights, wounded over twenty times, and left for dead twice! Anyway, I just love it that he's my great-uncle! Lindsey, can you tell me a little about your brothers and parents? I'm just nervous about meeting them, and it would help if I knew what to expect, you know?" I asked nervously.

"They're going to love you, Carol. My older brothers are both married. Businessmen now," he answered. In a proud voice he told me that his brother Greg won a silver medal in the 1964 Olympics for swimming. Jeff was even more of a hero to Lindsey. He lost part of his leg in a bad car accident and had an artificial limb below one knee. Jeff jogged, and unless you knew his leg was prosthetic, you'd never realize it. Lindsey's love for both of them shone in his eyes as he spoke.

His mother was widowed, as she lost his father to a heart attack during the fuel shortage of 1974. "My dad was in a line for gas. There were cars lined up for blocks and he had a heart attack. All alone in his car in a fucking gas line." Lindsey abruptly took an exit into a rest area and turned off the engine. I tried to look into his face in the dimly lit wooded area, but all I could see was his profile. His voice, however, carried so much pain that I wanted to reach out and take him into my arms. Sensing that he needed to talk, I sat still as he told me in words full of tears of the day he lost his father.

"I was in L.A., living with Stevie, when I got a phone call from my mom. I flew home that night and spent the night in my old bedroom. It was the worst night of my life."

"Baby, I'm so, so sorry."

Squeezing my hand tightly, Lindsey spoke of how much he missed and loved his father. How much he wished he could be here to share in what was happening in his life. I reached over and took his face into my hands and told him that I believed that his dad was with him, that he was watching over Lindsey, and how proud his father must be of him.

Speaking softly, Lindsey said that he wanted to believe that. He told me that his family grew up in a beautiful house with a pool and belonged to a country club for half of his childhood. Then his dad's coffee business started going downhill and they had to sell their big house for a smaller one. Father and sons handled it well, but it was hard on Lindsey's mother to give up the home and the country club life that she loved. And then, after Lindsey left home to follow his dream with Stevie, his dad passed away. As he told me, his face filled with a grief that left me speechless with the knowledge that it could never be healed or soothed.

He took a moment to collect himself and then leaned over and kissed me. "We're only about an hour away. I've booked us into the Santa Clara Marriott. Tomorrow I'll take you on a tour of my old neighborhood, and then we're going to dinner with my family."

"Sure, great," I said weakly. My nerves were on edge about the family gathering, but I knew that at least I'd have a whole day to work up my courage as Lindsey showed me his hometown.

We took the promised driving tour and spent a wonderful day. By the time we left to pick up his family for dinner, I was much more at ease and immediately felt welcomed by his brothers. His mother, Rutheda, in contrast was polite but distant. *I'll win her over eventually*, I said firmly to myself. *After all, Lindsey is her youngest. All mothers are extra protective about their youngest child.*

We went to Scotty's Steak House in Palo Alto. Lindsey had been going there for dinner with his family since he was three years old. The food was so-so, but the garlic bread was to die for. It was the bread, Lindsey said, that kept the Buckinghams coming back year after year. The topic of conversation: *Rumours*. His family was stunned over the success of Lindsey's album and I sat next to him happily as they praised his achievement. I could see in Lindsey's face how much it meant to him to have his brothers and mom so proud of him. I could also see that the three Buckingham brothers were very, very close—and it made me glad for all of them. Watching the three of them talk made me miss my own sisters and I vowed to call them as soon as we were back in L.A.

Lindsey Buckingham, Greg Buckingham, Jeff Buckingham, Laura Buckingham, Amy Buckingham, Daryl Buckingham.

On Sunday morning the weather was gorgeous and we drove to Point Lobos, a nature preserve that was a few miles outside of Carmel. Located on the edge of the Pacific Ocean, its miles of wild wetlands and cliffs are absolutely amazing. As I would discover over the years to come, it was one of Lindsey's favorite places to spend a day smoking weed, walking, and thinking about music.

As we walked through the beautiful trees and climbed down the rocks to watch the waves crash below us, I clung to Lindsey's arm and a sense of wonder overwhelmed me. Looking up at his chiseled cheekbones, long, brown-black curls, and piercing blue eyes, I couldn't believe that I was with him. *I must be in a dream,* I thought to myself. *I'm walking in one of the most beautiful places on earth with a man who takes my breath away. If this is a dream, I don't ever want to wake up.* As though reading my thoughts, Lindsey looked down into my upturned face and smiled. And I knew that I had never, ever been so in love.

After a few hours of walking we climbed into the car for our long drive back to L.A. First, though, Lindsey wanted to stop for lunch. We pulled into a roadside diner and on the way inside he saw a newspaper dispenser holding copies of the Bay Area's free alternative newspaper, *Bam*. It was San Francisco's answer to New York's *Village Voice* and on the cover was a small picture of Fleetwood Mac, with a caption that said, "Album review, page 3."

Lindsey grabbed the newspaper with excitement in his eyes. Stopping dead in his tracks, he almost tore the paper trying to get to the review of *Rumours*. I stood expectantly beside him as he started to read. Within seconds his face darkened and looks of horror, despair, and rage swiftly moved across his features. He looked up at me and said in a tight voice, "They fucking hate the album!" His voice rose in volume. "They basically say it's crap! They trash it! *Jesus, Carol, they hate the album!*"

He started to rip the newspaper into shreds and threw it on the ground. "I'm not hungry anymore. Let's grab a couple of burgers to go. I want you to eat. I don't think I can."

I felt helpless. I knew I had to make him feel better, but looking at his face left me lost for words. It seemed that in just one moment our world had come crashing down. Even though the afternoon sun was warm, I felt chilled to the bone. We ordered our food to go and climbed back into the car. We'd both lost our appetites, and the food sat forgotten between us.

Lindsey headed out of the parking lot and back onto the freeway. He was driving about ninety miles an hour, pushing the gas pedal down hard with rage and disappointment. I struggled to think of something, *anything,* to say that would make him feel better.

"It's only one review, Lindsey. In a crappy newspaper. *Rumours* is brilliant! Look at all of the airplay it's been getting. It's on every radio station!" I said desperately as the car swerved in and out of traffic.

Suddenly he took his foot off the gas and hit the brakes. Roughly, he steered the car over to the side of the freeway, pulled onto the shoulder, and turned off the engine. As traffic flashed by us he lowered his head onto the steering wheel and I swear that I could hear a silent scream fill the air. He turned his head, looked at me, and said simply, "It hurts so much I can hardly breathe. What if he's right? What if the album is shit? I can't tell any more, Carol. Am I crazy? I think it's good. Fuck, I thought it was great. But what if I'm wrong?" His face was that of a child, dismay and confusion etched across it.

The words of one reviewer had opened the door to Lindsey's darkest fears and it would take the words of another to close it. Until that next review, I would have to try to close the lid of his Pandora's box and help him with the pain that he was feeling.

Leaning over, I grabbed his face between my hands. "Listen to me," I urged him. "You're not wrong. You're not! This album is amazing. When I first heard it at the studio, I was stunned! It's that good, baby. You have to believe me; I'll never, ever lie to you. I think it's the best album I've ever heard! Why do you think every radio station is playing it before it's even sold one damn copy?"

Lindsey looked at me, calmer now, listening.

"You have to forget about the idiot who wrote that review. He doesn't get it, Lindsey. And if he doesn't get your music, *then fuck him. I hate him!*"

Lindsey blinked, startled at my ferocity, and then started to smile. "Maybe you should write our next review."

I kissed him hard and said, "I just did."

The ride back to L.A. was quiet, with none of the celebration that we had on the journey north. As we pulled into Lindsey's driveway on Putney in West L.A. he said, "I have to call the band. I have to tell them about the review." I nodded and followed him inside his house, leaving our suitcases forgotten in the trunk.

We entered Lindsey's bedroom, decorated with a shabby-chic, threadbare Persian carpet, a chipped wood bureau, and his ever-present guitars. The only wall decoration was a creased black-and-white poster of a Victorian house standing on a cliff, looking sinister as a storm wreaked havoc around it.

I stared at the poster. I'd seen it before, but tonight its stark bleakness made me uneasy—as Lindsey called first Mick, then Stevie and Christine to tell them about the piece in *Bam*. As he vented his rage and disappointment and received obvious reassurance from the voices at the other end of the line, I listened to the first of many occasions when the members of Fleetwood Mac would become one entity against the world, to support one another against an attack. Hearing confidence slowly creep back into Lindsey's voice with each call, I knew that *Rumours* had weathered its first storm.

In fact, the *Bam* review trashing *Rumours* would be the only time, to our knowledge, that the album wasn't heralded as the truly defining golden accomplishment in music that it was. Literally hundreds of magazines showered glittering praise on the record. *Rolling Stone* gave *Rumours* such a rave review that it was almost embarrassing to read. The album as a whole and the band members' individual songs were lauded to the heavens, with Lindsey's work getting special accolades: "joyous," "timeless," "angelic," and, best of all, "classic." Over the next year the same magazine would give Fleetwood Mac not one but two covers accompanied by main features: one of the highest honors a band could receive in the 1970s and '80s. We didn't realize it that night, but the golden curtain of fame was lifting for Fleetwood Mac.

Rumours was about to make history. The clock had started ticking on my days as a participant in everyday, normal life. Without realizing it, I was about to leave behind everything that I'd ever known.

4

LADIES AND GENTLEMEN: FLEETWOOD MAC!

Warner Bros. released *Rumours* in the last week of February 1977. It was the largest advance order that Warner Bros. had ever shipped. In one week the album sold enough copies to reach platinum status. The music industry had never witnessed anything like it before. Eight hundred thousand copies were shipped to record stores in the first week alone. Every radio station in L.A., and across the country, was playing each and every track on the album. I'd pull up next to someone in traffic with "Gold Dust Woman" on my car radio and hear "Go Your Own Way" blasting from the car next to me. The album hit number one on the charts within days of its release.

Lindsey's phone was ringing off the hook; people were beginning to stare as we went to restaurants. It was insane, exciting, and scary. Promotions, interviews, and magazine articles were appearing daily. I'd leave work at six, drive to Lindsey's for a dinner date, and have to wait in the living room while reporters interviewed him and photographers shot close-ups for yet another article in a newspaper or magazine. After a month of this I got as used to it as the rest of the band

Carol Ann and Lindsey arriving at the Jacques Cousteau show.

did, and the surreal world of rock icons quickly became part of my daily life. As the *Rumours* tour began, Fleetwood Mac was on the brink of becoming one of the greatest bands of all time.

The first show of the *Rumours* tour, in San Francisco, was fast approaching and after weeks of rehearsal at SIR Studios, the band was ready. Lindsey asked me to go with him barely a week before the show. I was beginning to wonder if perhaps he was too nervous to have me there at his first big show of the tour, but he made it clear that he needed me there. It seemed very important to him to have me at his side. I soon realized why.

Yes, I'd been to gigs before. I'd been in the music industry for years, and I was pretty laid back about most things. But I was totally unprepared for this. Believe me, there is no drug, no adrenaline rush, no high that compares to going onstage with Fleetwood Mac.

This was my first experience of a Fleetwood Mac performance, behind the scenes, up close and frighteningly personal. The band members were all clearly preoccupied on the flight to San Francisco and in the Fairmont Hotel, where we stayed. There was little of the amiable joshing and joking that I'd seen at the studio or in the rehearsal hall. I think they all realized by this time that this was way out of control—that the fast track they now found themselves on could head beyond fame into the unknown region of legend. The attention from the press and the fans was so overwhelming that it had almost become a physical weight—and it was beginning to choke everyone.

The sense of urgency and responsibility also transformed our charismatic English road manager John Courage. He appeared out of nowhere as our limo pulled up outside the venue, an instant butler—composed, deferential, and completely in control.

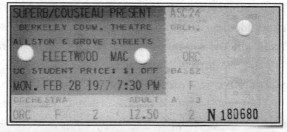

"And how are we tonight, Mr. Buckingham? Miss Harris? Let me get you to your dressing *Jacques Cousteau concert ticket.* rooms and I'll personally make you your first drink of the evening."

Lindsey needed one. He was deathly pale. The hand that held on to mine was clammy.

We followed J.C. past rows of huge anvil cases with the Fleetwood Mac penguin logo on them. Coils of gray cable snaked under our feet, boxes were piled in the corridors we stumbled through, there were racks of lights, roadies everywhere, technicians barking out orders, and, beyond it all, the hum of distant voices, whistles, screams—the audience taking its own place in the panic.

We were led through this madness and movement into a huge room furnished with tables piled high with food, exotic floral arrangements, and bottles of every conceivable alcoholic drink. It was also filled to capacity with men in suits, milling to fill every gap, networking, on the move, cuff links flashing.

Lindsey grabbed J.C. by the arm. "Get me out of here!" he pleaded, his voice frighteningly quiet. But he'd been seen and heard. The milling stopped for a moment. The shark pack of bodies seemed to inch toward him. There were hands outstretched, shit-eating smiles on faces.

J.C. quickly told Lindsey that he'd take him to the tuning room where Ray was waiting with Lindsey's guitars. Lindsey squeezed my hand and pulled me close. "You'll be all right here for a while?" he whispered to me, then, turning to J.C., "I'm leaving her in your care. Make sure no one bothers her!"

J.C. nodded at me and, taking Lindsey by the elbow, made way for him through the glad-handers. I stood where he left me, marooned, shaking. I wasn't expecting it to be like this. Not like this.

And then I heard Christine's warm, throaty laugh, and she was suddenly by my side. She threw her arm around my shoulders as she told me in a loud voice not to pay any attention to the flashy men swarming around us. Explaining that they were "money men," Warner Bros. execs and lawyers, she guided me to the drinks table and told me I'd be wise to keep away from them. She ordered me to have a drink to calm my nerves.

"I don't drink—" I started to say, but Christine, holding on to her usual vodka tonic, was already pouring the same for me.

"Get that down you," she ordered. She winked at me again, poured another drink for herself, and spun away. Immediately someone came up to me, introducing himself as Mickey Shapiro, attorney for Christine, John, and Mick. The name didn't register with me at the time. He was an attorney for just three of the band, not all five. Fleetwood Mac, with its separated affiliations, wasn't quite the unified organization it pretended to be. Lindsey and Stevie were each represented by different attorneys and when contracts needed to be signed there were multiple law firms happily billing multiple hours. I returned his handshake, hoping that I could manage a smile to match his leer, and then caught J.C.'s eye. He was waving to me.

"Hey, you!" he grinned. "Lindsey's asking for you. Let's ferry you through to him." He crooked his arm for me to slip mine through. I needed the support.

Lindsey was in a small room along the hallway, sitting on the floor, surrounded by guitars, strumming an Ovation quietly. "Hey," he grinned. "Mickey Shapiro just stopped by to congratulate me on my new girlfriend. I guess he thinks I chose well!" He stood and hugged me. He seemed back to his old self, there, in that tiny room, hemmed in by instruments. It was where he belonged. He always preferred to be among objects rather than people, I later discovered, especially if they were objects over which he could have total mastery and control. Instruments obeyed him. They spoke the words he wanted them to say and did whatever he instructed them.

Lindsey pulled me close and kissed me. He handed me his guitar, stroked it lovingly, nodded to a stand where he wanted me to set it and then began to change into his stage clothes, pulling a loose white cotton shirt over his head. With long full sleeves it was cut exactly like a pirate shirt that looked as though it was straight out of the wardrobe department of a film company. Standing there in his faded blue jeans, swirling shirt, cowboy boots, and dark curling hair, he looked like a fairy-tale prince. I wanted to tell him how much he meant to me, but at that moment, just as his lips touched mine, John McVie loped into the room.

"Hey, unhand that woman and pick up your Les Paul!" he shouted. Lindsey laughed, but picked up the guitar with the same tenderness that he'd just touched me.

"Could you grab me a Myers's and Coke?" he asked me, over his shoulder.

With a shrug and a grin, I left the two guitarists to make sweet music.

As I walked down the hallway J.C.'s voice boomed, *"Ten minutes, everybody. Ten minutes!"*

I'd soon learn that this was a ritual. Every show started the same way.

"Nine minutes! Christine, are you OK, dear?" he asked her as I stepped into the dressing room. The room was buzzing. It was empty of all but Christine, Mick, Stevie, and, of course, me, fixing Lindsey's rum and Coke.

I swear that you could feel the electricity in the air as the band members did their final preparations before taking the stage. I tried to hold the glass steady as I poured.

"*Seven minutes!* Mick, you have a question?"

Out of the corner of my eye, I saw two apparitions. One was Stevie, the White Witch, Rhiannon. Over a black leotard top she'd layered black chiffon, falling into points around her feet, then wrapped herself in three shawls, each with a different firework display of sequins, spluttering into rainbow light under the bright glare of the makeup mirror.

Then there was Christine, the Warrior Queen, in silk skirts and a velvet-embroidered waistcoat. Neither was quite real. Both were as fictionalized as the fans demanded. But the fans would recognize the legends. And on this night, their stage personas were already beginning to wipe out their real-life personalities. Christine's hands shook. Was it only nerves? She grabbed a stray glass and downed the contents.

"*Five minutes!* Stevie, are you ready? You look pale!"

"Fine, J.C. You'll make sure of that, won't you?" Stevie croaked. *What did that mean?*

"I will indeed, Miss Nicks! Don't you worry! *Four minutes!*"

John came into the room, drinking from an almost empty bottle of Scotch, with Lindsey following, his Les Paul guitar strapped around his neck.

"Your drink!" I smiled, handing it to him.

"Perfect!" he whispered. "Thanks, angel."

Mick was resplendent in a knickerbocker outfit of black velvet with a pair of wooden balls suspended from a cord and hanging between his thighs, just as he'd been photographed on the *Rumours* album cover. He leaped around the room with his drumsticks, hitting every solid surface. Then he held both sticks to his groin, standing proud from his crotch, and wiggled his hips, making the balls bounce and click. It was as crude a sexual gesture as I'd ever seen. Stevie Nicks giggled shrilly and I caught the glance he gave her, then the coy look she returned. *No, surely not?* I thought. *Mick's married, and Stevie has her choice of every available man in the world! But if Lindsey looked at me that way, I'd be left in no doubt what it meant.*

"*Three minutes!*"

Lindsey downed his drink, and glared out of the corner of his eye at Stevie, still giggling at Mick's mimed suggestions. My heart stopped for a second. It really wasn't over between them, was it?

"Line up and let's send you out in style!" J.C. ordered.

They seemed to know what came next. Like obedient schoolchildren, the band formed their line, holding out their fists. J.C. poured a small pile of cocaine onto each wrist. "*Two minutes!* Let's toot and get those roses in your cheeks, Stevie!" he commanded. Lindsey snorted, then looked at me. His blue, blue gaze held mine and for the first time in our relationship, I could see naked fear in his eyes.

"*One minute* and let's go."

I fought my inner instinct to run to him, and I hung back. Even at this first show I knew they were crossing into territory I could not enter. Once they left the inner sanctum of their dressing room they'd abandon their separate identities and forge themselves into the power that was Fleetwood Mac. Lindsey was gone, his eyes not leaving mine until he was out of sight and into the roar. They were fused. They were one. They still loved and hated in all the most dangerous places, but that was personal. This was different.

Lions and Christians. I'd never heard anything that could shake a floor and a ceiling at the same time—oh, but this noise did. It was human need. It was demand. And it was primal.

The lights dimmed in the auditorium as I drifted into the wings, then the stage lit up in brilliant colors and "You Make Loving Fun" made a deafening irony out of the frenzy. The audience response to this sound was a physical force so powerful that I took an involuntary step backward as though warding off an attack. It hit me and I felt as though I couldn't breathe, while onstage jeweled silk and black chiffon swirled and shimmered hypnotically to Lindsey's melodic spell of sound.

I was stunned. Until this precise moment I hadn't completely understood who Lindsey was. I knew he was a member of a well-known band. I'd been there with him in the last stages of producing the album. I knew he was special and talented. But up to now I'd felt, warmed there with him in bed at nights, laughing, being with him during the days, that I was the only person who could shower him with love. I thought that was all he needed to make him happy. I had no real comprehension of what it was that drove an artist to put himself through fire. Lindsey the man was happy enough with me. But his talent demanded the recognition of this mass of open mouths, open arms, open desire. His talent was a separate entity, an energy that fed off and into this voltage.

I was totally unprepared. I was sharing him with something that I could never match.

Just then I felt an arm on my elbow: J.C., pulling me toward the stage. "Lindsey wants you to come up," he said. "Come on. Come over. Inspire him!" I found myself pushed into the edge of that audience glare, face to face.

I stood helpless, panic-stricken, as the spotlight caught my stage appearance. Lindsey was no more than five feet away from me, playing to me, *to me*, as well as to that fan mass. His fingers were bleeding all over the guitar. He'd opened up the calluses on his fingertips, but didn't seem to notice. He smiled brightly at me, stepped toward his captive girlfriend, ice-cold with stage fright as I was. But in the roar of approval from the audience I felt like Alice in Wonderland, in a mirror image of the world I'd always inhabited. This was to be my new world, this strange, deafening, chaotic otherness that Lindsey was lovingly exposing me to.

And then, as I trembled back to my place in the wings, I heard sounds that would haunt me each and every time I heard them. It was the opening chords of Lindsey's song "I'm So Afraid" and the aching loneliness of his clear, tear-drenched voice. A supernatural quiet descended. This was just Lindsey, on guitar, picked out by a solitary spotlight, Mick on drums in the darkness behind, and a man crying out in pain and fury.

Why had I never heard it this way before? In rehearsal it was just a sad, beautiful song. Now it was uncomprehending, plaintive rage. The words spoke of his fear of his own demons and his loneliness. He was begging the world to break through to save him from darkness. His anguish was raw. He was terrified that he'd slip, fall, and die. He let his guitar speak for him now, as he moved to the edge of the front of the stage, playing notes of pure despair.

I didn't dare breathe. The man and the myth fused into a presence that was awe-inspiring. I stood with my palms pressed hard against a black speaker, in the song with him, living through it, whether I wanted to or not, along with all those hushed thousands who knew that he was speaking for them, just for them, each one of them stranded in separate emptiness.

Lindsey Buckingham was taking us all into black, black magic in each touched guitar string.

Silence greeted the final echoing note. I let out my breath. So did the audience, so clearly that I could hear the rush. Spontaneously everyone leaped to their feet for an almost unending standing ovation.

As I listened to the screams of the crowd, I felt pride that it was Lindsey and Lindsey alone who had inspired the audience to react in uncontrolled awe. Love for him swept over me as I watched him wipe away the sweat that was pouring down his face and slowly walk toward the darkness of the back of the stage.

I also felt fear. For the first time in our relationship, I felt dread descend upon me as I looked at him—and all I wanted to do was run from what I'd just experienced.

So I did. Turning blindly, I ran toward the curtain that opened into the backstage area, past the stares and calls of people who looked at me in surprise and concern, and I didn't stop until I hit the door of our dressing room. I threw it open and slammed it shut behind me. Leaning against it, I tried to catch my breath.

Looking wildly around the room, I was more than grateful to see that I was alone. Walking shakily toward the bar, I caught a glimpse of myself in the makeup mirror and I gasped. My hair was wild and tangled, my shirt had come untucked and the neckline was plunging much more than it should have. My image drew me closer. My face was so white it was almost translucent. A sheet of sweat on my skin glistened in the light and gave me an otherworldly look—an apparition dressed in black velvet. My eyes were huge and as I stared, I saw a very terrified girl looking back at me.

Shocked, I turned away and sank down onto the couch, the night's images playing through my mind. Lindsey and I kissing in the tuning room . . . the terror in his eyes as he gave me one last look before heading on stage . . . the crazed audience . . . Stevie's swirling black chiffon . . . the glare of white spotlights during the final notes of "So Afraid"—blood on a guitar, tears on faces, silence exploding into chaos . . . small white hands pressed against the blackness of a speaker . . . faces blurring as I ran and ran . . .

I laid my head down on my knees and tried to will the pictures out of my mind.

"Are you OK, sweetheart?" J.C. asked.

His was the face I saw through swirling black chiffon mist. His was the voice I heard, more distant than the sound of my furious heartbeat. I blinked. Whatever I'd been was now obliterated. What I thought I owned, Lindsey's total devotion, I'd lost to the masses.

"What happened? Carol, talk to me. I'm here to help you. I can take care of anything."

I gasped for air, struggling to find a small voice. "It's just," I whispered, "it's just the song. Never heard it that way before."

That was the easiest explanation, for me, as well as for him. How could I hope to put into words the initiation I'd just experienced? The bloodlust of the crowd—demands that can't be satisfied. Our love wasn't enough, and never would be.

"Look, I'm sorry," I sobbed. "Maybe it's all been a bit too much for me. Do I belong here? I just want us to be like everyone else!"

"But you're not. You're the lady of a very special man. And he has this job to do. And he chose you because you're special, too." J.C. tucked a stray lock of my wet hair behind my ear.

"Carol," he murmured, "you're one of us now. D'you know what that means? You're part of the Fleetwood Mac family, and we're a small tight band of people. It's a link stronger than blood. With or without Lindsey, you're one of us! Lindsey adores you. We all do. Except perhaps Stevie. And she'll adapt. Listen: Fleetwood Mac takes care of our own!"

He paused, wiped my tear-stained face. "Now next time you're upset or nervous, you come looking for me, no matter what. Lindsey'll be onstage, but I'm always here. You'll get used to this, trust me, you will. There's a long road tour ahead but after a while it'll feel as normal to you as living in L.A. It's going to be a great year, and Lindsey loves you and needs you with him. Understand? Now, watch this magic trick!"

J.C. pulled out a small glass vial half full of cocaine and poured some on the yellow plastic table next to me.

"Let's line that up and get it down you. Come on, Carol Ann, didn't I tell you you can trust me? Hey, I know what's best for you, and right now, this is! Just do it."

Just do it.

Why not? I couldn't feel any worse.

I nodded, took the rolled-up note he handed me, and did it like Julie had shown me once in rehearsals. And I could do it! It was so easy!

My heart pounded. The room was brighter. I wasn't small, I wasn't scared. I was so, so happy. A rush of exhilaration hit my bloodstream. Incredible. In one second I could go from being the scared waif from Oklahoma to feeling like I could do absolutely anything.

"Now, that's good, huh? So, freshen up, darlin', and let's have you back where you belong!" J.C. laughed. "And there's much more where that came from, so no need ever to feel anxious again, is there?"

I laughed with him. "None at all, J.C.!"

I quickly freshened up, as he waited, then, giggling quietly, walked back with him to my proper place in the wings.

"Gotta go!" J.C. said. "But here's a little toot if you find yourself getting tearful again!" He pushed a paper wrap into my hand. "You stay here, and remember, when you hear 'Go Your Own Way,' that's the last song, so stand next to the platform stairs. I want you safely back in the dressing room before the first encore's over. Got all that?"

I nodded. God, I felt great—energized, happy, and, most of all, like I could handle anything. *Is this what Julie meant in rehearsals? She's right, I totally love this feeling!*

Songs washed over and through me. Christine's poignant "Songbird," clearer than daylight, dedicated to Curry Grant. And Lindsey's "Second Hand News"—only a man could write that to his ex-lover! Suddenly it was "Go Your Own Way." The entire hall was on its feet. Ray, Lindsey's loyal guitar roadie, was onstage, accompanying Lindsey, and Stevie was racing round like a spinning top, wearing a top hat, beating a tambourine, whipping everyone

Photography © Ed Roach, roach-clips.com

Stevie sitting on the side of the stage.

into a frenzy. Flowers were sailing toward the stage, people were packing the aisles, trying to edge closer to the dream they'd just shared. There was laughter and celebration in those final words, "Thank you, San Francisco, and goodnight!" and then the stage was plunged into darkness.

I positioned myself by the stairs as instructed. It was eerie standing there, looking over the audience instead of being a part of it with a ticket stub in my back pocket. In a little over three hours my world had tilted on its axis and started turning in a different direction.

"You're part of the Fleetwood Mac family . . . You're one of us . . . It's a link stronger than blood."

I shivered. J.C. had whispered those words to me not just to comfort me. He wanted to make sure I understood something—that just as Lindsey and I knew we had fallen in love, so did the band, so did the organization, so did the "family." And they knew that this meant I had to be admitted to the circle. I didn't want to think about the implications of that, not just then. I'd done enough thinking for one night.

The clamor from the crowd changed in tone, and I turned to see flash-light beams through the curtains, newly parted. The stage was a riot of color—gold, blue, red. Stevie took center stage, a sheer scarf draped over her head. A star. Her voice rang out, husky, sensuous, taunting. Pure Stevie Nicks, "Gold Dust Woman," the ancient queen who uses men to satisfy her lust. Her sexual presence was mesmerizing. I was so caught up in it that I almost forgot J.C.'s command to get down to the dressing room by the end of the first encore.

I slipped through the curtain and back to our sanctuary. In minutes Lindsey would be offstage. I had to look my best, but exhaustion was catching up with me. I locked myself in the bathroom, made up my pale face, then inhaled J.C.'s gift and smiled thankfully. It was having a positive effect already. I felt stronger, more confident, happier. Wasn't that positive?

I heard one final bone-shaking roar from the crowd as I unlocked the bathroom door. Their show was over. Mine was starting. I counted to ten and walked into the dressing room, assuming the entire band would be there.

But there was only Stevie, pacing, clasping and unclasping her hands. She stopped dead when she saw me and stood silently, staring at me. I smiled, tentatively, but she glared and whirled round, throwing herself onto a couch, sobbing hysterically.

STORMS

I didn't know what to do. Should I comfort her? Would she accept that from me? She'd avoided me whenever she could, and part of me understood that. She and Lindsey were a musical partnership, had been lovers, now were being forced to perform and smile with their deep sense of betrayal pushed into some dark region where past loves are buried and new hatreds breed. I took one step toward the sobbing heap of black chiffon and layered sequined shawls.

Mercifully, Robin Snyder, Stevie's voice coach and best girlfriend, raced into the room at this very moment and swooped down on her, cradling her, rocking her, murmuring to her.

"It was horrible! I hated the show! I missed a cue in 'Rhiannon' and Lindsey had to cover for me! I hated it! I can't do it!" Stevie's sobbed. "I won't do it any more! I can't!"

I slipped by them. I had to get to Lindsey. If this was Stevie's reaction to the stress of performance, what might be happening to the man I loved, whose agony tonight during "So Afraid" had both shocked and devastated me? Would he be hurting this way? I rushed down the hall, flanked by security guards, and headed for the tuning room. And there he was—face to the wall.

The hush was like a rain-drenched night in Oklahoma after a storm. Heat engulfed me, burning from the lights around the mirror and Lindsey's sweat-soaked body. I spoke his name softly, and without turning around he stretched out his hand to me. Blood dripped from his slashed fingers.

I felt a wave of protectiveness, pure compassion. How could he do this to himself? This was his guitar style, this finger-picking, this refusal to use a pick, but it was self-harm, too. I grabbed a towel and gently took his damaged fingers in my two hands, wrapped them in the towel as he turned, exhausted, to face me.

"Baby, was it OK?" he breathed, almost too tired to speak.

"You were amazing!" I told him, taking him in my arms. I helped him into the chair, eased off his wet shirt, now grimy and transparent, and slipped into the bathroom to soak paper towels in cold water for his face and body.

He sat with his eyes closed as I pushed his long brown curls out of the way and gently washed his face and bound the towel, torn into strips, around his fingers. No rock star now, he was a small, helpless child needing tenderness.

"You're my angel, Carol," he whispered, tipping my chin up with one bandaged hand. "I love you."

There was no running away from this. I was going to heap his shadows in one corner and let in light. However damaged he was, bloodied, pursued by the monsters of his past or his childhood, or whatever it was that gave him no rest, I'd find those creatures and destroy them.

Our roles, in this one night, had reversed. He wasn't my fairy-tale protector. I must be his. This was the part I had to play, this part, kneeling at his feet, watching over him. Making him better.

He pulled me to him and kissed me, hard and desperately. The door was flung open suddenly and Ray Lindsey almost fell into the room. "It's crazy out there! Keep this door closed!" he barked over his shoulder at one of the security guards. "They've let the punters in already! It's hell!"

"Carol," Lindsey asked, his voice drained, "I hate to ask you this, but could you go across to the dressing room and get me a Myers's and Coke?"

"Whatever you need," I said.

"You'll be OK?"

"Fine!" I said with a courage I didn't feel, but the cocaine created the courage for me as security men formed a cordon to keep the crowds off my back and I struggled through the crush of bodies to the dressing room, expecting to find Stevie, sobbing still, distraught. Instead I found an empty room reeking with the stench of stale tobacco, spilled alcohol, and raw fear. There were linear tracings of white dust on the bar, where empty bottles perched drunkenly. And there, on the shabby sofa, was one abandoned sequin-scattered shawl.

As I moved across to mix Lindsey's drink I caught sight of myself in the scuffed mirror—a thin, pale girl with pale hair wearing a white satin blouse smeared with blood. Lindsey's blood. And that image will remain clear for all time: the sequined shawl—cheap, gold, splaying out rainbow light—and on my shirt a deep slash of blood, dried to black.

This Carol, this reflection in a mirror, wasn't the same person who'd arrived five hours earlier. That Carol had been a young girl who felt as if she were on the outside looking in. Starry-eyed, feeling as through she were arriving at a party—a guest who was only there to see how the beautiful people lived, dressed, and behaved.

She now knew that she was not a guest. She was one of the hosts of the hottest party in town. Lindsey and his fellow band members were the party; and as the woman he loved, I was now a princess in the royal court of Fleetwood Mac. Cinderella had come to the palace to stay. In every fairy tale I'd ever read, once the heroine of the story found her prince or knight in shining armor, she was automatically transformed into a great lady who lived happily ever after within the walls of her lover's kingdom. I didn't recall ever reading anything about her having doubts that she belonged in that kingdom. No—love and love alone was all she needed.

This is my fairytale, I said to myself, *and it's no time to change the rules.*

5

THROUGH THE LOOKING GLASS

During the first month of the U.S. *Rumours* tour I stayed behind in L.A., working at Producer's Workshop, for, unlike everyone else in my new world, I had a "normal" job. The time seemed to fly by, and things once again stabilized for me. I loved my little apartment and I loved my job. I missed Lindsey every minute, but his calls every night helped to ease the loneliness. On show nights he called me at 1 A.M. or later and we would talk for at least an hour.

After being away only a week Lindsey insisted that I fly out on the weekends to join the band. So every Friday night a long, black limousine was waiting for me in the parking lot of Producer's, attracting stares and attention from the ragtag group of tourists, junkies, and hookers passing by on Hollywood Boulevard. Upon arrival in whatever city Fleetwood Mac was playing that night, I was whisked straight to the venue to meet up with Lindsey and the band.

Just like a reverse Cinderella, when the clock struck six I was off and running to my prince, instead of away from him, for the next three Fridays. As each weekend came to an end, Lindsey and I found it harder and harder to say goodbye.

The tour was going great. The album was selling out in stores, breaking sales records, and getting so much airplay that it seemed that every station across the country had only one artist on their playlist: Fleetwood Mac. Rumours had sold one million copies in the first eleven days of its release, going platinum. Within a month it reached number one on *Billboard*'s album chart and was on its way to making history, for it would stay at the top for an unprecedented thirty-one weeks. Interviews, magazine cover shoots, and sold-out shows were now an everyday occurrence for the band.

Fleetwood Mac returned to Los Angeles and Lindsey once again appeared in the doorway of Producer's Workshop to sweep me off my feet and take me home with him. The band had a three-week break before leaving for Europe and the next leg of the tour. I refused to think any further ahead than the next few precious days.

As the first week passed by we resumed our routine of being together every night at either his house or mine. We didn't speak of the upcoming European tour. I couldn't bear to think of being separated from Lindsey, and like most people faced with painful dilemmas, I put it out of my mind, hoping that if I ignored it the horrible problem would go away.

During the second week of Lindsey's break he called and asked me to drive over to his house after work. "I can't pick you up today, angel. I forgot to tell you, we're shooting the cover of *Rolling Stone* with Annie Leibowitz here at my house. Come on over right after work, OK? The band's driving me insane."

Although I couldn't wait to see Lindsey, I looked at my clothes in horror. I was dressed in a short pleated black skirt and a man's white shirt, with black ankle-strap low heels on my feet. Very Mary Quant and English, but not exactly drop-dead sexy. I looked like a schoolgirl rather than the rock 'n' roll femme fatale that I tried to be at all Fleetwood Mac gatherings. The fact that I rarely succeeded in achieving the sophistication I struggled so valiantly for was beside the point. *There's nothing for it,* I told myself. *If I take the time to go home to change, I'll be an hour late getting to Lindsey's and, by the sound of his voice, he wants me there ASAP. The drive itself takes at least thirty minutes!* I sighed as I fixed my makeup, adding Brigitte Bardot–style eyeliner. *Better than nothing, I guess.* I giggled as I saw my reflection in the bathroom mirror. *Sheesh, I look as though I'm twelve years old . . . with attitude. In Lindsey's eyes, that might not be such a bad thing!*

When I pulled up in front of his house it was obvious that something big was happening in this modest little neighborhood in West L.A. The street was lined with limousines and Mercedes, and Lindsey's front yard was littered with photography lights shining in through the windows. Fluffing up my hair, I checked my face in my rearview mirror, jumped out of my little VW Bug, and, walked carefully through the confusion of cables strewn over his lawn.

Taking a deep breath—always wise before an encounter with Fleetwood Mac—I knocked softly. Lindsey threw the door open and yelled, "Thank God you're here! They're driving me crazy!" He stopped talking and looked me over slowly. "Hey, little girl, looks like you're looking for your daddy. I like it, Carol. You should wear this stuff more often."

I could tell by the gleam in his eye that he meant every word and I felt confidence flood through me as he pulled me into the house. Mick got up from the couch, leered, and began making a few suggestive "school-girl" remarks of his own. John and Christine started laughing as Mick and Lindsey each took one of my arms and played a tug of war with me caught in the center. Stevie sat silently, apparently not thrilled by my arrival and the happy reception I was receiving.

After I was finally allowed to sit down, I got a good look at the band. Everyone was dressed in varying outfits of nightgowns, T-shirts, and boxer shorts except for John, who was bare-chested and wearing blue jeans. Stevie had on a beautiful peach gown, a 1930s lace-and-satin boudoir piece. She looked amazing. Leaning over, Lindsey whispered into my ear, "This cover is going to be totally cool. Annie has the five of us lying on my bed . . . very incestuous." He looked at my raised eyebrows and laughed. "It's Fleetwood Mac, Carol—are you surprised?"

Suddenly I heard a loud voice calling out from Lindsey's spare bedroom. "Come on, you guys, quit fuckin' around in there. I need you in here now!" The voice was followed by the appearance of a woman with cropped short brown hair, dressed in shorts and a T-shirt. It was clear that Annie Leibowitz was used to being obeyed and she carried herself with an authority that spoke of numerous encounters with crazed rock 'n' rollers. Famed for her *Rolling Stone* covers and gorgeous pictorials of models as well as the rich and famous, she had reached a level of fame in photography shared only by Richard Avedon and Francesco Scavullo. For her to be shooting Fleetwood Mac's first *Rolling Stone* cover for *Rumours* was a sign that Fleetwood Mac had truly arrived.

The band members followed Annie meekly into a back bedroom as I made myself comfortable on Lindsey's couch. Knowing the size of his extra bedroom and the number of people and the amount of equipment that had been crammed into it, there was no way I could follow them. I flipped through magazines and listened to the laughter echoing down the hall. In less than an hour the shoot was finished, and forty-five minutes after that the house was empty except for Lindsey and me.

He pulled me up from the couch and led me into his bedroom. As he showed me the Polaroids that Annie'd left for him, I could see that the cover shot was amazing. *Rolling Stone* was going to be thrilled. Mick had Stevie curled up beside him, looking like a child next to his gangling frame. Lindsey and Christine were wrapped around each other and John, shirtless and barefoot in jeans, was reading *Playboy* off on the right side of the bed. It was a classic shot which really did tell the story of the *Rumours* album. I knew the underlying big message as I looked at it: incest!

Lindsey took the pictures out of my hands and laid them on the battered little table beside his bed. Brushing my hair out of my eyes, he said, "Carol, I have two things I need to talk to you about."

I looked up at him and saw with a start how unusually pale and gaunt his face looked, his cheekbones sharp. "What is it? Is something wrong?" I asked fearfully.

"I want you to come to Europe with me," Lindsey replied quietly.

I started to speak, but before I could say anything he placed two fingers over my mouth. I sat stunned as he told me how much he'd missed me over the past month and that he felt another month was far too long for us to be separated. So, he finished, I had to go with him to Europe.

Without hesitating I answered, "God, Lindsey, of course I want to come. I haven't even been able to think about what it would be like for me when you leave again. I hope I can take a leave of absence from Producer's—"

Lindsey cut in quickly. "You have to. I want you there and that's that."

I felt as though a huge weight had been lifted from my shoulders. I wouldn't have to say goodbye to Lindsey in a week and a half! At the back of my mind, though, nagging doubts tried to force their way to the surface. *We've only been together five months, and for the first time we're going to be with each other twenty-four hours a day, seven days a week, in a foreign country. Is it too soon for us to handle that?* I pushed the thought away as hard as I could, but still it lingered inside my head. I'd been to Europe with John twice, and Japan once, before I met Lindsey. I knew how hard it could be on a relationship when you're jet-lagged, eating bad food, and dealing with winter weather. And it wouldn't be just Lindsey and me. We'd be with the entire entourage of band, roadies, and technicians. Not to mention Stevie Nicks.

Will my being there with him make the uneasy truce between them break down and become an all-out war? I thought nervously. I knew from talking to Julie that Lindsey had never taken another woman on the road with him. I'd be the first. I thought back to the vow I made during rehearsals: *I'll never do anything that will come between Lindsey and his music.* Biting my lip, I wondered how hard it would actually be for me to keep that vow if I went on tour with him.

I knew that the working relationship between Lindsey and Stevie was very precarious, and thus the balance within the band itself. *Of course,* I told myself, *with or without me on the road, that's a storm waiting to break.* One look at Lindsey's pale, gaunt face and the wistful look in his eyes made me lock my fears away and cover his face in kisses as I said, "Yes, yes, yes . . . I'll come!"

Almost as an aside, Lindsey casually informed me that his wisdom teeth were impacted and he had to have oral surgery. I looked at him in concern. *That's why he looks so pale! Why didn't he tell me sooner that his mouth was hurting him?* I wondered.

"'I'm obviously not looking forward to it—I just hope that it goes well. I've been warned that getting your wisdom teeth out is a major deal. Richard will take me tomorrow, but can you come over after work? I'll try not to be too boring." I quickly nodded yes and for the rest of the night we tried not to think about hypodermic needles and drills.

For the first few days Lindsey seemed to weather the surgery well. The dentist had given him Percodan for the pain and he was stoned but happy when I arrived to spend every night with him. We lay in his bed and watched TV, talked about the upcoming European tour, and listened to his collection of the Beach Boys. Lindsey idolized their music. He played each song for me, pointing out the harmonies, the beautiful arrangements, and the sheer genius of Brian Wilson. I listened quietly as he told me stories about Brian's life as a tortured musician. Lindsey believed it was just the sheer weight of Brian's genius that was his greatest enemy.

And as he said these words I felt an inner chill. Lindsey was also a musical genius—and even in this early stage of our relationship I had seen a glimpse of his own tortured side. Every time he played "So Afraid" on stage, it was there for everyone to see. But I kept this to myself as I listened to him and tried not to think of it. Instead we listened to *Pet Sounds* in the darkness of his bedroom and fell asleep to the haunting sound of Brian's voice.

On the fourth day after Lindsey's surgery, I let myself into the Putney house and walked into the guitar-strewn living room. "You better go check on Lindsey, Carol. I think something's wrong! He wouldn't let me do anything for him . . ." Richard said in a rush of words as soon as he saw me. "He's been curled up in a ball for most of the day and won't talk. I think he's in a lot of pain." Looking at Richard in surprise, I rushed into the back bedroom and sank down onto the bed by Lindsey's side. His face glistening with beads of sweat, he was lying with his eyes closed, the bedclothes twisted around him.

As I called his name softly, he opened his eyes and grabbed my hand. "It hurts, Carol, really bad. I feel like shit. I've taken three Percodan, and it's not helping. Call Dr. Silvers for me, OK?" I ran to the bathroom to get a cold washcloth for his face and then frantically looked around for his dentist's number. Finding it, I clumsily dialed the phone with one hand while holding Lindsey's clammy palm with the other. After the answering service put me through to the dentist, I told him about how much pain Lindsey was in and that he seemed to be running a fever.

Alarmed, Dr. Silvers told me to ice Lindsey's jaw, give him painkillers, and, above all, keep him in bed. I scheduled an 8 A.M. appointment, hung up, and called my boss to tell him why I wouldn't be coming to work the next day. Ed, as usual, was wonderful and told me to stay by Lindsey's side.

At the dentist's office we were given very bad news. Lindsey had dry socket, which essentially meant that the sites on both sides of his lower jaw where his wisdom teeth had been extracted weren't healing; bone was exposed and it was infected. The pain was made worse by air hitting the wounds every time he opened his mouth.

"I've given him numbing shots of Novocain and another one of Demerol," said Dr. Silvers. "I want Lindsey to gargle at least five or six times a day with saltwater, take antibiotics, and I'll give him more Percodan. Stay on a liquid diet, use straws—absolutely no chewing or smoking. With rest, in a few weeks he should be fine."

"Um, sir?" I asked as the full impact of what he'd just told us started to sink in. "Lindsey is supposed to leave in a week for a monthlong tour of

Europe with his band. He has to sing and play guitar for two hours at every show. Is he going to be able to?"

Aghast at my words, Dr. Silvers sharply told us that we were running a huge risk with Lindsey's health and he wouldn't be responsible for what happened. Lindsey and I looked at each other, rolling our eyes as soon as the dentist's back was turned. We took the prescriptions and left.

As soon as we were in the car Lindsey lit a joint. He stared at me steadily and, by the look in his eyes, I knew better than to say anything about the warning about smoking. I mentally shrugged as I turned the key in the ignition and drove out of the parking lot. Lindsey would do what he wanted, regardless of his dentist's warning. *At least I can make sure he takes his antibiotics,* I told myself. Since Lindsey was now truly stoned out of his mind on Demerol and weed, I took him home first and then ran to the pharmacy for his prescriptions.

In the car I started to freak as my mind raced. *How is he going to be able to perform? He's in agony, can't eat, has a fever, and can't rest after this week. I don't know how he's going to be able to manage!* I felt a fierce protectiveness consume me as I drove at twenty miles over the speed limit to get back to him. *Tomorrow I'll talk to Ed about Europe,* I told myself. *It's no longer just about us not wanting to be separated: Lindsey's going to need me to take care of him. Ed will understand.*

I had a feeling, though, that he might not be so willing to let me take off from work and go with Fleetwood Mac on the road. I'd been putting off asking him for exactly that reason. Not only would it interrupt my training as a sound engineer, but Ed didn't seem that keen on my relationship with Lindsey. I wasn't sure why, but I could sense it. *Well, nothing for it, girl. You're going to talk to Ed in the morning and that's that,* I said firmly to myself as I pulled into Lindsey's driveway. Grabbing his prescription, I ran into the house to take care of the man I loved.

Giving Lindsey strict instructions to follow his dentist's orders, I left him drowsing in bed the next morning and drove from West L.A. to Producer's Workshop. I checked that day's bookings and waited nervously for Ed to arrive. As if my thinking of him had made him materialize, he was suddenly there, looming over my shoulder.

"How's Lindsey feeling?" He asked as he walked over and poured himself some coffee.

At six foot four, with longish sandy-brown hair and a handlebar mustache, Ed Cobb cut an imposing figure. I could tell that he'd ridden his new Harley to work that day. His hair was completely windblown as he stood in the office in cowboy boots, blue jeans, and a denim shirt, cigar smoke billowing around his head—the exact image of Tom Selleck as the Marlboro Man.

Ed carried himself as someone who was used to getting respect. He'd been a teenage music sensation when he sang in a folk group called the Four Preps. They'd had a string of top 100 hits in the late 1950s and early '60s. After that, Ed had gone on to produce, coproduce, or write records with total sales of forty million. Famous as the writer of such classics as "Tainted Love," "Good Guys Don't Wear White," and "Dirty Water," he'd been nominated for three Grammys and received two Record of the Year Awards for sound. Ed's outstanding career had brought him a total of thirty-two gold and platinum records to hang on his wall, for producing and/or sound engineering Pink Floyd, Steely Dan, and Fleetwood Mac, to name just a few.

"Not good, Ed."

I told him about Lindsey's dental nightmare and then asked him if he had a few minutes to talk to me. I quickly told him about Lindsey's invitation to me to join him on the road in Europe and tried to explain why I wanted and needed to go. He looked down at me from his imposing height, his eyes gentle and questioning. "Are you sure you want to do this?"

I nodded and he sighed, leaning back against the doorframe, letting an uncomfortable silence hang in the air. And then he shook his head wearily and started to speak. He told me that he was worried that I might not realize what I was getting into: the lifestyle, the drugs, the press, the fans—all part of the rock 'n' roll world that I was about to enter. He reminded me that Fleetwood Mac was on the verge of becoming a very big band, and anyone with them had better be ready for the glare of a huge spotlight.

"I can handle it, Ed," I said firmly.

He looked at me, smiling slightly, and asked simply, "Do you love this guy?"

"More than anything in the world," I answered ferociously.

"Well, then, I won't say no. Your job will be here when you get back. Don't worry about that. Listen, hon, if you change your mind once you're over there and want to come home—call me. I'll wire you the money and get you back home safe. I'm here. Remember that, Carol. If you need me, I'm here."

I walked the few steps between us and gave him a long hug, feeling that I might start to cry. I was feeling as though I'd disappointed him somehow, but also knew that he understood why I felt the need to go with Lindsey. I was in love and my guy needed and wanted me with him. I really didn't feel that anything else mattered.

Relieved but subdued, I followed Ed back into the office. Once I was alone, I phoned Lindsey to tell him that Ed had given me a leave of absence. Speaking like his mouth was full of cotton balls, he told me to start packing my suitcases right away. I hung up the phone and went back to work. At exactly 6 P.M. I grabbed my jacket and walked out into the dark night.

It started to rain again as I pulled out of the parking lot and into traffic. Suddenly, there was a crack of thunder as a jagged bolt of lightning lit the sky. The buildings along Hollywood Boulevard looked stark and gray, like monoliths from an ancient time. The figures moving along the sidewalk in dark coats, heads aimed at the ground, seemed sinister and solitary, sharing only the cold, hard rain falling from a sky that had turned L.A. into an unfamiliar landscape of moving shadows and wet terrain.

Palm trees bent as their fronds were ripped from their tops, blowing haphazardly in front of my car and onto rooftops. I strained to see the street, afraid to drive faster than fifteen miles per hour or turn on the radio, as I always did, to listen for Fleetwood Mac's songs. *I've never seen it rain this much in L.A.,* I said to myself. *If I didn't know better, I'd think that God was trying to tell me something.* I shivered as the cold and dampness seeped through the windows into the car.

I don't believe in omens anyway, I told myself fiercely. Yet I knew that I did, and with Ed's warning words repeating in my head, it was with an uneasy mind that I pulled into Lindsey's driveway. I was leaving in six days and I had no time for doubts or omens. *I'll take it one day at a time and it's going to be great,* I said firmly to myself. Ignoring the thunder and lightning, I opened the car door and ran toward Lindsey and the warm, safe haven by his side.

The past few days had been a whirlwind for us, packing, picking up prescriptions, keeping our heads down whenever we were out and about. I was glad for Lindsey's sake that he'd be leaving the country. People were starting to stare at us whenever we ventured out and it was a bit disconcert-ing, especially because he was still feeling so bad after his surgery. He'd lost at least ten pounds over the past week and was in constant pain. It was a relief to climb on board the 747 and take off for the start of the European *Rumours* tour.

During the long flight I got to know Judy Wong, Fleetwood Mac's secre-tary. I'd seen her countless times at rehearsals, but really didn't know her history with the band. She was only too happy to fill me in. Judy had long been a member of the Fleetwood Mac family. The ex-wife of Jethro Tull's bass player, Glenn Cornick, she'd arranged the introduction of Bob Welch to Fleetwood Mac and was instrumental in bringing about his four-year stint with the band. Immortalized in the *Kiln House* album by the song "Jewel Eyed Judy," she'd been indispensable to Fleetwood Mac. She was bright, funny, and had the energy of a thousand people. You'd swear she was a speed freak, but she never did drugs. Always moving, always talk-ing, and always happy—it was like having an Asian Mary Poppins in our midst. I felt drained as she flitted away to visit with Mick, and I laid my head on Lindsey's shoulder for the rest of the flight.

As the 747 landed in Birmingham, England, every member of the band's entourage groaned with relief. All of us felt like death. Lindsey was sick and in pain from his mouth infection and I felt ill from exhaustion. And every-one else looked as bad as we felt. Luckily, we cleared customs quickly and climbed into our separate limousines to drive in a convoy through the gray, fog-shrouded industrial city.

Our cars pulled up in front of a drab square building that was, to our dismay, our "luxury" hotel for the next two days. We gathered in the tiny lobby, huddled like refugees in the cold, plain entry hall and waited for J.C. to give us our keys to our suites.

Lindsey let out a loud *"Fuck! I hate this!"* and kicked the wall with his cowboy boot. Like cross, bedraggled children, we wearily trooped into the dark, cold elevators and proceeded to our rooms. The "suite" was a large bedroom furnished with threadbare carpet and a single lamp on the bed-side table next to a sagging bed. It was freezing cold, with the radiator against the wall giving off only tepid heat. Among the shadows in the cor-ners, I saw a spider making its way across the floor. As Lindsey and I looked at each other in dismay, there were no words to express how much we absolutely hated the hotel, even though, for fifteen minutes, Lindsey gave it the old "college try"—using his entire vocabulary of swear words. If the hotel was any indication, the tour was not off to an auspicious start.

The mood was not lightened the next evening when we arrived at the venue. Fleetwood Mac was booked into an old, decrepit theater that looked at least a hundred years old. The chandeliered interior resembled a Gothic stage set from *Phantom of the Opera*. Heavy, red velvet curtains covered with dust were pulled back over balcony boxes that circled the second tier. The seats in front of the stage were narrow and wooden, so small that they seemed

as if they wouldn't hold anyone over the age of ten. The theater had a seating capacity of roughly four thousand. While it was true that *Rumours* only opened at number thirty-four in the British charts, the band had been play-ing for sellout crowds of twenty thousand back in the States. It seemed strange to be in such a small hall for the first European show. And the band was not pleased.

Backstage in the tiny, cramped dressing rooms, each member of

Lindsey and Carol Ann backstage during the European Rumours tour.

Fleetwood Mac was letting J.C. know their displeasure in their own special way. Christine was bitching about the "nasty" theater; Lindsey was pissed off about the audience size; John was cold and couldn't get the radiator to work in the tuning room; and Stevie, whose wardrobe changes during the show were too numerous to count, was almost in tears over the one stingy hanging rack she had been given. Last, but not least, Mick was in a churl-ish mood over the lack of cocaine.

I felt sorry for J.C. as he ran around in circles trying to soothe, solve, and explain his way before the show started. "Stevie, I'll get you another rack . . . Chris, Lindsey, sorry, but this is the biggest hall in Birmingham . . . Mick, you know how hard it is to get blow over here. Even if I can eventually get my hands on some, it's going to take days, not hours. This isn't the U.S., mate. I feel your pain. I'd kill for a line right now, believe me. Don't you think I could use one, having to deal with you lot?"

Mick stared at him belligerently. "That's crap. Totally unacceptable, I'm afraid. You know I play better with it. Don't blame *me* if the show sucks tonight." As he finished he pointed his finger directly in J.C.'s face.

"What about weed, J.C.?" Lindsey asked in a surly tone matching Mick's. "You don't expect me just to drink my way through the show, do you? *Jesus!*"

"Look, lads," J.C. thundered through the tiny dressing room, "*there are no drugs here!* I'll do the best I can, but don't count on it for at least a few more days. Drink vodka! Drink champagne! Drink whatever the hell you need to get you through it . . . I mean, what are you thinking, boys? That I can fuck-

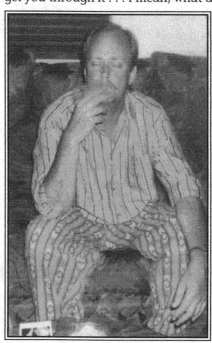

John Courage, a.k.a. J.C.

ing call a Colombian cartel? By the way, as for this theater, how the fuck could I know that *Rumours* would be a fucking monster record? Mick and I booked this tour five months ago, based on the results of your friggin' *last* album, not this one! *Shit!*" Muttering to himself, J.C. stomped out of the main dressing room and slammed the door behind him.

As soon as he was gone the whole room exploded in laughter. It was almost impossible to get J.C. rattled, but Fleetwood Mac's bitching and moaning had managed to break him down, destroying his cool demeanor, at the very first British show. Sadistically, the band felt better as a result. Now that someone had paid for their discomfort, they could get over it and go on with the show.

Despite the lack of drugs and the Vampire Lestat–style theater, the show was one of their best. The acoustics of the old hall were brilliant and the band sounded tight and energized. Gratified by the show and the reaction of the audience, albeit small in numbers, the band was in much better spirits when we all met up again backstage. Having recovered from his earlier lapse of decorum, a cool and calm J.C. ushered them to their limos and, with relief, left the theater with his ruffled feathers back in place and his silver Halliburton briefcase clutched firmly under his arm. It was time to move on.

After a show in Manchester, the band finally arrived in London. We were thrilled. Our hotel was large and, by English standards, very modern. We still had radiators and old wallpaper, but the beds didn't sag and the furniture was halfway decent. On our third night, everyone in the Fleetwood Mac entourage gathered in the bar, desperate for entertainment.

Decorated in traditional English pub style, the place was dark, smoky, and loud. Lindsey and I sat down on bar stools and as he ordered a pint of beer I looked around at the scene. John and Christine were laughing uproariously with their heads bent like conspirators over their mugs of beer. The band roadies were trying to pick up the few Englishwomen who mistakenly wandered into their paths, scaring them off with loud, off-color remarks that would make even the most jaded girl blush. Mick and his wife Jenny were nowhere in sight and J.C. was holed up in a corner with a couple of drunken English promoters. Stevie was holding court at a table with Robin Snyder. As though sensing my gaze, Stevie looked up and stared at me with no trace of emotion on her face, yet that one look said it all: *I don't like you and I don't want you here, Carol.* She then turned her back on me and rejoined the conversation around her table.

Tell me that there's a stare more intimidating than that of a woman who has transferred her feelings of rage from her past lover onto you and I'll tell you that obviously you're not a woman caught between Stevie Nicks and Lindsey Buckingham. To Stevie at that time, it obviously made no difference that I had no part in the breakup of their relationship. I was the new woman in his life and although her feelings about me personally were to remain unspoken—on *that* tour—it was obvious to me that they hovered somewhere below the sub-zero freezing point.

Whether I deserved it or not, her dark look made me feel as though I'd just had a black hole burned through me. And it made me sad, for I admired Stevie a great deal. Who wouldn't? She was beautiful, talented, and mysterious. With a sigh, I shrank back against the bar, thinking maybe it was not going to work out between her and me, and maybe I'd better watch my step. I looked over at Lindsey and saw that he too had seen the look that Stevie had thrown at me. As he leaned over and kissed me on the cheek in a show of support, Richard and Ken appeared from out of nowhere, almost jumping up and down in their excitement. They'd managed to score some weed! Lindsey told me to sit tight and leaped off his bar stool, disappearing like smoke.

So I sat by myself, feeling conspicuous, lonely, and completely out of place. The thought of beer made me want to gag, and with no one to talk to I had absolutely no reason to stay. I knew that Lindsey could be anywhere from twenty minutes to two hours, depending on exactly what was waiting for him to smoke in the boys' den of iniquity. Picking up my purse, I dug out my room key and went back upstairs.

Opening the door, I was hit with the overwhelming odor of unwashed laundry. The hotels in Birmingham, Manchester, and Liverpool had been so substandard that the idea of turning over our clothes to them to wash was ludicrous. I sighed as I looked at the jumble of garments spilling out of our suitcases. *Might as well do something useful,* I thought forlornly. I sank down onto my knees and started pulling out clothes and sorting them into piles, feeling exactly like a much put-upon Cinderella. An internal dialogue kept me company as I worked. *This is not exactly how I pictured being on the road with Fleetwood Mac. Actually, so far, none of the past week has been what I imagined it would be: crappy food, crappy hotels, Lindsey still sick . . . I miss L.A.—even if it is raining there constantly this year, it's better than the thirty-two degree winter weather over here!* Surrounded by towering piles of clothes, I felt myself gearing up for a real pout.

Suddenly the door burst open and Lindsey came running into the room. "Oh my God! Get dressed in something sexy! Put on some makeup! *Get ready!*" Startled, I dropped the handful of dirty socks I'd been sorting and looked at him as though he'd lost his mind.

"What are you talking about? It's almost midnight! What's going on?"

Lindsey grabbed me and pulled me up from the floor. *"We're going to Eric Clapton's castle!* Mick and Jenny already have two cars waiting for all of us downstairs! Where are my good jeans? My black cowboy boots? *Jesus!* I can't believe I'm going to *meet Eric Clapton tonight!"*

"Lindsey, you're kidding, right? We're meeting *Eric Clapton?*" I had loved Derek and the Dominoes since high school. Not to mention Cream and Blind Faith. I knew, of course, that Jenny's sister Pattie was married to Eric, but if anything, I thought he might come to one of the shows. I never in a million years expected that we would be going to his castle.

For the American contingent of the Fleetwood Mac family, meeting Clapton was on a par with meeting John Lennon. We weren't groupies, but who in their right mind wouldn't want to spend time with a musician who was a living legend? And thanks to Mick and Jenny, we were about to do just that.

I threw on my favorite velvet top, put on lipstick, and laughed at Lindsey hopping around the room with one boot on and one off as he desperately hunted for a matching sock. Swearing, he grabbed a dirty sock that was at least the same color as the one on his shod foot and collapsed onto the bed. Boots on, he shrugged into his black velvet jacket, wrapped his maroon wool scarf around his neck, and threw me my long, black, antique coat from the closet. "This looks great on you, baby. You have to wear it!"

Sighing, I took the coat from him, knowing that I was going to absolutely freeze in it. With a last longing look at my heavier coat thrown over the bed, I grabbed my purse and ducked under Lindsey's arm as he impatiently held the door open for me. He slammed it behind us and we raced downstairs to the waiting limousines. I could see that the two limos were crammed full with the entire band, along with J.C., Robin Snyder, Judy Wong, Jenny, Richard, and Ken. I sat on Lindsey's lap for the entire hour-long ride to Eric Clapton's home in the Surrey countryside.

When we finally drove slowly through the gates of Clapton's estate, we saw a huge stone house that did, indeed, resemble a castle. The weather had turned bitterly cold and even the short walk to Pattie and Eric's massive front door left me shivering in my thin coat. The door suddenly opened, spilling light and incense smoke and revealing the face of a rock 'n' roll legend haloed in candlelight.

Mick and Eric pounded each other on the back and we followed them into Clapton's large entry hall, where Jenny's famous sister, Pattie Boyd, stood waiting, wrapped in a cashmere shawl. Slender, with dark blonde hair and wearing pale pink lipstick and Brigitte Bardot–style eyeliner, she oozed sexuality. Pattie, of course, had had two of the most famous men in the world madly in love with her. She was married to George Harrison when she met and fell in love with Eric. No matter what else she might do in her life, she would forever be a part of rock 'n' roll history just because of that, as well as for the classic songs "Something" and "Layla" that she inspired.

After Mick and Jenny made hasty introductions, we were shown into a shabby-chic Gothic sitting room that was decorated with faded velvet couches, floor-to-ceiling brocade drapes, and wonderful little tables full of knickknacks and pictures of Pattie and Eric with just about every well-known musician in the world. Incense sticks trailed smoke while candles burned on every available surface, and velvet pillows were tossed haphazardly around the floor over an ancient Oriental carpet.

Lindsey grinned at me as we looked at each other. It was exactly how one would expect a rock star's "castle" to be. We were beyond thrilled. We were soon to find out that two-thirds of the twenty or so rooms had no furnishings whatsoever, but we didn't care. What counted was the ambience, and Clapton's home had that in spades.

We made ourselves comfortable on couches and pillows and Mick and Eric disappeared into the hall, returning within minutes with gleeful expressions and a silver platter. In the middle of the beautifully etched tarnished plate was a mound of white powder. Mick's shadow loomed on the wall as he slowly, ceremoniously showed the platter to one and all, reciting, "The woods are lovely, dark and deep, and we have miles to go before we sleep." It was the ritual call for the Fleetwood Mac family to gather around for a line of blow and a cheer went up as thirteen pairs of eyes glittered with anticipation. No one had had cocaine since we left America and there was a sense of bloodlust in the air as we impatiently waited our turn to sniff up a line. I was surprised to realize that I craved a line as much as everyone else in the room, who had all been doing blow far longer than I had.

Unlike the other members of the Fleetwood Mac family, I disliked alcohol, hated weed, and didn't take pills. Before meeting Lindsey, my only vice had been cigarettes, so I was pretty much a babe in the woods in the company of my new family. Christine told me during rehearsals that my almost total sobriety made everyone a little uncomfortable. *Not to worry,* I thought to myself, *I have found something that I can do right along with everyone else—and I like it! Nice to fit in!* I smothered a giggle, trying my best to maintain a cool composure. As though reading my thoughts, Chris winked as she held the plate in front of me, handing me a rolled-up pound note. I smiled back at her, feeling the familiar rush hit me as the blow went up my nose.

After everyone had finished off all the powder on the platter, Eric and Pattie told us to follow them upstairs to their "pub" room. As one, we all got up from our various corners and followed them up a sweeping staircase to the third floor. As I trailed behind Lindsey, I lingered to glance into darkened rooms within sight of the staircase. Eric's home looked very, very old and the empty bedrooms and sitting rooms that we passed seemed ghostly, filled with shadows and faint echoes of past occupants. Grabbing Lindsey's hand, I clung to him until we reached Eric's warm, bright den.

John, J.C., and Mick immediately challenged Eric to a game of darts. Christine, Stevie, Robin, Jenny, and Pattie headed off to Pattie's bedroom for "girl talk," leaving Judy and me behind with the guys. I mentally shrugged, glad to stay with my man and where the action was. Soon Lindsey joined in the game, and for the next hour the noise was incredible. More cocaine was brought out and snorted up immediately by one and all, and by 3 A.M. everyone was so wasted that I worried that one of the boys would throw a dart in someone's eye.

Every man in the room was falling-down drunk and, sure enough, they started throwing darts at one another—trying their best to make my prediction come true. Pattie and Jenny swept into the room just in time, grabbing the darts out of their hands and ordering everyone to behave. Like chastened children, we meekly followed them downstairs to the sitting room, stumbling a bit on the now too-steep staircase.

It was close to four in the morning and the room was painfully cold. The fire had gone out in the stone fireplace and the candles were rapidly melting into shapeless forms. Lindsey sat down in a chair and I pulled a pillow over by his feet, leaning against his legs as I shivered in the icy chill, still wearing my light coat. Outside the wind was howling and the air felt damp. Suddenly the front door echoed with the pounding of a heavy fist and Eric ran into the entry hall, to return with yet another legend on his arm.

It was Ronnie Lane, guitarist of the Small Faces and the Faces. With his black T-shirt and jeans and tousled dark hair, he looked more like a rebellious teenager than the respected, world-renowned artist that he was. He smiled shyly at all of us, saying, "Welcome to England, mates!" then walked quickly toward an acoustic guitar in a corner of the room, lifting it off its stand. There was a childlike quality to him, like a kid holding a piece of treasure, as he cradled the instrument in his arms. Looking straight at Lindsey, he smiled and said, "Wanna jam?" I felt Lindsey jump nervously and I placed my hand on his knee, looking up to see excitement shining from his eyes.

Eric grabbed Pattie by the hand, pulling her with him as he shouted over his shoulder, "I'm going up to my studio for some guitars . . . We'll be right back!" A murmur of excitement went around the room when Clapton returned with three acoustic guitars and handed one to Lindsey and one to John McVie. He settled down on a stool with the other well-worn, scarred guitar lying across his knees.

Pattie and Jenny raced around the room, lighting new candles, throwing more wood onto the fire, and pulling open the heavy brocade drapes to reveal a flurry of snowflakes outside. Jumping up, I ran to the window. I hadn't seen snow for at least three years and I was now looking at not just snow, but the beginning of a major winter storm. *No wonder the wind sounds like it's going to tear the house apart,* I thought as I stared through the smudged window. Hearing each of the guitars being tuned behind me, and excited whispers coming from everyone, I tore myself away from the window and walked quickly back to my place on the floor beside Lindsey.

Silence descended upon us all as Ronnie began to play, the snowflakes falling behind him creating a Christmas card backdrop. The opening chords of "While My Guitar Gently Weeps" filled the room and, as one, we all held our breath as Lindsey and Eric joined in on their guitars. Eric began to sing and Stevie and Christine joined in with perfect harmony, singing one of the most beautiful songs ever written by George Harrison—or anyone, for that matter.

Looking at Lindsey's face, I saw bliss shining in his eyes: he was living a dream that any musician in the world would give their weight in gold to experience. And the dream continued when Eric launched into "Layla," making everyone smile as Pattie stood up and took a little bow during the song. "The Sounds of Silence" followed, Simon and Garfunkel's words coloring the room in shades of dark blue and silver as Stevie's beautiful, husky voice gave them a plaintive longing that touched us all to the depth of our souls.

I sat on my velvet pillow, leaning my head on my hand, listening to the music in wonder while studying the faces of Lindsey, Eric, John, and Ronnie. Each one was filled with the special look of joy that master musicians have when they are lost in the music, playing with their peers and aware of one another as only musicians can be. Yet each man, for that short moment in time, was also lost in his own individual ecstasy as he played his heart out just for the sake of the music. And I knew with certainty that I was experiencing a moment so perfect that it would stay with me for the rest of my life.

Dawn broke as the music continued, fingers of weak light penetrating the dark sitting room, replacing the muted candlelight. The spell was broken by the crash of a large branch falling from a tree outside, making everyone jump up in fright, so lost were we in our world of music. Outside, the snow was now forming an opaque blanket of white, while the howling winds of a blizzard accompanied the guitars. The room was icy cold and I felt as though I'd been woken from a dream as I looked in surprise at Lindsey's face, blue with cold, and realized that I was absolutely freezing.

Nervous laughter replaced the singing, and Ronnie abruptly got up and placed Eric's guitar lovingly back on its stand. He looked so happy, so healthy standing there. A few years later, he was diagnosed with multiple sclerosis and had to fight a long, losing battle with that horrific disease. But this morning he seemed at peace with himself and with his friends both old and new. Looking back today, I believe that Ronnie treasured those few hours of music shared during Fleetwood Mac's first *Rumours* tour as much as we did.

Dazed and tired, we began to get up from our various pillows and sofas and walk in groups to the windows, staring in shock at the ferocity of the blizzard raging outside. As we watched, another branch was ripped from a tree and flung across the road in front of the house. "There's no way you're going to make it back to London in this," Eric declared.

"No shit, Sherlock," Mick sniggered, hitting him on the arm.

Ignoring him, Eric continued, "We've got plenty of bedrooms . . . everyone just wander around until you find one. See you in a few hours. If you need anything, don't bother me. I'm going to bed with m'lady here and I'm locking my door!"

STORMS

Lindsey looked at me, shrugged, and took my hand. We trudged upstairs, looking into room after room, trying hopelessly to find a room with a bed. At last we found one that had a narrow mattress on the floor and, surmising that we were lucky to have that, we went in and closed the door. Exhausted and cold to the bone, we laid down in the little room with our clothes on and pulled up the thin sheet—the only cover that was anywhere in sight and huddled together for warmth.

Our sleep was fitful. With the blizzard still howling outside, the twenty-degree temperature in our room, and the stone floor under our thin mattress, we were both pretty miserable as we lay there. I tried to focus on the hours that I'd just spent in Eric Clapton's sitting room, desperate to keep my mind off how brutally cold I was. Eventually Mick knocked on the door, looking as haggard as we felt, and told us that it was time to go. With no sign of Pattie or Eric, we trudged through the knee-deep snow, wet clothes adding to our morning misery, and climbed into the limo for the ride back to London.

The next day we flew to Paris, arriving only to find that the blizzard had followed us. I loved Paris and, having been there twice before, I happily pointed out my favorite shops along the Champs-Elysées and chattered about the impressionist museum that sat in a beautiful park across from the Louvre as Lindsey and I rode through the snow-shrouded streets.

We were booked for four days into a beautiful hotel overlooking a park with a black wrought-iron fence and gaslights mounted on lampposts. It was completely nineteenth-century and I adored it. I blithely made plans for shopping and sightseeing around the band's concert, which would be in three days.

By that evening I had a sore throat, a headache, and a cough. Lindsey gave me one of his Percodan and I took half of it, hoping against hope that I'd be miraculously cured. It knocked me out and the next morning, feeling light-headed and a bit shaky, I knew that my plans for shopping that day were gone. I couldn't seem to get warm even after turning up the radiator full blast and wrapping myself in the hotel's heavy chenille robe. It was obvious that my hours spent in Eric's freezing house had taken their toll. I spent the rest of the day under a mound of blankets, drinking hot tea and holding onto Lindsey's hand.

By morning I couldn't stop coughing. I could see by Lindsey's eyes that he was scared as he called the front desk and asked for a doctor. His pale face turned even paler as he listened to the clerk on the other end of the line. Hanging up, he rushed over to the window and pulled the drapes. It was a total whiteout outside. Another blizzard had hit Paris and even though our room overlooked the park, the shapes of the trees and the iron fence that I'd so admired the day before were lost in the haze of snow. "Carol, darlin', I know you're really sick. I've asked the hotel to call a doctor, but he can't make it here through the storm. He's calling in some prescriptions for you. Don't worry, I'm going to take care of you."

I tried to smile and nodded as I listlessly turned on the television. There was an Easter service on TV, with the pope on the steps of the Vatican. My throat burning, I whispered, "It's Easter, Lindsey! I can't believe I forgot that today is Easter!" As if by signal, church bells started ringing, echoing across the park outside our room and, together with my fever and the choirs singing on TV, I felt as though I were in a dream.

Lindsey leaned over and stroked my hair as he told me that he had to go out to pick up the medicine for me. Nodding, unable to speak again, I watched as he threw on a black overcoat and left the room. I turned on my side and felt the tears that I'd been trying to hide from him run down my face.

I couldn't remember ever feeling this ill, and I was scared. Right then I would have given anything to be in my bedroom in Tulsa with my mother watching over me. I stared out the window and suddenly I saw Lindsey walking through the park. My view of him became hazy as the snowflakes obscured his shape, and he grew smaller and smaller as he braved the blizzard for me. I had an otherworldly feeling as I listened to the choral music and watched the man I loved disappear in a swirl of white. Yet even in my fever-induced delirium, I could see that the balance in my relationship with Lindsey had shifted.

Until that day I had been the one taking care of him, feeling I had to be a rock for his musical genius and his needs, both emotional and physical, after his awful dental surgery. Now, suddenly, I was helpless and he was taking care of me. And I knew that, for both of us, our relationship would never be the same again. We had proved that, no matter what, we were there for each other. Until then I'd felt that I was his shelter in a storm, and that day he was braving one for me. As ill as I was, I fell asleep with a smile on my face. No longer afraid in a French hotel room so far away from home, I felt secure that Lindsey would do everything he could to keep me safe.

He returned, dusted with snow, holding a vial of pills and a large bottle of codeine-laced cough syrup. Spilling it over the bed covers as he tried to measure it into a teaspoon, he talked in a soothing tone to me, but in my fever the meaning of his words became lost.

The following day I was diagnosed with "walking pneumonia" by the hotel doctor and given more prescriptions. Between us, Lindsey and I had about seven bottles of different pills and syrups on the bedside table in our hotel room. By the night of the band's concert I was tired of being ill and determined to go to Fleetwood Mac's show, no matter what. And I did.

To everyone's disgust, a bullfight had taken place in the concert venue the previous day and the smell of blood permeated the arena. Everyone bitched and moaned, but this time it was with good reason. The stench was so strong that I felt my stomach churning as I laid on a couch watching Fleetwood Mac prepare for the show. And, by the looks on the band's faces, they were faring little better than I. Stevie was positively green under the fluorescent lighting and I knew that I must have looked the same. Still, everyone managed to make it to the stage and the roar of the crowd greeted them as they began to play.

Lindsey Buckingham on the European Rumours tour.

Following slowly, I walked through the curtains into the arena. As I looked at the audience I could see that they didn't seem bothered whatsoever by the smell of carnage in the air and the reddish-stained sawdust on the floor. The Parisian crowd was clapping and screaming, every single one of them on their feet as Fleetwood Mac launched into the set, pressing closer and closer to the stage in a frenzy as the music washed over them. I shrank back from the crush of fans and climbed onto the metal stairs to stay within reach of Lindsey should I need him. It looked as though the crowd might swarm the stage in their rapture.

The audiences in Britain had been good, but not like this. With the whole ground level of the venue open and without chairs, the kids were going insane. I saw a few of them fall, only to be picked up off the sawdust and surge toward the stage again as soon as they were on their feet. The band was possessed, reacting to the audience's crazed adulation as they performed. I stood silently, watching, accepting.

As I stood in the relative darkness of the stage stairs, I thought back to the band sweating out the final mixes of *Rumours* at Producer's Workshop and their first shaky rehearsal; to Lindsey's middle-of-the-night fears and that first bad review of the album; and to when Fleetwood Mac had barely dared to dream of the success that was unfolding before them that night in a blood-soaked arena in Paris. It was obvious that Fleetwood Mac was now an international sensation. And there was no going back.

John McVie and Lindsey Buckingham.

The snow accompanied the band as it swept across Germany and Holland, leaving rave reviews and crazed audiences in its wake. Fleetwood Mac's fame was growing by the day and it was putting pressure on everyone. The punishing schedule, the brutal weather, and the intensity of performing to ever-greater adulation had, by the end of the tour, exhausted every member of the Fleetwood Mac family. Lindsey had lost so much weight on the road from the aftereffects of his surgery that he looked skeletal, and I was still recovering from my walking pneumonia. Christine, John, Stevie, and Mick were hollow-eyed, cranky, and ready for a break.

The European *Rumours* tour had been a phenomenal success for Fleetwood Mac, but it had taken its toll on us all. It was time to go home—time to go back to the States and the superstardom that was waiting for the band.

6

IF YOU DON'T LOVE ME NOW

The Pan Am flight landed at LAX and the exhausted members of the Fleetwood Mac family staggered into the smog-laden air of Los Angeles. With a mumbled chorus of goodbyes, the band climbed into waiting limos, heading off to their (barely) separate lives and a three-week break in L.A. before the next leg of the *Rumours* tour.

Lindsey and I headed home. Because the band had about a thousand back-to-back interviews to promote the album and tour during their so-called break, a vacation was out of the question. To unwind, we spent three days secluded in Lindsey's house, playing records, making love, and giving thanks that we'd survived the tour.

We desperately needed the time off: just the two of us, with no band, no roadies, no concerts, and no grueling timetable to follow. The European tour had taken our relationship to another level. An exhausting tour schedule, blizzards, Lindsey's dental troubles, and my illness in Paris had shocked us out of the "honeymoon" period that every couple enjoys in the beginning of their relationship, driving us without mercy into the hardcore rock 'n' roll reality of being together on the road 24/7.

Our month in Europe had been a make-or-break time for us. Even at my young age, and with Lindsey only the second man I'd ever slept with—I still knew that not many couples could have survived such an ordeal with their sanity intact, much less their relationship. And I believed that the fact that we'd come out on the other side more in love than ever was not just a miracle, but fate. We were meant to be together.

After a too-short long weekend I returned to work. Ed was glad to have me back—glad, I think, to see that I'd actually survived the tour. The studio was busy. The Babies were still recording in Studio One so I was not surprised when Bob Ezrin walked in and leaned against my desk. He welcomed me back and then got straight to the point: he wanted to offer me a job.

"I'm sorry, what did you say, Bob?" I asked stupidly.

He needed a personal assistant and had decided that I'd be perfect. I would accompany him to Miami, New York, or wherever his work as a producer took him. The pay was four times what I was receiving at Producer's Workshop and best of all, he explained, it was not just a job—it was a career. I sat in stunned silence as I tried to take in everything he was telling me. Feeling a flicker of excitement as his words started to sink in, I replied, "Sounds great, Bob, but I'm not sure . . . I'm pretty happy here at Producer's."

Bob cut in quickly. "You'll be even happier working for me. I'll prove it to you. I have to go into this session right now, but I want us to sit down and discuss it." So we set up an interview on Saturday at Producer's Workshop.

My head spinning, I watched him disappear into Studio One. I couldn't believe what had just happened. *I can't wait to tell Lindsey,* I thought as I sat and chewed on my fingernail, staring at the phone. *Hell! He's doing interviews all afternoon. It'll have to wait until tonight. But he's going to be so proud of me! He'll be touring again soon, so it shouldn't be a problem if I have to travel as well for my job. It's going to be a lot easier for me if I'm busy while he's out on the road.* With a smile on my face, I went back to scheduling bookings and waited for the clock to strike six.

After work I headed straight for Lindsey's house and almost ran inside. "Lindsey! I've been dying to tell you! Something really amazing happened today! Bob Ezrin, Pink Floyd's producer, wants me to be his personal assistant. He said the pay would be really good, and that I would travel with him . . . and I'd be his representative in meetings with record companies when he couldn't attend them . . . and he wants me to come down to Producer's on Saturday to talk to him about it! Isn't it exciting?" I finished breathlessly.

Lindsey had been sitting playing his guitar when I rushed in talking a mile a minute. Expecting him to jump up and congratulate me, I stopped talking and looked straight at him. He sat deathly still, staring back at me with a brooding look on his face. I stood frozen, knowing that something was wrong, but not sure what I'd done or said to cause the shadows that I saw flickering across his narrowed eyes. And I had no idea that when I did find out, the entire course of my life would be changed in one afternoon.

After what seemed an eternity he carefully laid his guitar on the floor, got up, and walked toward me. "That's great, Carol. I'm going with you on Saturday, OK?" As I nodded he pulled me to him in a tight embrace. "I'm going house hunting on Saturday morning and I want you to come with me. We'll go to your studio after that."

Saturday morning dawned bright and glorious. The sky was a shade of flawless, intense blue that only appears after an L.A. rainstorm. As Lindsey and I drove through the Hollywood Hills, I gazed at the pink bougainvillea cascading down the walls and entry gates of old Spanish-style mansions that lined each side of the narrow, twisting street. The scent of jasmine hovered in the air and I felt incredibly happy. Not only was I spending a gorgeous morning with the man I loved, but also that afternoon I had a job interview that I was completely excited about.

As Lindsey pulled over and parked his Beemer next to a huge white Spanish house, I heard a voice echoing above our heads that I recognized. Looking up, I saw Stevie Nicks standing on one of the balconies overhanging the street. Lindsey swore as he grabbed my hand, pulling me up a flight of stairs that led to the open front door of the house.

"I can't believe that Stevie got to this house first! Damn it! I'm going to find a new realtor, I swear to God!" Lindsey tossed over his shoulder at me as we raced into the house and up a huge staircase inside.

Stevie laughed as soon as she saw Lindsey's scowling face from her perch on the balcony of the huge living room. "Great house, Lindsey. What a surprise to see you here!" she teased in her husky voice. "I just might buy it. You really must see the fireplace in the master bedroom! It's perfect for me!"

"Whatever, Stevie. Who's your realtor? *Satan?*" Lindsey snapped back.

"I wouldn't say that . . . but my realtor has enough mystical powers to know to bring me here an hour before you! And anyway, he got the listing last night from *your* realtor!" Laughing at the dark scowl still on Lindsey's face, she continued. "Oh, Lindsey, don't be such a spoilsport. This is a perfect girl's house . . . I really like it . . . oh, hi, Carol," Stevie added as an afterthought.

I threw a hello in her general direction as Lindsey continued to pull me up another set of stairs onto the next floor, stopping abruptly when he spied his realtor hovering in an alcove. Stomping up to him, Lindsey was breathing fire as he asked him why he didn't *mention* that *Stevie was also seeing the house?* The red-faced realtor mumbled his apologies as he handed us real estate brochures. Lindsey silently fumed as we walked through rooms and up and down staircases. After less than ten minutes, he declared that he hated the house.

We could hear Stevie's voice ringing out beneath us, talking, apparently, to Robin Snyder. Lindsey and I trooped back down into the living room and walked over to where Stevie and Robin were sitting on the floor.

"You can have it, Stevie. I don't think I could live here. You're right, it suits you better. Take it."

Stevie brightened at his words and a genuine smile replaced the smirk that she'd been wearing. "Do you think so, Lindsey? I want to think about it, but I just might! Hey, why don't you follow us back to my rental? It's only ten minutes from here. Chris is there and you know what that means. You really should come over."

"Really?" Lindsey said, his mood lightening immediately.

"He'd love to see you. Come over, both of you," Stevie replied, directing a warm and friendly smile at me.

Lindsey wrapped his arm around my waist, pulling me close to his side. "Do you want to go, Carol?" he asked.

"Sure!" I said forcefully as I smiled back at Stevie. *Maybe things are going to be easier between us,* I thought. *It's a start anyway. I don't think she's ever really smiled at me before.*

Stevie and Robin led the way back onto the street and Lindsey and I followed their BMW in *our* BMW to Stevie's rental home. It looked so much like the one we just left that I couldn't help wondering why she wanted to move. As we pulled through the iron gates, I saw life-size statues of pink flamingos in her yard, and one side of her house was covered in the same bougainvillea that adorned almost all of the homes in the Hollywood Hills.

The door opened as we climbed out of our car, and Chris Nicks, Stevie's younger brother, came racing out to greet Lindsey. I'd seen him at rehearsals, but had never really had a chance to speak with him. He stayed well within the circle of Stevie's girlfans and I can't say that I blamed him. It was a delicate situation between Stevie, Lindsey, and me, and no one wanted to get caught in the middle of it.

"Hey, Lindsey! Great to see you!" Chris gushed while shaking Lindsey's hand. As a light breeze blew his long shoulder-length blond hair, I noticed again how much he resembled Stevie. Delicately featured, his slender body and "barely there" mustache made him look like a Victorian poet rather than the ultra-hip brother of a rock 'n' roll goddess. "Uh, hi, Carol! Come in, both of you!"

As I walked into Stevie's home I tried not to be too obvious about my curiosity. It was beautiful, I realized quickly. Lamps were covered in fabulous scarves and blond wood floors gleamed under Persian carpets. The room was furnished with light wicker furniture that was almost buried under pillows covered in Laura Ashley fabric. Hanging from the ceiling by braided rope was a wonderful wicker swing that moved gently back and forth in the warm breeze coming through the open windows. Candles were everywhere, sitting on delicate tables next to photographs of Stevie and just about everyone in the Fleetwood Mac family—except me, of course. In one corner stood a baby grand piano that had a shawl thrown over it and fringe hanging down the sides. It was here that Stevie wrote her songs. And on a beveled-glass coffee table lay a large leather book that looked at least one hundred years old, titled *Magical Beings*. It was a room for Rhiannon and I absolutely loved it.

In less than two minutes, Chris and Lindsey were rolling joints. Stevie left the room, returning in mere seconds carrying a mirror with a mound of cocaine on it accompanied by a rolled-up dollar bill. "Here," she said as she handed the mirror to me. "Do as much as you like. I have to go get ready for a photo shoot. I can't even remember which magazine it's for. At least they're coming here to shoot it, thank God. Lindsey, we have a band meeting tomorrow. I'll see you then."

A cloud of smoke came billowing out of his mouth as he mumbled, "Sure." Frowning in annoyance at the lost smoke, he waved goodbye to her and went back to concentrating on the joint in his hand.

"Bye, Stevie, have a good shoot," I said in a soft voice. I was still a little in shock over the fact that I was sitting *invited* in the middle of her living room. *I would love for us to be friends,* I thought. *Maybe, just maybe, we will be.*

As though reading my mind, Lindsey reached over and grabbed my hand. "It's a nice house, isn't it?"

I nodded, smiled, and then inhaled a much bigger line than I'd intended to. "Oh shit!" I gasped as the powder went burning up my nose. Chris and Lindsey started laughing as the tears rolled down my face.

"Nice one, angel," Lindsey snickered.

Turning pink, I shrugged apologetically, setting the mirror down carefully.

Glancing down at my watch, I saw that it was already 1:30. *I have to be at Producer's for my interview with Bob Ezrin in half an hour! And I'm totally wired! Crap!* I realized with horror. "Lindsey, I have to be at the studio in thirty minutes!"

The smile that had been on his face was replaced with a frown. "Shit, that's right. We'll leave now, I guess. Chris, man, thanks for everything. We gotta run. See you later, OK?" I picked up my purse, waved goodbye to Chris, and followed Lindsey outside to the car.

I freshened my lipstick and tried to brush my hair that was blowing every which way in the warm wind streaming through the car windows. The smoke from Lindsey's joint swirled around our heads as he sat silent, lost in his own thoughts, or perhaps just stoned. Twenty minutes later we pulled into the parking lot of Producer's Workshop.

As we walked inside I could hear rock music coming from Studio One. Bob was obviously still recording and I sat down next to Lindsey to wait for him. As the minutes ticked by, I found it impossible to sit still. Jumping up, I asked Lindsey if he wanted a Coke and without waiting for an answer, I walked out to the machine just outside the front door to get one for each of us.

Returning minutes later, I stopped dead in my tracks when I saw Lindsey's face. He was staring straight ahead, a look of utter misery—and anger—upon his features. His jaw was clenched and his hands were wound so tightly into fists that his knuckles were white—a sure sign that he was deeply upset. *But about what?* I thought worriedly.

"Lindsey, what's wrong?" I whispered as I sank down beside him on the old stained couch.

He looked at me and in a halting voice said, "If you take this job with Ezrin we'll lose each other."

"What? What are you talking about, Lindsey?" I felt a physical wrench inside my stomach as his words sank in. At first I thought that he was joking, but from one look at his face I knew he wasn't. Anxiety was etched in every angle and his eyes were full of unshed tears.

In a voice that was now cracking with emotion he told me that I'd spend all my time working and that he needed me to be there for him—not for Bob Ezrin. Too stunned to speak, I sat silently, staring at him. I suddenly realized that in his mind, for reasons I didn't really understand, he felt that I'd be turning away from my commitment to him, our relationship, and any future we might have together by accepting a job that he clearly didn't want me to take. And I knew, as a chill went through me, that it didn't matter if I understood why. It was enough to know that he felt that way, and I saw that if I said yes to Bob's offer I would be running a huge risk of losing Lindsey.

Even though I realized he meant every word, I didn't want to believe it. *Maybe if I explain it better to him, he'll change his mind,* I thought desperately. So I tried. "Lindsey, you'll be on the road while I'm working and so what difference does it make if I'm working at Producer's or as a personal assistant? I'm still interested in becoming a recording engineer, but perhaps through this job I can discover another field that would be perfect for me. Let's face it, Lindsey, I'd have to be twice as good as any man to be accepted as an engineer in the music industry . . ."

"Carol," Lindsey answered, eyes still wet with unshed tears, "I need you. I need you to be with me. Not running around the country with some other guy. I've been thinking about this a lot since you told me about this job offer a few days ago." He stopped, took my face in his hands, and continued. "Carol, I want you to move in with me. I want you to go on the road with me. I want us to be together."

Still holding my face between his long fingers, he looked straight into my eyes and said, "I hate being away from you and I have a huge year ahead of me. Maybe if I wasn't touring, your having a job would work for us, but I *am* touring—for the next year at least. If you work we're never going to see each other and it's going to break us up. Trust me. If you don't love me enough now to do whatever it takes for us to be together, then you never will."

"If you don't love me now / you will never love me again . . ." In the back of my mind I could hear "The Chain" and Lindsey's anguished voice singing those words to an audience of thousands.

As I stared at his face I felt something give inside me and with no more questions—of either him or myself—I knew that I would never put anything as selfish as a job that I wanted before my relationship with him. And I realized that Lindsey felt that if I accepted this job, I was choosing a career—and Bob Ezrin—over him, and that made my answer to both of them crystal clear.

"Lindsey, I won't take the job. He'll have to find someone else." As soon as the words were out of my mouth, he leaned over and kissed me passionately.

"Let's get out of here, Carol. I can't stand it here. I want to leave. I want to take you home. We have plans to make, angel, and I don't want to do it here."

As we stood up to leave, the door to Studio One opened and Bob Ezrin called my name. Smoothing my hair back into place, I turned to Lindsey and said, "Let me go tell him I won't take the job. I'll be just a minute." Without hesitating, I walked into the studio and told Bob that I couldn't accept his offer. A look of surprise passed over his face as he stood and stared at me. With a nod he abruptly turned away, clearly displeased. He was offering me a dream job. What woman in her right mind would turn that down? A woman in love.

Without another word I walked outside into the beautiful afternoon and took Lindsey's hand. We stopped and looked at each other in the waning warmth of the sun. We had just made a huge commitment to each other. I was moving in with him and into his life completely. I was, as of that moment, a fully committed member of the Fleetwood Mac family and their future, like Lindsey's, was now mine. Instead of breaking the chain, I had become another link, and the enormity of what had just happened threatened to overwhelm me. Suddenly frightened, I took a deep breath, held his hand tightly, and walked away from Producer's Workshop and into my new future.

On Monday I gave Ed Cobb my two weeks' notice. Almost crying, I told him that I was moving in with Lindsey and that because of the upcoming American tour, I wouldn't be able to work full-time any longer.

Ed was visibly upset. "Are you sure, Carol? You'd make a great engineer. Are you sure this is what you want?"

Tearfully I nodded, and with a sigh he let go of me and walked quickly outside. Throwing a long leg over his motorcycle, he roared off, leaving me staring wistfully after him.

For the second time in a year my entire life had changed. The first time I'd claimed my independence by leaving a long-dead relationship, moving into an apartment of my own, and starting a new career. This time I was joining my life with that of the man I loved and embarking on a future that held almost everything that a young woman could want: love, excitement, travel, fame, money, and rock 'n' roll. That this future would also hold a darkness that would scar my life forever was beyond my comprehension.

As the days flew by Lindsey seemed to spend every waking hour doing phone interviews, band interviews, or photo shoots for magazines and newspapers across the country and the world. Dinners were spent every other night with various band members at favorite restaurants as, over tropical drinks or wicked margaritas, they worked out the last-minute details of the upcoming second leg of the American *Rumours* tour.

Mick, John, and Christine were frantically trying to get their green cards and had added some political benefit gigs to the tour schedule in the hope that if they greased the palms of different politicians, the cards would be granted without further delay. The band's English contingent was in America on extended visas and desperately needed to be declared permanent residents of the U.S. None of them wanted to be forced to return to England. It was a matter of supreme importance to Fleetwood Mac's future, and one that would take us to the White House.

"Don't Stop," the second single from *Rumours*, was released in Britain but stalled at number thirty-four on the charts there. This worried Mick, Christine, and Lindsey, but since the album was still at number one in America (and selling an astronomical number of copies), they adopted a "can't-win-them-all" attitude and hoped that the single would fare better on its release in the U.S. Radio airplay was as heavy as ever, and there was so much momentum going for both the album and the band that it was completely overwhelming if we let ourselves stop and think about it. So no one did. Lindsey, the band, their girlfriends, and one wife just went through every hour focusing on the mundane details of that day's schedule.

Now that I had officially moved in with him, Lindsey had made it a priority for us to find a home. Or rather, he'd planned to hire a new realtor and I'd do the house-searching while he continued his interviews.

He ended up choosing a realtor named Pam Sorens, and she and I had the exciting but heavy responsibility of finding a suitable "mansion." Over the next week and a half, Pam and I looked at a dozen houses that seemed better suited to geriatrics than rock 'n' rollers and I was beginning to despair of ever finding the right home for Lindsey and me. And then, like yet another fairy-tale ending, I was shown a house built over fifty years before we were born that seemed to have been waiting for us to find it.

After looking at two disastrously inappropriate houses that morning, Pam and I pulled up dejectedly in front of a huge brick Tudor-style home in the heart of old Hollywood's Hancock Park. As soon as I stepped through the huge wooden front door, I felt with a rising excitement that I had found our home. One look at the stained-glass windows depicting knights in armor, medieval princesses, daggers dripping blood, and at the stadium-size living room with its thirty-foot-high wooden ceiling made of hand-painted, four-foot-square drawings of unicorns, King Arthur, and Lady Guinevere, and I knew that I'd found a "castle" that was perfect for two inhabitants of the Court of Fleetwood Mac.

"It's so Fleetwood Mac, Pam!" I exclaimed as I turned in a slow circle in the living room, trying to take it all in.

I'd fallen in love with the two-story, five-bedroom house in just three minutes. A huge entry hall surrounded a sweeping staircase that led to both sides of the upper story. Here, there was a small, creepy library (it locked from the outside), three bathrooms, and four bedrooms. The house had a lot of dark wood panels throughout it, with Victorian lamp sconces to light the interior.

Downstairs, along with the gigantic living room, there was a glassed sunroom, kitchen, dining room, two dens, and a maid's quarters of two rooms. Huge upstairs balconies overhung a backyard with a large swimming pool and landscaped grounds. Because the yard backed up to a golf course, the green grass seemed to go on forever. Within twenty-four hours Lindsey put an offer on the house and it was ours. After three months of bank escrow, that was. We could wait. We were leaving L.A. almost immediately for the road. From this point on, I would be by Lindsey's side.

After the hardships of Europe, touring the U.S. was fabulous: no bad weather, no horrible food, and both Lindsey and I were healthy. But the most important thing was the change in our relationship. We were now liv-

ing together. Our feelings for each other were deeper and, most importantly, there was a permanence about us that wasn't there before. And, on the
road, it was obvious to not just the two of us but to everyone around us.

Our happiness was pretty hard to miss. We constantly held hands, whispered into each other's ears, and finished each other's sentences in conversations with everyone. We were
aware of the disgusted looks being
thrown our way by one and all, but
we simply didn't care. Even if we had
cared, we wouldn't have been able
to change how we were with each
other. And yet being so happy amid
the wreckage of other band members' old relationships was unnerving not just for Lindsey and me, but
for everyone in the inner circle.

The band's fame had grown
astronomically in just a few short
months, and so had their fan base.
Even though I knew in theory how
big Fleetwood Mac was getting, seeing it with my own eyes was exciting and a little scary. Now when the

Luggage tag on the Rumours *tour.*

band's plane landed at a city for a
concert, there were always at least seventy-five to one hundred fans waiting behind temporary wood barriers some two hundred yards from the
plane, and after the shows there were kids waiting at our hotels clamoring
for autographs. We never registered under our own names at hotels. Just
like all famous rock musicians, every band member had a fake name that
changed with each tour. For the *Rumours* tour we were "Mr. and Mrs. Pat
Pending." Later, on the *Tusk* tour, Lindsey would insist upon "Mr. and Mrs.
Russ Hunk," just to see me squirm every time I ordered room service.

As the concerts zipped by, the Fleetwood Mac family settled into a series
of concert rituals that would be followed for the next eight years. These rituals never varied. Like the special handshake of a child's secret club, they
were a routine that Fleetwood Mac believed in and followed every time.

The rituals began as soon as we entered the venue for that night's show. Everyone was treated to back-of-the-wrist bumps of blow the minute we walked into the band's main dressing room in the backstage area. An hour and a half before the show, if there were any local press or VIP visitors roaming around the dressing room, they were kicked out of the backstage, leaving the inner circle of Fleetwood Mac free to do whatever it was they needed or wanted to do. The band members got dressed, snorted blow, made drinks, and threw sarcastic remarks at each other—remarks designed to wound and cut just enough to peel back the surface of old scars without, God willing, causing a full-scale war before the concert.

Sitting watching this battle of words show after show, I wondered if there would ever come a time when the rage and hurt between John and Christine or between Stevie and Lindsey would end. As the years passed, this pre-show verbal sparring would escalate from sarcastic entertainment into vicious battles.

The banter stopped when J.C.'s ten-minute countdown began. On cue, Christine morphed into a gentler, English-rose version of Janis Joplin, with her raucous jokes and laughter—all she needed to complete the incarnation was a feather boa. Lindsey was Lord Byron, brooding and beautiful, his long fingers stroking the polished surface of his guitar in a completely unconscious caress as he leaned seductively against the wall. Mick's eyes became manic as he pounded his drumsticks harder and faster, looking at least a foot taller than his near-skyscraper height in his black velvet suit, ballet shoes, and trademark wooden balls.

Stevie turned pale and fragile-looking, her seductive power simmering on a low heat as she waited for the spotlights to hit her before she let its fire flare on stage. John stood dressed in shorts and casual shirt, giving me a wink and a wry smile as intelligence and sardonic wit shone from his eyes. His biting sarcasm and wicked humor were only on display for the trusted family members. Unlike the other four, John's stage persona was the exact opposite of what he was in everyday life. While playing a quiet, unassuming soul on stage, he was anything but that when among us.

"*One minute*, everyone—line up and I'll send you out in style," J.C. intoned as he dumped blow on the backs of the band's extended fists, and then, as our private security surrounded them, they walked silently out of the dressing room. Down endless corridors strewn with ever-present black and gray cables they walked, past anvil equipment cases adorned with Fleetwood Mac's penguin mascot, up metal stairs, and onto the blacked-out stage. Another show was up and running.

The audience's reception had become almost complete adulation and, for some, obsession with the band and their music. Even if some nights Christine's, Stevie's, or Lindsey's voice was ragged, every fan in the sold-out venue went insane over each and every song. "So Afraid" always got a standing ovation, "Don't Stop" brought thundering cheers, and Stevie's "Rhiannon" was an absolute showstopper. I never tired of watching her perform what had become her trademark song. The track itself was amazing, but on stage it became sheer theater as she sang out the lyrics in her husky, sexy voice and twirled like a possessed spirit behind the microphone.

Halfway through the song the stage would go dark. A lone blue light encased Stevie as she crouched on the right side during Lindsey's intricate guitar bridge. The backdrop of the withered tree and full moon was hit with red and gold spotlights and the forest of Rhiannon came alive. Haloed in blue, Stevie slowly stood, arms crossed in front of her face, her sheer black chiffon cape shadowing her features as she crossed to the center of the stage. With her back to the mike, she started singing the haunting lyrics about love and a white witch.

Stevie Nicks.

Photography © Ed Roach, roach-clips.com

Whirling around feverishly, Stevie screamed the words again as every one of us stood frozen watching her. "Rhiannon . . . Rhiannon . . ." she wailed, stomping her five-inch platform boots to the music, and then the stage went dark and the fans exploded in applause. There was no doubt in anyone's mind that they had just watched a potent incarnation of the witch Rhiannon—and they had. It was just another piece of Fleetwood Mac magic.

While the band played, the "family" continued its rituals backstage. J.C. began to run the scene. First, the band's personal security washed and dried beer-bottle caps and filled each one with a huge hit of cocaine. After the caps were lined up on separate cheap trays, a napkin was thrown over the whole shebang and a trusted band bodyguard carried them down the hall to the stage.

He climbed the stairs in the shadowy darkness and placed the trays on the tall black speakers at the back of the stage. During the show the band would fade back to the speakers at every opportunity and give themselves a bottle-cap pick-me-up. On Christine and John's side of the stage, vodka tonics were replenished as needed, and on Lindsey's side, Ray Lindsey, his roadie, always kept a joint going. Between songs an ever-present cloud of smoke hovered around Lindsey's head as he strolled back to toke up as often as he could. Mick ducked down behind his drums, tooting up like the master that he was, and Stevie tripped off to stage right during every single break to change a shawl and snag a bottle cap of blow.

In the last ritual of the night, after the show each band member was offered a folded white paper bundle of cocaine to take back to their room for personal use. It was a sheer miracle that a stray local policeman patrolling the auditorium or backstage didn't make world headlines by busting the entire band and entourage for drug possession.

But things like that happened in the real world. Not in ours. That it could happen simply didn't occur to us in those days. We lived by a set of rules that didn't exist outside the golden curtains that surrounded us. And there wasn't anyone with enough power to tell us that we were wrong.

The fact that blow was illegal didn't bother us at all. The fact that this drug was dangerous and not only could—but *would*—rule and damage the lives of almost all of us didn't even cross our minds. Never once did any-one voice any concern about the fact that cocaine had become not just commonplace but seemingly as necessary as the band's mikes. Basically, cocaine had become just a fact of life within the world of Fleetwood Mac, and for some of us, myself included, it would become one of the most important band rituals of them all.

After weeks on the road Fleetwood Mac returned home to play the Forum in Los Angeles. It was the biggest venue in the city and it was completely sold out. The acoustics were fabulous and playing in it was like being on the cover of *Rolling Stone*. If you sold out the Forum, you'd "arrived" in the music industry. The band was to play to an audience of over nineteen thousand fans and they were feeling completely, insanely freaked. It wasn't the size of the audience that had them on the edge of a nervous breakdown: it was the simple, brutal fact that in L.A. they would be playing in front of their musical peers—rock giants like Bruce Springsteen, Tom Petty, Don Henley, David Bowie, Mick Jagger—any or all of them could be sitting in the audience. It didn't really matter who you were or how much commercial success you had in the record industry, playing in front of people whose opinion matters to you and who are themselves your musical idols was a recipe for high-octane stress.

Rumours was already a phenomenon in the record industry: the reviews, interviews, and chart position couldn't be better. A history-making performance at the Forum was not only expected of Fleetwood Mac but was of absolute critical importance: to their fans in the audience, to their peers, and, most of all, to the band themselves.

After a three-day break it was countdown time for the Forum show. As usual, Lindsey's housemates Richard Dashut and Bob Aguirre were running all over the house in stages of undress, joints passed hand to hand as they ironed their shirts and wiped the dust off boots that hadn't been shined since they brought them home from the shoe store.

Carrying my clothes on hangers, I paused for a minute to watch their clowning as I headed into the bath-

Bob Aguirre.

room to get dressed. Because Richard was with us on the road in Europe, I knew him much better than I did Bob. Even so, Bob was quickly becoming one of my best friends. With his long, black, wavy hair, bandito mustache, and ever-present wicked smirk, he looked more like a pirate than the session drummer he had become in L.A. As the drummer in the band Fritz with Stevie and Lindsey, Bob had known Lindsey for years and, like Richard, was one of his best friends.

After ducking into the bathroom I locked the door behind me. Having grown up with six sisters, I found it ironic that I was now living in what amounted to a frat house. *I can't wait until we can move into our new house!* I thought to myself. With a sigh of relief to be away from the *Animal House* scene taking place in the living room, I hung my clothes on the door and jumped into the shower. An hour later I was dressed for that night's huge show. Wearing a white chiffon baby-doll shirt and a gorgeous antique beaded blue skirt given to me by Judy Wong, I felt like a fairy princess as I applied my makeup in the cracked mirror above the sink. Excitement and anticipation of the night that lay ahead seemed to put extra color in my cheeks and for once my hair had turned out exactly as I liked it: long, silky, and completely straight. Within an hour my hair would be the only thing "straight" about me.

Dressed in our finery, we all trooped out to the waiting limo and headed for the show. Lindsey gripped my hand as we rode through the streets of West L.A. His clenched jaw betrayed his nervousness as we got closer to the venue. I talked soothingly to him, doing my best to get his mind off the upcoming show. As my fingers started to go numb from his grip, I sighed in relief as our car neared the hall.

The Los Angeles Forum is a white circular building that looks as if a Roman emperor with horrific taste built it. The limo pulled into the back of the building and fans lined up on each side of us, waving programs and pressing their palms to the glass of the tinted windows of our long, black car. Smiling, Lindsey opened the window and shouted, "Thanks for coming!" as we barely missed running over a few stray kids who were trying to block the car from entering the security doors.

"We're going to kill all the punters!" Richard screamed, laughing hysterically as the driver desperately tried to thread his way through the throng of fans.

"Since each of those 'punters' has paid money to see us, try to keep the death toll down! *Jesus!*" Lindsey yelled at our driver.

Smiling at Richard, I had to laugh at his use of the word "punters." It was a term that everyone in the Fleetwood Mac family used to describe the fans, but one that was perhaps less than flattering. Usually reserved for rowdy English sports enthusiasts (or sports thugs), the word *punters* had become a mainstay of the Mac family vocabulary. After a harrowing few minutes the car made it through the horde of punters without leaving fatalities and the gates slid shut behind us.

"Fuck it," Lindsey said as he prepared to exit the limo. "Let's get this fuckin' show going!" A sheen of excitement was on his face and I smiled knowingly as I crawled out behind him and followed my frat brothers into the fluorescent lighting of the venue's huge loading dock.

Richard Dashut.

This was a metamorphosis I'd seen over and over again: Lindsey Buckingham, "rock star guitarist of Fleetwood Mac," had replaced the nervous guy riding beside me just a few moments before. And tonight he was ready to play the Los Angeles Forum.

Time raced by backstage. The dressing rooms were packed with the band's relatives and friends and the level of excitement was almost through the roof. This night meant a lot to not just the band but also everyone close to them who had watched the five members of Fleetwood Mac work, starve, struggle, and suffer for the success that they were now enjoying. Lindsey and I were as caught up as everyone else in the air of celebration that swirled around us. It was the most fun we'd had so far backstage.

But things turned bizarre within half an hour of the band taking the stage. It all began with Rod Stewart. By the side of his manager, he was roaming the backstage area freely—a privilege that was never allowed dur-

Christine McVie and Bob Aguirre.

ing the show to anyone outside the Fleetwood Mac family. But thanks to the close friendship of Rod's manager to J.C., Rod was allowed to wander wherever he pleased. It was a breach of security that would end up biting Fleetwood Mac's road manager on the ass after Rod became fixated on one of the women backstage.

I noticed him, of course, as I walked back and forth to the stage area. It was hard to miss Rod Stewart leaning nonchalantly against a wall. I smiled at him, said nothing, and kept walking. Up close and personal, I didn't really find him very attractive—not my type at all. My type was playing on stage with a guitar strapped around his neck. Next to Lindsey, Rod seemed washed out and more than a little pretentious with his perfectly coiffed blond hair, skintight pants, and long scarf carefully knotted around his throat.

Twenty minutes after the show had started, I saw him huddled deep in discussion with his manager. Dismissing them both from my mind, I headed back to the stage to watch Lindsey play.

The audience was going crazy, the band was on fire, and, as was now my own ritual, I wanted to have a hit of blow before Lindsey launched into "So Afraid." Wandering back through the black curtains, I went to the dressing room in search of a bottle cap. I found J.C. inside, red in the face and laughing hysterically as he talked to the band's security guys, Greg and Dwayne. Everyone stopped dead as I came in and then a fresh burst of giggles rocked J.C. as he stared at me standing in the center of the room.

"What's so funny, J.C.? What did I miss?" I asked as I looked around at the roomful of guys who were obviously trying to pull themselves together in front of me.

"Ah, Jesus, Carol, you're not going to believe what just happened," J.C. said as he wiped tears from his eyes caused by his hysterical laughter.

"Uh, OK. What?" I asked.

Trying to talk between fits of giggles, J.C. stammered, "Well, hell. Rod Stewart's manager just came up to me and told me that Rod has found the girl that he wants to have for the night . . . and, uh, he told me to fix it for him so that good old Rod can go home happy."

"Really? That seems kinda gross, J.C. Who is she? Some fan who got backstage?"

"Well, not exactly, Carol . . . I told his manager—with Rod standing right there beside him—that I'd be glad to try to help and asked him to point out the girl that Rod liked and I'd see what I could do—" J.C. stopped speaking as Dwayne and Greg sniggered in the background. "The thing is, Carol, he pointed out you! And so I had to tell him, 'Sorry, man, that's the guitar player's old lady!' Swear to God, man . . . I've never seen Rod Stewart look so fuckin' embarrassed. I think he's split, man. Which is a good thing. Lindsey will friggin' rip him a new one when he hears."

"You're kidding me, right? He just walks around pointing out girls and his manager 'gets them' for him? That's sick, J.C.! And anyway, do I look like someone he could just pick up that way? Do I?" I spluttered as I looked down at my relatively demure baby-doll chiffon blouse and knee-length skirt. I was also wearing suede boots with stiletto heels, but I really, really didn't think I looked cheap. Feeling my cheeks burn with embarrassment, I glared at J.C.

"Carol, honey, calm down. I know this is a nasty little shock, but you shouldn't take it personally. Listen, Rod has a thing for blondes. You're his type. That's all it is. You're blonde, pretty—exactly the kinda girl he goes for. I'm sorry, sweetie. Really." I looked suspiciously at J.C. as he tried to keep the grin off his face. Reaching for a nearby bottle cap, I tried to snort it with dignity—a rather difficult feat.

As I flounced across the room I could hear Greg's laughter echoing down the hallway as he made his way back out to the stage. Greg Thomason had been with the band only a few months less than I. Lindsey and Richard had met him on their skiing trip to Aspen in January. They'd both really taken a liking to this six-foot-two, 225-pound, blond, handsome surfer dude with a puppy-dog personality. He had a bodyguard's build and the charm of a little boy. Lindsey hired him immediately to tour with the band. In return, Greg worshipped Lindsey. Greg was the exact opposite of Dwayne. Dwayne was tall and thin with wire-framed eyeglasses that made him look like a high-school geek instead of the seasoned security man that he was. The band loved both of them.

I knew that Greg was rushing off to tell Lindsey what had just happened. The first short break that Lindsey had, Greg would spill the whole story to him. With a sigh I sat down on the couch to wait for whatever fall-out was about to come. That there would surely be some I had no doubt. Lindsey was pretty territorial when it came to me. Sure enough, Greg came rushing back into the room barely ten minutes later with a grim look on his face.

"J.C., Lindsey's a little pissed off. I think you better go talk to him. I told him what happened—I thought he'd think it was funny! Um, he didn't. He wants to talk to you, J.C. He told me to find you."

"Shit!" J.C. muttered as he stomped out of the dressing room.

Keeping his head down, Greg then shuffled out, leaving me alone in the room. As I walked over to the cheap vanity mirror hanging on the wall, I couldn't help smiling a little as I thought about what just happened. *It is a little flattering,* I thought to myself as I reapplied my lipstick. *But then again, it's totally creepy that Rod Stewart thinks he can just point his finger at a girl and she'll swoon at his feet and go for a one-night stand!* I shuddered as a picture of his disheveled manager flashed through my mind. *That's an even bigger creep! How can he act like that?*

As I turned from the mirror J.C. ran into the room and grabbed me gently by the arm. "Lindsey wants you up on stage with him, Carol Ann. He wants to know you're 'safe.' I have to make sure that Stewart has left backstage. Lindsey told me to throw him out. Shit, Carol, he's really pissed off. Tell him after the show that I protected you, OK? Please don't tell him that I laughed my ass off—he doesn't think it's funny, and I can see his point. I'm supposed to watch over you. Sorry, hon."

"It's not your fault, J.C. Don't worry about it. Of course I won't tell Lindsey. But J.C., I really would be totally embarrassed to run into Stewart. Are you sure he's gone?"

"Gone forever from Fleetwood Mac's backstage, I think. Come on, we gotta get you up on that stage before Lindsey fires my ass."

Walking up onto the metal stairs, I stood where Lindsey could see me and smiled as he blew me a kiss. He then turned toward J.C. and gave him a cold, dead-eyed stare. Looking sheepish, J.C. quickly beat a hasty retreat down the stairs and back through the curtains.

As I sat on one of the chairs at the side of the stage I wondered idly what Lindsey was going to say to J.C. after the show. *I've never really seen him angry, but if he'd looked at me the way he just did at J.C., I'd be more than a little worried. Actually, I'd be downright scared!* I thought to myself in surprise. There was definitely a sense of menace in Lindsey's glare and I winced as I watched him break a string on his guitar during "World Turning," curse at Ray Lindsey, and almost throw the guitar at him. He was pissed off all right. I decided to remain on stage. I didn't want to do anything that would distract him from the show. As I watched and listened to Lindsey play like he was possessed by a demon, I knew that that night's show was one of the best the band had ever played.

And just maybe a little of Lindsey's power was fuelled by his anger over an English rocker trying to make off with his girl. Just for the night, of course.

I was so caught up in the music that I jumped in shock when I felt a hand wrapping around my wrist, pulling me to my feet. The hand belonged to J.C. and the look of dark intensity on his face made me follow him without question down the stairs and through the curtains into the hallway. I knew that something was very, very wrong.

"J.C., what is it? What happened? Is someone hurt?" I stammered.

"Carol, hon, the police just called. It's bad news, I'm afraid: your house has been robbed," he said bluntly.

I looked at him in horror. My mind flashed mental pictures of Lindsey's guitars, Bob's drums, recording equipment . . . the new TV that I'd bought from my Producer's Workshop salary . . . Lindsey's prized record collection.

"Oh my God. What did the police say, J.C.? Did they catch them inside the house? I don't understand how they knew to call here . . . is everything stolen? How bad is it?" I looked down at my hands and saw that they were shaking. I'd never had anything like this happen to me, and I felt sick inside.

"Look, sweetie, I don't know for sure . . . but I think it's bad. All the police would tell me is that they've dusted for prints and they need Lindsey to call them immediately after the show. I guess one of the neighbors reported someone breaking into your house, called the cops, and they came out. They told me that they saw Lindsey's publicity photos lying around, knew that Fleetwood Mac was playing the Forum tonight, and I guess they put two and two together and knew to call here. I mean, who doesn't know where Lindsey is tonight?"

J.C. gently put his arm around my waist and led me into the dressing room. "Let me get you a drink, Carol," he said as he poured a splash of Myers's into a glass and added Pepsi to it. "After what happened with Rod Stewart tonight, I don't want to be the one to break the news to Lindsey. You tell me what you want me to do, hon. I can have security go out and find Aguirre or let Richard know . . . but I don't want to fuck with the show and Lindsey really shouldn't be told until he's offstage. It's your call, though."

"No! Don't tell Lindsey! It'll ruin the show if he finds out before they're offstage!" I said sharply. "I'll tell him. He's going to be really upset and I should be the one to tell him." I felt totally sick just thinking about it. "He has guitars there that he absolutely loves. Why did this have to happen tonight? This is one of the biggest nights of his career. Oh, J.C., why does shit like this happen? It's not just that our things have probably been stolen, it's just the thought that someone could do that to us, you know?"

For me, the show was already over. The shocking news that I'd just been given filled me with a sense of dread—I just wanted Lindsey. I needed him to be offstage and with me. I felt completely upset and I didn't want to be the one in charge. But for now, I was. For now, I'd let Richard, Bob, and Lindsey enjoy the rest of the evening. After all, the damage was already done. The robbery had driven our night of Hollywood glamour into the seamy dark world of Hollywood crime—and Lindsey's starry evening was now tainted. It had become a night for sordid memories.

There would be no after-party celebration for Lindsey and me. We had the LAPD waiting for our call and God knows what waiting for us at our house on Putney. I swallowed the drink that J.C. had handed to me and felt the rum burning my throat. Even though I rarely drank, I downed this one in thirty seconds. If ever there was a time when a stiff drink was needed, this was definitely one of them. With my eyes still tearing from the rum, I reached for another bottle cap of blow.

I had a feeling I was going to need to have my edges blurred before I walked into our house. Leaning my head on my hand, I sat and waited for the end of the show, staring forlornly at the floor. As soon as I heard the closing chords of "Blue Letter," I mixed Lindsey a drink. Like me, he was going to need it.

Fleetwood Mac burst through the doors of the dressing room like a tornado. Dripping with sweat, red-faced and triumphant, their bodies gave off so much heat that you could almost see the steam rising from their stage clothes. After a five-minute standing ovation they'd given two encores. When a show didn't go well, the band only played "Gold Dust Woman" and then left the stage in a pissed-off mood. Tonight they'd added "Blue Letter" and that meant that Fleetwood Mac considered the show a success.

As I looked at Lindsey's smiling face, I died a little inside, feeling as though it were my fault that I had such bad news to tell him. My mind knew this wasn't true, but my stomach didn't. I felt completely nauseous and walked into the bathroom to take some deep breaths. I decided to wait for Richard and Bob to come backstage before I told him. Squaring my shoulders, I went back out into the dressing room and watched the band congratulate each other on the show.

Stevie was absolutely glowing as she talked excitedly to Mick, leaning down to whisper something into his ear that made his already flushed face turn crimson. He looked up at her adoringly and gently touched her cheek. *Uh-oh, they're at it again,* I thought idly as I looked around quickly for Jenny. I was glad to see that she had her back turned to them—it was obvious to anyone watching that sparks were flying between Mick and Stevie. On any other night I'd watch this encounter with sharp eyes and my usual sense of watching a soap opera within a soap opera, but tonight it seemed absolutely trivial to me. The weight on my shoulders was almost unbearable as I stood there knowing that I was about to deliver news to Lindsey that would shatter his night.

Bob, Richard, and Ken came bursting through the door, yelling Indian war cries, lighting joints, and grinning from ear to ear. Grateful to have Lindsey distracted for a few minutes, I hung in the background, wanting to give him as much time as I could to enjoy the evening's brilliant success.

J.C. moved up behind me and whispered into my ear, "Sweetie, you have to go tell him. The cops are waiting to hear from you guys. I have a limo ready to leave at the loading dock. I'll go get Lindsey for you and bring him to the tuning room. Meet us there." He squeezed my shoulder, gave me a look that said "Be strong" and moved across to where Lindsey was standing.

I slipped quietly out of the now-packed dressing room and headed for the tuning room. Minutes later Lindsey walked through the door, a troubled look on his face.

"What's wrong, Carol? J.C. said you needed to talk to me right away. Are you OK? Did that bastard Stewart do anything to you? I'm going to kick J.C.'s ass as soon as I have five minutes alone with him!"

"Oh, Lindsey, I don't know how to tell you this, so I'm going to just say it. Our house was robbed tonight. The LAPD needs us to go straight home and call them." I could feel my eyes filling with tears as I looked as his shocked face. "I'm so sorry, baby. I can't believe it, either . . ."

"*Fuck!*"' Lindsey screamed. "You're fuckin' kidding me, right?" As the tears started to slip down my face, he pulled me close and stroked my hair. "It's OK, baby. Let me get changed and we'll go home. Don't cry. Whatever's happened, we'll fix it. Go get Richard and Bob—tell them what's up—they need to come with us," he said grimly.

Walking back into the dressing room, I made Lindsey a new drink—hoping that the alcohol would help numb the shock. On my way out I grabbed Richard and whispered into his ear the horrible news about the Putney house, asking him to bring Bob and meet Lindsey and me at the loading dock in five minutes. Looking as though someone had just slapped him across the face, he nodded, grabbed Bob by the arm, and pulled him out of the room. I left right behind them, stopping at the tuning room to find Lindsey dressed, depressed, and angry. As I handed him his drink he tried to smile at me but it came out more a grimace. Putting my arm around him, I leaned against him as we walked silently to the waiting limousine.

When the car pulled up in front of the house, we all looked at each other in dismay. On the ride there we'd tried not to talk about what might be waiting for us at home. None of us wanted to think about it—as though pretending it hadn't happened would make it go away. The sight of a pitch-black house brought reality crashing down on us and we all stared at one another without speaking. The driver opened the door to let us out of the car and we reluctantly climbed out. Holding on to Lindsey's hand, I huddled close to him, trying to find a little shelter before we walked through the front door.

The usually untidy living room was now in complete shambles. The first thing I saw was a pillowcase filled with lumpy objects lying abandoned just to the right of the door. My hand tightened on Lindsey's arm as we stepped farther into the entry hall. The house was dark and shadowy. Our living room lamps were knocked off their tables onto the floor, the broken glass from their lightbulbs glittering in the dim light coming from the streetlamps that were filtering in through the picture window. Scanning the room, I could make out empty guitar stands, electrical cords flung haphazardly across the couch, and an empty table where my Sony TV used to sit. All that I seemed to see was the emptiness that I knew should have been filled with amps, precious Les Paul and Gibson guitars, and recording equipment. Bob's drums were still sitting in the dining room, but that appeared to be the only piece of equipment left in the house.

Lindsey kept muttering, "Fuck, fuck, fuck . . ." as he made his way across the living room. He flipped the light switch in the hall and it felt as though someone had sucked all of the air out of the room. It was a total disaster. It was also sickeningly obvious that whoever did this had no qualms about not only stealing everything but also trashing the place as much as possible.

Lindsey grabbed my hand and we slowly entered our bedroom. The sheets had been stripped off the bed, and probably used to carry out whatever was stolen. The drawers to the bureau were open and clothes and lingerie were tossed onto the floor, lying on top of books that had been thrown out of the bookcase, their pages scattered across the floor. The nausea I'd felt backstage returned with a vengeance and it was all I could do to keep from throwing up. Sinking down onto the bare mattress, I stared at my underclothes lying on the floor, at the pillowcase left abandoned in the doorway, and I knew that I had never felt so violated or so angry.

It wasn't the material value of our stolen possessions that made me feel the way I did: it was the realization that a stranger had come into our home and completely violated our personal space and belongings. I knew then and there that I would never feel comfortable in that house again. And if I felt that way after living there only a few months, I could only imagine how bad it was for Lindsey, Richard, and Bob. I felt like crying, but for Lindsey's sake I blinked back the tears and took a deep breath. I wanted to be strong for him—it was his big night that had been ruined, his beloved guitars that were stolen, his special belongings and memories that no amount of money could ever replace.

While Lindsey was talking to Bob and Richard, I went to the hall cupboard to pull out clean sheets for our bed. Weariness swept over me, and it was all I could do to stay on my feet. Summoning my last bit of energy, I made up the bed, closed the door to our bedroom, and slowly took off my shimmering skirt and delicate blouse.

Feeling as though I were in a parallel universe, I climbed into bed and curled up on my side to wait for Lindsey to join me. Exhaustion took over and I started to slip into the nether land of sleep. *Coming home tonight was really scary,* I thought drowsily. *I hope I never have to feel this way again. I want to move into our new house. It's a fairy-tale house, and nothing bad can happen to us there.*

7

LIGHTNING FLASHES

There had been warning signs. We knew that something was terribly wrong with Lindsey. Over the summer he began to experience bizarre episodes of disorientation, nausea, and shortness of breath. Striking without warning and lasting between fifteen and thirty minutes, they left him pale, weak, and shaky. They were severe enough to send us rushing to our family doctor, who scheduled a myriad of tests for him. Blood tests, brain scans, X-rays—all were done by the leading medical specialists in Los Angeles. And none of the tests or any of the specialists we consulted could find anything wrong with Lindsey. Yet the attacks kept happening. We began to refer to them as "flashes" and tried to cope as best we could. Despite the doctors telling us that nothing was wrong, I didn't believe them. I knew something was wrong. And it terrified me.

As I packed to go back on the road with Lindsey for the next leg of the *Rumours* tour, I tried not to think about what would happen if he had one of his flashes while performing. The thought of thousands of eyes staring at him on stage as he was helplessly locked in one of his trance-like episodes made me feel powerless. We hadn't told any of the other band members about Lindsey's "problem"—after all, the doctors had given him a clean bill of health. *Maybe the flashes will just go away,* I thought hopefully. *They came from out of nowhere, so maybe they'll just stop. He's going to do just fine . . . stop worrying . . . he's going to be fine.*

And he was—for the first few weeks of the tour. I thought the biggest problem he would have to face was exhaustion. Playing a tour schedule of three shows in a row and two nights off, then two or three shows again and one day off, and playing the same set, the same songs, night after night, left every member of the band completely wrecked by the third week of the ambitiously scheduled *Rumours* tour. They were using more cocaine, more alcohol, more weed, more *everything* to get through the shows with the quality of the music intact. By now Fleetwood Mac had done close to seventy-five shows in the U.S., and the band was booked to be on the road well into 1978. Tempers were shorter, the partying wilder, and the hangovers more severe.

Even so, the show that was next on the schedule had all of us excited. The band was to play in front of one of its largest audiences ever. In Philadelphia, seventy thousand people would be waiting in the hot sun to hear Fleetwood Mac perform in an afternoon festival that was completely sold out. It was just what they needed to shake off the jaded routine that the *Rumours* tour was becoming and bring back the thrill for all of us.

After we'd checked into the huge hotel in Philadelphia, Lindsey immediately set up his portable recording equipment in the living room of our suite. Over the summer he'd ordered a reel-to-reel portable recording machine with a mixer and speakers—the works—to be built into three large anvil cases on wheels. Once set up, it spanned seven feet and stood three feet high. Lindsey loved it. He'd already started to work on new songs for the next album. Every night off that we'd had so far, he spent recording. Sitting cross-legged on the floor with his guitar in front of the red anvil cases of his portable studio, he laid songs down on tape as a cloud of smoke from an ever-present joint hovered around his head.

And this night was no different. I left Lindsey to his music and climbed into bed, knowing that he would probably work for hours. Waking briefly when he crawled in next to me, I looked at the clock and saw that it was almost 4 A.M. *He's going to be tired tomorrow—our wake-up call is for eight*, I thought sleepily as I curled up against his body.

At 8 a.m. the phone rang shrilly and as I lifted it to my ear I heard J.C.'s cheerful voice booming, "Rise and shine, kids!" With a mumbled OK, I hung up and climbed out of bed. Grabbing a long summer dress, I slipped it over my head and clumsily tried to button the bodice as my long hair got tangled in the intricate lace of the fabric. "To hell with it," I muttered, leaving my dress half unbuttoned as I walked into the bathroom to wash my face. When I came back into the bedroom I was pleasantly surprised to see that Lindsey was awake. After only four hours of sleep, it was a sure sign that he was excited about the show that afternoon. He gave me a quick, glancing kiss, grabbed his robe, and headed into the bathroom. As I heard the shower turn on I climbed back onto the bed, picked up the phone, and ordered our breakfast.

Room service arrived quickly and as I transferred our plates of scrambled eggs and hash browns onto the dining-room table, I thought idly about what outfit to wear to that day's huge show. Just as I reached for a glass of orange juice, Lindsey came walking out of the bathroom, a billow of steam escaping from the open door.

My welcoming smile froze on my lips when I saw his face. He had the same vacant stare that I'd become familiar with during his flashes. His lips were moving but there was no sound, just horrible silence.

"Lindsey! Baby! I'm here, baby, I'm here!" I cried as I rushed to his side. Taking him gently by the arm, I eased him over to the couch and lowered him onto it.

Before I could speak again, before I could touch him, he fell to the floor and started to convulse. He kicked and thrashed, his eyes beseeching me for help, and I didn't know what to do. I threw myself onto the floor next to him and tried to hold his shaking body still, but he seemed as strong as ten men and I was thrown backward, hitting my head on the edge of the coffee table.

Pure animal fear swept through me as I realized that whatever was happening to Lindsey was not going to stop. It was getting worse and I didn't know what to do to help him. *He's dying*, I thought hysterically. And I started to pray. *Dear God, help me . . . help Lindsey . . . help Lindsey . . .*

Out of the red veil of fear that threatened to send me into shock, a voice of reason echoed in my head, speaking to me as if I was a child. *Get help, Carol. Get Richard. Get up off the floor. Go to the door and start screaming for Richard. Richard will know what to do.* Hanging on to the words I was hearing in my head, I struggled to my feet and ran to the door, throwing it open with a force that sent it crashing against the wall.

"*Richard! Help us, Richard! Richard, help! Lindsey's dying! Richard, help me!*"

Down the endless corridor I saw a lone security guard staring at me as though he were seeing an apparition. In a heartbeat he started running toward me, and my screams continued as I watched him coming closer.

"*He's dying!* Please help us . . . *Lindsey's dying . . .*"

Breathing hard, the security man rushed past me into the room and knelt by Lindsey's still convulsing body. I looked in horror at Lindsey's face.

It was turning shades of gray-blue and his lips were colorless. "Get me a spoon!" the guard shouted over his shoulder. "We've got to keep him from swallowing his tongue!"

I grabbed a teaspoon from the table and handed it to him as I knelt down beside him and Lindsey. "Hold his head," he continued, "I have to get this into his mouth." I watched as he slipped the silver spoon between Lindsey's bloodless lips, and my hands shook as I tried to keep Lindsey's head still, but his convulsions were so violent that I couldn't hold on.

The phone started to ring and with a desperate look at Lindsey, I jumped up and grabbed the receiver. It was Greg Thomason with our second wake-up call.

"Are you guys up—?" Greg began as I cut him off and started screaming into the phone.

"Greg! Get help—Lindsey's sick—he's bad. Get J.C. down here now!" With a shocked gasp, Greg mumbled "OK" and I hung up and immediately called the front desk. *Answer the damn phone!* I thought desperately as I listened to the rings going on and on, waiting for someone, anyone, to pick up.

After what seemed an eternity I heard a voice say "Front desk," and I yelled shrilly into the receiver, "Get an ambulance for room 7322! Lindsey Buckingham needs paramedics and an ambulance. Now!"

After a short silence the horrified desk clerk answered, "Yes, ma'am, right away, ma'am!" I threw down the receiver and rushed back to Lindsey.

My feeling of helplessness seemed to have left me. I no longer felt hysterical. I felt a great sense of calm and purpose, my mind locking away the terror and fear for Lindsey and replacing it with a resolve so strong that I felt completely focused as I returned to his side.

Whatever it takes, Lindsey is going to get through this. I will get him through this. I will get him through this, I kept saying over and over in my head as I knelt by Lindsey.

"Carol, what's happening? What's wrong with Lindsey?"

I looked up to see Richard standing shirtless in the doorway, staring in horror at Lindsey twisting and turning on the floor. "My God! Lindsey! Carol, I heard your voice. I thought I was dreaming, but when I woke up I could still hear you screaming! What's happening to him, Carol? What's wrong with him?"

Not willing to leave Lindsey's side again, I reached my hand out to Richard as he crossed the room and, grabbing it, he sank down on the floor next to me.

"I don't know what's wrong. He's had flashes and I thought it was just another one and then he fell, and he started shaking and I can't make it stop, Richard. He won't stop—and I think he might die and I need help, I need help for him . . ."

In the background I could hear the security guard on the phone talking, making sure that paramedics were on their way to our room. And then the room filled with people. J.C., Mick, Greg, Dwayne, and Christine rushed to our side, staring in stunned silence at Lindsey's convulsions. Behind them three paramedics rushed in, ordering everyone out of their way so that they could get to their patient.

Everyone moved back except for me. I didn't want to leave him. I couldn't leave him. In my head I could hear Lindsey's voice pleading with me, "Carol, don't leave me. Stay with me. Don't leave me alone."

I just could not—and would not—move away from his tortured body lying on the floor. I kept stroking his forehead, willing his eyes to open in his contorted face as I murmured over and over to him, "It's OK, Lindsey, I'm here. It's OK."

Then I felt two hands reaching under my arms, pulling me to my feet. As I struggled against them J.C. spoke urgently into my ear. "You have to let them help him, Carol. You have to give them room. Come on now, come on."

Blinking back tears, I nodded and numbly stepped back and leaned against him as I watched the paramedics working over Lindsey's still con- vulsing body. One of them filled a syringe and shot it into Lindsey's arm. Lindsey slowly stopped moving and lay there, still as death. Talking urgent- ly to each other, the paramedics began to hook up monitors and tubes and I couldn't bear to watch.

I let J.C. guide me into the bathroom and leaned over the sink as he turned the faucet on. "You have some blood on the back of your head. Give me a washcloth, I'll wash it for you, sweetie. Doesn't look too bad. Button the front of your dress—we have enough excitement going on . . . put some cold water on your face, honey, and tell me what hap- pened," he said as he dabbed the back of my head with the washcloth.

He then tenderly held my hair back from my face for me as I splashed the freezing water over my burning skin. Turning to face him, I haltingly told him everything, starting with the minute Lindsey came out of the shower and finishing with the attacks that he had gone through over the summer.

J.C. listened without speaking and then told me to stay in the bathroom—which I didn't—and walked out into the living room. Following on his heels, I rushed over to Lindsey's silent form still lying on the carpet and looked up at the paramedics. "What happened to him? Is he going to be OK? Are you taking him to the hospital now?"

"Ma'am, we've been told that a doctor has been called. We want to take him to the hospital—it's just across the street—but Mr. Fleetwood says to wait for the doctor, so that's what we're doing."

I stood up slowly, looking at the faces of Mick, Christine, and J.C. They all looked away from me guiltily and I knew in a heartbeat what was going on. "You're thinking about the show today! You don't want to cancel the show! My God! Lindsey almost died! Are you insane? Mick, Chris, you saw how bad he was—is—he has to go to a hospital right now!" I stared in disbelief at everyone in the room and I suddenly felt very, very cold.

Stunned, my mind raced. *They don't care about Lindsey! They don't care about what just happened! All they care about is saving the damn concert! How can that be? How can they not care about Lindsey—about what they've just seen with their own eyes?*

Looking at Richard for help, I started to plead. "Richard. Tell them he has to go to the hospital—you saw how horrible it was! Richard, tell them!" Richard looked about to speak but then shook his head and stared at the floor. His face was almost as white as Lindsey's and I knew that he, too, couldn't believe that the band and the powers that be were putting the show first over Lindsey's ghastly attack.

Taking a deep breath, I whirled to face Mick and J.C. "We have to take him to the hospital. There's no way he can play today. He almost died! His face was *blue*, J.C.! He couldn't breathe and if the security guard hadn't gotten here in time, I can't even think about what could have happened. You don't know. . . you weren't here . . . I almost lost him and I'm not going to let you hurt him." I could hear the hysterical tone to my voice but I couldn't help it.

I felt like I was in a nightmare as I looked desperately at Mick. Why was this happening? What was wrong with them? How could they not care? I thought they loved Lindsey.

Without meeting my eyes, Mick told me that it was best to wait for the doctor. Talking to me like I was a child, he said that the show was huge and it was too late to cancel it. And anyway, maybe Lindsey would be "fine" when he woke up. He wanted to ask *Lindsey* if he thought he could play the show after his "little attack."

"A 'little attack,' Mick? Have you lost your mind? He was in convulsions for almost ten minutes! He turned blue from not breathing! I won't let you do this, I won't . . . Lindsey won't let you. You'll see. He can't play, and that's that!" I shouted, and Mick hastily stepped back from me.

Behind him the crowd parted as the hotel physician rushed into the room. Taking one look at Lindsey, he barked orders at the paramedics to carry him into the bedroom. He then brusquely asked me to tell him exactly what happened. He listened, nodded once, and then walked into the bedroom, closing the door behind him.

Richard crossed the room and put his arm around my waist, guiding me to the couch. "Sit here with me, Carol. I need you to sit with me, OK? Lindsey's with the doctor—he's safe for now. You need to sit down, honey."

Sitting together holding hands, we waited for the doctor to come out of the bedroom. I looked out into the hallway and saw J.C. huddled with Mick and Christine. I could see that John McVie had now joined the crew and I knew that they were desperately trying to figure out how to do the concert. Feeling disconnected from them, I leaned my head back and said in a low voice, "Richard, we almost lost him."

Richard nodded and we both sat in silence, tears running down both our faces, waiting for the doctor to come out of the bedroom.

Finally the door opened. With a stethoscope hanging around his neck and his sleeves rolled up, the doctor looked fatherly and trustworthy. As I jumped up from the couch and ran to him I trusted that his face would, God willing, give me the reassurances that I so desperately needed to hear.

"How is he? Will he be OK? Can I see him? Are you taking him to the hospital?" I asked in a rush of words.

"He's awake. He's seems to be recovering well. I believe that Mr. Buckingham has endured a grand mal seizure and he's going to be weak and sore for a few days. We need to run a lot of tests to find out what caused it. I don't want to speculate before I have more facts," the doctor answered in a kind voice. "He definitely has to be checked into the hospital, but Mr. Buckingham mentioned a big concert that he's supposed to perform in today. He doesn't want to check in until after the show. Maybe you can talk to him. I really don't feel it's wise to wait, but it's up to Mr. Buckingham. I can't force him—his life isn't in immediate danger—but I won't be responsible for what happens if he doesn't go."

J.C., Mick, and the rest of the band family had gathered quietly in the background as the doctor spoke to me. I could hear a sigh of relief coming from Mick when the doctor said that Lindsey wanted to play the show. A flash fire of anger went through me, but I kept my eyes on the doctor's face and tried not to think about the unseemly lack of empathy and *love* for Lindsey that I felt his "family" had displayed during the past hour.

"I'll talk to him, doctor. I'm going in to see him and then I'll let you know what his decision is," I replied with a disdainful glance over my shoulder at the band members.

The bedroom was thrown into shadows by the closed drapes keeping out the late summer sun. Lindsey's face was pale against the dark rose color of the sheets and I winced inwardly at the bruises already starting to show on his thin arms as they lay on top of the bedcovers; bruises that he'd gotten as he'd convulsed on the dirty carpet of the living room. His eyes brightened as I sat down on the edge of the bed and reached out to stroke his cheek. Pulling me to him, he held me tightly with hands cold as ice. We lay there together for a moment without speaking. "I'm so sorry you had to go through that, Carol," he whispered into my ear and it was all I could do to keep from breaking into sobs. My mind reeled at his words. I'd just watched the man I loved almost die in a grand mal seizure and he was worried about *me*!

Willing my voice to remain steady, I said softly, "Lindsey, please . . . I'm fine . . . God, don't even think about *me*. How are you feeling, baby? The doctor says—"

Lindsey pushed me away from him a little and looked into my face. He said he felt a bit weak and dizzy but otherwise fine. He thought he'd just passed out from a very bad flash. After the show he'd go to the hospital for tests, but with a dry laugh he added that he was sure they wouldn't find anything wrong with him. The other doctors didn't in L.A., so what was different this time?

I sat in shock as I listened to him speak. *He doesn't remember. He doesn't know what just happened to him! Oh my God, the doctor didn't tell him!* As I looked into his eyes I realized that the doctor didn't want to be the one to tell him. Staring down into Lindsey's wan face, it was obvious how fragile he was—and I knew that if I told him the truth about what he'd just gone through he'd be as terrified and shocked as I was.

But my God! He needs to go to the hospital! If I don't tell him, he won't know that he has to go. Yet how can I tell him the truth when I know it's going to shatter him? He's so sick—but he wants to play the biggest show of the tour. Am I ready to take that away from him?

My thoughts were jangled, confused, and anguished as I tried to decide what to do. If I told him he'd go straight to the hospital—no questions asked. If I didn't, then he'd play the show and at least have those few hours of happiness. I wanted him to have that after what he'd just been through and before he went through the hell of hospital tests. But did I dare?

I needed to talk to the doctor and J.C.—and I needed to do it fast. "Lindsey, honey, will you be all right for a few minutes? I have to go talk to the doctor for a second. I'll be right back, OK?"

"Sure. I want to rest for a little bit. Take your time," he answered quietly as I leaned over and kissed him.

Opening the door, I saw Mick and J.C. jump up from the couch and almost fly across the room to where I was standing. With my arms firmly crossed in front of me I told them that Lindsey had no recollection of what had just happened and that I hadn't decided if I was going to tell him. "I have to make absolutely sure that he won't be harming himself by playing this afternoon, J.C. Where's the doctor? I need to talk to him."

J.C. pointed to the hallway and I walked out to find the doctor. J.C. followed, talking quickly and reassuringly to me as I tried to ignore him. He told me that they would arrange for a nurse and ambulance to be backstage at the show, and then he pleaded with me not to tell Lindsey the details about what he'd just gone through.

After a brief conference with the doctor and a promise to take Lindsey straight to the hospital after the concert, it was settled. He'd play the show. Filled with a sense of dread about what *could* happen that afternoon, I returned to the bedroom and helped him get dressed. He was pale, of course, and a little off balance—but he swore he could make it through the show without having another flash. If he didn't, I'd never forgive myself—or the band. But it was a risk that everyone else seemed willing to take, so with fingers crossed—and fear in my heart—we left for the show.

Feeling as though I'd never smile again—much less laugh—I followed Lindsey across the hotel lobby in a daze. Suddenly a hand pulled insistently on my arm and I looked up to see Stevie Nicks.

"Carol, I heard about what happened this morning and I know just how you must be feeling!" she said in her low, husky voice.

"You do?"

"Of course I do! My poodle Jenny—I just love her to pieces—got shut inside the sunroom of my house in Phoenix and she almost *died*! It was horrible! The room was so hot that she collapsed and by the time I found her she was lying in a little heap, gasping for breath. It scared me to death, you know. I cried and cried. Anyway, I just wanted to tell you that." With a squeeze of her hand to bolster me against the horror of her personal tragedy, she swept away regally and walked out into sunshine.

What? She's comparing what happened to Lindsey to a near-death experience of her poodle? Standing frozen in my tracks, I tried to make sense out of what she'd just told me.

And I started to laugh, giggling hysterically, as I followed her outside to the limos. I felt like banging my head on top of the car to try to get back to planet Earth. *Jesus! Has the whole friggin' world gone crazy?*

Lindsey looked at me as though I'd lost my mind. "What's so funny?" He asked with a puzzled look on his face, unable, I'm sure, to understand how I could be laughing after that morning's events.

"Oh Lindsey, oh Lord, you're not going to believe what just happened!" I gasped, trying to stop giggling long enough to get the words out. His eyes widened in disbelief as I told him the exact words of Stevie's "comforting" story.

Now laughing as hard as I was, he spluttered, "That woman's wacko, I swear. Even for her, that's pretty out there! But seriously, Carol, did she make you feel better?" As I nodded we both broke into fresh peals of laughter and it felt wonderful. "Hey, Carol, you should have asked Stevie if she was sure it was the heat in her sunroom or if maybe 'little Jenny' had just OD'd on blow." And we started to laugh all over again. Stevie's poodle Jenny was infamous for its love of cocaine. Stevie had told many a story backstage of her poodle's fondness for the taste of blow. She said that she couldn't leave a packet on any of her tables at home—if she did, the dog would eat it, paper and all—and then run around in little energetic circles.

After the horrific morning we'd had, we both owed Stevie a solid "thank-you" for inadvertently making *both* of us feel better. Even if we were laughing *at* her this time, all that mattered was that she did, indeed, lighten our spirits. *Who knows, I mused, maybe Stevie's so brilliant that she knew it'd take a bizarre out-of-left-field story to cut through my shock.* I smiled as I replayed our encounter in my head.

As soon as we arrived at the venue Lindsey and I headed straight for our motor home so that he could rest for the twenty minutes left before the show. The weather was glorious and our camp of seven large trailers was teeming with people and activity.

We hadn't done that many outdoor shows, but I absolutely loved them. There seemed to be more of a sense of theater at an outdoor venue—sitting in movie star motor homes, breathing fresh air that carries the scent of marijuana and cigarettes mixed with grass and flowers. It made me think of newsreels that I'd seen of Jimi Hendrix at Woodstock. That afternoon's show was, in my eyes, almost on the same level. There was an ocean of seventy thousand people in front of the stage, extending back until they were mere dots on the horizon. And they were all there to see not a lineup of huge artists, but just one superstar band: Fleetwood Mac.

As J.C. promised, a nurse and an ambulance were backstage. Feeling relieved, I surrendered myself to the inevitable and prayed that Lindsey would make it through the show without another horrible incident. Before going on stage he made me promise to stay backstage and rest. As I looked at him standing there with a guitar strapped around a body that looked as fragile as glass, all I could do was nod. I knew if I tried to speak I'd burst into tears.

Feeling dazed and exhausted, I went into the semi-dark interior of our trailer and lay on the small bed in the back. Closing my eyes, I tried to relax. After thirty minutes I heard a break in the music. A sense of panic swept over me, as I knew that an unexpected break in a song could mean that Lindsey was in trouble. Jumping off the bed, I set out for the arena at a dead run. *Please God, let him be OK . . . please, please, please . . .*

Lindsey was at the back of the stage, head down, leaning against a speaker. The nurse and J.C. were whispering to him and as I watched, he nodded. I knew that he was saying that he wanted to continue the show.

A few minutes later J.C. came down from the stage and put his arm around me. "He just got a little dizzy, Carol. We're taking him straight to the hospital after the show. He's in good hands out here. Don't worry. I won't let anything happen to him. None of us will, Carol."

As I looked into J.C.'s eyes I was struck once again by the unbalanced world in which I now lived. On stage was the royal family of the court of Fleetwood Mac. To the seventy thousand hungry fans who were worshipping them in front of the stage, they were beloved idols who had few, if any, flaws. As I watched the band play I could see the smiles on Christine and John's faces, the winks that Mick was giving to Stevie, and I heard the roar of approval from the audience as the band members interacted in a public display of affection and love for one another. Thinking back to that morning in our room at the hotel, I knew without a doubt that those smiles and winks covered up hearts that could be cold and unfeeling.

Forget the soap opera of the broken love affairs—that was part of the Fleetwood Mac mythology and though painful, it was beneficial to the band. Lindsey's illness wasn't. Fleetwood Mac was first and foremost a business machine. And as I'd seen with my own eyes that morning, God help any of us that got in the way of that machine—even its crown prince, Lindsey Buckingham.

Blinking back tears once again, I looked up into J.C.'s face and could only shrug; I had no more words left. All I could do was keep praying that nothing would happen to Lindsey. As I watched him playing I started to shiver as a kaleidoscope of images flashed before my eyes. The stage disappeared and in its place I saw Lindsey convulsing on the floor—his eyes pleading for help . . . blue face . . . white lips . . . and the sound of my own voice screaming and screaming for help.

With a gasp I willed away the images as I struggled to keep myself from fainting. A wave of nausea swept over me. Stumbling along the dirt path, I tried desperately to make it back to our trailer before I vomited. Falling to my knees in front of the small toilet in the trailer, I started to throw up bile. I hadn't eaten anything that day, so all I could do was dry heave over and over again until, finally, the nausea passed.

Suddenly J.C. pulled open the bathroom door and picked me up off the floor. Laying me gently down on the bed, he stroked my face and said, "Carol, rest, honey. Lindsey would be very upset if he could see you like this. You need to stay strong for him. I'll watch over him for you out there, I promise." I nodded meekly and pulled up the cover that he'd thrown over me. As the afternoon shadows lengthened outside, I lay curled up on my side waiting for the show to end and Lindsey to appear. For the first time on the road I couldn't wait for a concert to end.

Finally Lindsey walked into the trailer, ashen-faced, exhausted, and dripping with sweat. Quietly and quickly, he changed his clothes and we walked outside to our limo, where J.C. was already waiting. The drive to the hospital was somber and silent. Lindsey was too sick, I was too drained, and J.C. was too worried about Lindsey and the effect his seizure would have on the tour for any of us to make small talk. Within an hour Lindsey was checked into the best hospital in Philadelphia for four days.

Those days passed by in a blur. The hospital was directly across the street from the hotel and I walked over every morning at eight and stayed by Lindsey's bed until ten each night. He looked defenseless and almost childlike in his blue and white hospital gown. The hours passed by as doctors and nurses came and went, running test after test to try to find the underlying cause of his grand mal seizure and his flashes. I stepped out into the hall while his blood was drawn and waited in an empty room as they took him for MRIs and EEGs.

The band hadn't come to visit him. There were phone calls and flowers from them, but there was no mistaking the air of resentment that surrounded Lindsey's hospitalization. J.C. had canceled two major shows and no one knew yet how many more dates would be lost because of Lindsey's "problem." Fleetwood Mac was not happy. Lindsey pretended not to care that the band was staying away, but I knew that it bothered him. It bothered me too, but I was much more worried about his health than I was about the band's not-so-subtle signs of displeasure.

Lindsey now knew that he'd had a seizure. The specialist who'd taken over his care, Dr. Williams, had told him exactly what had happened to him in our hotel room. He took this brutal news with a nod as dark fear shone from his eyes. We didn't speak of it. We waited for the test results. And, just like before, each test was coming back "normal."

On the third day he was given a spinal tap. It's one of the most brutal tests anyone can have: a large needle is inserted into the spine and fluid is drawn out for testing. It left Lindsey with a bruise the size of a fist on his lower back and a hole in his spine that would take three or four days to close.

On the final day of his stay Lindsey was diagnosed with epilepsy. He'd have to be on medication for the rest of his life. Dilantin—three pills a day, forever. He was ordered to change his entire lifestyle. No drugs, no alcohol, eight hours of sleep a night, and no driving a vehicle for at least a year. If he didn't follow these rules, Dr. Williams told him, then he'd have another seizure. And depending on where he was and who was or wasn't with him when he had it, he might possibly die.

We sat in stunned silence as the doctor gave us the news. Looking at our shocked faces, he went on to explain exactly what epilepsy was. It's not a disease, he explained, but a neurological disorder. The brain cells misfire—and when they do, it causes a blackout, or seizure. His flashes were blackouts. That he'd suffered a grand mal seizure was a worst-case scenario. With medication and vigilant health care, we were told, it was possible that we could keep his epilepsy under control and reduce the risk of his having another one.

"You can leave the hospital today, but you can't travel for at least three more days. You have a hole in your spine and it needs to close before you get onto an airplane. The pressurized cabin of a plane could cause your spine to leak fluid and that would be a very nasty problem."

"But Dr. Williams," I interrupted, "we have to leave for Washington, D.C., tomorrow! The band has already canceled shows and there's a huge party being thrown tomorrow afternoon for Fleetwood Mac by Hamilton Jordan. It's a White House affair and the rest of the band has to attend! The Fleetwood Mac plane is leaving at ten in the morning!"

Lindsey solemnly nodded his head in agreement. "Sir, I've put my band seriously behind schedule as it is. I can't ask them to sacrifice anything else. I have to be on that plane—I'll be careful. It's a big plane. I can lie down and Carol will be there to watch over me. I'll be fine," he finished firmly.

"I think it's an unnecessary risk, but I understand you have commitments. I must warn you, however, it's dangerous. I want you off your feet as much as possible for the next three days. Do what you must, but at the first sign of trouble, you need to go straight to a hospital in Washington. OK?"

"Thanks, Dr. Williams. I'll take care of him. Lindsey and I won't be attending the party, I can assure you," I said as I looked meaningfully at Lindsey. "As soon as we get to our hotel, I'll put him straight to bed. I promise."

The next morning on the plane, Lindsey, looking thin and wan, lay down on a couch under a pile of blankets, his head resting in my lap. Once we were in the air, J.C., Mick, and Christine made a beeline for us.

"Lindsey," Mick began, "the band has talked about what's the best way to handle the publicity on what's happened to you. We think it's in everyone's best interests to keep it private. We're really concerned about what's best for you, mate. I mean, it's no one's business, is it?" Mick asked with a tone of hearty bluster in his voice.

Lindsey just stared at him, his eyes cold and distant—perhaps thinking of the four long days he'd just spent in the hospital. Days where the band's "concern" would have meant a lot more if only one of them had come by to see him. Inexplicably, none of them had.

Mick cleared his throat and gamely continued. "We'll just tell the press that you were seriously ill with the flu and that you're better now. We'll make up the shows we've had to cancel and, well, everyone's just glad that you're going to be OK."

"Mick," Lindsey replied in an icy tone, "I'm not ashamed of having epilepsy. It's a big deal, I know—but I'm not going to hide the fact that I've been diagnosed with it. I'm issuing a press release about it in Washington."

"Why do you want to do that?" Chris asked incredulously. "I'm not saying that you should be ashamed of it, but I'd want to keep it private if it were me. There's no need for the whole world to know our personal business, Lindsey," she finished with a haughty sniff.

"This has nothing to do with you, Christine. It's *my* personal business—not the band's. You don't really have a say in it. I've made my decision and that's that. If you have a problem with it, too bad!"

Looking sullen and embarrassed at the same time, the band's envoy took an abrupt leave of us and stalked back to the front of the plane. Looking in concern at Lindsey's forehead now furrowed with pain, I murmured, "Hey, I'm really proud of you, Lindsey. You're doing the right thing. It's idiotic to hide what happened to you in Philadelphia. I don't understand why they would even consider trying to cover it up!"

"Oh, it's the English contingent's old-school belief that one must never air 'dirty laundry' in public. Well, I don't think my epilepsy is 'dirty laundry.' They're idiots sometimes." Lindsey snarled through clenched teeth. Suddenly, his back arched in a spasm and he gasped in pain. "Jesus, Carol, it hurts. I think maybe something is happening with my back. It hurts really bad."

"J.C.!" I cried out toward the front of the plane. "Can you please come back here?" Grabbing some Kleenex off the side table, I wiped Lindsey's now sweat-soaked face and hair.

Appearing by our side, J.C. took one look at Lindsey's face and turned almost as pale as Lindsey. "Mr. B., are you OK? What's happening? What's wrong?"

"It's my back, J.C., it hurts like hell. How soon before we land?"

"Twenty minutes. Can you handle that?" J.C. asked worriedly. "Do you want me to phone ahead for an ambulance to meet us at the airport?"

"No, I think that I just need to get on the ground. The doctor said the altitude could cause problems for me. I can make it for another twenty minutes."

"The hotel's only fifteen minutes from the airport, Lindsey. We can have you in bed within the hour. I'll help Carol take care of you until we land. Just hold on, mate," J.C. said in a soft voice.

With a nod of his head, Lindsey held my hand tightly as I waited for J.C. to bring me a cold washcloth for his face. I spent the rest of the flight wiping his face—trying not to let him see the fear that I was feeling. In the back of my mind, I heard the doctor's warning words about flying. *Could Lindsey's spine be leaking fluid? Just let me get him to the hotel and into a real bed. Once we're off of the plane, he's going to feel better*, I said to myself firmly, unable to let myself think the unthinkable that the doctor's dire words of horrific side effects from flying too soon after the spinal tap could be coming true.

In the limousine on the way to the hotel, Lindsey's pain seemed to ease and a little color came back into his face. Nonetheless, I cornered J.C. in the hotel lobby. "Look, J.C., I know the big party is this afternoon—but Lindsey's obviously not feeling that great. You have to promise me that you'll leave one of our security guards here and a limo in case we need it. Lindsey didn't want to make a big deal of it with the band, but the doctor in Philadelphia said that Lindsey could have some really bad problems with his spine from being on a plane. I don't want to be here all alone if, God forbid, anything happens to him!"

J.C. listened distractedly as he passed out hotel keys to Stevie and John McVie—rolling his eyes as they impatiently grabbed them from his hand. Patting me on the shoulder, he said cheerfully, "Duly noted, Carol. This is a huge party and everyone wants to go. But after all, we do work for Mr. B. and the band. All you have to do is call my room and someone will be there to help you!"

I should have known better than to believe him. The entire entourage had been looking forward to this event for over a month. Hamilton Jordan, President Carter's chief of staff, was hosting an embassy party in Fleetwood Mac's honor at 3 P.M. sharp. Jordan—young, brilliant, brash, and famous for wearing tennis clothes in the White House—was, along with President Carter's sons, a huge Fleetwood Mac fan. To say that this party for Fleetwood Mac was an *honor* was a major understatement. It was a rock 'n' roll coup of the highest order. No one in the Fleetwood Mac family wanted to miss it—and as I would soon find out in the most brutal way—none of them did.

Putting Lindsey to bed immediately, I watched with relief as he fell into a restless sleep. I was sure he'd feel better when he woke up. *Thank God the flight was so short,* I thought as I kicked off my heels and curled up into an armchair next to him. Turning on the television, I changed the channels listlessly, unable to focus on any one program for more than five minutes.

In less than a week's time, our world had turned upside down. Sitting there as Lindsey tossed and turned in his sleep, the reality of the past days went through my mind like black shadows. For the first time in my young life I had watched the extreme physical suffering and torment of someone I loved. Seeing Lindsey endure his grand mal seizure—watching him convulse and suffer while I stood by helplessly—made me feel completely inadequate. I knew that logically I was not to blame for his seizure—but the intensity of that morning revealed a shocking side to human suffering beyond anything I could have imagined. A suffering that was almost pure in its nakedness. I never wanted to see it again—and I never, ever wanted to feel that *helpless* again.

Since that horrible morning in Philadelphia, I couldn't shake the feeling that I was walking around in a living nightmare. Alone. Lindsey didn't remember anything about his seizure. I was the only one among the Fleetwood Mac family who had witnessed it from the beginning. The others had arrived almost fifteen minutes after it started—and after the first few seconds, they had turned away from what was happening. Rightly or wrongly, I felt that I was the only one who truly knew the terror of it.

But the nightmare was about to continue.

An hour passed.

Lindsey snapped awake, crying out in pain and thrashing about on his pillow. My heart stopped as I looked in shock at his frenzied movements. *No, NO, NO, NO! NOT AGAIN . . . PLEASE GOD, NOT AGAIN!* I thought as I rushed to his side.

"Carol, it hurts, it hurts, it hurts!" Lindsey moaned as I leaned over him. Grabbing my arm, he squeezed it painfully as his back arched off of the bed in a spasm. He cried out again. He was in agony and we needed help. Now.

"I'm here, baby, I'm right here." Reaching for the phone, I knocked it to the floor and had to drop onto my knees to grab the angrily buzzing receiver. Pulling the Fleetwood Mac room list out of my pocket, I dialed J.C.'s room. The rings seemed to mock me as they went on and on and on. *Oh my God, there's no one there!* Cursing J.C. under my breath, I clicked off and immediately dialed the front desk.

Trying to stay calm, I told them that I needed a doctor for Lindsey ASAP. I was stunned to hear the harried voice of the desk clerk telling me that they had no doctor on staff or call. "You'll have to take him to the closest doctor. There's one about four blocks away. I can get the address for you and call ahead. That's all we can do, I'm afraid. Unless, of course, you wish for us to call an ambulance."

"*Yes!* Call an ambulance!" I shouted into the phone.

Beside me on the bed, Lindsey tearfully pleaded, "No, Carol, no ambulance, please. I can't stand going to another hospital. Please, just get me a doctor. I don't want to go. I don't want to move."

Looking at a face that had now taken on the qualities of what Lindsey must have looked like at the age of ten, my heart broke. "Cancel the ambulance. Call the doctor's office. I'll be right down for the address," I told them. My instincts told me to call the paramedics, but Lindsey's pleading, trusting eyes convinced me that I had to find another way to help him. Knowing the horror of the tests that he'd already been subjected to in Philadelphia, I knew that I had to at least try.

With Lindsey uttering painful cries behind me, I desperately picked up the phone one last time to find the Fleetwood Mac security that J.C. promised to leave behind for us. I dialed his room—no answer. Frantically dialing room after room, I realized with a sinking feeling of despair that I was totally alone.

What was I going to do? I couldn't leave him alone, he might have another seizure! But I had to get help for him. I'd have to leave him for a few minutes to go downstairs to find the limo driver. I could be at the doctor's office in five minutes and bring him back with me. I was going to have to risk leaving Lindsey alone. I had no choice.

Trying to keep the terror out of my voice, I leaned over him. "Lindsey, I have to go downstairs for a couple of minutes. Do you think you'll be OK? Do you feel like you're going to have a flash?"

"No." He answered through clenched teeth. "It doesn't feel like that, it's just the pain. My back—my back hurts, Carol—it hurts. It feels like someone is twisting my back hard enough to break it."

"I'll be right back with help, Lindsey. Hold on, OK? Just hold on until I get back . . ." With a quick kiss on his sweat-soaked forehead and a last desperate look at his anguished face, I picked up my purse and ran out of the room.

Not wanting to wait on the elevator, I rushed to the dimly lit stairwell that was next to our room and started running down it. As soon as my feet hit the metal stairs, I realized that in my panic, I'd forgotten to put my shoes on. *To hell with it* . . . I swore as I ran down and down until finally I hit the lobby floor. Racing outside, I looked around expectantly for a black limousine. Nothing. Not one single car from the Fleetwood Mac fleet was parked where it should have been.

I CAN'T BELIEVE THIS! I CAN'T BELIEVE THAT THEY WOULD DO THIS TO US! I'M GOING TO FUCKING KILL J.C. WHEN I SEE HIM—I SWEAR I WILL!

Angry enough to tear just about anyone who got in my way limb from limb, I ran back inside to the front desk and tersely asked for the doctor's address.

Seeing that it was, indeed, over four blocks away I knew that I had to make a decision and I had to do it now. There was no way I could get Lindsey out of bed and into a cab. He couldn't be moved and he wouldn't go to the hospital. Precious minutes were ticking by and I had to act—fast. Throwing my purse over my shoulder, I took off through the lobby at a dead run and sprinted down the street. My bare feet burned on the hot pavement, but I kept going. Ignoring the amazed and curious faces that passed by me in a blur, I ran and ran until my breath was coming in gasps and my face was dripping with sweat in the 85-degree humid air of downtown Washington, D.C.

Seeing the door to the doctor's office, I burst through it like a tornado and almost threw myself across the room. A nurse stood openmouthed, staring as though she couldn't believe her eyes. With my Armani dress, Gucci purse, tangled sweaty hair, and dirty bare feet, I looked like a well-dressed lunatic.

"You've got to help me! I need a doctor to come with me right now! It's my boyfriend—he's in agony at the hotel and . . . Oh, Jesus, I'm scared and I need a doctor!" I screamed at her, ignoring the shocked looks of the seated patients in the waiting room. In my head I started a mental countdown of the time I'd been away from Lindsey.

Ten minutes gone. How is he? What's happening in our room?

A doctor came out of one of the examining rooms, took one look at me, and walked briskly to my side, guiding me gently but firmly back behind the reception desk to his office. The smells of metallic antiseptic cleansers assaulted my senses as I walked down the air-conditioned, white-walled corridor. It was a welcome change from the smoggy, hot air outside. As I looked into the face of the balding, cherub-faced doctor walking beside me, I could feel some of my panic receding, believing that help for Lindsey would soon be on its way.

"Start at the beginning," he told me as he led me to a chair. Sticking his head back out the door he yelled, "Nurse! Bring a glass of water in here for this young lady. She looks as though she could use one."

I poured out my heart to him, quickly telling him about Lindsey's seizure, the spinal tap, and the agony he was in back at the hotel. "Can you come with me right now?" I pleaded tearfully. "I'm so scared. He might go into another seizure. I don't know what to do. He doesn't want me to call an ambulance, and I need help. The band left me alone—I'm all alone—*we're all alone . . . please, please, come to the hotel with me!"*

As the doctor reached for his prescription pad, he shook his head no. "I've got five patients left to see. I can't come with you. I'll give you some muscle relaxants and some pain medication for Mr. Buckingham. And then I'll come to the hotel as soon as I'm done here."

"But you don't understand! You *have* to come! He could be having a seizure! Please, *please come with me!"* I begged.

"Listen, Miss, er . . ."

"Harris," I said softly.

"Miss Harris, you told me that he had a spinal tap in Philadelphia four days ago. That's a *very* nasty test. I believe that he has fluid leaking from his spinal cord. I know you're scared, but you've got to get this medicine for him and then get back to him as quickly as you can. I'll come straight there after I see my patients—shouldn't be more than an hour and a half. The hotel called before you got here. I know that your boyfriend is the guitar player for Fleetwood Mac, and I know that you're going to take good care of him before I get there. I'm a fan of the band myself. We're not going to let anything happen to him."

He kept his voice soothing as he continued. "Now get out of here and go straight to the pharmacy. It's a half a block away on the next corner. I'll see you at your hotel soon. I promise."

I nodded my head numbly, grabbed the prescriptions, and walked quickly out of his office. I felt like screaming and bursting into tears.

But I did neither.

Lindsey needed me and I had to keep it together. I couldn't fall apart. If I did, he'd have no one to help him. For now, I was all he had to get him through this.

I would not, could not, fail him.

Twenty-five minutes gone. Is he as scared as I am?

I started running as soon as I hit the street. I made it to the pharmacy in two minutes flat and paced like a caged animal as I waited under the suspicious eyes of the pharmacist for the pills. Store patrons and clerks alike gave me a wide berth as I glared back and forth from the clock on the wall to the white-jacketed technician behind the counter. I didn't care that I looked like a madwoman with my tangled hair and dirty bare feet. All I cared about was grabbing Lindsey's medicine and getting back to him.

Finally, my name was called and I rushed to the counter to pay for the prescriptions. Clutching the bag in my sweaty hand, I took off at full speed back to the hotel. As the smell of exhaust filled my lungs and the sound of traffic filled my head, sweat ran down my face, seeping into the collar of my now-ruined dress. The muggy heat enveloped me as I concentrated on putting one foot in front of the other. I could see black clouds gathering in the sky and knew that a storm couldn't be far off, bringing welcome relief to a stifling D.C. summer heat wave. The soles of my feet were burning and blistering from the red-hot pavement. I tried to close my mind to the torture of it and I kept running.

Run—run—run—just keep going. You've got to get back to him. You've got to get back . . .

My stride was broken as excruciating pain went through the heel of my foot. Looking down, I saw smears of bright red blood staining the sidewalk. I'd sliced my foot on a shard of glass and I could feel the sharp stabbing edges of it with every step that I took.

Even though I knew that it was insane not to stop and try to get the glass out, I wouldn't do it.

Blaming myself for Lindsey suffering all alone in a hotel room because it had taken me so long to get help for him, it somehow made me feel better that I was bleeding and hurting. It was like a penance that needed to be paid. Hysterical as I was, the blood and pain focused me and I started running even faster.

Fifty minutes gone. I'm sorry, sorry, sorry, baby . . . try to hold on, Lindsey—I'm almost there.

And I was.

As I threw open the huge door of the hotel lobby, relief hit me like a battering ram—staggering me, shattering the false energy I'd used in my hour-long frantic run for help. Used up now—gone. I limped across the lush carpet of the hotel lobby and leaned heavily on the elevator button. I had no choice but to wait for the slow-moving elevators—if I tried to take the stairs, I knew I'd have to crawl. With my feet throbbing in agony and my breath coming in gasps, I stumbled into the elevator car that would take me upstairs to Lindsey.

Using the wall of the hallway as a crutch, I tried to keep my weight off of my slashed foot as I limped toward the door of our room. Blood was streaming from the bottom of my foot, and it seemed as though the last twenty feet back to Lindsey was the longest walk I'd ever taken.

I was terrified of what I might find when I opened the door of our suite.

Had he had another seizure?

Was he unconscious?

Had he been screaming in pain with no one to hear him?

God help me, was he even now lying on the floor, not breathing?

My hand trembled as I pushed the key into the lock and threw open the door. The bedroom was cast in shadows. Through the half-open curtains, the sky had turned an ominous shade of purple and black. Flickers of lightning teased the horizon, followed by the soft rumble of thunder. The summer storm that had been threatening seemed about to break and the air felt thick and heavy with humidity. It seemed to hang like a tangible veil as I made my way across the ominously silent room.

I could make out Lindsey's body lying among the snarled covers of the bed. Afraid to breathe, afraid to look—terrified of what I was about to know—I closed my eyes for a split second, summoning up the courage to look at the deathly still form of the man I loved.

His eyes were closed in a face that was slack and white. I felt my stomach twist into knots as I sank down beside him on the bed.

"Lindsey, baby . . . *Lindsey. Wake up, please, please wake up . . .*"

He moaned as his eyelashes fluttered open, giving me a look that was both dazed and bewildered. His eyes were midnight blue in the semi-darkness of the room, pain lines reaching out from the corners and etched across his forehead. Trying to keep the panic out of my voice, I brushed his sweat-soaked hair out of his face.

"I brought you pills, baby. The doctor is coming—he's on his way. How do you feel?"

Trying to smile with bloodless lips, he whispered hoarsely, "It hurts so fucking much, Carol. I've never hurt like this before. It won't stop. The pain won't stop. Can you help me up? I'm going to be sick."

He held out his hand to me and I grabbed it, struggling to bear his weight as we made our way to the bathroom. Holding his hair back, it took all of my strength to support his body as he threw up violently into the toilet. With his arm over my shoulder, I strained to get him back into bed before he collapsed. As terrified as I still was, I breathed deeply with relief.

Because my prayers had been answered.

He hadn't had a seizure. He wasn't unconscious. It broke my heart to see him in so much pain, but I knew that we'd been very, very lucky—and very blessed. This time. It could have been so much worse. An image of Lindsey on the floor in Philadelphia flickered in my mind and I forcefully pushed it away.

Thank you, thank you, thank you, God.

"You're going to feel better in a minute, Lindsey. I'm just going to leave you for a second to get you a glass of water. You have to take your pills right away. Soon you're going to feel better, I promise." Jumping up from the bed, I ran to the bathroom for water and then dumped the pills into his hand. I held his head as he choked them down and I climbed into bed beside him. Relief and worry waged war inside my dazed mind as I studied his face.

He looked like death. Only twenty-nine, Lindsey looked at least fifteen years older than he had only a week before. His face was so thin and lined that to me it looked as through he'd walked through the fires of hell. And I knew that he had—with me right by his side.

I tried to keep my voice strong and positive as I stroked his hair, telling him of the hour I'd just spent running through the streets of Washington, D.C. Barefoot. He tried to smile as he listened—the image of me running, sweat-soaked in my designer dress with no shoes and snarled wild hair, was so incongruous to us both that in any other circumstance, we would be laughing hysterically at the absurdity of it. Not so much at the fact that I could look like shit, but at the mere thought of me running anywhere. I was an L.A. girl and only walked when I had to. If a car could take me where I wanted to go, even if it were only half a block away, then I took the *car*. Grateful for the smile that I'd been able to bring to his pain-lined face, I sat and watched over him, counting the minutes to the doctor's arrival.

Just as the storm broke, unleashing its fury on the streets below, I heard a soft knock on the door. Ignoring the stabbing pain from the cut on my foot, I leaped up and crossed the room in two seconds flat. Opening the door for the doctor who'd come to help us, I felt a surge of relief so strong that I almost collapsed under the weight of it. As the doctor examined Lindsey, I limped over to an armchair and curled up into the red velvet cushions, my eyes not really seeing what was playing out in front of me.

For now, I was able to turn the heavy responsibility of Lindsey's safety and well-being over to a professional and I was profoundly grateful for it. I passed the time easing the glass out of my wrecked foot and limped to the bathroom to wash and bandage it in a towel. Behind me, the doctor was giving Lindsey a shot of Demerol. I could hear him telling Lindsey that he had to stay in bed for the next twenty-four hours. In a slurred voice, Lindsey assured him that he would and I breathed a sigh of relief. He was OK, for now.

Telling the doctor thanks and to send a bill to the hotel, I let him out of the room and returned to the velvet chair. I watched as heavy rain spattered the window glass, the drops glowing red from the passing cars on the street below us. I sat and gazed at Lindsey, sleeping deeply—finally at peace after ten hours of agonizing pain. And I realized that I felt much, much older than I had a week before and I didn't think I would ever feel safe again.

I knew that this was only the beginning. The doctors had warned us in Philadelphia of the impact Lindsey's epilepsy would have on our lives. And I knew in my heart that their orders for life changes would be a warning soon forgotten by Lindsey once he'd recovered from this episode.

He was the guitar player for one of the biggest bands in the world. There was not a shadow of a doubt that everything that went along with that golden fame in the world of rock 'n' roll would define our existence for as long as the ride lasted. Drugs, alcohol, no sleep . . . endless concerts and endless partying. It was already written on the wall in indelible ink. Moderation and healthy living was, in the world of Fleetwood Mac, a ludicrous concept. No matter how important a concept it was for Lindsey's health, I knew that our life on the road, and in the studio, made it an impossible one to maintain. Even if Lindsey wanted to—which, of course, he didn't—it just wasn't going to happen.

As I watched the lightning flash outside our window, I swore to myself that I would do everything within my power to watch over him. For as that day had proved, I couldn't count on any help from the members of the Fleetwood Mac family—they either couldn't or wouldn't deal with Lindsey's "problem." As I listened to a crack of thunder, I knew that when it came to Lindsey's epilepsy, we were on our own.

I was so, so right. If I had known that night what lay before both of us in the years to come, I would have wept in despair—for there would be many more close calls.

But I had no idea what might lie ahead. All I knew then was that I never again wanted to experience the terror and helplessness that I'd felt since the morning of the band's biggest show of the *Rumours* tour. The images of Lindsey convulsing on a dirty floor—and screaming out in agony as his back arched in excruciating spasms in a downtown hotel in D.C.—were brutal. I didn't know if or how I could shelter him, but I knew that no matter what it took, I would do whatever I could to stop it from happening to him again.

I knew rationally that I had no power over what might happen, but logic had nothing to do with it. Emotionally, I only knew that I had to believe that I had that power. To believe otherwise was unbearable.

As time would prove, it would take every ounce of strength and will I had to try to keep Lindsey safe.

There would be nights when I would rush onto the stage in the middle of a show to give Lindsey extra doses of Dilantin as he tried to head off the sickening feelings of an impending flash.

There would be nights too numerous to count when I would sit up in a dark hotel room, my eyes burning from lack of sleep, head aching from that night's show and the partying that was a Fleetwood Mac ritual.

Keeping watch.

Keeping watch as Lindsey sat up in bed beside me, head on his knees, rocking back and forth, back and forth. Drunk, wired from blow, he would stay that way sometimes for two or three hours until exhaustion would finally make him slump over and fall into a deathlike sleep.

Keeping watch with the doctor's warning of what could happen if he drank and did drugs ringing in my head. For Lindsey ignored his warnings and mine.

Keeping watch as the images of Philadelphia and a desperate run through the streets of Washington, D.C., ran like a horror movie through my own exhausted mind. My heart in my throat, these hellish images of Lindsey's vulnerability (and mine) would play over and over again. And I would sit up a little straighter, watch a little closer, until I was sure that the danger had passed.

STORMS

He never knew of my late-night vigils.

I never, ever told him. To tell him, I felt, would open a door to his own defenselessness that he might not be able to face. It was a burden that I willingly took on.

Because I was hopelessly in love with him.

Because I was a young woman who truly believed—right up until the end—that love could conquer any darkness.

And I was so very, very wrong.

8

DREAMS OF A LIFETIME

Unlike the beginning of the year—when the band agonized in painful doubt over the fate of the soon-to-be-released *Rumours*—1977 ended with Fleetwood Mac on the fast track to becoming one of the biggest bands in the entire world.

We had stopped holding our collective breath now. We were, instead, enjoying the ride—for it looked as though *this* ride was going to last for a long, long time.

Rumours was still selling like it was the only album on the market after remaining at number one on the *Billboard* chart for an unrivalled six months. The album was breaking all records in the music industry. The momentum was growing with each passing day.

A two-word ad on *Billboard*'s back cover in the fall of 1977 said it all. "SIX MILLION," it read. And under those two words that were anything but simple was a picture of the album cover. Just that—nothing else needed to be said. The ad was the talk of the industry—so explosive and elegant that it got its own rave reviews from newspapers all across America. As if this salute to the album's sales figure wasn't sweet enough, one million of those sales had been in L.A. alone. To any artist, that meant a hell of a lot. To the five members of Fleetwood Mac, it was an astonishing affirmation of their talent.

It seemed like the whole world was feeling the same intense emotions that I'd felt at Producer's Workshop on that rainy afternoon barely eleven months before. On hearing *Rumours* for the first time in Studio B, I was blown away—and now it was clear that everyone else was too. *Rumours* was a phenomenon: one of those rare albums that seemed to touch everyone who heard it.

And despite the short setback from Lindsey's epilepsy that forced cancellations of important shows, the tour had been selling out in every single city. In the U.S., Australia, Canada, Europe, and Japan, a Fleetwood Mac concert was the hottest ticket in town.

Fleetwood Mac was now world-famous—rock stars, each and every one of them—idolized and loved by millions of fans.

And within the inner circle of Fleetwood Mac, we were all growing used to it.

Used to the fame.

Used to the cocaine.

Used to the money pouring in.

Used to the adulation that comes from being at the center of a new universe seemingly spinning around us—and only us.

In L.A., we were building personal kingdoms: each band member had a castle over which to reign, with all that money could buy within its walls. Everything seemed ours for the taking. And take we did . . . relishing each and every fucking minute of it.

But if 1977 seemed like a fantasy, then 1978 was about to blow our slightly jaded minds. And so the New Year began . . .

Lindsey bought a new silver BMW 733 to park in the driveway of our new home, our Gothic mansion on June Street in Hancock Park. For me, we chose a metallic-green Beemer 528i to replace my beloved Volkswagen Beetle, which was no longer seemly for a rock star's girlfriend to drive. The rest of the band members and their variations of live-in lovers were also spending money like there was no tomorrow. Mick was adding cars to his fleet at an astounding rate. Christine and John were shopping for new homes. And Stevie was renting yet another, bigger mansion, filling its closets with furs and designer dresses—and lots and lots of platform boots.

Most of this frenzied shopping took place in December during the start of a long break in the tour. Because of the many months on the road, no one had had time to spend and enjoy the money that was now rapidly filling the band's bank accounts. During one trip to Lindsey's business managers' office to pick up documents for him, I glimpsed three separate checks lying haphazardly across the desk of his accountant. Ranging from $600,000 to $900,000, they were his writer's royalties for just the past few months.

Barely five years before, Lindsey and Stevie were hocking guitars and bouncing checks for $7—the combined price of their "fine dining" meals at

Bob's Big Boy hamburger restaurants. Stevie's salary as a waitress was not quite making ends meet as Lindsey sat at home in their tiny apartment, working on new songs for Buckingham Nicks. But their years of hard work and sacrifice were now paying off. Big time.

Even though each of us relished our new cars, clothes, and mansions, none of us could truly enjoy our new bounty. We were all too freaked about what was looming ahead in January and February. Despite all of the record sales, despite the sold-out concerts, the last big test of the band's success and musical achievement would be two music awards shows: the American Music Awards and the Grammy Awards.

Both *Rumours* and the band had been nominated for major awards at both shows. It was bizarre, to say the least, to realize that we were now going to be one of the main attractions at two of the biggest events in the music industry calendar. The entire Fleetwood Mac family was anxious and excited. Lindsey was so nervous that he was pacing the floor like an expectant father in a maternity ward.

The day before the American Music Awards, I went shopping for a new outfit, choosing a sexy black velvet suit with a tight, knee-length skirt, similar to the one I'd worn at the band's first concert for the *Rumours* tour. Too nervous to shop, Lindsey decided to wear an outfit straight out of his closet: his signature blue jeans, designer shirt, and cowboy boots. Mick, John, Christine, and Stevie would, of course, be dressed to the nines.

Because the show was filmed a few hours before it was actually shown across the country, we had to leave at 3 P.M. for the 4:30 taping. As the limousine pulled up in front of our house, I handed Lindsey the three Dilantin pills that he needed to take each and every day to control his epilepsy, pills that he reluctantly took from me and then laid down on the side table by our couch. I sighed as I picked them up and held them out to him once again, answering his glare with a serene smile and a glass of water.

As I had surmised on that rainy night in D.C., it was primarily up to me to try to keep watch over the man I loved. Because he had no memory of his grand mal seizure—and therefore didn't truly understand what the big deal was—we went through a daily ritual of badgering and cajoling before he'd take his medication. Feeling back to normal, he didn't see the point. He hated the way the pills made him feel, he said—although through the haze of his daily joints, I found it hard to believe that the "downer" effect of the Dilantin could be *that* shocking for him. It was one ritual that he hated, however, and even though he was distracted by the excitement of the awards show, he still bitched for ten minutes (instead of the regular twenty) about having to take his pills.

The irony of this, as that night's events unfolded, was enough to make a grown man cry. Our first red carpet event at the American Music Awards would not be the evening of "rock 'n' roll cool" all of us had dreamed of. Rather, it would rapidly deteriorate into a real-life precursor to the film *This Is Spinal Tap*.

Embarrassing as this night would prove to be, the Fleetwood Mac family would, true to form, try to distance themselves from the public spectacle by pretending that what was happening in front of their eyes was a hallucination brought on by their own intoxication. And, par for the course, they would be only too happy to leave the damage control to me.

As we climbed into the back seat of our limo, Richard Dashut greeted us. He was hitching a ride in Fleetwood Mac style. With a joint burning and a flask of Jack Daniel's cradled in his lap, he was already wasted. Lindsey smirked as he took in Richard's crooked tie, wild red eyes, and wrinkled white ruffled shirt. Grabbing the joint from his hand, he took a long drag and told him he looked like the Marquis de Sade.

Too stoned to answer, Richard giggled insanely and offered the flask to Lindsey—which, of course, he took instantly. I shook my head and sighed. He had already consumed quite a few beers at home. *Not a good idea*, I thought, as I watched him down it, then follow it with a chaser of a new joint. The smoke was already so thick inside the back of the limousine that I could barely breathe. But the sight of the two of them giggling hysterically over nothing in particular was worth the unwanted contact high that I was sure to get. Waving the majority of the fumes away from my face, I once again wished that just *once* we could go out somewhere without being surrounded by a cloud of marijuana smoke.

But it was a part of Lindsey's everyday life and I'd grown used to it. I'd also grown used to trying to spend most of my time downwind of the potent fumes of the California Gold that he loved. Even though it was hard to do, I was becoming quite adept at it. I had to be. I'd learned the hard way that Lindsey's weed was so powerful that it had me walking in circles and bumping into furniture for hours—and it wasn't a pretty sight.

Before we knew it, we'd arrived at the show and it was everything I'd thought it would be. Hundreds of fans were grouped behind barricades watching as the limousines pulled up, hoping they would unload someone they recognized. As we stepped out of *our* long, black limo, flashbulbs blinded us as the paparazzi got busy with their cameras. Cheers from the crowds behind the barricades went up with a roar as Lindsey turned to wave to one and all, a huge, inebriated grin on his face. I clung to his arm, intimidated a bit and incredibly awed that we were walking down an actual red carpet! It was the stuff of dreams and for a little while at least, I would get to enjoy the star experience of being Lindsey's lady at our first awards show.

The band was waiting for us inside, seated in a place of honor: the second row of the auditorium. Aisle seats, of course—all the better from which to jump up and dash to the stage when their name was called for the two awards for which they'd been nominated: Best Band of the Year and Best Album of the Year.

Steering Lindsey toward the empty seats beside Christine, I focused on not falling as we both clumsily climbed over the rest of the already seated band members. We collapsed into our seats just as the lights dimmed and I let out a sigh of relief, grateful to have my butt in a chair—instead of sprawled across the laps of Fleetwood Mac.

Two minutes later, Lindsey reached back toward Richard, who was sitting in the row behind us, and grabbed the flask of Jack Daniel's. Out of the corner of my eye I could see that he was washing down a suspiciously large white pill. Looking to my left, I saw Stevie's purse lying open, revealing a bottle of pills on top of her myriad makeup items.

Stevie's penchant for pills to help her sleep, diet, relax, or get zonked was a well-kept secret within the band. With a mental shrug I assumed that Lindsey was taking one of her pain pills or tranquilizers, for which he had a fondness. In the excitement of being at the AMAs it didn't even cross my mind to ask him what kind of pill he was taking, or where he'd gotten it.

Suddenly music surged out of the orchestra pit. Grabbing Lindsey's hand, I felt his fingers tighten on mine. We looked at each other and I could see excitement and fear gleaming from eyes that were—thanks to the Jack Daniel's—more than a little crossed. As I reached over to give him a quick kiss, Dick Clark of *American Bandstand* fame walked across the stage and greeted the audience, and the show started.

The band members and their significant others paid little attention to the "lesser awards"—meaning, to us, Awards for Which Fleetwood Mac Was Not Nominated—as they were presented. Choosing instead to whisper, giggle, and squirm in our seats as we waited for the big awards to be announced, we didn't even stop to think about how rude we must have looked to those watching at home. Because, hey, it was *our* night and the Fleetwood Mac family was growing used to insulating ourselves from the opinions of others. As the band's fame had grown over the past months, we'd been establishing our own world, and anything that didn't fit or that we didn't like had absolutely *no* place in it.

The evening slowly progressed and huge television cameras swung our way repeatedly as they panned the front rows of celebrities. Vials of cocaine were dumped on the backs of wrists whenever the lights darkened, and a lot of sniffing was heard up and down our row—as it was in surrounding rows, cocaine being the drug of choice for large events. It seemed to be a requisite accessory for not only musicians but record company executives. At social functions a vial of illicit white powder was as likely to be found in a guest's pocket as a pack of cigarettes.

Next to me, Lindsey was starting to slur his words a bit as he whispered sarcastic remarks to me about any and everything. He was hysterically funny, but I was a little bit concerned about how wasted he appeared to be. I gave another mental shrug as I told myself that there was little I could do about it. I assured myself that he was just nervous. Once they'd won or—God forbid—lost, he'd be fine. After all, I'd seen him "party" after the concerts and he was, shall we say, a "pro" at it. Or so I thought.

Finally it was time for the award for Best Band of the Year. Fleetwood Mac's main competition was, of course, the Eagles. With the release of *Hotel California*, the Eagles had been in a dead heat with the band all year. The album had actually managed to knock *Rumours* out of *Billboard*'s number-one slot for one short week when first released, but much to our glee, *Rumours* was back on top within seven days. The Fleetwood Mac family was on friendly terms with the members of the Eagles, who, along with Boz Scaggs, had toured off and on with the band during the tour for the 1974 album *Fleetwood Mac*. And all of them were still remembered fondly by the members of the family. Stevie thought of some of the Eagles with a little more than fondness, having struck up a close friendship with Don Henley that was a constant topic of delicious speculation among us all. But business was business and a professional rivalry remained hot between them and "the Mac."

Glancing over at Lindsey, I saw that he was staring at the stage with a glazed look in his eyes as the announcer read out the list of nominees. As he held fast to my arm, his face was pale and a nerve twitched in his cheek. Placing my hand over his, I tried to psychically communicate calm to him as the entire row of the court of Fleetwood Mac held its breath.

"And the winner is: *Fleetwood Mac!*"

A huge smile broke across Lindsey's face as I screamed, Stevie gasped, and Mick and John pumped their fists in the air in a classic show of victory. Christine's raucous laugh almost drowned out the roar of approval from the music industry figures sitting behind us. Leaping to their feet, the band members hugged each other and headed for the aisle and the stage.

As the five of them climbed the steps to the podium I noticed with alarm that Lindsey seemed more than a little unsteady on his feet. Since he was holding on to Stevie and Christine, I put it down to the three of them throwing each other off balance and watched with tears in my eyes as they accepted their awards. They radiated joy as they gave their somewhat garbled acceptance speeches and then triumphantly left the stage to cheers and thunderous applause. That was one award down and one to go.

Ten minutes later all five returned to their seats, absolutely glowing (and perhaps gloating) from their win. Lindsey slid down into the red velvet seat next to me, reached over and took my face into his hands, and gave me a kiss that seemed to last forever.

"I love you, Carol. I just want you to know that. I really, really love you. You're my angel, aren't you?" he slurred after he let me up for air.

"I love you too, baby. Congratulations, Lindsey! I just *knew* you were going to win!" I answered happily as I leaned back from him. Suddenly I got a good look at his hair. It was completely flattened on top! His normal halo of curls looked exactly like the trademark locks of Bozo the Clown!

"Um, honey? What happened to your hair?" I whispered as I reached over to fluff the top of his curls back into place. *Sheesh, I hope no one got a picture of him looking like that,* I thought. *He'd absolutely die if he could see himself!* I gamely tried to keep a straight face as I waited for an answer.

With a fond smile Lindsey informed me that he'd been wearing a hat backstage—and by the way, he really, really, loved me.

STORMS

What the . . . is he totally stoned? I've never heard him gush like this in public, I thought, *except that time we both took quaaludes at Mick's house. Oh my God, please no! No he didn't—no one in his right mind would take a quaalude before the AMAs!* My mind reeled in horror as I looked into his completely stoned eyes.

Jesus, Joseph, and Mary! What has he taken? Is it just the booze and weed? I mentally slapped myself on the forehead as I remembered the suspiciously large pill that he'd washed down with Richard's flask of Jack Daniel's seconds before the show started. *I doubt that was a friggin' vitamin! Quaalude, tranquilizer, or vitamin, he's wasted—no doubt about it,* I said to myself miserably. As I snuck another look at his glazed expression, I knew that he'd downed, God help us all, a quaalude.

For those readers not initiated in the powers of a quaalude, a prescription drug of the 1960s and '70s, the pill's effect was literally mind altering. Manufactured as a pain pill, it was the side effects that made it beloved by all those who partook of illegal drugs. Quaaludes were the original "love drugs." Their effect was euphoric, mellow, and, best (or worst) of all, the poor hapless soul who was stoned on a quaalude *loved* everyone and everything in sight. It was a great drug for sex (trust me on this), and a great drug for wallowing in complete hippie-like abandon.

Quaaludes were so popular that their abuse was a national epidemic in the U.S. Even though most of the people we knew bought them illegally, anyone could get a prescription from a friendly doctor. It was a sad day for a lot of rock 'n' rollers (as well as middle America) when the alarmed U.S. government took them off of the market to stop their insane use.

Unfortunately, this was not soon enough to save Lindsey's ass.

As I looked at his lopsided grin, crossed eyes, and boneless posture, I knew that Fleetwood Mac's code of cool was in imminent danger of being blown right out of the water. Their lead singer and guitar player was completely whacked out of his mind. Knowing that it was far too late to do anything but deal with the situation, I propped his drooping head up against the back of his seat and kept a bright smile on my face while I mentally thought of ways to kill the fool who slipped him a pill.

Was it Richard? No, Richard wouldn't dare. He's too familiar with quaaludes to give one to Lindsey tonight, so who . . . ? An image of Greg Thomason wearing a goofy grin as he grabbed Lindsey in a bear hug while whispering into his ear flashed before my eyes. And I knew it was him. *He probably gave it to Lindsey right before we sat down! What an idiot!*

Busy with keeping Lindsey upright in his chair, I was startled to hear the announcement for the nominee list for Best Album of the Year. As the album names were rattled off, I anxiously watched Lindsey, hoping and praying that he'd miraculously sober up. At that point I was ready to spit over my left shoulder and turn in a circle three times to ward off the evil eye—using childhood voodoo as a backup was, I've always said, better than fuckin' nothing. Closing my eyes, I did it mentally, double-crossing my fingers and sneaking another look at Lindsey. As he sat there with a look of benign love and appreciation on his face that would have made a Holy Father proud, I knew that neither my prayers, voodoo, nor crossed fingers had helped and I surrendered myself to fate. Because Lindsey was still completely, totally wasted.

Once again *Rumours* was in a dead heat with *Hotel California* and the tension was so thick in our row that even Lindsey's benevolent priestly radiance failed to cut through it.

"And the winner is: Fleetwood Mac's *Rumours!*"

"*Oh my God! You won, Lindsey—you won!*" I screamed as I leaned over to hug his limp body. A look of tenderness was on his face, as though (of course) all he was feeling was *love*. All around us chaos erupted as Mick, John, Christine, and Stevie leaped to their feet. Laughing and crying, they started heading for the aisle as I desperately pulled at Lindsey's sleeve to try to get him on his feet. None of the other band members paid any attention to the fact that their guitarist seemed to be on another planet. Out of the five, he was the only one who was still seated, staring straight ahead like a Buddha on drugs. Which, I guess, was pretty close to the truth at that moment.

Suddenly he leaped up like someone had lit a firecracker under his butt and took off after the rest of his fellow band members. Already a full minute in front of Lindsey, they were all gathered on the left side of the stage behind the podium, posing and smiling for the cameras as they waited for him to climb the flight of about fifteen stairs to join them.

And then it happened. Lindsey began to ascend the stairs. His legs looked like they were made of rubber as he started to climb: first one stair, then the next. With each step his legs were getting shakier and looser as though the bones were dissolving in front of everyone's eyes. A stunned silence fell over the auditorium as every living soul watched Lindsey's progress in morbid fascination—for it was apparent to us all that the newly crowned guitarist of the American Music Awards' Best Band of the Year was running a 90 percent chance of tumbling backward and landing on his ass in front of millions of TV viewers.

Too stunned to move, I started praying again. Praying that someone—*anyone*—from the band would go to his rescue. And, once again, my prayers went unanswered.

Stevie and Christine, faces hanging slack in shock, stood in dead silence as they watched in horror his stumbling, bandy-legged ascent. Lindsey continued to climb, legs quivering . . . face beaded in sweat . . . looking like a character from a B-movie who'd been shot and was dragging out his last moments on earth as he mounted the steps to the pearly gates.

As if this spectacle weren't bad enough, Lindsey was not headed toward the podium on stage left. Instead, his superhuman effort was leading him to the *opposite* side of the stage. He was so cross-eyed, perhaps, that his line of destination was completely on the wrong side of the platform. Rising from my seat, I was on the verge of bolting to his rescue when, miraculously, he made it to the top of the stairs. Swaying and grinning like the Cheshire cat from *Alice in Wonderland*, he made a little bow toward his captive audience and waved hello.

Throughout this nightmarish exhibition I tried to keep a smile on my face. Frozen as it might be, at least it masked the sick feeling of dread that was coursing through me like electricity. At least I hoped it did. Just as I felt as though I might scream at the band, "For God's sake, go help him!" Mick and John raced across the stage and grabbed Lindsey by the arms, guiding him none too gently to the podium.

I went limp with relief from being paralyzed with terror over what was happening. Leaning my head back against my chair, I closed my eyes and counted the minutes until the band's return from backstage. *Thank you, God . . . Thank you, God . . . Thank you, God, for not letting Lindsey fall flat on his face,* I repeated like a mantra in my head.

As I heard the rustle of bodies moving back into the seats in my row I opened my eyes and prepared to help Lindsey sit down. That he'd need my help, I had little doubt. But, instead of Lindsey stumbling toward me, a huge, swarthy man who looked like an aging porn star in a tuxedo loomed over me.

"Um, ma'am? You need to come with me. Mr. Buckingham needs you backstage. ASAP!" he said in a low, gravelly voice.

"He does? Is he OK?" I asked timidly as I stood up to follow him. *Now what?* I wondered as I followed him through a door by the side of the stage. *Surely the worst is over. I mean, Lindsey made it up the stairs without falling! All I have to do is get him back to his seat and he'll be fine,* I assured myself.

"Oh, shit!" I cried out as I followed my escort into a large office. Directly in my line of vision was Lindsey—with his head between his knees—sitting on a couch. At the sound of my voice he raised his head and looked at me helplessly. For a split second time froze as I took in the bizarre scene that greeted me. In the opulent office of one of the music business's most beloved television and radio icons sat the man I loved . . . with a huge puddle of vomit between his legs on the expensive carpet under his puke-spattered cowboy boots. And not more than ten feet away was the icon himself: Dick Clark.

Looking on with distaste and disdain, he looked like he wanted to kill Lindsey. Actually, a more apt description would be that he was staring at Lindsey as though he were something nasty that he just scraped off the bottom of his shoe. And as I looked at Lindsey's white face, his slack mouth, and the pool of puke like a disgusting biohazard on the carpet, I had to admit that Clark might—at that moment—have a point.

My eyes quickly took in the glad-handing shots of the presenter on the wall with about a zillion rock 'n' roll legends, smiling his famous toothy smile as he posed boyishly next to each of them, decade after decade after decade, looking exactly the same age in each and every shot. It was totally creepy, actually. Without a hair out of place or one wrinkle in his shirt in any of the pictures, Dick Clark, I knew in a heartbeat, had never, ever thrown up in anyone's office. And now, here was the newly crowned legend of the AMAs vomiting all over his foot-deep carpet.

I didn't know whether to laugh or cry. With an inner groan I walked quickly across the room to Lindsey's reeking body and sat down next to him. As he leaned his head against my shoulder with the pleading, soulful eyes of a hound dog that'd just had an "accident" in his master's house, I knew that somehow, someway, I had to get him out of that office and home. Fast.

STORMS

As I put my arm around Lindsey's shoulders I looked over at Clark sitting behind his gleaming wood desk and felt a flash of anger begin to burn inside of me as I saw the coldness in his eyes. *Fuck him! How can he sit there and not even offer to help me? I don't care if Lindsey's ruined his stupid carpet—this can't be the first time he's seen a musician wasted!*

Fired up by my anger and worry over Lindsey, who was now sagging against me moaning, I spoke sharply to the TV celebrity. "Mr. Clark? Do you think I could have some help here? Or do you expect me to carry him out to our limo by myself?" *Asshole,* I added silently.

In one smooth movement he picked up the phone on his desk and barked a command into the receiver. In seconds the swarthy escort in the ill-fitting tux materialized and walked briskly across the room to where we were sitting. Without a word he heaved Lindsey to his feet and half-walked, half-carried him out of the room. Before the door closed behind us I turned and said, "It's been a pleasure, Mr. Clark." Getting an icy glare in response, I tossed my hair and smiled virtuously before I slammed the door.

Clark's security man got Lindsey to the waiting limo and wrestled him into the car. The driver took one look at Lindsey in his vomit-stained clothes and peeled out of the parking lot, undoubtedly counting the minutes until he could rid himself of our smelly, sick presence. Almost immediately Lindsey began to throw up again all over the back of the car. Projectile vomiting. Vile and disgusting as the smell was, I gritted my teeth and held on to him for dear life. He was as limp as a rag doll and it was a struggle to keep him in the seat as our driver turned the corners at breakneck speed.

Apologizing, I asked the driver to please put up the separation window that sealed us from his shocked eyes as he looked in the rearview mirror. I couldn't bear the thought of one more person witnessing Lindsey in that condition. *At least he didn't spew on stage,* I said to myself. *Thank you, Lord, for that!*

When we arrived at our home on June Street, the driver kindly helped me get Lindsey upstairs to the bathroom in the master bedroom. Thanking him profusely, I pressed into his hand a pile of money from Lindsey's wallet, knowing that he'd earned every damn penny of it. After I heard the front door close I started stripping Lindsey's clothes off as he leaned against the bathtub, then I pushed and pulled him into the shower with me. Fully dressed, I held him up under the warm water and stayed there with him until the smell of vomit no longer hovered around both of us. Throwing a robe over my own soaked clothes, I wrapped Lindsey in towels and pointed him toward the bedroom.

The shower seemed to revive him a little and he was able to stumble to bed under his own power. As I pulled the covers over him I could hear the beginning of the American Music Awards telecast from the television in the next bedroom. *Oh hell, I left the stupid TV on before we left! Please, please, Lindsey, don't say you want to watch it!* I thought. I held my breath as I furiously plumped up the pillows surrounding Lindsey, hoping to drown out the music from the next room.

No go, though. As soon as Lindsey heard the music, he groaned and grabbed my hand. "You have to go watch it for me, Carol. I just want to make sure that I didn't do anything stupid on camera. I can't remember much, but Jesus, I didn't do anything stupid, did I, baby?" he slurred in a desperate tone.

My mind raced. *Here we go—I gotta lie to him. What am I supposed to do? Tell him that by the end of the night he's going to be the star of about a billion jokes about the dangers of mixing alcohol and drugs? After tonight he's going to be the damned poster boy for the DEA!*

"Oh, no, Lindsey . . . you were fine. Really. I'm sure that no one will even notice that you got a little bit too wasted tonight. Don't worry, hon, I'll watch it to make sure. But I don't want you to worry now. Just go to sleep, OK? It's going to be all right, you'll see!" I tried to keep my game face on as I lied to him. I couldn't bear to tell him of his rubber-leg walk up the stairs to the wrong side of the stage in front of the music industry's elite—and soon the entire country. Obviously he'd had a complete blackout of his less than stellar performance at the show. *Well, it wasn't his finest hour, that's for sure. But he'll start puking again if I tell him what he did. He's been punished enough for one night by his stupidity in getting so wasted.* Shaking my head, I peeled off my soaked ensemble and robe and threw on jeans and a T-shirt.

With Lindsey sleeping in the next room, I curled up in our new Laura Ashley bedside chair and started to watch the AMA show by myself, trying to mentally prepare myself for what I was about to witness. As Fleetwood

Mac's awards were announced, I watched with morbid fascination as Lindsey's disastrous moment on film was about to unfold.

And there was no sign of it. The Best Album of the Year was announced, the camera showed the other four band members running up the stairs, scarves and hair flowing behind them, and then Lindsey miraculously appearing as if beamed down from a space ship to stand by their side. Kind of *Star Trek*-y, but I didn't care. It was a good edit and I was so relieved that I burst out laughing.

Oh my God. I can't believe they didn't show it! And then again, once the initial rush of relief was over, I smiled as I pictured the scene that must have happened in the few hours between the actual event and the telecast. I could only assume that the top Warner Bros. executives were burning up the phone lines to Dick Clark and the AMA brass to protect their biggest money-making asset of the moment: Fleetwood Mac.

Shit! That was a close one! Shaking my head, I got up and went into our bedroom and looked at Lindsey sleeping so deeply that it appeared he might be in a coma—or dead. Resisting the urge to hold a mirror up under his nose to make sure that he was still breathing, I stripped off my clothes. *All's well that end's well,* I thought sleepily as I slipped into bed next to him.

Waking up at noon, Lindsey and I climbed out of bed and stumbled down to the breakfast room for toast and coffee. He was nursing a major hangover and I felt like I'd been run over by a truck—after one of the most anxiety-ridden nights of my life. I made my way to the front door and grabbed the *L.A. Times* off the front steps. Sitting on the couch, I opened it to the "Calendar" section, wondering idly if there would be anything in it about the AMAs. I wasn't disappointed. Finding the page, I let out a string of expletives that would have made Christine proud.

Up in the right-hand side was a big picture of Fleetwood Mac taken the night before at the show. Stevie, Christine, John, and Mick were all smiling happily, holding their little gleaming awards—a fairly normal pose for a winning rock band at the AMAs. And then there was Lindsey. Wearing a gigantic Mexican sombrero on his head, he was grinning like an inmate from an insane asylum while snapping his fingers like a calypso dancer in front of the camera lens. *That explains the Bozo the Clown hair,* I thought miserably as I sat frozen, staring at one of the stupidest pictures ever taken of him.

Lindsey snatched the paper away from me, took one look, groaned, and said simply, "I'm going back to bed, Carol. Don't tell me anything about last night. I don't want to know. Jesus!"

With a sigh I watched him go. I knew that sooner or later he'd have to hear every horrible detail—but not from me. I couldn't even bear to think of it, much less talk about it. The horror of last night's debacle was still too fresh—I could still smell the scent of vomit wafting down from the upstairs bedroom. Or was it still in my hair? With a shudder, I followed Lindsey upstairs to purify myself in the shower.

He's going to hear all about it from the band, I thought as I climbed the stairs. He was going to hear every last, miserable, embarrassing detail—over and over again. It would be an opportunity too delicious for their malicious humor to pass up. I had no doubt that every member of the Fleetwood Mac family would make him pay in spades for quite a while for his off-camera performance. And it wouldn't be pretty for him. Not pretty at all.

As I washed the smell of vomit from my hair under the shower, I thought of the Grammys looming ahead in a little over a month. *I'll keep watch over him like a hawk there! There's no way I'll let a repeat of last night happen at the Grammys, for God's sake! I have to call Bjorn—I want to look really amazing at the show. I think I deserve to go all out after the shit I went through last night at the AMAs! I know that Bjorn watched the show, and since the band won he's probably already plotting my fashion debut. Wait until I tell him about what happened off camera!*

Bjorn was my new best friend. In fact, my relationship with Bjorn was my one and only new friendship outside the world of Fleetwood Mac and I prized it highly. In December he'd spotted me at Bullock's department store and introduced himself. With a face like Michelangelo's David and a body to match, he was gorgeous. Everything about him was physically perfect. He was six foot one, slender and well muscled, and had short, black hair and blue eyes that were always, always, enhanced by perfectly applied black eyeliner.

Bjorn was one of the top makeup artists in the U.S. Famous for his *Vogue* covers and his roster of celebrity clients such as Jaclyn Smith and Suzanne Somers, he'd taken me under his wing and was launching me into a new career: modeling. It was something I could do that would fit within my schedule of traveling with Lindsey on the road. I could work when I wanted—if I had what it took, that is. With Bjorn as my mentor and makeup artist, I'd already done four shoots for my portfolio. And the pictures were great.

I'd been shooting with one of leading fashion photographers in the industry: Charles Bush, father of now-famous Sophie Bush. Arriving in the studio, I was always nervous, awkward, and shy. But after Bjorn's two-hour magical makeup sessions, a person emerged in the mirror who was almost like a stranger. It was me—but then again it wasn't. Gone was the gawky schoolgirl, replaced by a pretty, waiflike, sophisticated young woman. Just like the girls in the fashion magazines that I'd grown up admiring. After slipping into one of the couture dresses that Bjorn always selected, I would feel a confidence unlike any I'd ever known. It wasn't just the confidence that physical beauty could bestow (I *never* felt beautiful), but the confidence of being, for the first time in my life, the center of a little universe that existed inside the creative world of a photography studio. That universe belonged, for those few hours, just to me.

Photography by Charles Bush, Bushstudios.com

Carol Ann.

This probably meant more to me than it would to other young women. When I was growing up in Tulsa with my six sisters, I'd always felt very insecure. I was insecure about my looks—I'd been very, very thin my entire life, and I despaired of ever being able to even look pretty, much less desirable. I was insecure about my clothes—my family didn't have a lot of money and I wasn't able to shop for most of my school clothes. I sewed my own dresses and I'd spend hours trying to make them look store-bought. And I was insecure about my ability to achieve as much as my older sisters, who all seemed to be absolutely brilliant in school. My sisters Tommie and Margaret both made the dean's list at Tulsa University and had put themselves through college. One of my other sisters, Sue, was literally a genius. She never got less than an A in any of her classes her entire life and had been offered full scholarships to several universities. She'd chosen OU in Oklahoma City for her bachelor's degree, and later, after moving to L.A., she would get her master's degree at Pepperdine University and her Ph.D. in psychology at USC. With sisters like these, my Bs and Cs just didn't cause a lot of excitement in our house.

So I tried to make up for it in other ways. I read every book I could get my hands on—I loved to read and this, at least, came naturally to me. Every year, I would pull down the lone A on my report card in English class—which kind of offset the perpetual C- I'd get in math. In the second grade, I fell in love with rock 'n' roll. I begged for Beatles albums and, later, Doors records, and I'd carry them over to my girlfriends' houses where we'd play them nonstop. In the sixth grade, I took a picture of John Lennon to a hair salon and had my hair cut into the classic "Beatle cut"—which, of course, looked ridiculous—and I spent all of junior high school trying to grow it out.

Carol Ann, second-grade class photo.

I would fall asleep each night with a transistor radio tuned to the one and only underground station in Tulsa. Every night, I would hear Creedence Clearwater Revival, Cream, the Kinks, Led Zeppelin, Ten Years After, and every other amazing band from the 1960s. I wasn't that interested in the band members themselves—with the exception of the Beatles in the sixth grade—I just wanted to hear the music. And by high school graduation, rock 'n' roll had become one of the most important things in my life.

Along with my best friend Lori, I was at every single concert ever given in Tulsa. I saw Jefferson Airplane, Three Dog Night, Gene Pitney, Joe Cocker with the Mad Dogs & Englishmen, and Grand Funk Railroad four times. Tulsa wasn't exactly a highlight stop for any band on tour back then, but if a band came to our hometown, Lori and I were there. My group of friends in high school were the kids who, like myself, grew their hair long, wore ripped-up jeans, and did everything to mimic the hippies that we so longed to be, but weren't because of our young age. And that's what led me to leave Tulsa three days after graduation. Lori and I wanted to be in the one place that seemed to be the mecca for all things rock 'n' roll—Los Angeles.

And now, in my photo shoots with Charles Bush, I'd found the one thing that I never thought I ever would—the chance to feel beautiful and special—and it meant everything to me. Holding those photographs in my hand fulfilled a childhood fantasy that I'd never, ever imagined would be filled—I looked like the girls in the fashion magazines. And after growing up as a middle child in a family of eight women, being the center of attention in the photography studio was a really big deal.

Within a few years Charles Bush would have an exhibition at the Los Angeles County Art Museum of one thousand of his favorite photographs. It was a prestigious honor befitting his status in the world of art and fashion. And hanging right next to pictures of Rene Russo and Cheryl Tiegs, one of the world's first supermodels, was a large photograph of me taken at one of his shoots. The title of the exhibition was *Girls of Our Dreams* and to this day I'm still amazed that I was a small part of it.

Lindsey seemed pleased with my decision to pursue modeling, and even though he called me constantly while I was in the photography studio, he seemed to accept my friendship with Bjorn. The fact that Bjorn was gay was a huge contributing factor to Lindsey's acceptance of him. To me, modeling seemed like the perfect career choice: I could be creative *and* I could have something of my own outside the world of Fleetwood Mac.

From the beginning I decided that no matter how many doors the name "Fleetwood Mac" could open for me, I wanted to try to make it in modeling on my own. Either I would have what it took or I wouldn't, but I knew that if I didn't do it the hard way—that is, without relying on Fleetwood Mac's power and status in the entertainment industry—then it wouldn't mean anything. And if didn't mean anything, then what was the point?

Sure enough, Bjorn had already decided to turn me into a "glamour girl" at the Grammys. We spent two days shopping for the perfect dress and shoes. Bjorn borrowed a silver fox stole from Alice Cooper's ex-girlfriend Cindy, one of his other protégées, and I was all set.

On the morning of the show he arrived three hours before departure time to do my hair and makeup and even applied black eyeliner on Lindsey. It looked amazing on him, making his blue eyes seem a little demonic. That night it proved to be a perfect touch for the wicked behavior that he displayed at the show.

Four hours later, our limousine pulled up in front of the red carpet at the Grammys. Dressed in his rock 'n' roll finery, Lindsey looked amazing as he got ready to step out of the car. His fervent wish to live down the AMAs should be easily accomplished tonight—unless, of course, he got wasted behind my back.

Cameras were already flashing as I put one stiletto heel of my new Charles Jourdan shoes out on to the sidewalk and emerged from the interior of the limo. As Lindsey proudly put his arm around me, I started the long walk with him down the red carpet. I was wearing a long, black lace dress with an underlining that stopped about three inches below my underwear. After that it was completely see-through. Complementing my perfect 1930s-glamour makeup, my hair cascaded over my shoulders in tiny, crimped-looking "angel waves" that were crowned with a small ponytail on the top of my head. Bjorn had wrapped my ponytail in black velvet ribbon that was, I had to admit, a lot like Suzanne Somers's trademark ponytail. Yet this variation looked, I hoped, completely rock 'n' roll on me.

Paparazzi cameras flashed like lightning as we walked down the red carpet, and for the first time in my life I discovered what it must feel like to be a celebrity. Amid shouts for me to turn this way and that, I smiled and waved as Lindsey took an amused step backward so that the photographers could have an unblocked view of me. Breathless with excitement, we finally made it through the doors and left the crowd behind. Lindsey burst out laughing as he wrapped his arms tightly around me.

"Oh my God, Lindsey!" I said. "I can't believe that just happened! Of course, the poor things are in for a shock when they take their pictures back to their editors and realize that I'm not a big deal after all."

"Oh, but you are, angel. You're my lady and the most important woman in my life. The best part of the night is yet to come—you're about to give the entire band a heart attack. Are you ready to go in?" Lindsey whispered into my ear.

With a smile, a nod, and a deep breath, I walked through the heavy doors of the auditorium, clinging to his arm. Everyone stared as we passed by. After all, Lindsey was instantly recognizable as the megastar that he was, and I felt like a fairy-tale princess as we walked down the aisle to our seats. When we reached the front rows, the entire band was staring at us with their mouths open.

John McVie was the first to speak. "Carol, you look like a star . . . Well done, m'dear!"

Mick let out a low wolf whistle, Richard Dashut beamed, and Stevie—well, Stevie was not so thrilled. She stared at me with shock and a dangerous glint in her eyes as she rose to her feet. She had chosen a somewhat 1950s look for her makeup, her hair was loose and very, very curly, and she was wearing one of her short stage jackets and skirts. It was an unusual moment for her and me. At every single Fleetwood Mac show, Stevie was always dressed in her fabulous stage clothes with perfect makeup and hair. I, on the other hand, usually looked nice, but there was no way I could compete with her. What woman could? She was a beautiful rock goddess and I was a mere mortal. She was also the ex-girlfriend of the man I loved and I wanted to, just once, look as glamorous as she. And with Bjorn's help I thought I'd managed it.

"Hi, Stevie. You look really nice," I said softly as I swept by her.

Through gritted teeth she muttered, "Thanks—you, too," and sat down abruptly, coldly staring daggers at Lindsey and me.

Christine leaned over and whispered, "Man, the two of you look amazing . . . but, um, Lindsey, is that eyeliner you're wearing?"

Lindsey smirked and answered, "Oh, no, Christine. Absolutely not."

Because Fleetwood Mac had taken home two of the top honors at the AMAs and had the number-one album in the country, as well as a hugely successful concert tour under its belt, the gigantic television cameras at the Grammys seemed to be constantly panning our row of seats. But I knew that it wasn't only in deference to the band's status. After the AMAs it was a sure bet that they were hoping to catch Lindsey in another social faux pas to liven up the broadcast. The band was on its best behavior, obviously hoping that this time around, no scandalous scenes would have to be edited out before millions of people watched the telecast. And, just as importantly, that no scandalous scenes would be played out before the eyes of the music business's elite.

Almost everyone had kept their drug and alcohol intake to a minimum before the show—after all, there would be plenty of time for that at the celebration parties later that night. But drugs or no drugs, Lindsey would find a way to make a scene. And he would prove within minutes that he didn't give a shit that we were surrounded by the living legends of the music world.

But I, less than six years out of Tulsa, Oklahoma, was not quite as blasé. Sitting in the fifth row, we were seated among the most famous people in the entertainment industry, and I couldn't help but be awed. Bette Midler, Tony Bennett, David Bowie—they were all sitting in sartorial splendor in the seats around us. As I glanced over my shoulder I saw Barbra Streisand settling into her aisle seat two rows behind and not more than ten feet away from us. Her famous nose seemed to accentuate her beauty rather than detract from it and I couldn't help but stare and marvel that I was sitting so friggin' close to her.

I nudged Lindsey with my elbow and he followed my gaze and winked at me as he whispered into my ear, "Pretty cool, huh? This audience makes the AMAs look like a poor man's barbecue. Hey! Check it out! Here comes Kenny Rogers!"

Suddenly Lindsey's sedate whisper rose in volume to a level that must have reverberated throughout the entire area in which we were sitting. "Oh my God! Look at the fuckin' pancake makeup he's wearing! It's gotta be four inches thick! Oh, man! Richard, take a look at Kenny Rogers!"

As Richard followed Lindsey's pointing finger with his eyes, he burst into hysterical laughter, which, of course, only egged Lindsey on. Kenny Rogers, now standing in the aisle before the second-row seats in front of us, turned and glared at Lindsey. It was a glare that reminded me of the one that Dick Clark leveled at him in the puke-filled interior of his office.

Uh-oh. Here we go again . . . shit! I thought miserably. I watched a devilish gleam shining from Lindsey's eyes—a gleam that always heralded a sarcastic tirade of the highest order, for Lindsey was a master of sarcasm. It was a trait that he and I shared, but nevertheless, I really, really didn't want to have my fairy-tale night spoiled by a fistfight between Kenny Rogers and my man. I placed a restraining hand on Lindsey's arm, but it was no use: he was enjoying himself far too much to give a rat's ass about decorum.

"Kenny, hey, Kennnnny! Man, love your makeup! Really, you look great, cowboy!"

Lindsey was standing up now, arms crossed in front of him as he nodded and smiled, waiting for an answer from Rogers. I glared down the aisle as Richard giggled hysterically, Christine let out a loud guffaw, and John sardonically nodded in approval at Lindsey. Every one of them was enjoying Lindsey's impious performance. I, too, was having a hard time keeping a straight face—but I knew that if I didn't, then God only knew what Lindsey might say next. Not even someone like Streisand would be safe if Lindsey got on a roll. And somehow, I was more afraid of tiny Barbra's retaliation than that of Kenny Rogers any day. She was a lady, I'd heard, that *nobody* fucked with.

"Lindsey, for God's sake! Please sit down! Jeez, Lindsey, I'm begging you—*please,* please, please sit down!" I whispered desperately as I stood up and pulled his head close to mine as though I could will him back down into his chair by my desperate grip on his hair. Smiling crookedly at me, he shrugged and allowed himself to be none too gently shoved back into his seat by my now sweaty hands.

"Jesus, Lindsey! Behave yourself!" Trying hard not to laugh, I gave him a schoolmarm's stare of disapproval as he continued to eye the back of Kenny Rogers's head after the country singer had sat down.

"Kenny! Hey, Kenny! Dig the makeup!" Lindsey barked out suddenly, sounding just like a disembodied voice from the heavens. Richard was laughing so hard by now that I worried he might choke. I leaned my head back against my seat and wearily closed my eyes. My plan for a starry night was rapidly going up in smoke as I listened to the sniggers and laughter moving up and down our row of family members.

Suddenly I felt Lindsey's fingertips under my chin, gently holding my face. Opening my eyes, I saw a chastened look on his features as he clearly realized that I was suffering at the thought of saying goodbye to my dream night at the Grammys. "Sorry, baby. I'll behave, I promise. I promise I won't do anything to spoil this night for you, OK? But, hey, you gotta admit that Kenny Rogers must have a pretty damn awesome supply of pancake makeup, huh? Bjorn would die if he could see him! I don't know a lot about makeup, but Jesus, if I ever wear makeup like that, just kill me. Promise? Just shoot me and put me out of my misery."

I burst out laughing as I told him, "Don't worry, baby . . . if you ever walk around with four inches of pancake on your face, you'll already be in hell."

With the crisis averted to the extent that a fistfight hadn't started between Rogers and Lindsey, I settled happily into my chair for the show. And just in the nick of time, too, for the cameras were once again glued to our row of seats, their operators undoubtedly waiting for whatever Lindsey might do next. They seemed to constantly sweep our seats.

When it was time for the Album of the Year award, the band members were actually sitting in their seats like adults. Lindsey was smiling, nervous, and, most of all, alert. Except for the effect of the ten joints that he smoked each and every day, he was stone-cold sober. Clutching my hand tightly, he sat and held his breath as the members of Crosby, Stills, and Nash listed the nominees. *Rumours* was up against *Star Wars*, *Hotel California*, Steely Dan's *Aja*, and Jackson Browne's latest effort. All of them were amazing albums and Lindsey's nails were digging into my palm as Graham Nash stalled and goofed around for agonizing minutes before announcing the winner. Finally he came back to reality from whichever weird planet *he* was on and opened the envelope that would reveal Best Album of the Year.

"And the Grammy goes to: Fleetwood Mac's *Rumours!*"

"Oh my God, oh my God, Lindsey! Congratulations, baby!" I whispered into his ear as he sat frozen beside me. With a huge grin, he kissed me quickly, let go of my hand, and rose from his seat.

Stunned, euphoric, and victorious, the band members, along with Richard Dashut and Ken Caillet, raced up the stairs to the podium and said a few words before the Grammy orchestra cut them off.

In less than an hour's time we were all backstage in a large room reserved for the after-show press conferences that were given by the winners of that year's Grammys. While Lindsey stood in front of a dozen microphones with the rest of Fleetwood Mac, I stood alone in the back of the room, waiting for him

Suddenly, as if from nowhere, at least fifteen photographers surrounded me. Blinding me with the strobe lights from their cameras, they took my picture over and over again as I stood and smiled, enjoying and relishing every second of how it must feel to be a star. It didn't matter to me that I was not a famous person in my own right—I was quite comfortable in my role as "famous by association." But during those moments I felt just like Cinderella, covered by fairy dust as I got to live through ten minutes of focused attention from press photographers from all over the world.

It would remain a moment frozen in time for me, as it would have for most women who had grown up reading fairy tales. For, along with the members of Fleetwood Mac, I was living through a fantasy night when the dreams of a lifetime had come true. And on this one night, every single member of the sixteen-strong Fleetwood Mac family was blissfully euphoric.

But nights like these, when all of us were serenely, completely happy, would be few and far between.

9

IT'S NOT THAT FUNNY IS IT?

After the intense months of touring, nonstop interviews, and awards shows, it was a relief for the whole Fleetwood Mac family to be able to take four months off. For Lindsey and me, however, our much-needed break had taken on a dimension that made the pressure of being on the road pale in comparison.

Like most people, I thought that the awards Fleetwood Mac had received at the AMAs and the Grammys would be all the proof they needed that the band was recognized as a brilliant creative force. Maybe for the other four band members it was. For Lindsey, the awards inspired him, but they also terrified him.

The success of the album and tour was so great that it had become a heavy burden for him to bear. How does a musician top an album that has broken all records in the music industry? An album that had sold millions of copies and was beloved by people all over the world? The pressure of living up to the success of *Rumours* had become a living, breathing presence in our lives, and it consumed every minute of every day.

We sat and talked about it from morning until night. We went shopping at Tower Records, looking for the newest and most experimental bands on the market. Talking Heads and the Sex Pistols were played around the clock over the stereo system in our den. Lindsey was completely blown away by the music of these amazing bands and it triggered a hunger in him: a hunger to grow as a musician and to let his creative talent take him wherever it may lead.

He was also tortured because the world was waiting for another, newer version of *Rumours*. That fact was threatening to tear apart the man I loved, for Lindsey burned with a desire to create something new, something completely different. And his torment broke my heart with every discussion we had about his music.

The same anguished questions appeared again and again in our conversations. What if the new musical direction he craved resulted in music that was total crap? Should he play it safe and stay within the formula of Fleetwood Mac's music or trust his own creative urges and risk everything? And if he created radically different new music, then how would the band react to it? More importantly, how would the fans react to it?

I told him over and over that I believed he was a brilliant musician and a creative force, and that no matter what direction his music took him in, he had to go for it. If he didn't do that, then he'd never achieve his full potential as a musician. But this didn't mean he should follow in the footsteps of bands like Talking Heads and the Sex Pistols. It meant he should try to have them follow in his. And I asked him a question: whose admiration and respect means the most to you, the fans' or your musical peers'? "If you earn the respect of your musical peers with your new sound," I said, "then the fans will love your music as well. It might take them a little while to get used to your new sound, but in the end they'll love it. I believe in you, Lindsey. You have to go for it."

I knew I was only saying out loud what Lindsey himself knew to be true. But I also knew that even though I might be stating the obvious, he needed to talk to someone about his ideas and his fears, and who better than me? I was there, I loved him, and, unlike the band, the only stake I had in whatever decision he made was my need for him to be happy.

After each of these conversations Lindsey slowly but surely lost his doubt and anxiety about his creative abilities and became more and more excited about where they might lead him. And I was just as excited, for while I loved *Rumours*, I believed with all my heart that Lindsey was capable of breaking new ground with his music, and to me that was what it was all about. That was the epitome of achievement for any great artist. Lindsey had already proved how great a musician he was—who knew how much further his talent could take him?

But we both knew that the band was going to freak when Lindsey told them what he was planning to do. They wanted to do another *Rumours*-type record and it went without saying that their reaction to his striking out on his own—outside the winning formula—was not going to be favorable. That problem set off another intense discussion between the two of us, in which Lindsey made his feelings clear.

"I always use my best ideas for Stevie's and Christine's songs, Carol. This time, I want to use all of my creativity on my own songs. I don't have to see any of them for at least a few months. I'll tell the band when I'm ready for them to know what I'm doing. I have a lot of song ideas and I really want the freedom now to run with it, you know? You can be my sounding board, OK? You can tell me if my new stuff sucks."

"It's not going to, Lindsey. If you think you need to be on your *own* to create then that's what you should do. And I agree, you don't need to sit through a band meeting about this right now, do you? It's your music. It's that simple, Lindsey. It's *your music.*"

Within a week, Lindsey was setting up a recording studio in the maid's quarters behind our kitchen. Five days later he'd finished and proudly took me on a tour of his new home studio. Even though there was barely room to sit, much less walk through it, I stood and admired his handiwork from the hallway.

The two small rooms were packed full of equipment and instruments. The first held four professional tape recorders patched into a small mixing board. Microphones, guitars, cables, cymbals, and a child's piano that we'd bought at a toy store were all scattered throughout it. The second room was filled with so many different lead, acoustic, and bass guitars that Lindsey could have started his own retail outlet if he'd wished. In an adjoining small bathroom he'd set up drums in the bathtub and a snare drum and a microphone right in front of the toilet.

I burst into a fit of uncontrollable giggles as I pictured Lindsey sitting on the john playing the drums. "I'm sorry, Lindsey, but talk about *convenient*! Jeez! I mean, if you have to pee, you'll barely have to move a muscle. The minutes you save by not having to run to the bathroom could cut hours off your recording time." I tried to stifle my laughter as he gave me a look that told me he was not amused.

"Hey, the sound in here is fuckin' amazing, Carol. Don't give me any shit."

We both burst into hysterics at his unintended pun, Lindsey almost choking on the smoke from one of his ever-present joints. "Wait until you hear the sound I can get in here—the tiles on the wall and floor create some of the best acoustics I've ever heard," he said proudly. "I'm also going to do some vocals in here. I'll set up a different mike for that when I need to. It's gonna work, believe me."

Of course, he knew exactly what he was doing. In the weeks and months to come, Lindsey would record incredible vocals closeted within the tiny eight-by-ten-foot bathroom. Within hours of giving me the grand tour he was already working on his new songs. I didn't think I'd ever seen him so excited.

Our days fell into a pattern. Lindsey woke up early and raced downstairs to the studio.

And slowly but surely, the songs that would be his contribution to the new album began to emerge. As they did, I became intimately familiar with every step of their creation. Lindsey, being much more *technically* proficient than Stevie Nicks, composed his music in a radically different manner. Unlike Stevie, who composed all of her songs with lyrics and a melody line first, Lindsey created his from the ground up. He explained to me that as far as he was concerned, it was the "basic track" that was one of the most critical elements to a song. The basic track consisted of the rhythm section and drums, and the music created from it formed the song's fundamental structure. From this, a melody emerged that was almost organic in nature because it grew from the emotions expressed in the music of the basic track, emotions drawn from the wellspring of Lindsey's creativity.

The lyrics, Lindsey told me over and over, were almost an afterthought once the musical portion of the song was finished. He hated writing lyrics and felt that he wasn't good at it. I laughed in his face every time he said this, because I, along with millions of fans, had *heard* his lyrics. And I knew without a shadow of a doubt that the lyrics to each of his songs on the earlier *Fleetwood Mac* album and *Rumours* were absolutely friggin' brilliant.

Also, I knew the man I loved. There was no way that he could ever make me believe that his lyrics were "beside the point." The lyrics on "So Afraid," for instance, seemed to come from deep inside his soul; they were words that still upset me each and every time I heard them. When I eventually heard the lyrics to his new set of songs, I would be convinced that Lindsey's musical genius was all encompassing.

As I listened and watched him at work, I was fascinated by the complexity of making a song. Long familiar with the mechanics of recording and mixing music, I was seeing for the first time how that music was created—and it was unlike anything that I'd ever been exposed to. I was witnessing an artist at work, and opportunities like that are few and far between. It was a world that I'd been allowed to enter by invitation only.

For the first time in our relationship, I would not be just an observer or a good listener during Lindsey's creative journey but also an emotional participant as I willingly assumed a role that felt as natural to me as breathing. It was a role that would, from that point on, become a critical part of our relationship. For we discovered that I had the innate ability to be a muse for him. A muse who was not, perhaps, the source of inspiration, but one who cleared a path for inspiration to come to him in whatever forms he needed. And it consumed every minute of every single hour in my life. That my role in Lindsey's creative world would almost destroy me piece by piece during my years with him was, at that time, beyond my comprehension. I would eventually become a tool for Lindsey to use in his music and, as willing as I was to be so, I didn't see the insidious danger of it until it was much too late. And when I did, I would not have the strength to save myself—for when you give everything of yourself to another person, in the end, there's nothing left to give to yourself.

But, as with most things that later have a great impact on your life, it all began simply, as a matter of course. Lindsey and I were incredibly close to each other emotionally, having spent the majority of our time side by side, twenty-four hours a day, since we had met. We were so close that we seemed to be able to read each other's minds. Each night as he came out of his primitive studio, I could tell exactly what kind of song he'd been working on just by the expression in his eyes. Intensely aware of the deep fears that he harbored about this new creative road that he'd chosen to follow, I quickly learned how to use all of my emotional support as a kind of lifeblood that he could pour back into his music.

One of the first songs that he wrote was "That's All for Everyone," which was about loneliness and a man's search for someone or someplace in which to find refuge. It was so emotionally powerful to us both that we almost drowned in every single note. As this song was forming itself in the basic track, Lindsey's demeanor during those weeks was like that of a man holding on for dear life every time he came out of the studio and rejoined me. Sadness hung about him like a dark aura and I sensed that he needed every single bit of reassurance that he was not *alone*—that I was always waiting for him, no matter what. He told me over and over again how much he loved me, as though he were afraid that I'd disappear from his life.

The music was manifesting itself in our lives, and I was as protective, loving, and reassuring as I could possibly be. I didn't leave the house. I put my modeling shoots on hold. Not just because I couldn't bear the thought of him walking out of the studio into empty rooms where no one was waiting for him. But also because I felt that if I wasn't available to him whenever he might need me, the *music* might, in some indefinable way, suffer.

Finally Lindsey wrote the lyrics to "That's All for Everyone," and the song was essentially finished. We both sat on the floor of the studio with tears streaming down our faces as we listened to it again and again. Sitting with hands clasped tightly, leaning against each other, we didn't speak about what we were feeling—we didn't have to. I was sharing Lindsey's pain that was coming through the music and he knew it.

I felt that it was one of the most beautiful songs I'd ever heard, and it ripped my heart into pieces each time I listened to it.

During the recording of the next two songs I assumed an entirely different persona. As soon as he began to record "Not That Funny" and "What Makes You Think You're the One"—both songs tinged with anger and sarcasm—Lindsey's personality went through a radical change: he was sexually aggressive, ordered me around like I was his handmaiden, and strutted around the house like a friggin' king. Instead of being his refuge in an emotional storm, I played the part of the subservient courtier. I *felt* that this was what he needed from me. His behavior was the exact opposite of what it was when he was writing and recording "That's All for Everyone" and it took a great deal of submissive—and repressed—behavior on my part to survive the recording of these new songs. Honestly, sometimes I just wanted to scream at him to *get over himself*! But I didn't. For I knew, once again, that it was all about the music.

Nevertheless, it was with relief that I listened to the final mixes of these two brilliant numbers. I loved them, and I knew that Lindsey had found the "cutting edge" that we talked about during our New Wave listening parties. It had his completely original stamp of genius. It was a cutting edge that didn't sound anything like Fleetwood Mac. In fact, I had a foreboding that when the others heard his new songs, this new cutting edge could very well slice Fleetwood Mac's fragile truce into tiny, bloody shreds. And I knew that when this happened Lindsey was going to need all the moral support that I, so far his only emotional cheerleader, could give him.

But the song closest to my heart was "Save Me a Place." One day, standing on the balcony of our bedroom, I begged Lindsey to take a few days off so that we could spend time together. He answered that he didn't know how to explain it, but that he just couldn't—but "if I saved him a place, he'd come running" after the album was finished. When I heard that song for the first time I was overwhelmed by the love in it, and its harmonies were so beautiful that I once again began to cry.

Two days after the final mix of "Not That Funny," I awoke to the smell of coffee coming from our downstairs kitchen. Throwing on a short dress, I skipped down the stairs, following the heady aroma all the way into our breakfast nook. As I walked into the octagonal room I grabbed the back of an antique chair to keep from stumbling at the shock of what was waiting for me. And then I let out a scream. Lindsey was sitting at the table, trying to pull off an air of complete nonchalance as I stood and gaped at him, my eyes traveling back and forth between the long brown curls of hair lying on the floor at his feet and the short, uneven locks that were sticking out from his head.

"Lindsey! What the hell happened?"

"Uh, I just wanted to try something new. You know. Like we talked about," he answered sheepishly.

I stared at him with my mouth open for thirty seconds and then started to giggle. "Oh my God! I know we talked a lot about finding the 'cutting edge' with your *music*, Lindsey, but I swear to God I don't remember talking about your hair!"

As I collapsed into a chair next to him, trying to stop my giggling so as not to hurt his feelings, I took a close-up look at what he'd done while I was sleeping. Lying on the table in front of me was our pair of old kitchen scissors and a hand mirror. He'd used the dullest pair of scissors in the house to chop off all of his hair, and he now looked like a medieval prisoner about to be taken to the guillotine.

"You don't like it?" he asked in a small voice, his forgotten joint burning in his hand.

"Oh . . . huh . . . yeah, Lindsey, I do! I think maybe we need to even it up a little bit, and then it's going to look great! Really! But, uh, I don't think the mustache and goatee look that hot with your hair short, do you?"

"Really?" Lindsey grabbed the mirror off the table and examined his reflection. "I don't know—it seems like a lot to cut off my mustache and beard. I'm not sure if I want to."

I cringed before I answered slyly, making a point that I knew would surely shock him out of his reluctance to shave his now effeminate-looking facial hair. "Well, you *do* look a lot like Bjorn right now, actually. I mean, not that you resemble him—but it's the same kind of look he has, you know what I mean?" I said matter-of-factly as I looked at Lindsey's face. His cheekbones were much more pronounced with his hair short and with his blue eyes and strong chin he could have easily passed for one of Bjorn's close—in the biblical sense—friends. Despite the bad job he'd done in the actual overall haircut, Lindsey looked *gorgeous*. But I knew that wasn't the look he was going for. Lindsey wanted to look punk, not like a male model—and especially not like one of Bjorn's paramours!

Peering in the mirror again, Lindsey let off a string of curses that left little doubt over his horror of looking like he'd just stepped out of Studio 54 in New York. He glared at me as though it was *my* fault that he looked so "pretty" with his short hair, beard, and mustache. I put my hands on my hips and stared him down. "You could do worse, you know," I told him. "Bjorn's great looking. But it's not exactly rock 'n' roll, is it? And anyway, Bjorn would have a heart attack if he knew you cut your hair off with a pair of scissors that barely cut paper! God! You must have had to almost saw it off!"

With a shrug Lindsey calmly answered, "I couldn't find any other ones. Fuck it. Let's go upstairs. I'm going to shave my face clean and then we'll do the hair again. Will you help me?"

With that we ran upstairs together and an hour later Lindsey's transformation was complete. His hair was, at most, two inches long, sticking out in choppy pieces from his head, and he was now completely clean-shaven. And I fell in love with him all over again. He looked beautiful and, I had to admit, more than a little diabolical. We looked at each other and screamed, "*Yes!*"

His new look signaled a radical new Lindsey Buckingham. It was a physical persona that matched his new music and I, for one, couldn't wait until the band saw him. It might, just might, give them a forewarning of the explosive changes in musical direction that Lindsey was secretly shaping for Fleetwood Mac's next album.

As I was soon to find out, the changes wouldn't just be in the new direction that his *music* had taken. Lindsey's new sound and persona would literally transform the fundamental balance of power on stage and in the recording studio. And it would shatter Fleetwood Mac's uneasy peace.

Lindsey posing with his new look.

A few weeks after Lindsey's transformation I got an urgent call from Bjorn. He wanted me to start doing shoots again. "I know you've been 'standing by your man,' Carol, but we need to do lots more photo shoots for your portfolio. Surely Lindsey can survive without you for a few days or nights a week, can't he? I mean, you haven't left his side for almost two months! Aren't you bored?"

"I don't know, Bjorn. I do miss seeing you and of course I want to get back to work on my portfolio, but I have to make sure that Lindsey doesn't need me here while he's recording."

"What do you mean? He's in his little studio all day long while you sit in that huge house waiting for him to walk out of the maid's quarters at God knows what time every single night. How can you being gone while he's working behind closed doors matter? Doesn't he know your work is important, too? You and I have a lot of plans, remember?"

With a sigh I told him that I'd been doing what I felt I needed to do. But I promised that I'd talk to Lindsey about resuming work on my portfolio. While it was true that I'd been lonely and bored while Lindsey spent hours locked away in his studio, I felt it was a small price to pay for the music that he was creating. His work was going so well that sometimes he didn't come upstairs until midnight, having spent fifteen or sixteen hours recording. And when he did finally come to bed there was a sense of calm about him now that wasn't there in the beginning. I knew that he'd weathered his creative crisis and come out on the other side of it stronger and with a new depth to his writing.

After discussing it with him, Lindsey told me that he didn't mind if I went back to doing my modeling shoots—as long as I worked during the day. Within a week I was back in the photography studio with Bjorn orchestrating every single look that I needed for my model portfolio. And at home, Lindsey continued to work on the songs that would, months later, appear on the new album.

In May, Lindsey left the sanctuary of his studio and joined Richard Dashut and Ken Caillet in Studio D at Village Recorder studios in West L.A. Perhaps not so much needing as wanting a studio that had state-of-the-art sound for the next album, Fleetwood Mac had built one. Designed exactly to the specifications of Lindsey, Richard, and Ken, the new studio was an amazing accomplishment in sound and acoustics, as well as in comfort. In the outer listening room there were beautiful tiny stars on the domed ceiling hovering over a huge mixing console equipped with soundboards that were the best in the world. Cushy couches lined the walls and the coffee table was glass—perfect for laying out lines of blow.

And it was all being paid for out of Fleetwood Mac's pocket. The final tab: $1.4 million. Of course, there was English beer on tap in the outer waiting room, so the band felt that the money had been well spent. There had been talk of the band actually buying the studio in the beginning, but negotiations had stalled and no one seemed that upset about it. Not one of them worried about spending that much money on a studio that the band didn't even own. It was all for the future album, and anyway Fleetwood Mac had plenty of money and, with the last leg of the American *Rumours* tour only two months away, there soon would be plenty more.

Lindsey had yet to play his songs for anyone but me. And he wouldn't. He was going to tell the band what he was doing and what he wanted for their next album when we went back out on the road. He was hoping, I suppose, that the distraction of the tour would help cushion the shock of his announcement. And it would be even more of a shock than I expected.

Lindsey was so happy with how his songs were turning out that he'd decided that he didn't want the band to have any input whatsoever into them. No more collaborating, no more jamming in the studio as each member contributed his or her ideas to Lindsey's songs. He didn't want even one note changed in his masterpieces—and if he had to, he told me, he'd play all the instruments himself during the recording of them at Village Recorder. Afraid that their input might dilute—or even destroy—his new songs or, God forbid, give them even a *hint* of the sound on *Rumours,* he abso-fuckin'-lutely wouldn't risk it.

Despite his confident words, I knew that he was nervous and totally dreading the showdown that was sure to come. But I also knew that, true to his word, he wasn't going to change his mind. No matter how ugly and horrific it might get for him, he'd never bow to pressure from the other members of the band. The new creative road he'd taken was far too important and he'd worked too hard to allow *anything* to jeopardize it.

"Maybe it won't be so bad, Lindsey," I said hopefully. "I mean, if you play your songs for Mick and *then* tell him how you feel about the recording sessions, he'll be so impressed with the music that he won't care!"

Lindsey snarled as he reminded me that I wasn't present for the recording of *Rumours.* It was an ugly scene—and he believed that there was an even uglier scene waiting to happen when the band returned to the studio. I believed him. I only hoped that, if he did what he felt he must, we'd both survive the inevitable hideous fallout from the other four members.

During the *Rumours* recording sessions—as most of the world knew—Stevie and Lindsey, and Christine and John, had ended years-long relationships. Hysterical tears, furious accusations about real and imagined infidelities, and heartbreak over love that had been lost caused gut-wrenching scenes on a daily basis. Fueled by the band's cocaine and alcohol use, it was purgatory for the band at the Sausalito Record Plant in Northern California. Even though the songs that Stevie, Lindsey, and Christine wrote during that painful time were now beloved by millions, to the band members who created them they would forever be reminders of their own personal heartbreak and still-burning resentments.

Almost like the final meal served to a death-row inmate, Lindsey and I decided to throw a barbecue for the Fleetwood Mac family. A party, Lindsey told me with a wicked smirk, was the least we could do for them. After all, in a month's time he was going to tear the band's world apart. From the moment he broke the news about his music to Mick and the others, Lindsey and I were most assuredly running a high risk of landing on top of the band's most-despised list. And by doing so, we could stick any party invitations for the immediate future from *them* up our asses. As we lined the kitchen counters with bottles of daiquiri mix for our barbecue guests, I told Lindsey what I'd just been thinking. "We are," I said with a snigger and bravado that I didn't really feel, "dead men walking."

Every member of the family showed up on our doorstep around 1 P.M. Everyone that is, except the personally invited Stevie Nicks. At first I assumed that Stevie's absence was because of an aversion to making her first appearance at the home that Lindsey and I shared. But I soon found out that *I* wasn't the one that she was avoiding. In fact, when I heard the real reason for Stevie's unsociable behavior I knew that I'd become the least of her worries. She herself was now playing the role of "the other woman" and it was Jenny Fleetwood she was avoiding—not me.

Within an hour of her arrival Jenny asked me to go upstairs with her for a private chat. Seeing her white face and eyes that were brimming with tears, I immediately grabbed her hand and guided her up to my dressing room. As I closed the door Jenny broke down.

"What is it, Jenny? My God, what's wrong? What's happened?" I asked as I hugged her thin body against mine.

"It's Mick," she whispered.

"What about Mick? What did he do, Jenny? Don't be upset, sweetie— talk to me!" I said gently, stroking her hair as I waited for her to compose herself. *Shit*, I thought, *whatever's he's done, it's bad this time. I've never seen Jenny so upset. That bastard. It can't just be another groupie. I've already gone down that road with Jenny, and she survived it. This has to be much worse.*

I thought back with an inner shudder to last fall when the band was still touring, to a morning when the phone rang in our hotel room and I heard Jenny's tearful British voice at the other end of the line. She'd just phoned Mick's room and a woman answered his phone. Even though Mick tried to tell her it wasn't true, Jenny knew that he'd spent the night with a groupie. I consoled her as best I could. After that day she never again mentioned Mick's philandering on the road, so I assumed she'd come to terms with it.

As Jenny delivered her earth-shattering news, my mind reeled. Mick, she told me, was having an affair with Stevie Nicks.

Jesus, Joseph, and Mary! They went for it. I knew it! I knew all last year that Stevie and Mick had their sights set on each other! Oh my God. This is going to be interesting—another friggin' band soap opera is about to unfold. I bit my lip to keep from saying these words out loud.

Mick and Jenny Fleetwood at June Street house barbecue.

In a soft voice Jenny told me that she just didn't care any longer; that she was tired of worrying about whether he was being faithful on the road and now, apparently, off. She didn't feel that it was good for her or her daughters. It wasn't just Stevie that had her upset. She was very concerned about the amount of drugs—mainly cocaine—that now proliferated her home. It was not a healthy environment for their children and she'd made up her mind to leave Mick, take her two little girls, and go home to England. It seemed that she was not even that angry with Stevie. It was Mick's betrayal that had her upset. She wanted to make a fresh start—away from the madness of Fleetwood Mac's world.

"Oh, Jenny, I'm so, so sorry!" I told her. "Sweetie, no matter what is going on between Stevie and Mick, I know he still loves you. Stevie's the last person in the world who would confide in me, so I don't really know what's going on with them. I'm sure she doesn't want to hurt you—but damn, I know it's awful for you. I think you have every right to feel betrayed. Did you talk to Stevie about it?"

With a shrug of her shoulders Jenny answered that she hadn't, nor did she plan to. She just wanted to get away and have a chance to think about what was best for her.

I told her that Lindsey and I loved her and that if there was anything we could do to help we would. Then I asked her if she wanted Lindsey to have a talk with Mick. For the first time since we closed ourselves into my dressing room, Jenny started to laugh. She told me that she knew that Mick was absolutely terrified that Lindsey would go ballistic when he found out that he and Stevie were sleeping together. It seemed a fitting retribution to let Mick just suffer from whatever his vivid imagination created as "punishment" for his most recent transgression with Stevie. To put it bluntly: let him stew in it.

We both giggled as we pictured Stevie and Mick's clandestine hand-wringing over the exposure of their illicit affair. Brushing Jenny's sweat-soaked bangs off her forehead, I softly said, "The irony of it is I really don't think Lindsey's going to give a shit. Except for the damage to you, Jenny. I'm not going to say anything to Lindsey. Let Mick be the one to tell him!"

As I stood holding Jenny my mind reeled with the news that she'd just delivered. *I won't tell Lindsey—no friggin' way,* I said to myself. *The situation is another nightmare in the band's soap opera and I absolutely will not get caught in the middle of it. Lindsey loves me—and whatever and however he feels when Mick and Stevie finally have the guts to tell him about their affair has nothing to do with me. But Jesus, why are these friggin' people so incestuous? It's totally bizarre. Would it kill one of them to actually get involved with someone who's not a Fleetwood Mac family member? Christ!*

Jenny Fleetwood.

When we went back downstairs Mick gave both of us a worried look, knowing, I'm sure, that Jenny had told me what was going on. He looked at me pleadingly and I stared back at him with a blank expression. Because Jenny was right: he deserved to squirm a *lot* for what he'd been doing behind her back and I, for one, had no intention of soothing his nerves. *Let him think that I'm going to tell Lindsey,* I thought as I walked away from Mick. *It's the least I can do for Jenny right now. I love Mick, but jeez, can't he keep it in his pants?*

Lindsey's new look drew lukewarm reactions from the Fleetwood Mac family, but that was not that big of a surprise to either of us. The band members' onstage personas were seen as money in the bank to the Fleetwood Mac band members and the powers that be. And anything that messed with that formula was looked upon with suspicion and uneasiness by everyone concerned.

But despite this, the barbecue was a great success—which, in our world, meant that everyone was incredibly drunk on margaritas, stoned on weed, and, most of all, whacked on blow. As was normal for a band social gathering, the supply of cocaine was enough to keep us all going until we dropped dead from cardiac arrest. None of us were in any shape to handle the shock of suddenly having on our doorstep a party-crasher who was, in every sense of the word, a living legend. A living legend who had, according to band lore, been to hell and back.

Steve Steinberg, Richard Dashut, and Lindsey at the barbecue.

Hearing a timid knock on our front door at 6 P.M., I threw the door open and looked in confusion at the man standing there. He seemed familiar, but I couldn't place him. *Where had I seen this guy before?* I tried to focus on his face—which was a little hard with my dilated eyes—but before I could ask his name, John McVie came rushing up behind me screaming, "Jeremy! You made it, old man . . . you made it!"

What the—? I thought as the sound of feet pounding across our huge living room followed John's reverberated welcome.

"Carol, I'd like you to meet Jeremy Spencer. Jeremy, this is Carol Ann, Lindsey's lady," John said as he guided Jeremy into our foyer, which was

John McVie.

now packed with the entire Fleetwood Mac family. I was stunned to find out that this man, who looked more than a bit unkempt with unwashed, shaggy hair and wrinkled clothes, was *the* Jeremy Spencer of Fleetwood Mac's original heyday in the 1960s and very early '70s. Over the past year Mick and John had told me stories about him—about his amazing talent and how he would wear a gold lamé suit on stage and impersonate Elvis during the band's shows, but most of all, about how he was one of the world's greatest blues guitarists.

Jeremy Spencer, always religious to an obsessive degree, had disappeared hours before a show while on tour with Fleetwood Mac in the U.S. According to band lore, it had happened right here in Los Angeles in 1971. He walked out of the band's hotel room announcing, "Just going out to a bookstore," and never returned. Somewhere on Hollywood Boulevard he climbed into a van belonging to members of a religious group who called themselves the Children of God. After a long, frantic search involving the police and close friends, Jeremy was finally tracked down to a ramshackle house that was the headquarters of the Children of God.

He'd become a full-fledged member of a religious group that some would label a cult. And there he stayed. He refused to come back to either Fleetwood Mac or his wife and children, choosing instead to join a group of religious fanatics and leave all that he had ever known behind.

And now he was standing in my entry hall with a ghost of a smile on his pale face. It was obvious to me that whatever life Jeremy had been living had been a hard one. His face was lined, his hair shot with gray, and there was a bewildered air about him as though he was not quite sure where he was or what he was doing here. Stepping out of the way of the surge of people who had gathered around to greet him, I looked for Lindsey.

He was staring at Jeremy, an excited look on his face similar to the one he'd had when he met Eric Clapton. That excitement would be replaced with a sense of sadness in all of us as we spent the next hour trying to talk to Jeremy. He barely spoke at all, choosing instead to sit at our piano in the living room and play simple melodies as though there were no one else in the room but himself.

It was obvious to everyone that he was extremely uncomfortable being surrounded by people, so we left him alone and let him play the piano in solitude. We checked on him at regular intervals to offer drinks that were refused and quiet conversation that was rebuffed. After an hour and a half he disappeared. But somehow it was enough that he had chosen to pay a call on old friends and new ones, even though he left in his wake a sense of loss for us all.

At the barbecue Julie Ruebens and I spent hours talking about her upcoming marriage to John McVie. They would be wed on June 1 in a small ceremony before their closest friends—the Fleetwood Mac inner circle—and their own family members. After the private wedding vows they would throw open their house in the Hollywood Hills to a reception that promised to be a huge blowout. Julie thought it was quite hilarious that their wedding would take place in the same house that John once shared with Christine. We agreed that it was another sure sign that the band's incestuous way of life was all-inclusive—even when it came to their weddings.

The morning of the nuptials Lindsey and I dressed in our finery and arrived in time to see John and Julie exchange their vows in a moving ceremony that brought tears to my eyes. Julie looked so beautiful, so happy, and John was the typical nervous groom as he stuttered through his marriage vows.

Within half an hour of the ceremony the house was full of people. Ron Wood, guitarist for the Stones, was there with his girlfriend. Bill Graham, the famed concert promoter, was in attendance, along with John Mayall. Derek Taylor, the dashingly handsome Englishman who was a close friend of the Beatles as well as their official press officer (a career that would span thirty years), was making the rounds with a martini glass in his hand. To everyone's surprise, Peter Green and his new wife Jane were also in attendance. One of the original members of Fleetwood Mac, Peter looked cherubic and happy in a long, flowing caftan. He was in preproduction for an album that Mick was supposed to produce and was warm and gracious to everyone who spoke to him—which was just about every living soul at the wedding. He was, after all, a legend who had only recently rejoined the world after a long battle with drugs and alcohol.

The reception was fun and charming, but the real action wasn't in the living room or patio area where the famous guests were making small talk, nor in the bathrooms where lines of blow were being laid out for the wedding guests. The action was in Julie's walk-in closet.

For it was there that Stevie Nicks and Jenny Fleetwood were having themselves one hell of a "clearing-the-air" session—at top volume. At the sound of female voices raised in anger, I rushed to where they seemed to be emanating from and I found the two women behind the partially closed door of Julie's cedar closet. Jenny was screaming, *"How could you?"* as Stevie, looking more than a little embarrassed and defensive, did her best to talk herself out of a corner. And in a corner she surely was. Jenny beckoned me into the closet and I stood by her side as she glared, hands on hips, breathing fire, at Stevie.

Apparently Stevie was trying to deny that she and Mick were having an affair, while Jenny, not listening to one word that was coming out of her mouth, was going on and on about how Stevie should think of Mick's children, Amy and Lucy. I stood paralyzed. I didn't know what to do to stop the rapidly escalating fracas.

Oh my God, why did they have to pick Julie's wedding to have this out? I can't believe this! What should I do? I thought desperately as I looked at the two rigidly angry women squaring off in front of me. *I think I need help with this—they're going to ruin the wedding! Damn! John and Julie's parents are out there—this is so trailer park, I can't believe it! They're going to start pulling each other's hair out any second!*

I turned and bolted out of the closet, the sound of the two furious women following me down the hallway. As I entered the living room I saw that just about every coiffed head was swiveled toward their voices, trying, no doubt, to make out the angry exchanges in what was obviously a cat-fight. Seeing Robin Snyder standing outside on the patio, I ran to where she was standing and whispered in her ear what was happening inside. With a look of shock on her face, she grabbed me by the hand and we both raced back to the closet. Robin swooped in, grabbed Stevie, and spoke urgently into her ear. Whatever it was she said, it did the trick. With a haughty toss of her hair and a last glare at Jenny, Stevie regally swept out of the small room and slammed the door behind her.

Jenny and I looked at each other and I wrapped my arm around her. We could hear the murmur of voices outside the room, so we hurriedly touched up Jenny's tear-smeared makeup and walked outside together as if nothing had happened. Jenny told me that she was caught off guard seeing Stevie dressed in a long, white dress at Julie's wedding. It was, she said, the straw that broke the camel's back. We agreed that the dress was a faux pas of the highest order.

Lindsey and I had been shocked when we saw Stevie in her dress, too. Lindsey remarked that only Stevie would try to upstage a bride on her wedding day. The white dress was beautiful but it was, after all, Julie's wedding day—not Stevie's. Julie seemed unaware of the catfight in her closet and I didn't tell her about it. I was still committed to trying to stay out of the whole ugly three-way scene between Mick, Jenny, and Stevie.

I knew I wouldn't even share this delicious piece of gossip with Lindsey, because that would, of course, let the cat out of the bag in a huge way. And in the world of Fleetwood Mac, strange cats in bags had a bad habit of clawing mercilessly until they cut you to ribbons.

I found it incredibly exhausting to be living through a full-blown, sordid Fleetwood Mac love scene and I couldn't wait to leave the wedding reception and go back home, where at least the soap operas were on television instead of in the next room—or in this case, the closet.

Three weeks before we were due to go on the road, Bjorn had scheduled almost back-to-back shoots to finish my portfolio. Lindsey was not pleased. He didn't like me working this much, he told me. He didn't like it that I was shooting with photographers with names like François and Antonio—men who were every bit as good-looking as their somewhat smarmy names suggested. Even though Bjorn "chaperoned" me at each and every shoot, Lindsey's displeasure seemed to increase every time I left for a session. He became distant and sullen, and while it hurt me, I did my best to placate him by calling home as much as possible when I was between shots. *It's just a passing phase,* I told myself. *He just isn't used to me working, but once he is, then everything will be fine.*

The night of my last and final shoot I was so nervous I almost felt like vomiting. This was the shoot for my first real professional booking. I'd been chosen as the model for the print ad for Bobby Caldwell's new hit single "What You Won't Do for Love." It was the first song released from his new album and was getting heavy airplay and making its way to the top of *Billboard*'s singles chart. The physical appearance of the record itself was amazing. A heart-shaped pressing made of red vinyl, it was destined to be sought after by record collectors everywhere.

Bjorn, Andy, and I were doing the shoot in the living room of our June Street house. Bjorn and Andy had insisted upon it because they didn't want me to be distracted by Lindsey's concerns about who-what-when-where-why. Even though Lindsey was working at Village Recorder that night with Richard and Ken, he'd seemed happy that morning when he learned that I would be working "safe" at home tonight. And, unlike my other shoots, he hadn't called once to check on me.

We'd been shooting for almost three hours when the front door flew open and Lindsey came into the entry hall carrying his guitar case. He stopped dead center and stared at us without speaking, ignoring everyone's shouts of hello. Instead of offering a welcoming smile or even acknowledging that he was being spoken to, he glared at us and took the stairs two at a time, seeming to fly up to the master bedroom. The sound of the door slamming behind him made all of us jump as it reverberated through the ceiling of the living room.

Feeling my face flush with embarrassment, I quickly told Bjorn and Andy that he'd probably had a bad night in the studio and I was just going to run upstairs and make sure that he was OK. Bjorn handed me a fistful of Polaroids to take with me. "Show him these, Carol. He's going to be so proud of you when he sees them. They're absolutely stunning. Oh, and you might want to mention that this is going to be a full-page ad in *Billboard* and *Record World*."

"*What?* You're kidding, Bjorn! I'm doing a full-page ad? *Why didn't you tell me?* I thought this would be a little picture in the corner of a back page. Are you serious? Oh my God!"

"That's why we didn't tell you. Andy and I didn't want that kind of pressure on you while you were posing, but hey, the shoot's going great—and, well, just tell Lindsey, OK? This is a big deal for you—and us." Bjorn gave me a hug and a little push toward the stairs. I smiled gratefully at him and raced up to the bedroom to find Lindsey.

He was standing in the middle of the room, facing the door. Waiting for me.

"Lindsey, did everything go OK at Village?"

"Yes," he answered, as he stood frozen, giving me a thousand-yard stare. It was the same stare of fury that I'd seen him give J.C. on the night of the Rod Stewart incident at the Forum. A warning bell went off inside of my head as I slowly approached him. *What's wrong with him? Why is he staring at me like that?*

Reaching him, I held out the Polaroids as I kept a bright smile on my face. "Lindsey, look! Look at my pictures! Bjorn just told me that this is going to be a full-page ad in *Billboard* and *Record World*. Can you believe it?"

Silence greeted my words as Lindsey continued to stare at me with blue eyes that held no expression. His gaze dropped to the pictures and he knocked them out of my hand, sending them flying in all directions. Speechless, I looked down at one of them lying on the dusty carpet between our feet: a shot of myself dressed in a long-sleeved white lace blouse and holding a heart-shaped single to my breast as I smiled into the camera. The image seemed to mock me as Lindsey started to scream out words that stunned me.

"*No!*" Lindsey shouted. "I don't want to see your fucking pictures! I *hate* what you're doing! Leave me alone . . . go back downstairs and take your *stupid* pictures with you!"

Struggling to speak as tears started to stream down my face, I whispered, "Lindsey, what's wrong? Why are you saying these things to me? Look at my pictures! They're nice! They're pretty! Aren't you proud of me? Why are you so angry? I don't understand!"

"Goddamn it! *I fucking hate this!* Get out and go back downstairs—now!" he snarled. Turning, he rushed into the bathroom and the door crashed behind him as he kicked it closed.

Numbly picking up my scattered photographs with shaking hands, I felt as though my entire world had just been shattered. Never before in my life had anyone screamed at me with such anger. And that anger left me trembling in its wake. Hearing a soft knock on the bedroom door, I blindly turned to open it. Bjorn was standing there, his worried expression darkening when he saw the tears running down my face and soaking the high collar of my blouse.

Pulling me gently out of the room, he whispered soothing words into my ear. He guided me back down the huge staircase to the pool of lights set up in the living room. Taking one look at my face, Andy ran into the kitchen and came rushing back with a glass of water. Silently he offered it to me before turning away, fiddling with his cameras in the classic pose of a man who was completely at a loss for how to deal with the scene in front of him. Bjorn, however, was not at a loss.

"Sweetie, I heard it. I couldn't help it—I think the neighbors down the street must have heard Lindsey. Hey, I love you. You didn't do anything wrong, Carol. I don't know what Lindsey's problem is, but you didn't do anything wrong. I feel like going up there and giving him a piece of my mind—"

I held up my hand to cut off Bjorn's words. I didn't want to hear them— and I didn't want to talk about it. I *couldn't* talk about it. All I wanted to do was finish the shoot as quickly as possible and be alone. In spite of Lindsey's anger toward me, I felt a fierce protectiveness toward him and I couldn't bear to hear anyone criticize him—not even Bjorn, my closest friend.

"I'm fine. Really. Let's just finish this, all right? I'm sorry I ruined your makeup, Bjorn. Lindsey's just tired, that's all. I just want to finish the shoot, OK? Please?"

With a sigh and a shrug Bjorn forced a smile onto his face and nodded at me. As he went about touching up my makeup, he chattered and laughed, trying to distract me from the reality of what had just happened upstairs. Grateful for his understanding, I was soon standing in front of the camera again, ready to shoot the last roll of film. But the excitement and happiness that I'd felt only hours before was now gone—replaced with a feeling that I was posing for a senseless photograph of a blonde holding a record to her chest. And now that perfect heart-shaped red record seemed to taunt me as I picked it up to pose once again for the cameras. Staring at it, I wanted to throw it on the floor and watch it shatter.

I moved automatically to follow the directions from Bjorn and Andy, my mind wandering as the camera clicked away. The echo of Lindsey's words seemed to dim all the thrill of my first real booking as a model. Instead I felt ridiculous about being excited over an ad in a magazine.

And as the light strobes flashed from Andy's camera, my thoughts made a mockery of what was happening that very minute. *I don't know what's wrong. If Lindsey isn't proud of me, if Lindsey hates what I'm doing so much that he could scream at me the way he just did, then it really isn't worth it, is it? I've probably been kidding myself all along—my modeling career isn't going to go anywhere. I probably don't have what it takes. And that's what Lindsey meant with his horrible words. He must have been trying to tell me something—that kind of anger doesn't just come from out of nowhere. I mean, if he isn't proud of me, if he thinks so little of what I'm doing that he can throw my pictures on the ground, then he obviously doesn't believe in me. Maybe I'm just not beautiful enough . . . not skilled enough . . . or special enough to be one of the few who actually make it as a model.*

After Bjorn and Andy left I turned off the lights in the living room and climbed the shadowy staircase to the master bedroom, exhausted by the intense emotions that still screamed through my mind. A career in modeling seemed somehow more meaningless with every step that I took toward Lindsey, who was waiting behind the closed doors of our bedroom. Hesitating in front of the solid oak door, I took a deep breath, straightened my tense shoulders, and tried to get my thoughts under control.

I need to think long and hard about it while we're on the road, and make a decision about what to do. After all, I have a lot more important things to think of than my so-called modeling career. Fleetwood Mac is going on the road and Lindsey's going to need me—and starting tomorrow, I'm going to devote every minute of every day to him and only him. Because that's gotta come first. And who cares anyway? Is posing for a picture important? No.

As I turned the handle, opened the door, and saw Lindsey's sleeping body lying on top of the covers of our bed, a tiny, stubborn voice continued to whisper: *But believing in yourself is . . . believing in yourself is the most important thing in the world.* Shaking the voice out of my head, I quickly stripped, slipped into bed, and fell into a dreamless sleep.

10

On The Edge

It was wonderful being back on the road for the last leg of the *Rumours* tour. Neither Lindsey nor I had spoken of what happened the night of the magazine shoot only a week before. Instead, we concentrated on the here and now—and that here and now was being on tour again with the band. Anyway, the past months at home had been wonderful in so many different ways: having heart-to-heart talks with Lindsey about his new music and then sharing in the excitement and thrill as he created new songs—and, of course, working with Bjorn on my portfolio. But I was more than ready to leave the intensity of that time behind me.

It was a relief to be back in familiar territory, back to where Lindsey and I focused all of our attention completely on the band and the shows. And I

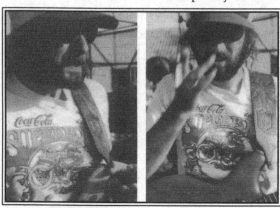

John McVie at soundcheck.

realized that I'd missed sharing that *outwardly* directed intensity with him. It was an intensity that had, from my very first days on the road with him, created a special bond between us, a bond that had made us an inseparable team.

After two weeks on the road the novelty of touring was beginning to wear off. It was all becoming routine again. But, unlike the marathon tour jags in the months before, the band now had something to look forward to that wasn't just routine: planning the next Fleetwood Mac album.

In the concert venues and on the plane, the band members began to speak of matters that never failed to electrify all of them: the new recording

studio and the upcoming album. Everyone was excited. Everyone seemed pleased and content with what they foresaw as just one big party in the band's new Disneyland: Studio D at Village Recorder.

Everyone, that is, except Lindsey. Like the others, Lindsey was also

Mick Fleetwood at soundcheck.

looking forward to starting the new album in the studio. But only he and I knew that the sessions were not going to be quite the "party" that the band was expecting.

The heavy weight of the secret that Lindsey was carrying was beginning to show. His smiles were fewer and further between and there was a constant troubled, far-away look in his eyes, as though he were glimpsing an apocalyptic event on the horizon. And I guess he was. Because it

was time to tell Mick about the new direction that he'd taken in his songs and the new rules that he wanted to lay down for how they were to be recorded. These were rules that would send the rest of the band into shock and could, in a worst-case scenario, destroy Fleetwood Mac.

On an overcast afternoon in yet another nameless city somewhere on the East coast, Lindsey was pacing frantically in the living room of our Hilton hotel suite. We had a two-day break between shows and the time had come for Lindsey to speak with Mick about his new songs and his creative deci-

Lindsey.

sions about recording them.

It wasn't that he was *afraid* to tell Mick or even that he was having doubts. He completely believed in what he was doing and the new direction of his music. He was, however, absolutely dreading the scene that he knew was sure to come when he delivered his either/or ultimatum for the new record. I spoke to him in soothing tones, doing my best to reassure him that no matter how Mick reacted, he would, once he'd heard the songs, understand how Lindsey felt, and why.

We both knew, of course, that my assurances were just words to bolster both of us. There was no way that Mick was going to calmly take the news he was about to hear. Throwing himself down on an overstuffed armchair, Lindsey let out a scream of frustration. With a few profound curses he told me (and himself) that he hated feeling bad over telling Mick what he needed to do for his music. Then, without another word, he picked up his jacket and stalked out the door. It was time to face Mick.

Mick Fleetwood.

The air of tension that had been hanging in the room like a black cloud barely dissipated with his departure, since I was every bit as nervous as he was. A part of me wished that I could be by his side when he sat down with Mick, while the other, saner part was grateful that I didn't have to be. I looked at the clock and started counting the minutes until his return. Smoking cigarette after cigarette, I curled up in a corner of an ugly plaid couch and stared out at the dismal gray sky.

I didn't try to imagine what was going on in Mick's room a few floors beneath me. I didn't want to. The mental image of Lindsey sitting on the floor, playing the tapes of his new songs and explaining why he *needed* to do what he *wanted* to do was too painful for me to even think about. We both had known that this day would come, but now that it was happening, the reality of it was harsher than we'd anticipated. And if it was that brutal for me to endure, I didn't even want to imagine what Lindsey was going through downstairs.

After two hours he came quietly into the room. Looking drained and exhausted, he sat down on the floor at my feet and stared up at me with the eyes of a man who'd just fought a hellish battle. Sliding off the couch, I put my arms around him and held him tightly.

"What happened, baby? Can you talk about it? Do you *want* to talk about it?" I whispered.

He nodded and in a halting voice began. He told me that he'd told Mick everything, told him about the new direction that he'd taken in his music, a direction inspired by the radical new bands that we'd been listening to. After playing a few of his songs for Mick, Lindsey had explained to him that he wanted to play every instrument on them *himself*, in the studio— with no help from the band, no "jamming," and no "constructive criticism" from his four bandmates. He wanted to follow his own creative voice and let it take him down whatever road it would.

The bottom line: he won't do another *Rumours*. And, to put it mildly, Mick was not happy. He was very upset. He pleaded with Lindsey to reconsider, afraid that the decisions that Lindsey had made would ultimately destroy the band. But after two hours of conversation Lindsey hadn't changed his mind.

But that didn't mean that Lindsey himself was not shaken by his talk with Mick. He felt horrible about upsetting Mick, and that was never his intention. He wasn't doing any of this to attack the band: it was all about the music. We both hoped that when Mick had a chance to calm down, he, along with the others, would understand this and work it out with Lindsey.

As I stroked his hair I said, "Lindsey, you did what you had to do. I'm sorry it was so hard, baby. I know that you love the band, and Mick knows it, too. I'm sure he's burning up the phone lines right now to Chris, Stevie, and John. Hopefully, they'll be able to all come to terms with it together. They'll come around. They're not going to risk losing you. And damn, when they hear your songs, they'll see how great the music is."

With a shrug and a dry laugh Lindsey added that he also pointed out to Mick that he was tired of using all of his best song ideas on Stevie's and Christine's music. He'd still contribute his talent to their songs, but this time he wanted to put *his* music first. And how could that be wrong?

Lindsey was as upset as I'd ever seen him. I sat on the floor next to him and held him in my arms as the sky outside the window darkened to a murky black. The room turned cold as we sat there for what seemed like hours—no longer speaking, just giving and taking comfort from each other's presence. We both knew now that our darkest fears had been realized. It wasn't as though we weren't prepared for Mick's reaction, but now that it had become a reality it felt like somehow we'd just purposefully crushed his world.

But it couldn't be helped and only time would tell how the band was going to deal with Lindsey's plans for the new album. I sent up a silent prayer that everything would work itself out, and focused on taking care of the deeply shaken man beside me.

I jumped up, turned on all the lights, and ordered us both a light dinner. While we waited for room service, I ran a hot bath for Lindsey, turned down the bed, and gave him his Dilantin. His face was so pale, so full of sorrow, that it almost broke my heart to look at him.

In the days that followed, on the plane and at the shows, the atmosphere was one of ever-changing levels of unspoken indifference, iciness, and resentment, depending on the mood of the other band members. No one talked about what everyone knew. Lindsey's conversation with Mick had, for now, been left up in the air, to be resolved once they were off the road. We were relieved. Neither Lindsey nor I had been looking forward to the aftermath of his bombshell decision. And for now, at least, it seemed we'd been given a reprieve. Quiet hostility we could deal with; it beat a bloodbath any friggin' day.

And then, overnight, the focus of the band was no longer on the album or the tour. Mick's father was seriously ill and everyone's thoughts were with him as he flew the Concorde to England to be at his father's bedside. His beloved father had finally lost his long battle with cancer. All of us were devastated over the pain that Mick and his family were enduring. His family was well loved within the inner circle. Being a consummate professional, Mick flew back to the United States and rejoined the tour and we all did our best to comfort him.

As the demanding tour continued, the band finally got a much-needed diversion. Personally invited to Washington, D.C., by Hamilton Jordan and Jimmy Carter's sons, Fleetwood Mac was to have two honors bestowed upon them. First, the band members and the inner circle were to be given a private tour of the White House.

Driving through the gates of the White House, and walking down the corridors of power through which so many great men of American history had walked, almost felt like a dream. To see the Oval Office where John F. Kennedy spent his days listening to the counsel of his brother Bobby was overwhelming. The effect of being in those corridors reduced the ever-raucous Fleetwood Mac family to starstruck tongue-tied children. As our cars left the grounds of the White House we were a somber, introspective group—every one of us awed by the experience.

The second tribute was a gala reception thrown in the band's honor by President Carter's sons, Chip and Jack. It was held in a beautiful room in one of the buildings on Embassy Row. The room was decorated with white silk drapes, satin chairs, and crystal chandeliers. Black-tuxedoed waiters prowled the room carrying trays of champagne as *Rumours* played over invisible speakers. Secret Service agents, linked by walkie-talkies, hovered in the corners, keeping watch over Hamilton Jordan and the sons of the president. The bulge of a gun was obvious under each agent's evening clothes as their eyes ceaselessly roved over every single corner and every person in the room. I felt like we were in a James Bond movie.

In a room filled with almost two hundred of the young, hip movers and shakers of Washington, the members of Fleetwood Mac and their entourage were the center of attention. Within ten minutes of entering the room, Carter's sons, surrounded by Secret Service men, moved shyly up to shake Lindsey's hand, gushing about how much they liked the band's album. Young and soft-spoken, they actually blushed when he introduced me. And I, in turn, blushed, too. I felt like Cinderella at the ball with her Prince Charming.

And just like in a fairy tale, it was on this night that Lindsey proposed to me. As we stood in a corner of the ornate room he grabbed my hand and whispered into my ear that he thought we should get married. Taken by surprise, all I could do was stare at him. With a shrug of his shoulders he told me that he hadn't had time to buy a ring, but thought we needed to be engaged. Thunderstruck, I haltingly told him that I absolutely agreed. Feeling a bit dazed but deliriously happy, we spent the rest of night ignoring the party. Sitting in a corner on satin chairs kissing and murmuring to each other, we were immune to the curious stares of passersby in designer clothes and the ever-present dark looks directed our way by the lavishly dressed members of Fleetwood Mac.

For the past few weeks, I'd been feeling a bit like Yoko Ono; loved by her man, but disliked by the members of his band. For they were well aware that I had been completely supportive of Lindsey's new direction in music— which was the focus of their angst. I was absolutely convinced, however, that Lindsey was doing the right thing and although it was uncomfortable at times, I was more than happy to weather their cold shoulders.

It was best for now, we decided, to keep our engagement quiet. Not that we were trying to hide it, but we were both tired of feeling at the center of a storm. Keenly aware that the members of Fleetwood Mac couldn't care less about our happiness at this point, I was not about to throw more fuel on the emotional fire that was already burning between the band members.

But, fortunately for us, two other band members also had their attention directed not on the upcoming album but on matters of the heart. And it was this relationship that was the focus of the Fleetwood Mac family's attention. The affair between Mick and Stevie was blatantly obvious to anyone who even looked in their direction. Secret smiles, loving soft touches, and long sessions of feverish whispering before and after shows left no one in doubt that they were an item. The fact that they were still apparently trying to keep it under wraps only added to the gossip, and I had to wonder if Mick would ever have his promised talk with Lindsey and finally get it out in the open. I think everyone was wondering.

Right before we left to go on the road, Mick had flown his wife and two daughters back to Los Angeles and had bought them a home on Little Rameriz Canyon in Malibu. He and Jenny supposedly were going to give their marriage another try. I'd been so busy before we left on the road that I hadn't had a chance to talk to Jenny, but I'd nonetheless been thrilled to hear that she was back in town. I knew that Mick loved his wife and daughters. But he was, apparently, also in love with Stevie Nicks.

I was still very determined to stay out of it. Besides, I knew that Mick, Jenny, and Stevie would—in typical Fleetwood Mac fashion—work out the love triangle. That meant, of course, that it would be worked out with as much drama as possible.

From the moment I first heard the news at our summer barbecue, I'd been waiting for Mick to tell Lindsey about his affair with Stevie. So as not to become involved, I hadn't broken the news myself. He seemed to be oblivious to their starry-eyed behavior, or maybe he really didn't care. It was hard for me to tell, since we never spoke of it.

Either way, it made no difference to me, because as far as I was concerned, the happier that Stevie was, the better it was for all of us—especially me. Her happiness was translating itself into overtures of friendship toward me and I was more than willing to reciprocate. To not be the target of her animosity was as welcome as a summer's breeze and for the first time since Lindsey and I had been together, Stevie and I had started to build a cordial relationship. I wouldn't go so far as to say that we were friends, but it appeared that we were no longer enemies, and that was good enough.

Lindsey and I made it to the end of the tour relatively unscathed and, with relief, headed back to the sanctuary of our home on June Street. Within days he was back in his studio, writing and recording feverishly before it was time to head into Village Recorder. He'd had another meeting with Mick at his Bel-Air house and, despite Mick's pleading, had not given an inch on his position. Finally, Mick had grudgingly said that the band would agree to giving Lindsey room to do things the way he wanted. But even though the pressure of breaking the news to the band was over, he was now under pressure to bring songs to the studio that would hold up under a seemingly hostile reception by the other band members. He'd put a lot on the line, and as the days passed by, this pressure would build and finally explode.

The first obvious sign of trouble appeared on a night that started out with the promise of being a fun-filled evening with J.C. and his girlfriend Fifi. Elvis Costello was playing the Palomino in the San Fernando Valley and both Lindsey and I were dying to see him. Huge fans of his songs "Watching the Detectives" and "Alison," we waited with eager anticipation in front of the club's small stage. We were all sober—after the road, everyone was tired of doing blow and drinking hard liquor. As I ordered a Diet Coke, J.C., Lindsey, and Fifi decided to share a pitcher of beer. While we waited for our drinks, Fifi and I giggled and gossiped.

J.C. broke in with his own tales of life on the road and I suddenly realized that Lindsey was looking increasingly irritated. Apparently not amused by the stories or the fact that Elvis Costello was now running forty-five minutes behind schedule, he didn't appear to be enjoying himself in the least. Finally the lights darkened and the show began as Costello took his place behind the microphone on the sawdust-covered floor. Even though he was wearing cuffed Levi's, cowboy boots, and a western bolo tie along with his trademark black-framed eyeglasses, it didn't occur to us that we were in for a musical shock.

Instead of launching into the rock 'n' roll hits that everyone in the club was eagerly awaiting, Costello began to sing country and western songs—one right after the other—very, very badly. There is nothing quite as *wrong* as an Englishman trying to pull off a country and western tune. It just doesn't work. After song number three I collapsed into helpless laughter as I watched the expressions on the faces of just about every patron of the small club turn gradually from disbelief to disgust. Lindsey's expression was sullen and rebellious as he began to curse under his breath. And he wasn't amused that J.C., Fifi, and I found the whole thing hilarious. He, it seemed, did not.

After six songs Lindsey stood up and stalked out of the club. Without a glance to see if any of us were following him, he got into his BMW and slammed the door. With a hurried goodbye to a confused J.C. and Fifi, I climbed into the car beside him and held on to the dashboard as he punched the gas and peeled out of the parking lot.

Trying to engage him in conversation, I was met with complete silence—until we got within six blocks of our house. In the middle of the street, Lindsey slammed on the brakes and sat still for three heartbeats. Without a word he lunged toward me and wrapped his hands around my neck and started to squeeze. Too shocked to scream, I grabbed his hands and tried to pry them away, but his grip tightened painfully around my throat. His eyes looked lifeless as he stared into mine and his teeth were pulled back in a grimace. Panic surged through me as I fought for breath and my struggles became stronger as the burning pain in my throat increased. Suddenly Lindsey let go, leaned back, and hit the gas. The tires screeched as we took off at a high speed down the dark street.

Tears were pouring down my face as I cried, "Oh God, Lindsey, what's wrong? What did I do? What did I do?"

In answer, he hit the brakes and lunged toward me, once again wrapping his hands around my throat. My head snapped back and forth as he silently shook me. All I could hear was the sound of my own ragged gasps for breath. Just as suddenly as it started, it stopped. He let go of me and put the car into gear. And as I sobbed, he slowly, carefully drove us home. As we pulled into the driveway, I jumped out of the car before it was even stopped and ran to the front door. Fumbling with my keys, I finally opened the door and took off at a dead run up the shadowy staircase into our bedroom.

I stumbled across the warmly lit room and collapsed into a large armchair, pulling my legs up under me, trying to make myself as small as possible. I wasn't crying now—I felt strangely calm as I watched Lindsey walk into the room and cross to where I was sitting.

"Why, Lindsey?" I whispered as I looked up into his face. His expression was cold and distant as he stared at me for long seconds. Then his lip curled and he snarled, "You're all alike . . . you're all fucking alike," as he once again lunged for me. Frantic, I pushed him away as I struggled to my feet and I started to run down stairs lit only by streetlamps filtering through the stained-glass windows of the foyer and into the even darker kitchen. I sank down onto the cold tiled floor, wrapping my arms around my shaking body.

Why, why, why, why? The word kept echoing in my head as I sat frozen in despair. Never in my life had I felt so shattered, so lost, and so utterly bewildered. I had no idea what I had done to cause such rage to be directed at me. Other than his harsh words on the night of my magazine shoot, Lindsey had rarely raised his voice to me. What had happened this night was beyond my understanding.

I sat with tears streaming down my face as I listened to the sound of his footsteps coming down the stairs. I just wanted to disappear and be somewhere far, far away, in a place where everything made sense again.

Silently walking into the room, Lindsey stopped and looked at me, as though seeing me for the first time. He then held out his arms to me, his expression now soft and welcoming. Slowly, I got up from the floor and stood trembling in front of him. He pulled me into his arms and I collapsed against him, sobbing. He gently, lovingly helped me upstairs. Easing me onto the bed, he lay down beside me, stroking my hair as I cried myself to sleep.

In the morning it was like nothing ever happened. Lindsey woke up, kissed me, and jumped up out of bed, heading down to the studio where he stayed for the remainder of the day. I stayed in bed, exhausted and spent from the night before. My mind however, was manic. I went through the events leading up to the incident over and over, but I couldn't for the life of me understand what caused it. But surely, I told myself, I must be to blame, because otherwise it made no sense at all—and I needed it to make sense.

I spent the day feeling numb and shaken, bereaved by a loss of something that I couldn't put a name to—a loss that seemed to haunt me as I listened to the music coming out of the studio. *Maybe*, I thought, *it's the pressure of the upcoming album that's responsible for what happened between us last night.* I felt chilled to the bone when I realized that this was only the beginning of that pressure. The band would be going into the studio in a matter of weeks and I had no idea what to expect. But nevertheless, just having something concrete to blame for what had happened between Lindsey and I helped me weather the emotional storm that had left me bereft.

A few days later Lindsey began to have excruciating stomach pains that left him doubled over in agony. After two days we rushed him to our doctor and he was admitted to Midway Hospital for a four-day stay for tests. Once the tests were back, we were told that it was stress, and even though I was distressed to hear it, I was secretly relieved. Now my excuse for what happened the night of the Elvis Costello show seemed to be confirmed. The pressure of the album and the long hours that he'd been working at home were taking a toll on his mind and body that was as dangerous as it was painful—to both of us. He was prescribed pills to help with the stress and pain and was sent home with instructions to take time off—which, of course, fell on deaf ears.

He went into the studio the minute we walked into the house and I headed straight for the phone. Bob Aguirre had been dropping by our house ever since we'd gotten back from the tour. He'd let us know in a straightforward fashion that if we ever needed a personal assistant or house sitter, he was the man for the job. While Bob already worked as a session drummer, he seemed to miss being around Lindsey. Unlike Lindsey's other close friend Richard Dashut, who traveled on the road with Lindsey as Fleetwood Mac's sound engineer, Bob had been left at home alone while his two former housemates traveled the world. And it had been hard on him. He was, after all, one of Lindsey's oldest friends.

Lindsey and I had talked about having Bob move in and Lindsey had pretty much left it up to me. He didn't want me to feel like I was giving up my privacy by having another man move in with us. And I, in turn, wanted to think about it.

But with the recording sessions approaching and Lindsey's obvious stress, I felt that a little *less* privacy was a small price to pay for the contribution that Bob could make to the serenity of our household. I knew for a fact that Lindsey seemed relaxed and happy when Bob was around. And I, too, had become close friends with him. Since our house had four bedrooms, I realized that having Bob move in to help Lindsey as a personal assistant—or just to be there as a friend when he needed it—was a brilliant idea.

Speaking with Bob on the phone, I asked him if he'd like to move in with us. Without a moment's hesitation he jumped at the chance. And within forty-eight hours we were living a version of *Three's Company* in the June Street house. Bob immediately set up a croquet set in our large backyard, and both Lindsey and he delighted in beating me game after game. I was hopelessly bad at croquet, but it was fun and, more importantly, it was relaxing. Our new living arrangements seemed like a match made in heaven and I breathed a sigh of relief. Lindsey's stomach pains disappeared and he returned to being loving and caring toward me, and that, in itself, was all the evidence I needed that we'd made the right decision in welcoming Bob Aguirre to our home. Since that night, Lindsey had not apologized or even mentioned what had happened between us—and neither had I. I was convinced that it would never happen again and honestly, I couldn't bear to think of it, much less talk about it. It had become my secret, my shame, and my guilt. I believed that somehow I must be to blame for what happened. I wasn't sure what I'd done wrong, but I felt that if I were loving enough, smart enough, and supportive enough, it would never happen again.

In the years that followed, Bob would become one of my best friends as he moved with us from house to house. With his dry wit, low-key presence, and constant mishaps with various girlfriends, he never ceased to entertain. Asking Bob to live with us would prove to be one of the best decisions

Lindsey and I ever made. He became a big brother to me and when push came to shove, he was always there when I needed him. His protectiveness when I needed some shelter in the world of Fleetwood Mac is a gift I'll never be able to repay, but one for which I'll forever be grateful.

In a few days' time Fleetwood Mac would officially begin their recording sessions for the new album. The studio was ready. Lindsey was ready. And hopefully, so was the rest of the band. I, however, was not so sure that I was ready. Never having been in the studio with the band as they recorded an entire album, I was more than a little worried. If Fleetwood Mac interacting in the studio was anything like the stories that I'd heard about the *Rumours* sessions, then I had every reason to feel a great deal of apprehension about what might lie ahead. There had been so many fights . . . so many nights of tears, accusations, and unbridled rage within the studio that even now, whenever the subject came up, it was spoken of in only general terms within the band. Nobody wanted to relive those nights when marriages and relationships disintegrated within the walls of a recording studio.

Lindsey and I had been together for almost two years now and, just as I had known it would be at the very first show of the *Rumours* tour, my life had become almost a fairy tale—a very twisted one, but a fairy tale nonetheless. As I sat outside on the backyard patio of our house watching Bob and Lindsey play yet another game of croquet, I leaned back in my wicker chair and propped my head up on my fist, staring past them into the vast green expanse of the golf course that backed up to the edge of our property. And I tried to remember what it felt like before I met Lindsey, before I became a real-life version of Alice in Wonderland and stepped through a looking glass into a world where magic was real and mundane reality could be changed to suit our purposes. And I couldn't. Not really. That world seemed like a black-and-white version of the one in which I now lived.

Listening to Lindsey and Bob's insolent taunts reverberate against the background crack of croquet mallets on wooden balls, I smiled at the innocence of the scene that was taking place in the backyard of the beautiful mansion that I now called home. It was a scene that went hand in hand with my many trips up to northern California with Lindsey to see his family during our breaks on the *Rumours* tour. Wonderful days when we walked around Point Lobos, stayed in Carmel, and lived a life that was as tame as it was beautiful.

And as daylight faded to a darkening twilight, I thought of Stevie's swirling black chiffon, bottle caps full of blow, spotlights of gold and red, and the spell that was cast over every single member of the Fleetwood Mac family as they listened to the band perform "The Chain" night after night on the road. Those lyrics, which had been a secret bond that held Fleetwood Mac together before the band's amazing success, seemed now to be too much to bear. I had no idea how much longer they could carry the weight of that golden chain. Or of the cost to us all.

11

MAKE IT, BABY

The weather was gorgeous in L.A. on the day that Fleetwood Mac was scheduled to begin recording the follow-up album to *Rumours. A good omen,* I thought, as I pushed my Ray-Bans onto my face. It was three in the afternoon—an *early* call time for the band. Even though we'd had the summer off, Lindsey and I were both deathly pale from "studio pallor." We wore it like a badge of honor as it proved its bearer lived a completely nocturnal life—in the studio, on the road, and at dusk-to-dawn parties. To look healthy and tanned in the late 1970s in the music industry was a sign that an artist's career was in the shithouse.

Fleetwood Mac's career was definitely *not* in the shithouse. As Lindsey and I pulled up and parked in the lot that belonged to Village Recorder, we checked out the cars that were parked around us. We spied Mick's red Ferrari, J.C.'s Jaguar, a couple of black Mercedes, and a few BMWs that may or may not have belonged to our clan. The band members changed their cars as often as their underwear, so it was hard to be sure who was driving what at any given time.

Lindsey pushed his own Ray-Bans firmly into place over red-rimmed eyes and took a deep breath. "Ready?" he asked as he reached into the backseat of our silver Beemer. Grabbing the small leather case that contained the cassettes of his home-recorded songs, he quickly climbed out of the car and started to walk away.

Carol Ann.

After checking my pale pink lipstick in the rearview mirror, I grabbed my purse and followed. I almost had to run to catch up with him as he made his way to the sidewalk. Lindsey was definitely looking forward to getting started on the album—so much so that I felt that I might as well have been invisible as I trailed behind him.

Having lived with Lindsey during his recording sessions at home, I'd grown accustomed to feeling like a ghostly presence when his mind was focused on music. As soon as I realized he was looking *through* me instead of *at* me, I knew that yet another song was brewing in his head. And once that happened Lindsey was oblivious to everything around him. I'd come to terms with the fact that his favorite place in the world was a recording studio—which meant that for the duration of this new album I'd better get used to being invisible at times.

Walking past the main entrance to Village Recorder, we headed straight for a gray iron door that had no markings on it of any kind. It was the private and only entrance to the new studio that Fleetwood Mac's dollars had paid for. There was a buzzer and intercom on the left side and when Lindsey pushed a button and mumbled his name, the heavy door opened almost immediately to reveal the grinning face of Greg Thomason.

Beckoning us inside like a butler, he walked ahead of us down a dark corridor to the outer studio reception room, which held about a dozen people. Lindsey's ever-valiant, ever-vigilant roadie, Ray Lindsey, was sipping a mug of the much-heralded English draught beer. The polished blond wood keg with its gold spigot held a place of honor immediately on the right side of the room. And already there was a steady flow back and forth of the band's other personal roadies, Greg, Dwayne, and the man himself, J.C.

Mickey Shapiro, a cigar hanging from his mouth, was hovering in a corner with Mick, wrangling over a legal document as Mick listened intently. Christine was standing with a cigarette dangling from fingers that also gripped a red plastic cup filled with her standard vodka tonic.

Tables were laden with salad, sandwiches, and assorted expensive cheeses and crackers that I knew, within a few hours, would make the inner circle gag when they came out of Studio D's interior. As soon as the band members walked through the double-soundproofed doors that guarded the studio itself there would be massive amounts of cocaine waiting for whoever wanted it. And once the blow was snorted, the food that now looked so delicious would become a source of stomach-wrenching loathing to the wired inhabitants of the Fleetwood Mac family.

After ten minutes Lindsey whispered into my ear that he wanted to go into the studio itself. Clinging to his hand, I double-stepped behind him and entered the private realm of Studio D, which would become the band's home away from home for the duration of the album. It was a room to which only the band and their close associates would be given access for the duration of the recording process. Any others—secretaries, Warner Bros. executives, lawyers, and outer circle friends—would never be allowed to stay longer than an hour. It would prove to be more inaccessible than even the band's personal dressing room on the road. It was the most exclusive room in Fleetwood Mac's world.

Richard Dashut and Ken Caillet were seated at the eight-foot-long mixing console. Ensconced like kings in executive-type black leather chairs, they were passing a joint back and forth. Spying Lindsey, they cackled out a cry of welcome and held it out to him as he crossed the distance between them. Within minutes Mick, Christine, and a newly arrived John McVie were breezing into the inner sanctum.

In the middle of the coffee table was a large paper packet. Immediately descending like vultures, Mick, Richard, and Ken waited impatiently as Christine made a big show out of taking her time opening the packet and daintily dipping a fingernail into it. She then passed it to me and I did the same.

"Christ, ladies! Hurry it up! We're dyin' here!" Mick groaned as his immensely tall, swaying body loomed over me. Giggling, I took my time closing the packet neatly before he snatched it out of my hand. "Gimme that, Carol! What's the point of closing it?" he screeched. He looked darkly around at the cluster of bodies pressing close to the paper packet as though it were the Holy Grail, then his voice dropped five levels as he intoned, "The woods are dark and deep and I've miles to go . . ." Sticking the end of a Swiss Army knife into the contents, he proceeded to snort a huge pile of cocaine up his patrician nose. "Ahhhh! That's fabulous!" he said, beaming happily at everyone in the room.

Energized by the white powder, Mick excitedly told the gathered clan that he'd just bought a new $70,000 sports car. As he went on and on about the luxurious seats, the huge engine, and yada-yada-yada, I tuned him out, completely uninterested in the long, wordy story about "horsepower," "cylinders," and "zero to one-sixty" in what seemed impossibly few seconds, leaving the oohing and aahing to the men.

Both Lindsey and Christine were digging cassettes out of their bags, laying them on the coffee table. Lindsey suggested that everyone listen to Chris's songs first, feeling, I was sure, that *his* tapes might not be the right ones to start off the recording sessions in a calm, cool, and collected manner. Better to start with the "expected" sounds of Christine's songs than shock the band with his. Even though they'd been warned by Mick, they had no idea what they were in for. And we had no idea how they were going to react. So, Lindsey's suggestion, made in the spirit of harmony, was a wise one.

As Richard and Ken scrambled to get the mixing board set up for playback, Lindsey held up his hand like a traffic cop signaling "Stop!" With a raised eyebrow he growled, "Where the hell is Stevie? It's almost five! It'd be great if she could make it here like the rest of us! Nice way to start the sessions—can't even be bothered to get here."

Just as he was getting himself worked up for a real tirade, the door slowly opened as though being pushed by an invisible hand and Stevie swept into the studio. Dressed in a flowing dress made of antique scarves, with jade and gold bracelets jangling against her thin wrists, she looked like the queen of rock that she most definitely was. Her girl fans followed her, lugging various "Stevie" bags and accessories. And hot on their heels was the yipping, squeaking form of Jenny—Stevie's poodle. It was an entrance that would have made Elizabeth Taylor proud.

"You were saying, Lindsey?" Stevie asked in her husky voice before gesturing grandly to Christie, her makeup artist, to drop her bags in a corner of the already crowded floor. Lindsey's response was drowned out in the chorus of greetings from the rest of the room's occupants and within five minutes everyone was happily gossiping, doing hits of cocaine, and guzzling their drinks of choice. It looked as though the night was going to be peacefully productive after all. And then the phone rang.

Richard answered and, with a puzzled expression on his face, handed the receiver to Mick. "It's some guy, man. He sounds freaked. Says it's an emergency," he said as he shrugged his shoulders. The room went deathly quiet after Richard uttered the word "emergency"—never a good word to hear over the phone.

"This is Mick, yeah. *What?* A semi hit the car while it was being *towed?* The fucking thing is in *two halves? Fuck!*" Mick's scream of anguish filled the room as we sat in stunned silence trying to compute what we'd just heard. After a few more minutes of profanity Mick hung up the phone and looked at us, his face slack with shock.

"What happened?" I meekly asked, as everyone leaned forward to catch Mick's mumbled response. "The car," he moaned, "was being towed up to my house in Bel-Air on a flatbed trailer." Mick looked forlornly around the room as he raised his hands toward the star-adorned studio ceiling as though summoning heavenly intervention before continuing. "The trailer was broadsided in Beverly Hills by a huge semitruck and it fucking *cut* the flatbed and my new car into two halves! They're still picking up the pieces—can you friggin' believe that? It's a total flippin' loss."

As Mick sank despondently down on the now-crowded sofa he morosely reached for the packet of blow and shoveled a huge hit up his nose. Holding his head in his hands, he was the very picture of a man who'd just lost his best friend—to a semitruck. He muttered that the driver walked away without a scratch, but the car was on its way to the scrapyard. Christine patted Mick on the back while telling him that his insurance should definitely cover every dime that he spent on the ill-fated car.

"That's just it, Chris! The car *isn't insured!* I was just filling out the paperwork with Mickey a couple of hours ago here at the studio. Why do you think I was having it *towed* instead of driving the fucking thing home? Why does this kind of shit always happen to me? Why, why, why?" he wailed.

Looking across the room at Richard and Lindsey, I saw with horror that their faces were bright red. *Oh, no. Please no. Poor Mick. Those two are going to burst out laughing any second and Mick is going to be crushed, poor thing,* I thought as I tried to catch Lindsey's eyes to send him a silent message: *Jesus, guys, hold it together!*

Seeing the look on my face and reading it for what it was, Lindsey gestured to Richard and the two of them slipped into the soundproofed recording room. Through the slanted glass, all of us watched as they fell to their knees, silently convulsing with laughter. Next, Ken got a peculiar screwed-up look on his face and quickly slipped into the recording room with them. He, too, collapsed in—to our ears—silent hysterics and the three of them looked like they were from some twisted comic book. Red-faced, contorted with sound-less laughter, and obviously choking on the force of their hysterics.

In under a minute Christine exploded into guffaws—not so much at Mick's plight, which was, in a sick way, hysterically funny, but at the sight of Richard, Lindsey, and Ken laughing and pounding the floor with their fists. Mick silently stood up and joined them. We all held our breath as we watched him cross the room to where they were lying prone on the floor. Within seconds he was in full Laurence Olivier mode as he acted out the part of tragic hero. And, like an audience at a movie theater, the rest of us gathered around the slanted glass of the control booth giggling and adding our own commentary on the impromptu performance being played out on the other side of the glass in the band's new $1.4-million studio. With Jenny the poodle adding her own yipping comments in the background, the studio had become a scene straight out of a Marx Brothers film.

And that set the tone for the whole evening. Instead of getting down to work, the band decided to party instead, using the need to cheer up Mick as an excuse to do what everyone wanted to do anyway: party until the sun came up.

At 6 A.M. Lindsey and I drove back through the streets of Beverly Hills, Ray-Bans once again firmly in place over our dilated eyes. Exhausted, wasted, and with hangovers the size of Texas insidiously creeping over us, we both agreed that the first night at the studio had been pretty much a washout. Absolutely no work was done, but then again, during the course of the evening's rave-up there was never a dull moment. It was Fleetwood Mac at its partying best, and that in itself made the evening a classic.

The next night Lindsey went alone to the studio. Mick had called for a few nights of "closed sessions" with only the band members and crew allowed in. Aware that this first week was a critical one, he didn't want any distractions for the members of Fleetwood Mac. Lindsey was going to debut his new songs for the band, as were Stevie and Christine—a process that I was more than happy to sit out. Thinking once again of the accounts of what happened in the studio during the recording of *Rumours*, I knew that things could turn ugly if the band hated his songs. I prayed for his sake that they didn't, but if they did, I knew that this was one battle he was more than ready for. Though I supported his every decision with his music at home, I didn't feel it was my place to get in the middle of band politics.

If there was to be a showdown between the band members, then they needed to work it out by themselves, without having their significant others chiming in. This band had way too much history between them for any-one who had a shred of sanity to even contemplate getting involved in an out-and-out battle over the music for their next album. Besides, I knew that Lindsey could and would handle it.

After the first week Lindsey came home to report that the band had somewhat grudgingly come to terms with the new direction of his songs. There was a lot of discussion about them not being "commercial," as well as not sounding *anything* like Fleetwood Mac's music, but Lindsey had slammed the door shut on further criticism. He had explained to them, as he had to Mick on the road, that he was "absolutely not going to do anoth-er *Rumours*." If they insisted upon trying to replicate that album, then he was out of the band. It was an ultimatum that was causing shock waves between the other four. But the good news was that both Christine and Stevie had brought in "good, solid" songs, according to Lindsey. Of course, he wasn't that excited about them—but since his entire focus was on his own music, this wasn't a reflection on their quality.

It took about two weeks of dusk-to-dawn studio sessions that seemed to be more marathon fights than anything else. As the sun came up I heard the door slam morning after morning, and when Lindsey appeared in the doorway of our bedroom his face was angry and despondent. He didn't say much. He just held me close and I hung onto him for dear life, trying to will away the frayed nerves and anger from the past night in the stu-dio. It seemed Lindsey's decision was indeed wreaking havoc on the band's fragile truce and I wondered what was going to happen when it was time for him to put his tracks onto tape in Studio D. I didn't think anyone knew the answer.

Playing it safe, Fleetwood Mac had decided to record Christine's and Stevie's songs first. This allowed the five of them to settle back into being a band working on a common cause instead of separate musicians who were fighting and clawing at each other over radical artistic differences. Lindsey was brilliant when it came to contributing vocals, musical ideas, harmonies, and guitar parts to the music of both of the women in the band. I was quickly learning that one of Lindsey's biggest talents was the ability to act as a producer on another artist's music. He seemed to know inherently what a song needed—and his song arrangements proved it. His guitar riff on "Rhiannon" helped make that song a classic. And despite his vow that this time around he didn't want to use his best ideas on Stevie's or

Lindsey at Village Recorder studio.

Christine's songs, he now appeared to be willing to contribute whatever he felt their music needed. Within a month Fleetwood Mac had seemingly put aside all differences—for now— and music was actually starting to be recorded.

Since things seemed to have calmed down, I once again returned to the studio with Lindsey. The official start time was now 5 P.M., which, in Fleetwood Mac time, meant that the band was expected to be there before 8 P.M.

Arriving at a little after 6 P.M., Lindsey was hoping to get inside and be at the mixing board before the rest of the band arrived. He wanted to work on the mix of one of Christine's songs before they started recording back-up vocals. Walking right by the usual cluster of Fleetwood Mac secretaries, publicists, and record executives in the reception room without even saying hello, Lindsey went straight to the drinks table and mixed a cocktail.

It was a completely different atmosphere from the one I remembered at Producer's Workshop, where the band mingled freely with their friends and business associates as they put the finishing touches on *Rumours*. At that time they were just a successful band with a new album coming out. Now they were superstars, working on the world's next big musical phenomenon. Worth millions to the record company and beloved by fans all over the world, Fleetwood Mac was now accustomed to its slightest wish, need, or command being granted without question. Even if that wish was to act like a pissed-off king.

Without a word to anyone Lindsey took his drink, ignored all pleas and comments directed toward him by the assembled crowd, and walked inside the inner sanctum. Ken and Richard were at the console and, much to Lindsey's disgust, John and Mick were collapsed and grinning on the couch. A mass of empty plastic cups sitting before them signaled that they'd been there for quite a while. The smell of vodka was wafting from the near-empty bottles like some kind of Smirnoff air freshener. Last but not least, there was a large packet of blow open and waiting on the coffee table.

The smell of weed also permeated the air and Lindsey automatically walked to Richard to grab the joint out of his hand. Lindsey's wish to have a somewhat sober Richard and Ken in an empty studio to work seriously with him on Christine's mix was obviously completely out the window. It went totally up in smoke when Stevie walked through the door in a shockingly unexpected early appearance in the studio. She was dressed in an outfit that put even her most lavish stage costumes to shame—a long blue velvet skirt covered with crystal beads and a matching jacket. Her clothes sparkled as she walked into the room. To finish it off, she had about four silk and gauze antique scarves wrapped around her neck. She looked as though she were on her way to an after-party at the Academy Awards.

I looked down at my blue jeans, cowboy boots, and black sweater and once again sighed in resignation. Next to her, I looked completely under-dressed. Of course, next to her, *everyone* looked completely underdressed.

When I saw the coquettish look she gave to Mick under her eyelashes, I mentally slapped my forehead with the heel of my hand. *No friggin' wonder she's dressed like a friggin' fairy princess. It's for Mick! Damn! She didn't even dress up this much for the gala parties on the road—this should be interesting tonight!* I thought, delighted with the prospect of witnessing the two of them in action.

Lindsey still hadn't said a word to me about Mick and Stevie's affair. He didn't miss much of anything that went on around him, so I knew for a fact that he *had* to be aware of it. I mean, you'd have to be completely in a coma to miss the interaction and chemistry that was flowing between Stevie and the new love of her life. But, aware or not, Lindsey didn't seem concerned. If he were, then I think I would have known. After all, I was with the man twenty-four hours a day.

Upon seeing Stevie, Mick segued from inebriated slob into a suave, debonair Englishman who looked like the cat who'd just caught the canary—with Stevie playing the part of the canary. Richard raised an eyebrow at me and we both smiled wickedly as Stevie sashayed across the room and struck a pose for the benefit of Mr. Fleetwood. After ten minutes, apparently happy with the sensational entrance she'd made, she contentedly came over to the couch and sat down next to me.

Smiling sweetly, she asked how I'd been and, before I knew what was happening, Stevie and I were talking like long-lost girlfriends. And it felt totally natural—it was like all the weirdness, all the competitiveness that existed almost as a matter of course between two women who had shared their lives with the same man was swept away in one minute flat.

Ignoring the guys in the room, we went on and on about clothes, makeup, and the latest gossip about the Fleetwood Mac family—of which there was a lot. Christine's three-year relationship with Curry Grant had ended and Curry had been busy trying to distract himself with just about every available female in the band family. Since it was apparently Chris's decision to end the affair, I felt more than comfortable exchanging stories with Stevie about what *I* had heard of Curry Grant's extracurricular activities. Because obviously, in Christine's opinion, what he did was no longer her problem.

As we compared notes we both realized that (present company excepted, of course) Curry was rapidly making his way through each and every woman in the band's inner circle. With his dashing good looks and enough playboy charm to make George Clooney jealous, he was drowning his sorrows with yet another typical cure for an inner-circle crisis: sex with women who were close enough to be your sisters.

We giggled and gossiped about Curry, but then a familiar voice started up inside my head. *What the hell is the deal with these people? Can't any of them go outside the small circle of people who make up the family and actually sleep with someone who isn't a person their best friends have already slept with?* I didn't say it out loud, of course, since Stevie herself had fallen for Mick Fleetwood, a close friend who once belonged to another family member. *But then again,* I told myself, *Stevie wasn't just sleeping around—she was in love. That did make a difference, didn't it?* As I looked at her happy face I shrugged mentally and assured myself that it did. And anyway, it definitely fit the

Fleetwood Mac code of conduct to *never* go looking outside that charmed circle if you could find what you wanted *inside* of it.

As Stevie and I passed the packet of blow between us I looked up to see Lindsey watching us intently. He smiled and nodded at me, as though telling me that he was glad to see Stevie and me finally having a *real* conversation. And I suddenly realized how nice it was to feel like I wasn't her adversary. For I never had been—not in my eyes anyway.

I wanted us to be friends. Now that she and I were actually speaking to each other, I knew that under any other circumstances we would have been girlfriends the moment we met. We were a lot alike—and yet not. And that was the essence of any great friendship. But as much as I hoped that our new camaraderie would last, I knew better than to count on it. With the history that Stevie and Lindsey shared, it was only a matter of time before I was once again caught in the crossfire.

But until that day came I planned to enjoy my newfound status as "girlfriend" to Stevie. With my sarcastic humor and her equally wicked quick mind, we were indeed, at that moment, a formidable pair of blondes. As though sensing my thoughts, Stevie reached over and gave me a long, heartfelt hug. A stunned silence fell over the room as every man stood frozen, mouth hanging open, as though witnessing a shocking hallucination brought on by their own overuse of the huge amounts of drugs in the studio. As Stevie and I sat and smirked at them, they hastily turned away, as if the sight of us being friends was going to make them spontaneously combust. Or, even worse, sober up.

Suddenly Christine entered the room with the force of a tornado. Talking a mile a minute and throwing her purse on the ground, she surveyed the scene and in two seconds flat saw that every single person in the studio was already whacked. And she was not too happy about it. "Think we can get some work done tonight, boys?" she asked in a tone that left no doubt in the minds of the band's sound engineers that they better get their act together—fast. With guilty looks on their faces, Richard and Ken rushed to thread a huge twenty-four-track tape onto one of the machines sitting in a corner. It was her new song, "Over and Over," and the plan tonight was to do a pre-mix of it and start on the vocals. A hush fell over the room as the basic track and Christine's lush voice reverberated around us, filling the air.

Lindsey rolled a chair over to the center of the mixing board between the lads and with eyes closed listened to the song, lost to the world and the people around him. As soon as the last note faded, he opened his eyes and briskly rubbed his hand together, then flexed his long fingers. Holding his hands suspended like a concert pianist over the controls of the board, he took one last hit of a joint and got to work. With head down, he made adjustments to a dizzying array of levers as Christine headed out to the large recording studio and sat on a stool behind a mike. The tape was rolled, Chris started singing, and Lindsey's hands moved constantly on the board as the song was rewound and played—again and again.

After an hour of listening I decided to go outside and get a 7UP, my drink of choice whenever I was with the band. Since I was the only person in the Fleetwood Mac family who didn't drink, having a glass of something that *looked* like a cocktail in my hand made me feel a little less conspicuous, for I still felt oddly embarrassed that I couldn't quite get the taste for hard liquor. It was one of my "schoolgirl" issues that I was trying hard to hide. When I was surrounded by the worldly, sophisticated members of the band, my alcohol sobriety made me stand out like an alien in their midst.

As I pulled open the heavy inner door I jumped in surprise as the outer door crashed open at the same time. And in the tiny space that existed between the two doors, I met Dennis Wilson—drummer and heartthrob of the Beach Boys—for the first time. With Mick looming behind him, Dennis stood with a grin on his spectacularly handsome bearded face and looked me up and down like he was taking my body measurements.

Once I got to know Dennis I'd realize that my first impression of what he was doing was exactly right. Dennis Wilson was not only the consummate (Bad) Boy of Summer, he was the West Coast's biggest playboy and a true connoisseur of women. I could say without a shadow of a doubt that, in the months and years that followed this first meeting, Dennis would never meet a woman he didn't like. He would soon become one of my best friends and to this day I miss him with all my heart.

As Mick introduced us, I stammered out a hello, and to my chagrin I knew that I was blushing—cheeks turning hot under the force of Dennis's gaze. Obviously used to having this effect on women, he grinned even wider as he lifted my pale fingers and kissed the top of my hand like a courtier.

As the two drummers giggled at my discomfort they kept me imprisoned for a few seconds longer before they finally released me from the claustrophobic space between the huge heavy doors. Trying to hold my head high, I breathed a sigh of utter relief as I stepped into the safety of the reception room. My knees felt weak and my fingers seemed to tingle from their brief contact with Dennis Wilson.

Damn! That guy is something else! I thought as I walked a bit unsteadily over to the drinks table and grabbed a cup as my mind raced. *Jesus! We have an actual Beach Boy in the studio tonight! It's going to seem like a dream come true for Lindsey—he's one of their biggest fans. How awesome is this? And how awesome is Dennis Wilson? Talk about charisma—the guy friggin' oozes it!*

Photography © Ed Roach, roach-clips.com

Dennis Wilson.

As it turned out, Lindsey *was* thrilled. But it was Christine McVie who was swept off her feet. When I returned to the studio I could see Mick, Chris, and Dennis laughing and talking in the outer recording room and even through the soundproofed glass it was possible to see that sparks were flying between Christine and Dennis. Stevie and I looked at each other and started giggling. We both knew that we were undoubtedly witnessing the beginnings of a love affair. There was no mistaking the looks and smiles that were passing between the now single Christine and the playboy of the West Coast.

When Dennis finally left two hours later—after snorting up an outrageous amount of his own stash of blow—Christine walked around the studio with a glow and a smile on her face that confirmed what Stevie and I already knew. She was entranced and in the first stages of infatuation with the drummer who would become the new man in her life. And the rest, as they say, was history.

While Lindsey was busy in the studio, I stayed home planning our first big party. For Fleetwood Mac, Halloween was the most important party night of the year. Actually it was the most important holiday of the year to us—a holiday that seemed tailor-made for the band and its court. After all, the five band members spent half their lives in costume, assuming their respective intense roles on stage as they toured the world relentlessly. Fleetwood Mac was all about costumes, hidden identities, and Gothic scenarios both on stage and off. So Halloween was kind of a no-brainer.

It was also a tradition for one of the band members to throw a huge bash. And this year the party was going to be at our house on June Street. Lindsey and I were both excited. With a guest list of the royalty of the entertainment industry, personal friends, and the entire Dodger baseball team, our home was overflowing with two hundred costumed and crazed party-goers on Halloween night.

It went down in band history as one of the best Halloween parties *ever.* Everyone was in full costume and the catered food went ignored as almost all of our guests helped themselves to the full bar and partook of their own personal stashes of illegal substances. Most of the executives left by eleven, and the party went into high gear: music blasting, people jumping into our pool, and others roller-skating across the polished wood floor of our huge living room.

Around midnight our front-door security man admitted a beautiful girl with long, brown hair into our foyer. As Stevie rushed to meet her I quietly asked Mick who she was. "Why, that's Sara Recor, Stevie's close friend. I'll try to introduce you when I get a chance, Carol. I know you'll like her," Mick replied as his eyes followed Stevie—not the girl with the long, brown hair.

Watching Sara climb our sweeping staircase with Stevie by her side, I studied her with interest. Then, distracted by another party guest, I soon forgot about her. But I'd be reminded soon enough. Within six weeks Sara would commit the ultimate *coup d'état,* turning Fleetwood Mac's soap-opera world upside down. And the next time I saw her she and I would discover that we were destined to become lifelong friends and allies.

Within two days of the party, a crime wave at our house began. As Lindsey worked at Village, I was spending the night at home alone, still recovering from our party. Upstairs ironing in front of the TV, I heard glass breaking down in the kitchen and the heart-stopping noises of someone walking through our house.

For the next fearful half-hour I locked myself in the bedroom, called the police, and sat on the floor, waiting in terror for help to arrive. After the LAPD thundered through our back door, I was told that an intruder had broken a window in the maid's quarters with the clear intent of burgling our house—and God knows what else if he found a woman alone. The arrival of police cars and sirens scared him away. Luckily for me, the heavily armed cops got there before the burglar made it upstairs to where I was hiding. As the police questioned me I told them of our recent party and they explained that although we lived on a beautiful street, the worst elements of Hollywood were only five minutes away. And the valets, limos, and beautiful people coming to our front door alerted every criminal in the area that ours was a house worth robbing. Lindsey came rushing home after my panicked call and we were told to put in an alarm system—immediately.

The next day we called an alarm company and had a $7,000 alarm system installed. We knew, of course, that our state-of-the-art system would only *warn* of us danger. It wouldn't keep it out. If someone wanted to get to us badly enough, then we were entirely dependent on how fast help could reach us. But for a while at least, it made us feel safe.

I spent the next two weeks in the studio with Lindsey. Alarm system or no alarm system, I hadn't gotten over the trauma of the break-in. It was much easier to not think of it as I sat, listened to the music of the next album, and partied along with Lindsey and the rest of the band and studio crew. But as much as I was relieved to be surrounded by the Fleetwood Mac family, the happy atmosphere that had existed in the studio a month before Halloween was no longer present. It had been replaced with an intense and strained mood. And it was pretty damn easy to figure out the source of all the tension. Stevie and Mick were barely speaking to each other. What had been such a love story only a month before had somehow gone terribly wrong.

Is it Jenny? Has Mick decided to go back to his wife after all? I wondered as I sat chewing my fingernail, trying to figure out what was behind the simmering tension that seemed to spark every time the two of them got within five feet of each other. *Mick seemed so in love with Stevie at our Halloween party! Obviously they've had a huge fight of some kind. But most fights get resolved within a few days, and whatever's wrong has been going on for two weeks now— at least as long as I've been here. I haven't seen Jenny, so I doubt if Mick's gone back to her. She would have put in an appearance in the studio by now. So what the hell has happened?*

Stevie wasn't talking about it. She was keeping pretty much to herself and not speaking to any of us. I could understand her not confiding in me— after all, she and I were still getting used to being friends. But she wasn't speaking to Christine or John or Richard either—at least not in the studio. She seemed angry, frustrated, and, from what I could tell, deeply hurt.

There was a look in her eyes that didn't go away: it was the look of a woman who felt betrayed. And although the communication between Stevie and I had finally, after almost two years, become comfortable, it wasn't on a level where I felt I could reach out to her and see if I could do anything to help. And even if it were, I had a feeling that whatever the problem was, there was nothing that any of us could do that would make it go away.

And I started to notice that Stevie was writing constantly in her notebook, her eyes following Mick as he walked back and forth across the studio. There was sadness in her gaze. Her eyes were so full of pain and tenderness that my heart ached when I looked at her. As she sat next to me on the couch I caught glimpses of what she was writing in her large leather-bound book and I saw that she was working on song lyrics. In a month those lyrics would belong to one of her greatest songs, "Angel." And it was all about Mick.

But before I heard the song, I'd already know what happened between them, and I'd know the reason behind her feeling of betrayal. I'd find that out the night I met the woman who would become my best friend for the next twenty-five years: Sara Recor.

12

DON'T SAY THAT YOU LOVE ME

As I stepped out into the dark, rainy night I hesitated before I punched in the alarm code outside our front door. Even though I'd been bored beyond belief at home in studio-widow solitude, Mick and Lindsey's solution to my restlessness left me with mixed feelings. They'd urged me to pay a first-time visit to Sara Recor, Mick's new live-in girlfriend.

I'd heard from Lindsey a couple of weeks earlier that Sara Recor had moved into Mick's mansion in Bel-Air. With this news, everything about Stevie's mood in the studio just a month before became crystal clear. Mick hadn't gone back to Jenny. He'd fallen in love with a new woman—a woman who was one of Stevie's close friends.

I felt a slight twinge of guilt as I climbed into my car. Was I betraying Stevie by going up for a friendly night with the girl who had supposedly broken up her relationship with Mick? I wasn't sure. But Lindsey and Mick wanted me to go and I shrugged off my uneasiness as I tried to justify going. *There are two sides to every story—and anyway, if it's weird when I get there, if I don't like her, then I'll just come home,* I thought as I drove through the streets of L.A. *I really have no idea what happened between the three of them, but I'm about to find out. In my place Stevie would do the same. It's the Fleetwood Mac way, after all. Everyone always knows everyone else's business—and this mystery needs to be solved.*

After a harrowing drive through the hard rain, I pulled up to Mick's open front gates in exclusive Bel-Air and drove as close as I could to the front of the huge house. Clamping my hat down tight on my head, I jumped out of my car and ran to the front door. Icy rain soaked through my clothes as I waited impatiently for Sara to answer it. Suddenly the door swung open and there she was, with a bright smile on a face surrounded by long, brown hair, dressed in a flowing dress that reached down to her bare feet. As we stood and looked at each other we somehow knew that we were kindred spirits. It would be, to quote *Casablanca*, "the beginning of a beautiful friendship."

Pulling me in out of the rain, Sara gave me a long hug and then pushed me away at arm's length, to look me up and down. "I was so excited when Mick called and told me you were coming! I'm so *bored* tonight!" And before we knew it, we were laughing and talking as though we'd always known each other. She immediately ran upstairs to grab a dress for me out of her closet to replace my soaked jeans and T-shirt and once I put it on, we stood side by side in one of the many full-length mirrors throughout Mick's house and started to giggle. We looked like sisters—one blonde, one brunette—but our facial features, hairdos, and the way we stood were almost identical.

After we were done admiring ourselves Sara led me into the living room, where the only light came from an open fire and a dozen candles sitting on the floor and on tables scattered throughout the exquisitely furnished room. As we sank down onto a rug in front of the fire Sara whispered into my ear, "Wait here! I have a surprise for you!"

She left the room briefly, returning with a plate containing a huge heap of cocaine. "Mick doesn't know this, but I found his secret stash!" With a silvery peal of laughter Sara quickly made a row of lines and handed me the plate. Snorting it up through a rolled-up dollar bill, I almost choked as the powder went straight up my nose and down my throat. After slapping me on the back, Sara handed me her glass of wine and I took a swallow, grimacing at the bitter taste.

Suddenly I noticed movement in the background, like a shadow that had crossed the doorway and then disappeared from sight. Before I could say anything Sara grabbed me by the shoulder. "She's doing it again!"

"Who is? Is there someone here with us?" I asked nervously. With the rain and the candles, the atmosphere conjured up a ghost story and I half expected to see a white apparition appear next to us at any second.

"It's Mick's secretary! She's always creeping around in the background. I feel like she's eavesdropping but I can never really prove it. It gives me the creeps. I don't think she likes me very much. Actually, I don't think anyone likes me very much, Carol," Sara told me with a forlorn note in her soft voice.

"I do," I said immediately, meaning it.

She gave me a hug, her eyes brightened for a second and then, with a sigh of resignation, she asked me if I'd like to know the story of how she and Mick fell in love. Once I'd heard it, she said, maybe then I'd understand why she felt so alone. I nodded and she reached out and took my hand, before telling me one of the most convoluted stories I'd ever heard.

She began by explaining that her husband was Jim Recor—Kenny Loggins's manager—and that although she was living with Mick, she was still technically Jim's wife. During the 1975 Loggins and Messina tour, Fleetwood Mac was the opening act at a few of their shows. It was during this time, Sara said, that a friendship was struck up between Jim Recor and Stevie Nicks on the road. Sara wasn't touring with her husband at the time, but she soon found out that Jim really, really liked Stevie. And Stevie liked him. Sara was modeling in New York when Jim flew there to see her. During that visit, he told her that he was very close to Stevie, but assured Sara that nothing untoward had happened between them. He raved about Stevie so much, Sara said, that it was a bit hard to take. But nonetheless, she took Jim at his word and tried not to worry about it. Jim urged her to meet Stevie and this put her mind at rest, because why would he suggest that if there were hanky-panky going on between them? Sara didn't want to go into it, but I got the feeling as she told me the story that there was more to it than she was willing to admit to me—or herself.

So Sara flew out, met Stevie, and introduced herself with the words, "So you're Jim's little road friend?"

We both burst out laughing, almost choking as we tried to catch our breath. Finally able to speak, I gasped, "Oh my God! You actually said that?"

"Yep. I didn't know her. And I didn't know if I wanted to . . . so yeah, I said that."

"What did Stevie say?"

"Well, not much, actually. She just kind of nodded and it was pretty awkward. She just kind of got up and left the room really fast." As we both began laughing again, Sara and I took a moment to savor the thought of Stevie Nicks at a loss for words, for this was not something that occurred often.

"Anyway," Sara continued, "Stevie and I slowly became friends and I really grew to love her. She's really special and we got along well. I mean, after a while, I didn't really care about what *might* have happened between my husband and Stevie—it was pretty much over between Jim and me at that point anyway. I mean, I love Jim and we're good friends, but that's what my marriage was about by then—*married* friends. And I know that at the very least Jim had a major crush on her—but whatever. Who wouldn't? So I didn't ask either of them, because I really didn't want to know. And I still don't."

Sara went on to tell me that by the time she came to our Halloween party, she was over at Stevie's house all the time. She said that she kept making eye contact with Mick on the night of our Halloween party and that she was immediately attracted to him. And that was when she first started falling for Mick. But because of his relationship with Stevie, she tried not to pursue it. But every time Mick came to see Stevie, she couldn't help but see him as she was always there with Stevie. And, well, sparks started to fly between Sara and Mick.

One day she and Mick were left alone in Stevie's house and they decided to go for a drive. Not just a drive to any old place. Oh no, that would have been too *normal*. Mick took her to the small house he'd bought for Jenny on Little Ramirez Canyon. That house was now vacant because Jenny had once again packed her bags and gone back to England with Mick's two daughters. He'd told her that his affair with Stevie was now over, but of course it wasn't and she rightly believed he was lying.

Once there, Mick declared his feelings for Sara and she for him. Neither of them wanted to hurt Stevie. And she didn't want to hurt her husband, with whom she was still living. Everyone involved felt like crap about destroying Jenny's world and it was a huge mess.

As Sara broke off to catch her breath and snort a line I sat open-mouthed, trying to keep it all straight in my head. I felt dizzy from trying to follow the trail of women and homes that all had one thing in common: Mick Fleetwood. But Sara wasn't finished with her story yet. The next thing, she said, is that she started spending as much time with Mick as she could, but there was still a big problem. She hadn't told her husband Jim that she'd fallen in love with Mick. And, of course, Mick and Jim were also friends!

So—to make a long story not that much shorter—Sara went home to pack her things to leave Jim for Mick, and when Mick came to pick her up and whisk her away to his castle, *that's* when Mick told Jim that he'd fallen for Jim's wife and he hoped that everyone could just be civilized about it. And believe it or not, everyone *was* civilized. Jim shook Mick's hand, said farewell to Sara, and in half an hour Sara and Mick were living together in blissful harmony.

Sitting in stunned silence, I had to admit that what Sara had just told me was one of the best stories I'd heard all year. But it was going to take me a little time to get all the details straight in my head. Because damn, that was one twisted circle.

Seeing the confused look on my face, Sara nodded and said, "It's a little much, isn't it? But what could I do, Carol Ann? Mick and I fell in love. It just happened. I love Stevie and I would never intentionally do anything to hurt her. But I fell in love."

As she stopped to take another line before she completed her story I watched Sara's face and saw her pain playing across it. I reached out and took her hand and held on tight. *Damn. Poor Sara. Poor Mick. Poor Jim. And poor Stevie*, I thought as my head started to ache a little—this story was beyond bizarre, even for Fleetwood Mac.

As happy as she was to be with Mick, Sara said, it had been hard for her. Everyone was angry with her, or seemed to be. All of the fallout from Mick's failed marriage, his breakup with Stevie, and Sara's own breakup with Jim seemed to be landing on *her* slender shoulders, not Mick's. At least half of the members of the Fleetwood Mac clan were friends of Jim and all of them were close to Stevie and Jenny. She told me that Mick's family *also* blamed her for his breakup with Jenny.

I looked at her in shock. *What the hell? What about his affair with Stevie? Did he keep this under wraps from his family and let them think that it was Sara—not Stevie—who was the catalyst for Jenny leaving Mick for the final time? That's really unfair!* I thought indignantly.

But in the world of Fleetwood Mac a band member was *never* blamed when something went wrong. It was *always* someone else's fault, not his or hers. It wasn't the *band* who asked for this absolution, but, asked for or not, it was given as a divine right by the band's inner circle as well as their blood relatives. So Sara was the bad guy in this situation from about fifty different angles—and she'd been feeling pretty damn friendless.

She and I forged a bond that night. I, too, knew what it felt like to be the new girl on the block. And I could easily empathize with her. Caught in the middle between Stevie and Lindsey, I had few friends in the band's inner circle for the first few months I was with him. It'd been only recently that I'd been able to count Stevie as a friend, and that friendship still felt very tenuous. Of course, I was still only *tolerated* by the girl fans around her.

But the other band members had welcomed me with open arms from the very beginning, and I had no doubt whatsoever that they would do the same with Sara. I told Sara all of this as we sat in front of the fire's dying flames. She smiled gratefully and gave me another hug.

"I hope so, Carol. I just want to be happy with Mick. I'm so glad that you came up tonight. I've really been feeling so, so alone," she quietly said.

"Just give Stevie some time," I told her. "Obviously the two of you have a deep bond of friendship—and even though *I* haven't been very close to her, I believe that Stevie will ultimately welcome you back with open arms."

The phone rang and we almost jumped out of our skin. We had been so engrossed that time had flown by. It was 3 A.M. and our guys were checking in. Both Mick and Lindsey told us to have fun and to stay up as long as we wanted, because neither of them would be home before 7 A.M. Sara and I spent the next few hours roaming all over Mick's house, trying to evade the lurking presence of his live-in secretary, and giggling and whispering like teenagers.

By the time I left for home at 6 A.M. I realized that I'd had more fun than I could remember having in quite a while. Having grown up with six sisters, I'd sorely missed having a girlfriend, and since I'd moved to Los Angeles straight out of high school I had spent my time surrounded by men. First I lived with John and our roommate Mike for five years, and then with Lindsey in his Putney home, with Richard and Bob in their rock 'n' roll fraternity. It'd been a long, long time since I'd spent a night doing "girl-friend" things with a woman that I had so much in common with. I silently thanked Mick for sending me up to his house to meet my new best friend.

As the weeks and months passed I began to spend more and more time hanging out at Mick's house with Sara, and less in the studio. It was starting to become a little boring for me at Village Recorder. It had also become very uncomfortable. The band was working on both Stevie's and Lindsey's songs and it was a battle scene in Studio D almost every single night.

The pattern was always the same. The sessions began peacefully enough. Everyone trooped through the door anywhere from 6 to 9 P.M., got his or her drinks, busted out the blow, and mostly fucked around until about 10 P.M. Then, when they finally began to get down to the business of recording music, I would get the dubious pleasure of seeing firsthand just how bad things must have been when they were making *Rumours*.

And it was not a pretty sight. On a balmy spring evening I decided to go with Lindsey and watch the band record—hoping that *this* night, at least, would be a happy one. But, as I found out again, happy nights in the studio were now few and far between.

Tonight Stevie had brought in one of her songs with melody and lyrics already laid down over a simple basic track. Even though it was obvious that the song needed to be recorded professionally, to me it already sounded great. But not good enough, apparently, for Lindsey.

Stevie, standing in the middle of the room, kept a serene smile on her face as the band listened to her new song, "Storms." As the last note faded away she looked around the room, waiting for the positive comments and feedback that she obviously felt the song would garner from everyone present. And then it all started to turn ugly.

With a slight twisted smile on his face, Lindsey drew first blood. Going over her new song bit by bit—pointing out how this part was crap, the next part needed to be raised or lowered by two octaves and this section desperately needed a new melody line—he tore it apart. By the time he was finished dissecting everything in detail about what was *wrong* with the song, he smiled serenely and said, "I like it, Stevie. It just needs some work, that's all."

As Stevie listened to Lindsey's comments you could almost see the steam coming off her. With sarcasm and hurt dripping from every word, she began to lash out at Lindsey and his suggestions. She knew what she wanted for her songs. And while she was more than willing to accept his input and his creative genius, she wouldn't let him take over her musical creations *completely*. She just wouldn't have it. And the end result was always the same: a snarling, vicious battle over her music.

For, without fail, the parts of a song that Lindsey didn't like or outright hated were the parts of that song that Stevie loved. Their angry debates would quickly escalate to a screaming match, with stomping around (by Lindsey) and tears (from Stevie). More cocaine was snorted, the liquor flowed, and, after a couple of hours of soothing talks by the other band members, Stevie headed out to the recording booth and Lindsey sat at the controls and, before you knew it, peace was restored. But the damage was done. For these fights left their bloody marks, over and over again. Added to the weight of the battle scars from Lindsey's and Stevie's past personal relationship, they made the atmosphere of the studio even uglier with each passing day.

And it got worse when it was time to work on Lindsey's songs. First of all, nobody *ever* said to Lindsey, "That part sucks, it's gotta go," even if they were right and the part in question sucked big time. There was an aura to Lindsey, a certain look in his eyes and way he walked into a room that screamed, "Don't fuck with me. I know what I want and no one can do this better than I can." And if some hapless person did disagree—if he or she had the guts to speak out—then that person had better be ready for the hellish fallout. For it would surely come. In sharp words that came fast and furious, Lindsey reduced whoever spoke out to a shell-shocked mass of quivering humanity. He didn't need to threaten to quit the band, for his intrinsic value to Fleetwood Mac was there for all to see. His genius was not disputed. It was *his* artistic input that polished and put the guitar riffs into some of the band's most famous songs. Without him those riffs and harmonies would never have materialized. And everyone knew that there was a very good chance that those songs wouldn't have gone to number one on *Billboard*.

Lindsey was a hit maker. His genius at producing was recognized by all, as was his volatile personality. He could be the gentlest, sweetest person in the room and, in a heartbeat, turn into your worst enemy. And when that happened, believe me, you'd give anything not to be on the receiving end of his angry disdain. Lindsey commanded in the studio—and by April he ruled.

On most of his songs he completed almost all of the basic recording in the studio at our house on June Street. There were, of course, parts that needed to be recorded or backtracked in Studio D. And every single note, whether a vocal or a bass or a drum part, was done exactly to Lindsey's specifications. Standing over John as he put down a bass part on a song, Lindsey played the part *for* him and then insisted that he copy every note as closely as was humanly possible. The same happened with Mick and the drum sections on Lindsey's masterpieces.

It was really painful and embarrassing for everyone in the studio to witness two great musicians having their musical input dictated and orchestrated by Lindsey. To say that neither John nor Mick appreciated being told what and how to play was to put it mildly. The resentment and animosity was so thick that it hung in the air like the black, swirling mists of J. R. R. Tolkien's Mordor. Put all of this together with the fuel of alcohol, cocaine, and exhaustion from the all-night sessions and things were not good.

And none of us was immune to this seething, intense environment. We were all suffering. Unhappy people breed unhappy lives, and the mood of the studio was carried home. Every single member of the Fleetwood Mac family was struggling to survive the sessions with their relationships and sanity intact.

Hanging over it all was the unanswered question: how would the public react to the new sound that Lindsey's avant-garde musical direction had created for the band? It didn't matter that Stevie's and Christine's songs sounded similar to the ones on *Rumours*—it was Lindsey's departure from the Fleetwood Mac sound that had changed the new record radically, so that the Fleetwood Mac album that the public was waiting for was *not being recorded*.

What was being recorded, thanks to Lindsey, was a whole new Fleetwood Mac sound. And that made the album an unknown quantity—and an unknown risk. The tension that the entire band was feeling about how the record would be received by the world, and by Warner Bros., had become a living, dangerous presence within Studio D.

Lindsey was waiting to be its first victim. He was just as aware as every other band member of how his new songs had changed the sound of the album. That was his aim. But as positive as he was that he was right in changing his musical direction, it was a heavy burden for him to bear. He knew that if the album failed, it was his head on the cutting block.

It could become known as "Buckingham's Folly" or maybe something far less polite. We spoke of it often when we were home alone, and it took every ounce of support I had to bolster his decision to let his talent take him wherever it needed to go. Not because he didn't know how great his songs were, but because the pressure of doing the album was overwhelming. And when artists are overwhelmed, doubt about their creations is an understandable byproduct.

But it wasn't all bad times. Good things were happening as well. Christine was head over heels in love with Dennis Wilson. He had moved into her home just off Coldwater Canyon, and I didn't believe I'd ever seen her so happy. While she, too, had doubts and worries about the album, she had Dennis to distract her. And Dennis Wilson was some kind of distraction, that's for sure. He was a party monster. Able to drink and drug just about any member of the Fleetwood Mac family under the table, he did so with regularity and charm.

Before Sara and I knew it, he began to become a normal fixture at Mick's house in Bel-Air on our "girlfriend" nights. He'd chosen to hang out with us instead of in the now-claustrophobic studio with the band, and we welcomed him with open arms. Who wouldn't? We began to call ourselves "The Three Widows" in reference to our mates being otherwise fixated on their music instead of us—and we made the most of it. Which wasn't hard.

As the sun was setting one crisp fall day, Sara and I glanced through her upstairs window to see a gorilla sitting in a black convertible Rolls-Royce Corniche, waving gaily as we stuck our heads outside. With screams of hysterical laughter we watched as Dennis, dressed in a full black-fur gorilla suit, climbed out of his car, gesturing for us to come down and join him. Running barefoot to the front lawn, we climbed into his car and went for a spin through the tony streets of Bel-Air with our gorilla chauffeur alternating grunts and Tarzan yells.

On other nights Dennis regaled Sara and me with stories of his seemingly endless history of sexual exploits. It seemed to me that he'd bedded about half of the attractive women in Los Angeles.

We also got to listen to stories about Dennis and his time spent with the Manson family. This wasn't so funny; it was both fascinating and frightening. It all began when Dennis picked up a couple of girls on Sunset Boulevard and took them to his mansion on that street. He left them there while he went to a recording session and got a huge surprise when he returned. Climbing out of his car, he was shocked to see a small man literally stumbling out of his house. It was Charles Manson. Falling to the ground, he kissed Dennis's feet. While thinking this was bizarre, Dennis said, he just thought Manson was another harmless acidhead.

He told us that he actually didn't mind having Manson and his family of women and hangers-on living in his home—at first. They cooked, cleaned, and kept Dennis entertained sexually. But as the weeks passed, his house became a commune, with over a dozen people coming and going at will. Manson's charisma was so strong that Dennis fell under his spell for a short period of time. And before he knew what hit him, he was deep in a bizarre and frightening situation.

As Sara and I listened in rapt attention Dennis talked in a hushed tone. "I probably spent over $100,000 on them—food, drugs, alcohol, clothes, doctor bills for their STDs. You name it, I paid for it. One of the Manson family guys totaled my Mercedes, which wasn't insured. In the beginning, there was music and singing and it was like living in hippie paradise—in a twisted way. Charles Manson considered himself an artist and I even recorded some songs of his. He was a horrible singer! But that music, Carol, was not of this earth. It was scary. I hated it and I destroyed the tapes. And I just knew that I had to get away from those people. It wasn't fun any more—it was fuckin' weird. With the help of my manager, I got them evicted from my house on Sunset."

A shadow crossed Dennis's handsome face whenever he spoke of Manson. Much to his everlasting relief, he made his escape from the Manson family before the horrific world-famous Sharon Tate and La Bianca murders. I could tell as he spoke that he was still deeply disturbed that he'd ever crossed paths with Charles Manson. And I knew that if he'd still had any kind of a relationship with him at the time of the gruesome murders, then he more than likely would never have gotten over it. It was terrifying to comprehend what self-imposed guilt by association would have done to Dennis Wilson's psyche. Because Dennis Wilson was the type of person who loved life, music, and people—the innate evil of a personality such as Manson's almost scarred him for life.

On nights when it was just Sara and me, we spent our time making cassette tapes of our conversations, in which we talked about our lives, adventures, and opinions on anything and everything that was happening in the realm of Fleetwood Mac. One of these tapes would, in a year's time, be the catalyst for one of the most horrific fights I'd ever experience with Lindsey. But, at the time, we felt that they were harmless and greatly enjoyed recording and listening to ourselves. After all, with all of the recording equipment at our disposal, it was only natural that we should make use of it.

Christine, Lindsey, and Mick were so preoccupied with the album that it was hard to tell what, if any, opinion they had of Sara, Dennis, and me hanging out together constantly. It seemed to Sara and me that they were probably relieved that we were not lonely or bored—or worse, running around to L.A. nightclubs while they toiled in the studio. Anyway, they never told us *not* to hang out together.

On some nights Dennis would bring Ed Roach along and the four of us would have a blast. Ed was one of Dennis's childhood friends. He was handsome, perennially tanned, and had the same cavalier, dashing presence as his buddy Dennis. Already a renowned photographer, he would become an L.A. club owner and entrepreneur in the years to come.

Jackson Browne also paid us a visit, espousing his latest political cause: nuclear energy. On that night, Stevie and Jim Recor also joined us and the sound of cocaine being sniffed could be heard in almost every room of Mick's house, as could the sound of Jackson's earnest voice trying to convince all of us that nuclear energy was not a good thing. It wasn't exactly the kind of light topic that any of us wanted to discuss while wired on blow at 1 A.M., but nevertheless, it seemed that that was the only thing on his mind.

As Sara and I listened, trying vainly to stifle our giggles, he was in a frenzy trying to convince Stevie and Dennis that they needed to contribute thousands of dollars to his anti-nuclear organization instead of to the "establishment" causes of heart and cancer research that Fleetwood Mac generously supported with their dollars. What had us so hysterical was that every time he tried to say nuclear, he would pronounce it "nu-cu-lar" or "nec-leer" instead of "noo-kle-er." And he was completely oblivious to our snickers as Stevie rolled her eyes and Dennis sneered every time the word came out of Jackson's mushy mouth. Finally, after realizing that no one was going to whip out their checkbooks and give money to his "anti-nec-leer" cause, he wandered off to his car and left us alone.

I didn't spend every night with Sara and Dennis. I continued my modeling shoots with Bjorn, putting the finishing touches to my portfolio, and at least three times a week I accompanied Lindsey to the studio. Sara joined me there, and as I'd predicted, she was made welcome by almost all of the band—except, of course, Stevie. While Stevie wasn't outright hostile, it was obvious that she wasn't thrilled to see Sara walk through the doors of the inner sanctum.

But Sara had an excellent excuse for being there, one that overrode any objections of Stevie's. Mick had been diagnosed with hypoglycemia and a mild form of diabetes. After weeks of being struck by uncontrolled bouts of shaking and weakness, he reached out for medical help and got the bad news. He was under strict orders to completely change his diet. Every night Sara made special health-food dinners at home and delivered them to the studio for Mick.

She dressed up in gorgeous outfits each and every time she came down, and it drove Stevie wild. One night, as Sara and I sat on the couch, Stevie walked over and told her that she would appreciate it if Sara didn't dress up so much for her visits. The whole band found it "distracting," she claimed. Since Stevie herself dressed head to toe in velvet, chiffon, and silk, it was all we could do not to burst out in hysterical laughter. With a sweet smile Sara nodded her head and got a curt nod in response. The next night Sara arrived looking as if she'd stepped out of the pages of *Vogue*. And Stevie was not amused.

One night, as on so many others, the partying had gotten completely out of control. We were all having a blast. Cocaine was being snorted like there was no tomorrow, the cognac was flowing, and by dawn no one was ready to call it a night. "Transcend, everyone! Transcend!" Mick cackled as everyone did their best to follow his instructions. Christine suggested that we all go to her house to continue our wild party. This invitation was met with almost unanimous cries of glee. Lindsey, however, said he wanted to call it a night. Telling me that I should go if I wanted to, he waved goodbye in the parking lot as I climbed into Christine's car to follow the convoy that was already on its way to Coldwater Canyon.

Dennis was at Christine's, waiting with relish, as the entire studio clan climbed out of their cars and spilled into the house. The insanity continued until the early afternoon—until Christine blurted out that she had a children's birthday party scheduled in two hours. Reacting in horror, the inner circle quickly dispersed and went running for the hills. The mere thought of being around children after an entire night and day of hard-core partying was more than any of us could bear. But I didn't have my car. I was stuck.

Before Christine headed up to shower for the party, she asked Dennis and me to run to the store for ice and sodas. Grateful for a reason to be gone when the guests started to arrive, Dennis and I hightailed it out of there in two minutes flat. Instead of driving straight to the store as we were sup-posed to, Dennis told me that he needed to stop by his permanently rented hotel room at the Hilton on Sunset to pick up a few supplies. Once there, we snorted some lines of blow and started talking. Before we knew it, over two hours had flashed by and we were in big trouble with Christine.

We sheepishly pulled up her driveway and found out within seconds that she was livid. She wouldn't talk to either of us, and I can't say that I blamed her. But, damn, if anyone should understand how time flies after so many hours of nonstop partying, you'd think she would. But no, she was pissed off and Dennis and I were *persona non grata* at the birthday bash.

Not to worry, Dennis told me. He was playing a show with the Beach Boys that night at the Universal Amphitheatre and he got down on one knee and asked me to be his official "date." As we both started to giggle I accepted and told him I'd go if he made sure that Christine didn't mind. She came upstairs and told me that while she was not amused by our two-hour absence, she didn't care if I went with Dennis. She couldn't go anyway, she said; the all-nighter and birthday party had been enough for her. "I'll tell Lindsey when he calls where you've gone. I hope he doesn't mind that you're going alone with Dennis."

Looking at her in surprise, I answered, "Of course he won't mind, Chris. He *loves* the Beach Boys. I'd think he'd be more upset if I *didn't* go!"

After borrowing a skirt from Christine, I hastily reapplied my makeup and within half an hour I was seated next to Dennis in his black convertible Rolls-Royce Corniche. It was late afternoon and eighty degrees, and with the Stones blasting out from the cassette player we drove down the twisted canyon road of Coldwater. Handing me a mirror and a plastic packet of cocaine, Dennis told me to dump the coke on to the mirror's surface.

"But we're going fifty miles an hour, Dennis! It's all going to blow away!" I yelled over the ear-splitting volume of "Midnight Rambler."

"That's what makes it fun!" Dennis shouted back with a huge grin on his face. "Live for the moment, Carol Ann. And this is a perfect moment in time. Dump the fucker, snort what you can, and pass it over here!" Laughing, I did as he said and felt the warm wind blowing through my hair as I held the mirror for Dennis. Driving with one hand, he leaned over and snorted directly off the mirror without the aid of straw or dollar bill—and we both laughed hysterically as the white powder softly blew away in puffs like tiny clouds around us. Laying the mirror on the floor, Dennis and I held hands and sang along with the Stones as our long hair flew behind us.

He's right, I said to myself, *this is a perfect moment and as long as I live I will never, ever forget it. I'm driving with a Beach Boy on a beautiful day in a Rolls-Royce on the way to his concert. It's a moment that millions of people would give anything to experience.* And I felt sublimely happy as we pulled up to the Universal Amphitheatre.

Backstage, Dennis got changed and I wandered around the dressing room as late afternoon changed to twilight. Carl and Brian Wilson entered from the outside stage area and Dennis ran out to greet his brothers. They were like giant teddy bears. Carl was so gracious and sweet that I found it hard to believe that he'd been in the music industry as long as he had. When Dennis introduced me to Brian, I stood tongue-tied in front of him. An aura of greatness radiated from the man. I shyly whispered, "Hello," and got a gentle smile in return.

Ten minutes later I was walking with Dennis to the stage area, excited over the show I was about to see. As we reached the platform, Mike Love, a Beach Boy cousin and off-and-on lead singer, walked up to Dennis and snarled, "You missed the fucking sound check—again!"

Without a blink of an eye, Dennis balled up his fist, raised his arm, and knocked Mike out cold. Lying crumpled in a little skinny heap, Love was administered to by the band's roadies as Dennis watched with a blank look on his face.

Shit! I can't believe he just did that! Lindsey told me that the two of them didn't get along, but damn! I can't believe that Dennis just friggin' knocked him on his ass! Oh my God! I thought. I didn't know if I should laugh or scold Dennis. After five minutes Mike Love struggled to his feet, glared at Dennis, and jumped onto the stage. Dennis winked at me and took his place behind the drums.

The show was fabulous and halfway through it Christine joined me. She told me that she felt obligated to Lindsey to act as a "chaperone" since she placed me in Dennis's care. *Whatever,* I thought to myself. Although I didn't take Lindsey's territorial issues about me lightly, I had the feeling that it was more a case of Christine wanting to chaperone us for her sake. But I was glad to have her company and when I got home later that night Lindsey listened to every detail and laughed himself sick over the Mike Love incident.

Two weeks later Christine called and asked me if I'd like to have a "sleepover" with her. The band was in the studio and she wasn't, she said.

With Lindsey's blessing, I arrived at her house and we stayed up all night laughing, gossiping, and partying Fleetwood Mac style. Lindsey called a few times and I had no indication that he was anything other than happy that I was with his bandmate. That would change.

The next morning I was upstairs in Christine's bedroom picking up my things and preparing to leave when I heard the screech of brakes in the driveway. Looking out the window, I was startled to see Lindsey's car. Dropping my purse, I hurried to the stairs and had almost reached the bottom when Lindsey stepped through the doorway.

"Lindsey! What's—" My words were cut off as Lindsey raised his arm and hit me hard enough to knock me off the staircase into the wall. I landed in a crumpled heap on the floor. Without uttering a word, he then turned on his heel and strode back out the door.

Too stunned to even cry out, I struggled to my feet and with halting footsteps followed him out onto the driveway. Lindsey was already seated in his car staring at me with a look of rage on his face. I was reeling in disbelief over what had just happened. And it felt as though I'd just been thrown into someone else's reality—for this just wasn't, *just couldn't,* be mine.

Without conscious thought, I ran toward him and leaned next to the car window, screaming, "Lindsey, what are you *doing*? You said that you were glad I was at Christine's! Why are you so angry? *Why?* I didn't do anything wrong—" Before I could say another word, he grabbed a fistful of my hair and floored the gas. Jerked forward, I desperately tried to hold onto the car door as I was dragged by the hair down Christine's driveway. I could hear her screaming, "Lindsey, *stop the car!* Stop! *Stop!*" over the sound of Lindsey's voice muttering unintelligible words as I stumbled to my knees, still trying to hold on.

Then I was falling as Lindsey finally let go and the gray of pavement filled my vision as I hit the ground. And suddenly it was quiet. I felt hands helping me to my feet and through blurred eyes I saw Christine's startled face as she asked me over and over if I was OK. I couldn't speak. I didn't cry. I was too shell-shocked to do either. There was a burning sensation in my scalp and I raised my hand to my head and it came away sticky, smeared with blood. I didn't feel anything else. I didn't feel pain, I didn't feel hysterical. I felt numb. And I welcomed it.

Strangely proud that I was able to walk, I turned and slowly made my way back upstairs and found my purse, a now-silent, white-faced Christine following behind. Mumbling an apology to her and goodbye, I used the wall for support as I went back down the stairs and out to my car.

I drove to the Century Plaza Hotel in Beverly Hills—a hotel that Lindsey and I often stayed at when we wanted to get away for a night—and shakily walked to the front desk. The manager took one look at my face and my bloody hair and asked in a shocked tone, "Ms. Harris, can I help? Do you need a doctor?"

"Please, just a room. I just need a room," I answered as I struggled to keep it together in front of him as he slid a hotel key across the desk. Walking unsteadily to the elevator, I slipped inside and shrank back into a corner as it rose to my floor. Closing the door of the room behind me, I walked slowly to the bed and almost collapsed onto it. And I cried. I cried for what felt like hours. My heart was breaking. I felt so lost and so alone and my mind kept going back to an image of Lindsey's face as he grabbed my hair and wrapped it in his fist . . .

The room had grown dark as I lay curled on the bed and the sound of laughter in the hallway brought me out of the semi-trance that I'd fallen into. I wearily rose and stumbled into the bathroom and turned on the light. I had to grip the sink as I stared at my face in shock. There were streaks of dried blood across a face so white that it seemed carved from alabaster. Haunted eyes stared back at me from the mirror, and I had to turn away from my reflection as I felt nausea course through me. Turning on the taps of the bathtub, I stripped off my clothes and climbed carefully into the bath . . . staring at nothing as the water gently rose around me.

My knees began to sting from the cuts and abrasions that laced across them and I winced in pain as I carefully soaped off the dried blood. My body ached and I had to force myself to slip down and soak my scalp—I tried to brace myself for the pain, but I gasped as my head started to burn in the warm water. Sitting up, I ran my fingers carefully through my hair and was stunned to see that my hands were full of strands of blonde hair that had obviously been torn from my head on Chris's driveway. And the sight of it, the *impossibility* of it, threatened to send me into hysterics. Taking deep breaths, I forced myself to remain calm. *You're OK, Carol, you're OK,* I kept saying over and over as I stepped out of the bath and wrapped myself in the large white hotel towels folded neatly on a wire rack.

I walked slowly back to the bed, pulled back the covers, and slipped in. *It's the album . . . the pressure has just made him crazy, that's all . . . It's just like after the Elvis Costello show,* I said to myself as I lay in the dark. *I didn't do anything wrong . . . I spoke to him several times while I was at Christine's and he seemed happy that I was there . . . and I know he didn't mean to hurt me. Lindsey loves me—he loves me and I know that he didn't mean it . . . that wasn't my Lindsey today . . . it just wasn't. I'll try harder to make it better for him . . . because this has to be my fault . . . I don't know how it is, but he wouldn't just do this without a reason, would he? Would he?* I forced the thoughts out of my head, too tired now to do anything but sleep.

The next day I stayed in bed, listlessly watching television, doing my best not to think of Lindsey or what had happened the day before. I felt detached from it—and just like after the night of the Elvis Costello show, I was glad to be numb.

At eight the next morning, there was a soft knock on the door. It was Lindsey. I opened the door and he took me into his arms, murmuring over and over that he loved me. He led me back to bed and climbed in beside me. Gently stroking my hair, he clung to me as I lay in his arms. There would be no apology—no explanation for what happened at Christine's. Only soft words of love and caring touches that made it hard to believe that any of it had ever happened. And I clung to the sound of his voice and the touch of his hand, as I told myself over and over that it would never ever happen again—for it was obvious that I was loved . . . wasn't it? I assured myself that I was and fell asleep in the dark, dark room.

After months of recording, the band hired Peter Beard (who was married to supermodel Cheryl Tiegs) to design and photograph the new album's inner sleeves. World famous for his photo-diary books and montages that focused mainly on elephants in Africa, he was, the band felt, the perfect man for the job, as the album had been named *Tusk.* To Fleetwood Mac it was a word that was regularly used in reference to a man's "male member" and every guy in the band unanimously accepted the album title. Stevie hated it and even threatened to quit Fleetwood Mac if the album was called *Tusk*, but her threats fell on unhearing ears and when all was said and done, she accepted the inevitable and lived with the majority vote.

Peter was in the studio for two weeks, shooting mainly Polaroids of the band and the inner circle. Resembling Peter O'Toole in *Lawrence of Arabia*, he was funny and a blast to have around. At one point he whispered into my ear, "Carol, I'm going to make your picture the biggest shot on the inner sleeve—wouldn't that be fun?" As I blushed and murmured, "Yes!" he winked and gave me a hug.

When the album cover design was finished, I'd find that a Polaroid shot of me was indeed bigger than any of the pictures of the band that Peter had taken. I looked like a misbehaving twelve-year-old in the shot and Lindsey loved it. Peter seemed unfazed by the amount of drugs that were everywhere in the studio, and I got the feeling that he saw us as just another species of wild creature to capture in his camera's lens.

Even though sometimes it wasn't that much fun because of the tension, I was starting to once again really love being in the studio with Lindsey. I wanted to be there to support him and, of course, hear the almost-finished music that would be on what had now become a double album. After much debate, the members of Fleetwood Mac had decided that they just had too many great songs to leave *any* of them off *Tusk*. Twenty to be exact. There was concern coming from Warner Bros. about the high list price of a double album, but then again, after the astronomical success of *Rumours,* the record company wasn't really in a position to object. Fleetwood Mac could do what it wanted. And what the band wanted to do was a double album.

As I listened to the nearly finished tracks I couldn't believe how amazing the record was. Because of Lindsey's songs it was a cutting-edge album, and he was really happy with it. To say that Mick was still apprehensive was an understatement. He was freaking. Even now, with the record almost finished after a *year* in the studio, he was *still* trying to convince Lindsey to change his songs, to tone them down. He tried everything, from calm talks to bitter fights, in his efforts to convince Lindsey to infuse his songs with the more traditional Fleetwood Mac sound—and Lindsey adamantly refused, over and over again.

The irony of this would be obvious to every member of the Fleetwood Mac family. It was Mick who first dreamed up the drum riff for the song

"Tusk." With Lindsey's screams, moans, and grunts over a jangled basic track, it was arguably the most radical cut on the album. And, with the *pièce de résistance* of recording the University of Southern California Trojan Marching Band at Dodger Stadium, it screamed "cutting edge."

With sound trucks full of recording equipment set up inside the perimeter of the stadium, the marching band, in full regalia, gave a brilliant performance on the field as it played along with the basic track and vocals to the playback of the studio-recorded "Tusk." There was a video crew shooting the entire day to get live footage that would be turned into a promo video for the song, the first single taken from the album.

Mick Fleetwood at Dodger Stadium.

All of us were there except for John McVie. To represent him, the band had made a life-size cardboard cutout to stand in the middle of Dodger Stadium. Having completed his bass parts, John was sailing to Hawaii with three friends—a trip that caused a great deal of worry for some of the Fleetwood Mac family. The boat was as well supplied with party treats as it was with food and water. I, for one, shuddered to think of what could happen to its potentially inebriated crew.

We would find out days later that John and his friends were almost capsized in the middle of the Pacific Ocean by a whale. It was a very close call and the other band members were shocked at how close they came to losing their beloved bass player forever.

In between getting takes of the marching band, the film crew moved about the field with handheld video cameras, shooting Fleetwood Mac throughout the day: Lindsey and Christine in USC Trojan helmets goofing with the students, Stevie twirling a baton with aplomb—a hidden talent that surprised us all. That she had the energy was in itself a miracle. She'd told me that she hadn't slept the night before the recording and video shoot and I watched in admiration as she breezed through the day—with, no doubt, a little help from the band's favorite energy booster.

Julie, Stevie, Robin Snyder, and I laced on roller skates around 3 P.M. and spent over an hour skating the perfect circle of concrete hallways above the seats in the stadium. Celebration was in the air. Not only was this track turning out to be brilliant, the album was almost finished! There was still some post-production work to be done in the studio, but the recording of the actual tracks was almost complete. The band had spent close to $1 million during the year that it had taken to record *Tusk*, and that's without including the $1.4-million cost of building Studio D.

Warner Bros. had informed the band that *Tusk* would need sales of close to 500,000 just to break even. But no one was worried, and at this point the band didn't care about how much money the album cost to make. All they cared about right then was that it was almost done, and they were individually thrilled with how their own personal tracks sounded. Within the band there was still controversy over the new sound of the record, along with a lot of concern about how the public would respond to *Tusk* when it was released in September, not to mention what the Warner Bros. executives were going to think when they heard the finished album. For none of them had heard it yet. The band had stuck to its exclusive "no access" policy throughout the entire year.

A short time later, the Warner executives were seated around a large conference table in a boardroom at company headquarters, anxiously waiting to hear the new album in its entirety. As we walked into the large room at the record company I held tightly on to Lindsey's hand. He'd said little on the drive there, but I could feel nervous excitement radiating from him as we took our seats among the already assembled members of Fleetwood Mac and Warner's top brass. After a few minutes of small talk, the first track, "Over and Over," blasted out of the hidden speakers in the room, and then the rest of the nineteen songs were played straight through. No one in the room said a word. After the final note faded away I looked around at the businessmen and every single one of them looked stunned.

A few had weak smiles plastered on their faces, but all in all it was obvious that, as Lindsey would so succinctly put it once we were on our way back home, "They're seeing their Christmas bonuses fly out of the window." The Warner Bros. executives, who told the band that they liked the record, gave hasty and subdued congratulations to Fleetwood Mac. But no one was fooled. The record company was sorely disappointed that it didn't get another *Rumours*-type album and it seemed that its executives simply didn't know what to say.

The meeting adjourned quickly, and as Lindsey and I headed home he made a few other choice remarks as he laughed bitterly over their reaction. As we stopped for a red light I leaned over and kissed him passionately.

"Lindsey, I am so proud of you," I told him. "I think your songs are absolutely brilliant! I can't wait for the release of *Tusk*! Just wait and see—everyone is going to be blown away by your music. Your music is like the Clash and Talking Heads—and that's exactly what you wanted. You did it, baby. You did it."

With a rueful laugh Lindsey smiled brightly for the first time that day. "Yeah, I guess I did, didn't I? I don't know about the world, but I'm happy with my music . . . and as you and I always said, that's all that matters to me."

13

STAR POWER

"Let's hope that Christine makes it to the shoot without being pulled over by the LAPD," I said with a smirk as Lindsey and I stood in front of the large antique mirror hanging above the dressing table in our bedroom.

Lindsey rolled his eyes at the memory of Christine's encounter with the NYPD a few weeks before and let out a loud guffaw as I gave him a glimpse of my lace underwear. After that unfortunate but undeniably funny event at the Richard Avedon shoot in New York, I'd been meticulous about wearing my best undies every single day of the week.

As Christine's misadventure proved, you just never knew what could happen to a girl innocently on her way to an album cover shoot trying to have a little wake-me-up in the back of a limo. Her close call and humiliating body search by the coppers in Manhattan wreaked havoc during the first album cover shoot for *Tusk*. Her near-arrest for possession of an illegal substance—which led to the now-infamous "granny knickers" being on display at NYPD headquarters—had now become yet another private band legend. And a warning to us all to never, ever get caught without your Sunday-best lingerie.

Christine with photographer Ed Roach.

Today's shoot was with the renowned photographer Norman Seeff. The band would be shot in an oceanfront house in Malibu with a call time at noon. It was 11 A.M., and I reeled in horror as Lindsey stomped out of our walk-in closet.

"I don't have a damn thing to wear. Nothin', Carol. I don't want to wear just the same old shit I've been wearing in the studio all year. What am I gonna do?"

Oh, I don't believe it! I thought he was going to wear jeans and a white shirt! That's what he said a few days ago! It's Sunday! Maxfield's isn't open! It's not like I can go to a friggin' department store and find a cool look for him in the men's section. Dammit! I said to myself, as I struggled to keep my frustration hidden. I narrowed my eyes as I looked over Lindsey's clothes, now tossed haphazardly all over the closet. "Your white shirts are totally trashed! You're right, you don't have one shitty thing to wear!"

Chewing my fingernail, I suddenly got an idea. "Here's what we can do, Lindsey. You take the limo to the beach and I'll take my car and go to Country Club Fashions. I mean, it's a women's store, but they carry a lot of designer labels and I know I'll find something that will work for the shoot. Don't worry—as long as it looks cool and fits, that's all that matters, right?"

With a smile Lindsey nodded in agreement just as the doorbell rang. The limo had arrived and as Lindsey climbed into the back seat I jumped into my car and raced off to Century City and my third-favorite store in L.A., Country Club Fashions. I quickly told the manager my predicament and we raced around the racks and found two jackets that were perfect: one single-breasted in tweed, the other a short, dark-green satin, military-style jacket in size forty-six. Unable to resist, I grabbed two jackets that matched them, in my size. Throwing all four items on the counter, I grabbed a couple of satin pirate shirts in silver and green and looked desperately at the clock. It was after one and I was still forty-five minutes from the shoot location. *Please let the clothes fit!* I chanted as I ran to my car and hit the gas.

The house in Malibu that was being used for the shoot was large and mostly unfurnished. Outside there was a beautiful gazebo overlooking the ocean and it was here that Norman wanted to do the pictures. Lindsey loved his new clothes and they fit perfectly. It was barely noticeable that they buttoned on the wrong side, and who cared? He looked great and that was all that mattered.

The day raced by and all of us were having a good time. Except, of course, for poor Norman Seeff. Every single time he got the band in position for a picture, he turned his back and one of them slipped away. Each had their own private agenda: they needed a drink, a toot, or a pee. By the end of the long shoot he was about to tear his hair out. The band was happy when they saw the pictures and Seeff had retained his status as genius photographer—even if the day had been complete bedlam.

The next week saw the third and final shoot for *Tusk*, with photographer Jayme Odgers doing the honors. The set was a room with furniture fixed to the ceiling and floor. It was a great concept and thanks to darkroom tricks and band contortions, the pictures were great. The work of all three photographers— Beard, Seeff, and Odgers—combined for the sleeve of *Tusk* and it was a masterpiece. Everyone agreed, however, that it was the shot of a visiting random dog biting a hapless second engineer's pant leg in Studio D that was the best shot of them all, and it was chosen for the front cover of the new double album.

Mick and Lindsey on set at a Tusk *photo shoot.*

After the shoots the band was notified that it was to receive a star on the Hollywood Boulevard Walk of Fame. Not only would they get a star, but Los Angeles Mayor Tom Bradley had declared that that day would officially be Fleetwood Mac Day. The USC Trojan Marching band would be there; Mo Ostin, chairman of Warner Bros., would give a speech at the presentation; and hundreds of fans were expected. It was a great honor, of course, but there was one tiny embarrassing detail. Fleetwood Mac's star was located right in front of Frederick's of Hollywood lingerie store. It was a store known worldwide for racy underwear that was the stuff of male fantasies—undies that were a stripper's dream and a Bible-Belt mother's worst nightmare.

Entering through the back entrance of the store, Lindsey and I sniggered as we threaded our way through the racks of lacy bras, crotchless panties, and feather boas. After walking to the front of the store and going outside, we turned and got a look at the unavoidable backdrop for the band and we almost died. The display window of mannequins dressed in lurid attire was so cheesy that it almost turned Fleetwood Mac's big moment into an X-rated farce.

Lindsey tried to keep a straight face during Ostin's dedication speech, but he soon lost his battle. After the star was unveiled and Stevie stepped up to the microphone and said, "Thank you for believing in the crystal visions. Crystal visions really do come true," Lindsey grabbed my arm and we both burst out laughing. I mean, we knew she was saying it from the heart, but it was just *so Stevie* to throw out her "crystal vision" line at every opportunity that we both cringed—and quoting it against a backdrop of push-up bras and fuck-me heels gave it a double entendre that smacked of stand-up comedy. After a few minutes Lindsey whispered into my ear that we had to get out of there, and we made a mad dash back through the unmentionables and into our car. Once there, we laughed hysterically for a full five minutes.

Later that night, a gala listening party for *Tusk* was held in Beverly Hills for over two hundred guests. It was a crazed scene and both Lindsey and I had a blast. Brian Wilson was there and Lindsey spent much of the night trying to talk to him. Brian was a man of few words, however, and for the most part Lindsey had to be content to just be in his presence. The rest of the time we wandered through the crowd as the record blasted. There was a lot to celebrate, and in typical Fleetwood Mac fashion, we did it until 3 A.M.

The band had booked six weeks' rehearsal time at SIR Studios for the *Tusk* tour. Only this time the soundstage was twice as big as the one used for the *Rumours* rehearsals. For this tour *everything* was being done on a scale that made the *Rumours* tour look like a poor man's road trip. There was a masseuse on staff for the rehearsals and the daily buffet was lavish, with food that went untouched and champagne that didn't. The road crew and personal security team had doubled, new backdrops were being made, and there was a mountain of new sound equipment with bright red anvil cases to hold it.

There was a new addition to the stage that everyone was thrilled about. Two black tents were being made that would be erected every night on either side of the stage. Each approximately ten feet by ten feet, one would hold Stevie's unending costume changes and both would be used by the band during breaks in the show for their private refreshments—both liquid and powder. Sara, Julie, and I would have unlimited access to the tents during the shows and while we never got in the band's way (much), we would absolutely adore the secret world that was enclosed inside each one.

Outside the soundstage entrance a long table was set up, manned by Greg, Dwayne, and a new security man, Jet. Jet was tall and skinny and had a long wild beard that made him look a lot like an insane biblical character. He was a fanatical defender of the door, and only intimate members of the Fleetwood Mac family were allowed in without a special pass. Anyone else would be turned away with a tirade of words explaining in no uncertain terms that no one—absolutely *no one*—got through the door without maximum clearance. Executives, band lawyers, journalists, and invited guests were double-checked for recording devices and cameras—and their visits were few and far between. This was the big time now, and the band was taking every measure necessary to protect the new music, and their new stage sound, that would be unveiled during the *Tusk* tour.

On the third night of rehearsals, arriving at my usual time of 5 P.M., I was surprised to see J.C. racing across the concrete lot to meet me. "Carol. I need to talk to you before you go in there. Apparently Dennis and Christine had a huge row last night and he told her that he slept with both you and Sara!"

"That's a lie!" I yelled as I looked at him in shock and anger.

With a sigh J.C. answered in a low voice, "He told her that during the band's recording sessions he had separate love affairs with both of you."

Looking him squarely in the eye, I said, "He's fucking lying. I would *never* sleep with Dennis Wilson, J.C. Sara and I hung out with him, that's it. I'm not like *some* members of the Mac family—I don't think it's OK to sleep with your friend's boyfriend. And I would never do that to Lindsey—never!"

With a nod and a quick kiss on my forehead, J.C. escorted me into the rehearsal hall. "Oh, one last thing . . . *People* magazine is on set today filming the band. Bad day for it, obviously, but who knew this shit was going to happen? Just be careful that whatever you need to say or do, you do it away from the cameras, OK?"

As I entered the hall on J.C.'s arm I couldn't help but think of the irony of it: how a band so infamous for its unhappy love affairs within its own ranks always seemed to live up to its image, whether intentionally or not, when the press was around.

Lindsey was standing on stage fiddling with his guitar as I left J.C. and walked across the cavernous room toward him. He watched as I approached, a quizzical half-smile on his face. As soon as I reached him he leaned over and kissed me.

"Lindsey, J.C. just told me what Dennis is saying. It never happened. God, I would *never, ever* do something like that to you. I love you! And I can't believe that Dennis has the nerve to say such a thing about me. I'm going to kill him!" I spluttered, my words sharp and angry.

After staring at me for a few seconds Lindsey took his guitar off and wrapped his arms around me. Looking into my eyes, he told me that he

Christine McVie, Tusk *rehearsal.*

believed me. Dennis, he said, could be crazy. It was Christine I had to convince—not him. As he pointed to a couch where Chris was scrunched up into the corner chain-smoking, he asked if I needed him there when I spoke with her.

"No, it's OK. I can handle it. I just can't believe that Dennis would use me to hurt Christine—that's just so *wrong!*" I felt like screaming, but aware of the cameras lurking in the background, I controlled myself and forced a grim smile onto my face. To have my faithfulness to Lindsey questioned by anyone was so beyond the bounds of what I'd tolerate that my normal mild temper had turned to fury.

With a last quick kiss I left Lindsey and went straight to an angry and upset Christine and sat down next to her. *What an asshole Dennis is,* I thought as I reached over and took Chris's hand in mine. "Christine, I just talked to Lindsey and I told him what I'm about to tell you. I never slept with Dennis. I would never do that to Lindsey or to you. Dennis and I are friends. That's it. And right now, if I could get my hands on him, I'd murder him."

Conflicting emotions played over Christine's face and although she said that she believed me, she asked plaintively, "Why would he say that if it weren't true?"

"I don't know, Christine. He's obviously trying to hurt you, but I can't believe he's using me to do it. Dennis is lying. I know that he loves you, Chris. He constantly tells Sara and me how crazy he is about you. I'd give anything to not be caught in the middle of something like this. But I'm telling you the truth. Lindsey believes me and I hope you do too. And right now I think Dennis owes all of us an apology."

Christine and a crew member, Tusk *rehearsal.*

Finally Christine smiled and gave me a long hug. That she was still upset was obvious, but at least I was no longer the cause. *What a friggin' putz Dennis is. I can't believe he'd tell such a lie!* I thought, as I looked at Christine. Hoping that all was now fine between Christine and me, I got up and sat on the floor close to Lindsey. He gave me a questioning look and I said softly, "I talked to her, Lindsey. I can't believe Dennis would hurt her like that. I just don't understand it."

With a shrug he told me that Dennis apparently had been awake for three days straight. *Well, no wonder he's acting crazy!* I thought as I stared glumly at Christine, who now had Sara sitting next to her, looking just as freaked out as I felt.

Years later I would read time and time again quotes from Lindsey in magazine interviews where he swears that Dennis and I did, indeed, sleep together. And to this day it's a complete mystery to me why he changed his mind and decided to believe the worst. But for the record, it never, ever happened.

Carol Ann, Tusk rehearsal.

As the night went on the camera crew photographed the band performing and roaming the soundstage. The article that would run two weeks later shows a picture of Christine and me deep in conversation on the couch, with a short caption saying, "Christine and Carol Ann are in a deep serious conversation during the Tusk rehearsals." *That's the understatement of the year,* I thought as I read it. *Thank God they couldn't get close enough to hear what we were talking about. Friggin' Dennis.*

Five weeks later I pulled our matching Halliburton suitcases out of the closet and into the middle of the bedroom. Sinking down on the floor next to them, I rested my head on my knees and stared at the empty interiors. A week before, Bjorn had given me the amazing and nerve-racking news that Eileen Ford of the world-famous Ford Modeling Agency in Manhattan wanted to see me—in person.

She'd seen pictures of me in his portfolio and she was thinking of signing me, he said. Of course, he didn't tell her I was only five foot six and therefore not runway material, but we were both hoping that she'd sign me with her agency for beauty ads. It was a huge compliment for Eileen Ford herself to be interested in me, and Bjorn and I were both nervous wrecks. Fleetwood Mac would be playing Madison Square Garden in three weeks and I had an interview already booked with her during our stay there. And I had no idea what to wear for it.

"Need some help?" Lindsey asked as he walked quietly into the room. Leaning down to kiss me, he looked long and searchingly into my eyes.

"Hey, Carol, do you want to buy new clothes for the tour and for this modeling interview you have? You can go to that new place in Beverly Hills that you like, Charles Galley. I want you to have new stuff. Let's get you a whole new wardrobe, OK? Would you like that?"

"Really, Lindsey? I have a lot of clothes, but you're right . . . I have no idea what to wear. I'm so nervous. Do you think I have a chance?"

"Yep, I do. I know you're nervous and so am I. I want you to model, but I don't know how it's going to work if you get signed in New York. I guess we'll figure it out. So why don't you go shopping, OK?" he asked in a low voice.

Knowing how nervous *he* must be about the upcoming tour, I felt conflicted and guilty. Even though I was beyond excited about the Ford Agency, the reality was if I signed with them, I'd be spending time in New York on my own. The interview appointment happened so quickly that neither Lindsey nor I had time to even think of its potential repercussions on our relationship. *I'll worry about it when and if I have to,* I told myself as I looked up into his eyes. Remembering my vow of two years before that I'd never do anything to come between Lindsey and his music, I was hit by divine inspiration. There was something I could do for him right then that would take his mind off my interview. And no, it wasn't sex.

"Lindsey, let's go shopping for both of us! I want to completely design a new stage look for you to go with your new haircut and new music. I've given it a lot of thought and I really want to see if my idea for you is right. It's something that will be completely different from anything you've ever worn before on stage. Will you let me do that? Please? That would make me really happy, Lindsey."

Seeing the pleased look on Lindsey's face, I jumped up and hugged him. An hour later we headed for Beverly Hills and my new favorite store. Focusing on the old-money elite of Beverly Hills, Charles Galley carried only top designers. With Armani and Versace clothes hanging on their racks, it was the perfect store for Lindsey.

I wanted the quality of Armani so that I could turn it into a one-of-a-kind cutting-edge persona for the guitar player of Fleetwood Mac. Of course, I made no mention to Lindsey of the actual look I had planned for him—because I knew there was a chance he might balk at trying the radical change that I had in mind.

As Lindsey browsed through the designer shirt section, looking for shirts to wear with his usual blue jeans on stage, I furiously pulled out Armani suits and handed them to the salesgirl. Within ten minutes a dressing room was ready and waiting for the surprise I had in store for Lindsey.

As I ceremoniously ushered him inside I watched his face with amusement as he surveyed the assortment of beautiful suits that were hanging from every available peg mounted on the walls. "Um, Carol? What are all these suits doing in here? You want me to wear a *suit* on stage?" he asked incredulously.

"Just try one on, Lindsey. I just want to see what you look like wearing an Armani suit. We'll go from there, OK? Please? Try one on for me—just one—and if you don't like it, then we'll do something else. But let's just see how it goes," I answered in a soothing tone.

With a shake of his head and a rueful smile, Lindsey stripped down and reached for a gray silk-and-wool suit. He had his back to the mirror as he slipped first into a white linen Armani shirt and then pulled on the suit. The jacket was single-breasted, fitting him like a glove, and the trousers were narrow with knife creases centered perfectly down each leg. Sitting in a gilded chair, I held my breath as he turned around and looked at himself in the ornate three-way mirror.

He stood silently, as though hypnotized by his own image, staring as though he were looking at a stranger in the mirror—and realizing that that stranger was himself.

A look of wonder crossed his face as he took in his reflected image. With his choppy short hair framing a face with chiseled cheekbones, dark brows, and blue eyes, he looked like a rock 'n' roll version of Cary Grant—incredibly handsome, incredibly sexy, and, most of all, incredibly *cutting edge.*

And as I watched him I suddenly saw that Lindsey had not, up until that moment, realized how amazingly handsome he actually was. My breath caught in my throat as I watched emotions play across his face that signaled a change in his self-perception. I knew exactly what he was feeling because I'd seen the same expressions cross *my* face when I first saw my own reflection after Bjorn had transformed me for my very first photo shoot with him.

It'd never even crossed my mind that Lindsey himself could ever feel even *remotely* the same basic feelings of insecurity about his looks that I did about mine. As I watched him turning this way and that I decided that it was more likely that Lindsey had never really given his looks or his stage persona much thought—until now. Never realized how much power physical beauty could wield—until now.

Watching him, I was aware that I had just given him another tool to make his creative transformation complete. I knew that, for the first time in his life, Lindsey understood that he could have the same hypnotic presence as Stevie Nicks on stage—the same sex appeal, the same ability to mesmerize, the same *power*.

For in the end, it was all about power. Stevie had *owned* the spotlight at their shows, but it was obvious to both Lindsey and me that he, too, could step into that golden light and quite possibly outshine her—or at the very least equal her in physical presence. We didn't even give it a thought that this ability could change forever the basic power structure of the band's performances. And that, once changed, there would be no turning back.

He looked at me, still thunderstruck, and I jumped up from the floor and threw myself into his arms. "Do you like it, Lindsey?" I asked breathlessly, even though the answer was now written all over his face.

"It's amazing, Carol. I love it. Jesus. I look so different. I don't recognize myself . . . but I guess that might be a good thing, huh? It's fuckin' brilliant, isn't it?"

"Oh my God, Lindsey! You're drop-dead gorgeous in that suit. And I want to do makeup on you for stage. You know, like what Bjorn did at the Grammys, only more. I mean, I think we should do your eyes with dark eyeshadow and shadow your cheekbones and darken your eyebrows . . . and God, I'm so excited for everyone to see you on stage! The band is going to die when they see this new look on you, Lindsey! The friggin' fans are going to go crazy!"

We grinned at each other and screamed, "*Yes!*" in unison before starting to giggle helplessly. For we knew that the band was in for yet another shock—and this shock would mainly reverberate with the one person who was in the most danger of suffering from it: Stevie Nicks.

"I can't wait until Stevie sees me at the first show. She's gonna die!" Lindsey sniggered.

"'Yeah, I know. She will. But that's not why we're doing this, Lindsey," I answered primly. "It's for *you*. It fits your new music, you know? Your music has changed and now so have you! So let's take the high road and try not to be too mean about it."

As we both started sniggering again we cried out together, *"Yeah, right!"*

From a pleased salesgirl, I quickly ordered two identical gray Armani suits for Lindsey and four white linen shirts. I then went happily back out into the store and grabbed some designer clothes for myself. *This should keep me covered for my interview,* I thought happily.

It took two store employees to help us load our treasures into the trunk of Lindsey's BMW and we sped off for a celebration dinner at El Cholo, Lindsey's favorite Mexican restaurant. Between sips of margaritas, we talked excitedly about the upcoming tour. We were looking forward with relish to the storm that we were about to unleash on the unsuspecting members of Fleetwood Mac.

It was a storm that would match the impact that the controversial new album would unleash worldwide. Lindsey insisted on releasing the title song as the first single off the record. He wanted the world to be prepared for a new Fleetwood Mac—and "Tusk" got heavy airplay. It was a brilliant track, but it sent shock waves through the music industry and Fleetwood Mac fans.

For a band that had seen such monumental success, it was an anomaly to mess with its winning formula—and nobody knew what to think. In October the album was released to mixed reviews. Everyone greeted Lindsey's songs with a love-hate reaction, and it was a little bit rough on him. But he believed in his music and I assured him that as soon as people heard his new songs played live, everyone would recognize how great they truly were. "And if they don't, then fuck 'em," I said with a smile.

In Pocatello, Idaho, the first show of the Tusk tour was only two hours away—and Lindsey and I were literally hiding from the entire Fleetwood Mac entourage in the small tuning room backstage. We were in the process of getting him dressed for the show, wickedly savoring every second we spent on creating his new look. Seated on a metal folding chair in his new gray suit, Lindsey kept his eyes closed as I applied dark brown eyeshadow to his lids, finishing it off with carefully drawn lines of black eyeliner to starkly outline his blue eyes. After adding brown shading to his already hollow cheekbones, I finished his makeup with a dusting of white powder and leaned back to admire my handiwork.

Photography © Ed Roach, roach-clips.com

Lindsey's new stage persona.

With his chopped hair, darkened eyes, and striking cheekbones, he looked completely satanic. And that was exactly the look we were going for. As he stood up and strapped his guitar around his neck I smirked, reflecting that it might seem a little strange to the world at large for a girl to get so much pleasure out of turning her fiancé into a rock 'n' roll vampire. But the world at large didn't live within the realm of Fleetwood Mac—where that fiancé was in heavy artistic competition with a woman who portrayed herself on stage as the goddess of witchcraft.

Admiring our achievement in the mirror, Lindsey turned and grinned at me. "What do you think?"

"It's killer, Lindsey. Really. I absolutely love this look on you. Do you? Are you happy with how everything turned out?" I asked anxiously.

"Come here and I'll show you."

I ran to where he was standing and happily returned his kiss with care, because I didn't want to mess up his makeup. We both started laughing as I inspected his face for smudges. *I wish Bjorn were here to see Lindsey—he'd be so impressed!* I thought as I grinned at my sexy rock vampire in the Armani suit.

Fiddling with the strap of his guitar, Lindsey told me that he couldn't wait until the band got a look at him. And neither could I. At the moment I was looking forward more to their reaction when they first got a look at the new Lindsey than I was to the actual show. Lindsey opened the door of the tuning room and strode ahead of me down the hallway to the main dressing room, where the rest of the band was already assembled—blissfully unaware of the surprise we had in store for them. Winking at me over his shoulder, he turned the handle of the door and walked inside.

There was stunned silence as we entered the room. Stevie stared openmouthed as Lindsey casually strolled to the drinks table and started to mix a Myers's and Coke. Christine almost choked on her vodka tonic, spluttering noisily as she gulped it down.

Mick, who was about to inhale a bottle cap of blow, froze, the cap clutched forgotten in his hand. And then he dropped his massive hit of cocaine. As the cap slipped out of his fingers and fell slowly to the ground, every pair of shocked eyes in the room moved briefly from Lindsey to follow the puff of white dust that drifted up almost weightlessly from the shiny piece of metal. In the reality of the world of Fleetwood Mac, a dropped hit of blow outranked the shock the band members were feeling at Lindsey's alarming appearance any fuckin' day.

Looking first at Lindsey and then at the tragically spilled blow, Mick let out a heart-wrenching screech. "*Aaaargh, shit!* Jesus Christ, Lindsey! What the hell?"

Lindsey surveyed the room, a smile of satisfaction crossing his now-satanic countenance. "What the hell what, Mick? Drag about your blow, man," Lindsey sniggered as he downed a huge gulp of his drink.

"I mean, *what the hell?*" Mick snapped as he pointed toward Lindsey.

"You don't like my suit, Mick? It's Armani . . . you of all people should appreciate an Armani suit," he answered smugly as he flicked imaginary specks of lint off one of his cuffs.

As Mick stared at him, speechless, Christine stood up, irritation radiating from her erect, stiff posture. Walking quickly to where Lindsey was now leaning nonchalantly against a wall, she stared closely at his face. "Christ! Are you wearing *makeup?*"

"Maybe," Lindsey smirked.

Chris turned to the rest of the band for support. And then she told Lindsey exactly what she thought of his new look. She gave the suit a backhanded compliment, stating that she liked it, even if it didn't really work with the rest of the band's "stage look." She then asked in a mocking tone if he didn't feel that perhaps the makeup might make him look "a little gay." As she looked again in exasperation for band support from John or Stevie—who remained completely silent—she gave Lindsey a withering stare, refilled her glass with more tonic and vodka, and almost stomped back to her chair.

Giving Christine a classic Lindsey look that said, "*Fuck you!*" he smiled smugly and sipped on his cocktail.

"I like it, Lindsey," John said with a shrug. "You look great. I take it you didn't do that makeup by yourself?" Turning to me with a smirk, he added, "Carol, you did a great job. He looks rather devilish, doesn't he?"

I blushed as I curtsied in John's direction, unable to hide my smile of triumph any longer. "Thanks, John. I think he looks amazing. The fans will too!"

"Actually," Lindsey said to John. "The suit's Carol's idea. She's a woman of many *talents,* I gotta say."

As Christine and Stevie glared at me, I cringed a little under the force of their obvious wrath. *Great. As if Stevie needs any more reasons to be mad at me. And now Christine's pissed off at me too! Well, too bad, girls. Lindsey looks great and you're just going to have to deal with it,* I thought with a bravado that was coming a little bit hard as their anger made me feel like running for cover. Walking quickly to Lindsey's side, I slipped under the relative safety of his free arm and gave them the sweetest smile I could muster.

As we both stood whispering in the corner, Stevie wrapped herself in another of her beautiful shawls. Studiously ignoring us both, she finger-combed her hair in the mirror. Over that night's choice of signature chiffon skirt, she was wearing layers of three different shawls, each one more stunning than the last. In the fluorescent lights of the dressing room she was absolutely gorgeous. And as anyone who's ever stood under a fluorescent light knows, that was a pretty hard trick to pull off. But she did. With a toss of her hair she turned and stared at Lindsey, as if telling him that *she* wasn't worried about being upstaged. And he stared back without even a trace of a smile.

Here we go again, I thought, as I not only watched but felt the intense rivalry flowing between them. It was like an unseen malevolent presence in the room and with a sigh I wondered if that was ever going to change. *Not friggin' likely,* I told myself. *Not on this tour anyway.*

"*Six minutes,* everyone, six minutes," J.C. called out as he entered the room. Looking at the frozen tableau in front of him, he followed the gaze of the band and saw Lindsey and me, standing as though we were in front of a tribunal.

"Damn, Mr. B. You've done it up, haven't you? I like it. You look quite the dandy in that outfit! The fans are going to be in for a bit of surprise, eh?"

Giving me a wink, J.C. walked over to the door and intoned, "*Five minutes,* everyone. Let's line up now. Time to play the first show of the tour! Make it a great one! There's close to fourteen thousand punters out there waiting for you. Let's give 'em what they want, shall we?"

Lindsey gave me a quick kiss as a long-familiar, faraway look came into his eyes. He was once again entering a place where I could not follow. And despite the small altercation minutes before, the merging of the band members' separate personalities into one powerful force known as Fleetwood Mac seemed to electrify the very air around them as they walked single file out of the room into the brightly lit hallway. It had been over a year since they'd taken this walk through cables and past anvil cases and I felt a surge of excitement. The first show of the *Tusk* tour was about to begin.

Keeping my usual distance from the band members, who were now congregated at the bottom of the stage, I watched Lindsey gleefully rubbing his hands together as he laughed at something Mick was saying to him. He looked so happy that I wanted to run and throw my arms around him. But I didn't. He was within the entity that was Fleetwood Mac and was therefore unapproachable. Instead, I hugged the moment to myself and realized that I was absolutely thrilled to be back on the road. The welcoming roar of the crowd rang in my ears as I watched J.C. move across the stage to the microphone.

"Ladies and gentlemen, please give a warm welcome to . . . *Fleetwood Mac!*"

J.C. stood aside as the band ran up the stairs to the stage. The voices of thousands of fans erupted into screams and cheers, echoing throughout the huge stadium with a deafening roar. As soon as the band launched into

"Say You Love Me," I sprinted up the short flight of metal steps and stood on the left side of the platform. There was no way I would miss a second of the audience's reaction to Lindsey in the debut of his radical new music and stage persona. And I was not disappointed. On the contrary, I was about to be shocked out of my naive little mind.

As I looked out over the ocean of faces it seemed that almost every pair of eyes was glued to Lindsey. He looked so different that I thought there was at first some slight confusion in the audience about who the hell he *was*. But then, as he crossed to the mike and began to sing, there was no doubt in anyone's mind that it was indeed Lindsey Buckingham on stage.

By the second song, "The Chain," I began to notice an audience reaction that I'd never seen (or heard) before. As Lindsey sang the lyrics, his voice was met with welcoming screams from thousands of women standing at his feet. Over and over again. Each time he sang another line, the noise of female voices threatened to almost drown out his. Lindsey started laughing, for there was no mistaking the screams for anything but what they were: the screams of women who were swooning in front of a sex symbol.

I was too stunned to do anything but stare first at Lindsey and then at the adoring faces of the women in the first fifty or so rows of the amphitheater. Realization hit me like a sledgehammer. *Oh my God . . . it's like he's friggin' Jim Morrison or something! Those women look like they want to rip his damn clothes off! What have I done?*

I felt like going to the nearest speaker and slamming my head down on top of it. *Fuckin' great! I'm going to have about a million women trying to get their hands on my man! Shit, shit, shit!* I thought as I sank down onto one of the folding chairs that were always set up for me, Sara, and Julie and stared glumly at Lindsey. He looked gorgeous. No wonder all the girls wanted to jump onto the stage and drag him off with them.

As I sat pouting I suddenly noticed something else that was different about Lindsey and my mind began to race. *He's standing at the front of the stage! He's playing every guitar solo standing ten feet in front of Stevie! He's never done that before!* I was incredulous and as I watched I realized that not only was he placing himself on stage literally as the front man, he was also playing and singing with a feverish passion that I'd never heard before. He was performing like a man possessed. Chewing my fingernail, I thought,

Jesus! He not only looks like a demon, but he's playing like one! I think I've seen enough for now . . . I need a toot.

With a last look at the new, improved Lindsey, I stomped off the stage. Walking quickly through the curtains, I headed down the dirty cement hallway. And as I walked, a feeling of triumph began to wash over me and suddenly all feelings of insecurity were swept away. The realization that Lindsey's new persona had unleashed some kind of inner power within him on stage made me feel incredibly happy. *Giorgio Armani would be proud!* I thought smugly. *It's kind of like a superhero suit that he's wearing . . . and, I have to admit, Bjorn himself couldn't have done a better job on his makeup!*

I almost felt like skipping the last few feet into the dressing room, so thrilled was I with the success of my grand plan for Lindsey's new stage look. As I entered the door, J.C. greeted me with a huge smile. "I take it you've been out on the stage, Mrs. B.? It's turning out to be one of the best shows the band's ever done! I don't think I've ever seen Lindsey play so well. I like the suit and hair. Well done." Gesturing to the tray of cocaine-filled bottle caps, he gave me a wink and waited while I treated myself to a hit of blow.

"Thanks, J.C. The new look is perfect for him—and right now there are at least eight thousand women out there who'd agree with me!" I answered dryly.

"You don't have to worry about that, Carol Ann. Lindsey doesn't fuck around—hell, it's band policy not to let groupies come within five hundred feet of their backstage. Fleetwood Mac protects their women from that kind of bullshit. You don't have a thing to worry about."

"I know—it's just going to take some getting used to. I mean he's a damn sex symbol on stage now, J.C.! But I'm excited about it. After all, I styled it! Want to walk back out with me to see the show?"

With a grin J.C. took my arm and we walked back outside and stood next to the stage. Once there, we watched in amazement as the band gave what promised to be the best performance we'd ever seen. It was like they were all painted with magic.

The energy that was being created on stage swirled over the crowd like crashing waves and then surged back again, sweeping through the air and coloring it with shimmering waves of sound. J.C. and I looked at each other

open-mouthed as we watched what was happening up on the huge platform. It was obvious to us both that what we were watching was a relent-
less power struggle on stage. Three members of Fleetwood Mac were mercilessly waging war against each other, using music and performance as
their weapons.

Fueled (and not amused) by Lindsey's showstopping guitar licks and
now undeniable stage presence, Stevie was giving the performance of her

life. Barely looking in
Lindsey's direction—
ever—she was doing
the show as though she
were the only person
on stage. Beige chiffon
swirling, voice wailing
and soaring, she was
doing her best to out-
shine Lindsey and put
herself back into the
spotlight that she had
so long been accus-
tomed to occupying
alone. Christine was
competing with Stevie,
and John and Mick
were caught up in the
fury of sound, feeding
the battle between their
three lead singers with
the raw power of bass
and drums.

Stevie Nicks.

"Jesus Christ!" J.C.
shouted above the
music. He gave me a wink and we grinned at each other, sharing a moment
that gave both of us a conspiratorial thrill. It was obvious that Lindsey had
turned a corner in his stage presence and performance. He was, in our eyes

and undoubtedly in those of the audience as well, winning the struggle to be the center-stage star at *this* show—and we both knew what that was going to mean to him.

Lindsey had long lived in the shadow of Stevie on stage. His musical genius and amazing guitar playing were often overshadowed by the powerful visual presence of a beautiful blonde dressed in revealing black chiffon. It was a visual presence that gave Stevie's amazing musical abilities a bit of an unfair advantage. But now that Lindsey had become a newborn sex symbol, it looked like all that was about to change—*was* changing—right before our eyes.

J.C. and I stayed by the stage, unable to tear our eyes away from Fleetwood Mac. Looking around, I saw that most of the road crew were standing with us, staring up at the stage as the band played through their set, as enthralled as we were.

And let's face it, when the Fleetwood Mac family itself—who at that point had witnessed over one hundred shows—was mesmerized by the band's performance, then you could bet your life that the show was the best that any of us had seen.

As the concert neared its end, J.C. insisted that I go back to the safety of the "unlimited-access only" barricaded area backstage, as the crowd out front was getting increasingly out of control. People were surging toward the stage, pushing and shoving their way into the aisles with looks of intense and scary determination on their faces. J.C. pulled a walkie-talkie out of his pocket, barking orders for security guards to rush down front, now!

Climbing onto the stage, I looked in shock at the chaos lying before me. I saw people falling and getting trampled as others climbed over their prostrate bodies in their frenzy to reach the band. I flashed back to the show in Paris during the *Rumours* tour and knew that history was repeating itself. I found myself shrinking away from the chaos in front of me. To my relief, the ones who'd fallen got back onto their feet and joined in the ocean of people, who were like sharks in a feeding frenzy. They were swarming and clawing their way toward the objects of their fanatical desire: the members of Fleetwood Mac.

Greg grabbed me by the arm and started to pull me off the stage. "Greg!" I shouted over the music. "Is the band going to be OK?"

"We've called for extra security—we're not going to let anyone get close to them, don't worry," he screamed back. "It's not safe out here, Carol! J.C. wants you back in the dressing room. This crowd is out of control. Man, the band really worked them into a frenzy, huh? Come on, Carol, we gotta *run* to the dressing room. I have to get right back out here. The band's gonna need all of us when they try to leave the stage. *Jesus Christ!* I've never seen anything like it!"

Looking over my shoulder at the mob of hungry faces behind me, I allowed myself to be taken by the hand and led backstage like a child, grateful for the protection of Greg's muscular physique.

"Come on, Carol, run . . . run! The show's almost over and I have to be out here for the band. Man, this show was bitchin'!" Greg yelled as we took off down the huge inner cement hallway. Getting to the dressing room, he threw open the door and pushed me inside. "Lock the door! Don't open it up until we bring the band back!"

Stevie and Lindsey on stage.

Photography © Ed Roach, roach-clips.com

Breathless with excitement over the success of the show and the audience response to their new songs, the five members of Fleetwood Mac burst through the doors triumphantly. Exhausted, sweaty, and happy, they crowded together, sharing the moment in pure celebration. The fact that the audience had gotten worked up into a mob-like frenzy had blown everyone's minds. There was a feeling in the dressing room of having just survived a siege. I knew that, in a sense, they had. It was a remarkable contrast to the aftermath of the first show of the *Rumours* tour, and all of the band knew it.

No more words were spoken about Lindsey's new "gay" stage persona. It was obvious to all of the band and crew that he rocked the house—and whatever caused him to play the best performance of his life was not open to debate. No one cared. All that mattered was that Lindsey fueled the fire behind the band's kick-ass show and it was clear that every member of the band thoroughly enjoyed trying to upstage each other.

And no matter what the critics might have been saying about Lindsey's songs on the new album, the next year on the road would prove that his radical change in musical direction and stage persona would be the star power that burned like fire every time the band took the stage during the yearlong *Tusk* tour.

14

BEHIND THE GOLD CURTAIN

When I close my eyes and think back to the *Tusk* tour, I see a hotel room with silver Halliburton suitcases thrown open on the floor. Dresses, shoes, blue jeans, wrinkled designer jackets, and beaded, hand-tooled belts spill

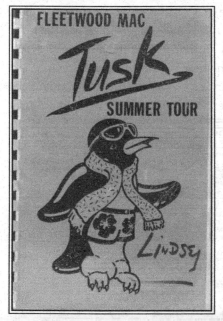

Tusk *tour book.*

across the carpet, creating a kaleidoscope of colors against the muted tones of the suite's interior. There's a room-service table sitting in the middle of the room, overflowing with dirty dishes and ashtrays full of cigarette butts and half-smoked joints. A cassette player sits on the end of the bed blasting the Clash or Talking Heads.

And in my mind's eye there I am, seated at a vanity mirror with a curling iron in my hand, burning waves and curls into my long, straight hair. I see myself turn and watch Lindsey as he paws through the pile of clothes on the floor, searching for a clean pair of jeans or a shirt to wear to that night's venue. Looking up, he smiles and asks what I'm wearing tonight. He knows that I always have a designer outfit ready and waiting to slip into. On this tour, Armani jackets, antique skirts, and couture dresses adorn my body at every show. And as

I stand before him Lindsey tells me how beautiful I look—and because he says it, I feel it.

The phone rings, summoning us downstairs to our waiting limousine, and I rush back to the vanity table to do yet another touch-up of my make-up before we walk out the door. Lindsey leans against the wall, taking one last hit of his joint as he watches me apply lipstick and, without fail, kisses it off before he lets me leave the room.

Other images from that year are not at all pleasant, but they are just as vivid. It is a year of enough events and memories to fill ten years of life for anyone not living within the inner world of Fleetwood Mac.

A sure sign that the band's star had risen since playing New York City during the *Rumours* tour was waiting for us in the limousines that were lined up at the bottom of the stairs of Fleetwood Mac's jet. Each car had four grams of bottled blow rolling around on the black leather seats—courtesy of the limo company. The bottles were met with cries of glee as we all piled into our individual rides. Later the band would agree that it was so very, very thoughtful of the limo company to welcome us in this way to NYC. Those bottles would pretty much set the tone for the entire tour.

It was going to be an exciting, delirious, nerve-racking week and a half for both the band and myself. There was to be a party at Studio 54 in

SUNDAY	MONDAY	TUESDAY	WEDNESDAY	THURSDAY	FRIDAY	SATURDAY
AUGUST 3	AUGUST 4	AUGUST 5	AUGUST 6	AUGUST 7	AUGUST 8	AUGUST 9
TRAVEL DAY HILTON INN 813/688-8484 LAKELAND, FLA.	REHEARSAL DAY HILTON INN 813/688-8484 CIVIC CENTER 813/682-6564 LAKELAND, FLA	SHOW DAY - 8PM HILTON INN 813/688-8484 CIVIC CENTER 813/682-6564 LAKELAND, FLA.	TRVL & SHOW 8PM SONESTA BEACH 305/361-2021 SPORTATORIUM 305/431-9100 MIAMI, FLA.	OFF DAY SONESTA BEACH 305/361-2021 MIAMI, FLA.	TRVL & SHOW 8PM COLONY SQUARE 404/892-6000 THE OMNI 404/588-9958 ATLANTA, GA.	OFF DAY COLONY SQUARE 404/892-6000 ATLANTA, GA.
AUGUST 10	AUGUST 11	AUGUST 12	AUGUST 13	AUGUST 14	AUGUST 15	AUGUST 16
OFF DAY COLONY SQUARE 404/892-6000 ATLANTA, GA.	TRVL & SHOW 8PM MOBILE HILTON 205/476-6400 MUNICIPAL AUD. 205/422-0959 MOBILE, ALA.	TRVL & SHOW 8PM BIRMINGHAM HYATT 205/251-2221 JEFFERSON CIVIC 205/328-8160 BIRMINGHAM, ALA.	TRVL & SHOW 9PM ROYAL ORLEANS 504/529-5333 RIVERSIDE COLSM. 504/383-0033 NEW ORLEANS, LA.	OFF DAY ROYAL ORLEANS 504/529-5333 NEW ORLEANS, LA.	OFF DAY ROYAL ORLEANS 504/529-5333 NEW ORLEANS, LA.	TRVL & SHOW 8PM FAIRMONT HOTEL 214/748-5454 REUNION ARENA 214/658-7072 DALLAS, TX.
AUGUST 17	AUGUST 18	AUGUST 19	AUGUST 20	AUGUST 21	AUGUST 22	AUGUST 23
TRVL & SHOW 8PM INN AT TURTLE CREEK 512/696-5600 CONVENTION CENTER 512/271-3124 SAN ANTONIO, TX.	TRVL & SHOW 8PM THE WHITEHALL 713/659-5000 THE SUMMIT 713/627-9470 HOUSTON, TX.	OFF DAY THE WHITEHALL 713/659-5000 HOUSTON, TX.	OFF DAY THE WHITEHALL 713/659-5000 HOUSTON, TX.	TRVL & SHOW 7:30PM GRANADA ROYALE 402/397-5141 CIVIC CENTER 402/346-1326 OMAHA, NEB.	TRVL & SHOW 8PM AIRPORT HILTON 405/947-7681 MYRIAD CONV. CTR. 405/235-1023 OKLAHOMA CITY, OK.	TRVL & SHOW 8PM HILTON INN 316/686-7131 KANSAS COLISEUM 316/755-1243 WICHITA, KAN.
AUGUST 24	AUGUST 25	AUGUST 26	AUGUST 27	AUGUST 28	AUGUST 29	AUGUST 30
TRVL & SHOW 9PM CROWN CENTER 816/474-4400 KEMPER ARENA 816/474-7841 KANSAS CITY, MO.	OFF DAY CROWN CENTER 816/474-4400 KANSAS CITY, MO.	TRAVEL DAY HOLIDAY INN 505/526-4411 LAS CRUCES, NM.	SHOW DAY - 8PM HOLIDAY INN 505/526-4411 PAN AMERICAN CTR. 505/646-4414 LAS CRUCES, NM.	TRVL & SHOW 8PM ARIZONA INN 602/325-1541 MCHALE CENTER 602/626-5824 TUCSON, AZ.	TRVL & SHOW 7:30PM LA POSADA 602/952-0420 COMPTON TERRACE 602/273-0980 PHOENIX, AZ.	OFF DAY LA POSADA PHOENIX, AZ.

Tusk *summer tour itinerary.*

Fleetwood Mac's honor and two back-to-back, sold-out shows at Madison Square Garden. And I would be going to my long-awaited interview with the Ford Modeling Agency with Bjorn by my side.

Lindsey had flown Bjorn in for the duration, not only to help me but also to do his makeup for the Manhattan shows. Playing Madison Square Garden was a dream come true for any artist and Fleetwood Mac was pulling out all the stops for this one. Press conferences, photographers, drug suppliers, and designer clothes were all in place for the highlight of this leg of the tour. Because, let's face it, being in the center of Manhattan as the hottest ticket in town was a little more exciting than being in Cincinnati, Ohio, even if the band was just as popular there. Manhattan was the shit—and all of us felt breathless with anticipation of the days ahead.

After playing three shows at the Veterans Coliseum, the band and the inner circle were en route to Studio 54. We couldn't wait to see the disco so long associated with Andy Warhol and 1970s decadence. As we pulled up in front of the club, I looked in wonder at the mob of hundreds of people clamoring to get beyond the red velvet ropes. A path cleared for us as we stepped out of our cars like royalty. It was Fleetwood Mac night and the band was the guest of honor. As paparazzi's cameras flashed and the crowd screamed, we entered the legendary Studio 54.

The music was blasting, the loud bass hitting my chest like a fist. Lavish bars surrounded a gigantic dance floor that held a raised platform dead center with couches behind silver velvet ropes and VIP signs. Studio 54 security men led us through the mass of sweaty, dancing bodies to this section and by the time we sat down I felt completely overwhelmed. We were used to big crowds, but we were used to seeing them from the distance and safety of a stage. On the long walk through the club I'd been pushed, shoved, scratched, and bruised by the huge mob of people in our way—and it was terrifying.

Lindsey grabbed my hand and shouted to make himself heard, asking if I was OK. Nodding, I clung to his arm as I looked in amazement at the chaos surrounding us. Under pulsing red strobe lights, drunk, drugged, and delirious patrons were either frenziedly dancing or literally stepping over the bodies of people lying on the floor. The unconscious unfortunates looked like they had either overdosed or just collapsed from the heat and the ear-splitting disco music pounding through the air—and no one was doing a thing to help them. I'd never seen anything like it. To me, it looked like a scene from Dante's *Inferno*—and I hated it.

Suddenly Steve Rubell appeared in front of us and, grinning from ear to ear, asked if we'd like to accompany him to the basement. With his unruly dark hair and little-boy smile, he looked more like a disheveled college boy than one of the owners of the world's most famous nightclubs. Ready at this point to be anywhere but in the middle of the club, Lindsey grabbed my hand as the rest of the band followed Rubell through the mob and into the lower recesses of Studio 54.

Grey walls dripped with moisture as we walked down gloomy hall-ways into a plain room where we saw a huge mound of cocaine piled in the center of a table. Steve gestured grandly for all of us to step up and have our fill, and we gathered around the pile of blow like vultures, need-ing every bit of false energy we could get just to survive the party. I looked at the faces of the band and it seemed that they too were feeling exactly as I was—and I just wanted to get out of there and back to the hotel in one piece.

"Lindsey, I don't think I can go back up there!" I said desperately. With a nod of his head he pulled me close and asked Rubell to show us the way out. Shrugging, the club owner pointed to a back door and Lindsey and I sprinted for our limo and the hotel.

Once there, I sank down onto a chair and looked at Lindsey, as tears began coursing down my face. Reaching for my hand, he asked what was wrong and I tried to put into words what I was feeling. I told him that as excited as I was about my interview, I hated the world we'd just left. And to me, the world at Studio 54 was symbolic of Manhattan and the life I'd be leading if I joined the Ford Modeling Agency. As silly as it might sound, I said, I knew that I didn't belong here. I belonged in L.A. and with him. I loved New York but I didn't want to live there. Ever.

Kneeling before me, Lindsey took my face into his hands and told me that he didn't want me to accept an offer in New York. He, too, was shaken by what he'd just experienced and there was no way he wanted me to be in Manhattan on my own. As I threw myself into his arms I felt overcome with relief. No matter how much I might have wanted a career, I wasn't willing to enter a world where I instinctively knew I didn't belong. *I'll find another way,* I told myself. And I did.

A head shot of Carol Ann for an Elite Modeling card.

During my interview the next day, Eileen Ford told me that while she loved "my look," I was just too short for her agency. She offered to make a call for me to Elite Modeling—John Casablanca's agency. As she told me that Elite also had an office in Los Angeles, I felt weak with relief. I went straight to their offices and got signed. My nightmare had once again become a dream. I was now a professional model signed to a top agency.

That night Fleetwood Mac was playing Madison Square Garden. Despite reports of countless celebrities in the audience, the band had its strict "no access" policy firmly in place. They didn't care who you were—this show was too important to let anyone distract them from the impending concert. After the unsavory episode with Rod Stewart at the Forum on the *Rumours* tour, it was a policy that they'd followed for every single show. Family and close friends were welcome for a short time, but after that it was the band's inner circle and crew whose footfalls echoed through the backstage area.

John McVie pulled me aside minutes before the concert. Shuffling his feet, he told me that he personally wanted to thank me for everything I'd done to change Lindsey's stage persona. The makeup and new wardrobe, he told me, seemed to have had a huge impact on Lindsey's stage performance, and speaking for himself and the band, it was much appreciated. I stood before him speechless at this unexpected thank you, and then he kissed me gently and walked away to join the rest of the waiting band.

Standing there silently, I realized just how much it meant to me to be finally acknowledged by Fleetwood Mac. Since meeting Lindsey I'd sworn vows, out of love for him, to help him in any way that I could with his music. I'd lived for him and his career. And it hadn't been all that easy: dealing with Stevie and her history with Lindsey; learning how to nurture a musical genius and coping with the ups and downs of his personality; navigating the creative process and the mood swings—the blackest of which I knew only too well; dealing with the way that his music seemed to rule our daily lives.

Lindsey constantly had music going through his head. Sometimes, late at night, the unrelenting mental music drove him to the verge of desperation. With hands clasped to his head as he lay next to me in our bed, he would scream that he just wanted it to stop and leave him in silent peace. But it never did—and after three years by Lindsey's side I knew I was grateful that I wasn't born with the gift of musical genius.

It meant the world to me that I was able to find a way to not only give him emotional support but also do something tangible to help him: creating a stage persona that seemed to be succeeding beyond my wildest dreams. In under a minute John had given me a reward in just a few heartfelt words. And it was enough, because I never expected to get any thanks at all. But now that I had, I treasured the moment as I happily ran up the stage stairs to watch the man I loved perform.

Over the next few weeks the whole world would begin to acknowledge Lindsey and his new stage persona. Without fail, a review of the band's show would appear in the pages of the local city newspapers. And as the band played shows in Boston, Rochester, Philadelphia, Washington, D.C., and Pittsburgh, slowly but surely the critics' focus seemed to be changing. For the first time since Stevie and Lindsey joined the band, the reviews were not centered on Stevie. They were focused on Lindsey.

When the *Tusk* tour first began, the critics didn't know what to make of Lindsey's new persona and music. It wasn't that they didn't like it—they just seem puzzled by his stiff-legged guitar playing and wailing, screaming vocals on his new songs. Not to mention his satanic stage presence. They didn't get it. But it seemed that was changing. Now the reviews raved about Lindsey's performance, with Stevie and the rest of the band members mentioned almost as an afterthought.

No one on the morning-after plane rides knew what to say as they read the reviews of their shows. To congratulate Lindsey would be insulting to the rest of the band and especially to Stevie, who had, up until this point, been the "leader of the pack" as far as the journalists were concerned. So no one said anything. But the silence said it all. A new Fleetwood Mac had been born with *Tusk* and Lindsey was a serious contender for the new darling of the media. In city after city after city, the same rave reviews appeared in the next day's local papers and Lindsey and I were ecstatic. His guitar playing was described as brilliant, his voice was "powerful," and the consensus was:

"Buckingham dominates the stage and the performance!"

"Thanks to Buckingham, Fleetwood Mac reaches a new level of achievement unlike any we've ever seen!"

"Buckingham brings a fresh New Wave approach to an already superstar band!"

Buckingham . . . Buckingham . . . Buckingham . . .

It wasn't as if the reviewers were trashing the rest of the band. Everyone was receiving applause and recognition from the media, and Stevie was always mentioned and applauded for her performance, but it was Lindsey who was now getting his day in the sun.

And if the band had any negative reaction to this, they were keeping it to themselves, for no one wanted to mess with success. After all, the truth was staring everyone in the face: so far these shows had been the most successful, in terms of media and audience response, of any tour since Stevie and Lindsey joined Fleetwood Mac.

After New York, Dennis Wilson and Sara joined us in Philadelphia. I was ecstatic to have them there. Dennis fell all over himself apologizing for what he said to Christine about both of us, and in a heartbeat it was forgiven. It was impossible to stay mad at Dennis. He was like a wicked little child and when he smiled at you, you had to smile back. Sara and I were joined at the hip backstage and we gossiped and giggled our way through the show. As we sat in the dressing room Dennis joined us, looking higher than God Almighty as he stumbled into the room.

"I want to go up on stage, you guys! Will you walk out with me? I tried to go on my own, but I couldn't seem to find my way. I got fuckin' lost and I had to come back here to do another line to have the energy to try again! Come on, girls, do a line with me and let's go see the end of the show. I want to watch Christine do 'Songbird.' OK? Pretty please?"

As Sara and I looked at each other we burst into laughter. The thought of Dennis wandering aimlessly backstage and more than likely bouncing off concrete walls was hysterical. As we got up to lead him to the band we had no idea that we were about to see one of the most classic Dennis moments we'd ever witnessed.

At this venue the only way to get around to stage right, where our chairs were waiting on stage, was to go under the actual stage itself. And it was a bit of a hazardous walk. Steel beams and girders threaded through our path, but it was well lit and not all that hard to navigate—for us. Dennis was following behind us, talking a blue streak, when suddenly there was a loud thunk and then dead silence. Whirling around, we saw Dennis lying flat on his back, knocked out cold. He'd hit his head on one of the beams and a huge welt was already forming over one of his eyes. As Sara and I knelt over him, about to shout for help, he opened his slightly crossed eyes and grinned. "Shit! Didn't see that one! Fuck! Help me up, girls . . . Let's get out there!"

"Damn, Dennis! Are you OK? Maybe you need to go lie down for a little while!" I said as he struggled to his feet using us as his anchors.

"I'm fine! Bit of a headache, though." Taking him firmly by the arms between us, now laughing hysterically, we managed to steer him out from under the stage and up onto it. Finally sitting him down on a chair between

Christine and Stevie on stage.

us, Sara and I gave our attention to the show and watched the band perform. And then it happened.

We heard another loud thunk as we felt a whoosh of air, and instead of Dennis's head between us, we were now looking at his feet. He'd fallen over backward in his chair and was lying as helpless as a turtle on his back right in front of fifteen thousand Fleetwood Mac fans. Still in a seated position with his chair under him, he blinked a few times and grinned.

Screaming with laughter, Sara and I knelt once again beside him, rolled him onto his side, and helped him to his feet. Lindsey was watching out of the corner of his eye and I could see that he was having a hard time trying to keep a straight face as he watched Dennis, Sara, and me struggle like Lucy and Ethel with Desi in the 1950s sitcom. Finally we got Dennis back into his chair and I stood behind him to make sure that he didn't fall over again on my watch. The good news was that he got to hear "Songbird"; the bad news was that he was going to have to endure a week's worth of vicious teasing by the Fleetwood Mac inner circle.

In the midst of all our good times and the band's success, tragedy was about to strike. In Champaign, Illinois, a horrific event took place during the show: a fan was knifed to death during a fight in the balcony. Halfway through the band's performance, J.C. walked into the dressing room, ashen-faced and shaken. Taking me aside, he told me in a low voice about the incident. The details were murky and we had no idea why it had happened—only that it had. As I looked at him in shock he asked me to not say a word to anyone.

"We have to let the police handle it, Carol Ann. It's not going to help anything to upset the band and the crew about it. I'll tell them about it tomorrow on the plane. I just can't believe that something like this could happen at one of our shows. This isn't Altamont—those are nice kids out there, not members of the Hell's Angels. I don't understand it."

As he poured himself a stiff drink, I sank down on a couch and stared into space. The incident at Altamont in 1969 when, during a Rolling Stones concert, fights broke out between the Hell's Angels guarding the Stones and the fans, was now legend. To think that a violent death had occurred in a place where people had gathered to enjoy the music of Fleetwood Mac was inconceivable to me. And I knew that when they heard of it the band would be devastated.

Photography © Ed Roach, roach-clips.com

John and Stevie on stage.

The death cast a pall over the next weeks on the road, and it was with relief that we returned to Los Angeles to play five shows at the Forum. The USC Trojan Marching Band would be a part of each concert and that, of course, added to our excitement. All five shows were sold out and each night the band's dressing room was packed with family, friends, and the usual glad-handing executives. An exception to the usual somewhat-smarmy executives was Danny Goldberg. Young, handsome, hip, funny, and brilliant, Danny was co-owner of Modern Records and had recently signed Stevie as a solo artist. Her future *Bella Donna* album would go to number one on Danny's label. He had a great friendship with Stevie and was also a close friend to the band. He was at many of the shows, and the Mac family was always glad to see him walk in. He, along with all of us, was eagerly anticipating the Forum shows. Like the rest of the tour, the band would be playing their hearts out.

But the highlight of each night was when the band performed the song "Tusk." Huge red curtains were hung around the stage shielding the USC kids from the eyes of the audience until the song began. As the band launched into the raucous strains of "Tusk," the curtains parted and the marching band, in full Trojan uniform, joined in, its members high-stepping down the aisles among the audience as they played their instruments. It was absolutely brilliant and it brought the house down.

The last three shows of the fall 1979 *Tusk* tour were in San Francisco at the Cow Palace. Even though these were amazing, the USC Trojan Marching Band was greatly missed by all of us. If we could have, we would have had them on the road with us for the entire tour. It was debated back and forth before the beginning of the tour, but the cost was astronomical, and in a rare moment of restraint Fleetwood Mac put cost over want and the marching band was left behind in L.A. But that was pretty much the only time budget came into play during this tour.

The money pouring in from record sales and box-office receipts was being spent hand over fist by every member of Fleetwood Mac. During the past seven weeks, grand pianos had been delivered to both Christine's and Stevie's hotel rooms whenever they wanted them. Hotel suites were painted pink if Stevie felt she needed to be surrounded by the flattering, soothing shade in order to perform. Cocaine was flown out on a regular basis by a dealer on the band's payroll, and Dom Pérignon was sipped like water by every member of the inner circle during all-night parties held in the best hotels across the country. While it was true that the tour had been grueling despite the five-star luxury, if we'd suffered, we'd done it in style.

By this time any little thing that the band wanted to do was done on such a huge scale that sometimes even we couldn't believe it. The last show in San Francisco happened to be on J.C.'s birthday. Before the concert, John McVie came tiptoeing up behind me and whispered into my ear that Lindsey and I had to hightail it out of the hall and back to the Saint Francis Hotel, where we were all staying, ASAP after the show.

"I'm planning a big surprise for J.C. and I want all the band to be there for it. Believe me, Carol, when you see what it is, you're going to absolutely die. And when you get to the hotel, go straight to J.C.'s room. Promise me you won't say a word to Courage, OK? Just get there as fast as you can," he said with a wicked laugh.

Whatever's going on, it's got to be big, I thought. *John has never in his life wanted to rush back to the hotel after a show. Damn, he's usually the last person to leave the hall. Yep, whatever's in store for J.C., it's big.* As soon as the band left the stage I whispered John's words into Lindsey's ear and within fifteen minutes all of the band members were in their limos heading back to the hotel, leaving a very puzzled J.C. behind. None of us had even wished him a happy birthday yet and he was worried. He knew that something was going on, and the entire evening he'd walked around with the look of a doomed man. And rightly so, I found out as soon as we arrived at his hotel suite.

Even before we knocked I heard weird sounds emanating from behind the door. Scratching, cackling noises that were distinctly out of place in a stuffy, conservative hotel like the Saint Francis—or at a motel, for that matter. A giggling Mick opened the door and ushered us into a room that was filled with chickens and covered with straw. With a high-pitched scream I ducked as three chickens went flying by my head in a flutter of wings. With a hysterically laughing Lindsey beside me, I stared in shock at the scene before me. Everywhere I turned there were chickens and roosters. Birds were perching in the middle of J.C.'s suitcase, on the television, on chairs and tables, and cackling happily on the straw covering the expensive carpet.

Hearing Dennis's voice coming from the bathroom, I dodged the chickens and poked my head inside. He was lying in the bathtub, fully dressed, with a cigarette in one hand and a bottle of blow in the other. He tossed me the bottle and gestured toward the rooster grandly perched on the toilet. "Pretty fuckin' cool, huh?"

Since it was pointless to even try to speak above the hysterical laughter coming from the rapidly filling outer room, I nodded my head and grinned as I dumped some blow on the back of my hand. Dennis looked completely demented lying in the tub, but not all that out of place in the shambles of a once-luxurious hotel suite. J.C. arrived and with laughter and good-natured curses, he accepted the inevitable and joined in with the serious partying going on around him.

With all of us coming and going at will, the chickens began to escape from the room and wander the hallway, pecking their way into open elevators and riding down into the lobby of the staid hotel. As the stunned hotel management chased hens around their plush lobby, they were not as amused as we. It would be the last time the band would be allowed to even walk through their hallowed halls—and it was with both relief and loathing that they wished us a firm goodbye forever as we departed for the airport the next day and headed back to L.A. for separate vacations for a six-week break in the tour.

STORMS

Lindsey and I went straight to Hawaii and spent three weeks in Oahu and Maui. Alone, drug-free (except for Lindsey's pot), and relaxed, we savored every single minute we were there. Tan, rested, and happy, we returned to

Lindsey and Carol Ann in Hawaii.

L.A. expecting to spend the next few weeks quietly enjoying our home. Instead, we were about to walk into a nightmare. Unlocking our door, we were met by a frazzled-looking Bob Aguirre.

Our house had been broken into again. During our vacation in Hawaii, Bob came home to find business cards from LAPD detectives stuck onto our

front door with a brief letter telling him that our house has been burgled. As he entered he saw chaos. Polaroids belonging to Lindsey and me lay all over the carpet in the den. Records, cassettes, and guitars had been taken off shelves and stands and also dumped onto the floor, as though someone had taken the time to examine them and then toss them wherever they pleased. Upstairs, in the master bedroom in which Lindsey and I slept, the bureau drawers were open, but unlike the robbery at the Putney house during the Forum show, everything was still lying neatly inside. The covers on our bed looked as though someone had rolled around on them—and there was one last piece of news that sent chills down our already frozen spines— because it made no sense whatsoever.

With wild eyes, Bob spoke in a hoarse voice, "Your bags of weed that were hidden in the closet were propped up against the wall, Lindsey. Just sitting there. It's totally freaky, man. I found a note Scotch-taped on the wall from the cops telling you to 'hide your weed better next time.' Thank God they're Fleetwood Mac fans, or the shit would have hit the fan. I called the Hollywood precinct this morning and the detectives told me that they found the weed exactly as I did. Just propped up against the wall. They were really nice about it—just said to tell you to put it away. I don't think anything has been stolen. Someone just came in and went through all of our things like a fuckin' tornado." Bob ran his fingers through his messy hair before continuing. "The cops think it's some deranged fan—but I dunno, Lindsey. I mean—did you hear about the murder?"

Now sitting on both sides of Bob, we looked at him in shock. "*What* murder?" we said in unison.

In answer, Bob got up and threw me a copy of the *L.A. Times* from a few days before. As my eyes scanned the story, I looked at Lindsey in disbelief. In the Hollywood Hills, a wealthy record executive and his girlfriend had been attacked in their home. Men with masks had walked into their bedroom in the dead of night and taken the executive downstairs after telling the girlfriend to stay in the bedroom—or else. The story went on to say that the executive was taken to his kitchen where he was beaten, stabbed, and left for dead. The girlfriend, who survived without physical injury, had listened to his screams and cries for help, but had been too paralyzed with fear to leave the bedroom even after the house had been deathly quiet for two hours. Finally, she crept downstairs and found her lover dead.

The killers were still at large and the motive was a mystery. Nothing was stolen in the house. The article went on to say that the entire music industry had been shaken to its core at the death of this much-loved young executive—and at the senselessness of it. If the motive wasn't robbery, then it looked like a thrill killing. The article finished on an even more sinister note, reminding L.A. that the Manson killings were not exactly ancient history and speculating that this murder had been perpetrated by another crazed cult. And that had everyone in L.A. absolutely terrified. Gun sales were up and alarms were being installed across the city in the homes of those who had felt safe only a week before.

I felt sick to my stomach as I told Lindsey everything I'd just read and we both sat and looked at each other. The burglary at Putney had been bad enough, but this was the second time our house had been broken into on June Street. It was just too much for either of us to contemplate what might have happened if we'd been home the night before when the break-in happened.

Lindsey looked at Bob and quietly told him that in the morning, he was going to buy a gun. Pulling me to my feet, Lindsey slowly walked me up the stairs to our bedroom and together we stripped the bed and threw the covers and sheets out into the hall. We never, ever wanted to have them on our bed again.

Two weeks later, Lindsey picked up his gun after the designated waiting period and slid it under his side of the bed. And he promised to take both of us to a shooting range to learn how to use it safely. But as it turned out, we were not going to have time.

The next night, we were shocked awake by the screeching of our alarm. On the panel in the bedroom, I could read the word "Intruder" flashing in red as I sat terrified in the dark. Within seconds, Lindsey dragged me off the bed onto the floor as he reached for the gun lying in its wooden case. In the moonlight, the dull silver finish gleamed as he took it firmly in hand and started for the door.

"What are you doing?" I asked in a panicked whisper. "Lindsey, please! Let's just lock the door and wait for help. The police will be here soon!"

As the phone rang and I answered it, I watched Lindsey cross the room and stand beside our bedroom door. The alarm company told me that help was on the way and I told them to hurry as I saw Lindsey open the door and start down the hallway, gun in hand. *No!* I thought as I threw down the phone. As I tried to pull him back into the room, he shook his head and tried to push me back. He whispered for me to lock the door behind him, but I was not about to let him go downstairs by himself. As the story of the murdered executive flashed through my mind, I knew that I simply couldn't stay behind while Lindsey walked into danger. And I was terrified, make no mistake about it—I was not feeling brave. I only knew that if something were to happen to Lindsey and I wasn't by his side to fight for him, I would never be able to live with myself.

My hands were slippery with sweat as I clung to Lindsey's arm as we made our way to the head of the stairs. It was hard to hear anything over the screaming of the alarm, but there seemed to be muffled sounds coming from the kitchen. Just as we began our descent down the dark stairs, our front door shook under thunderous pounding and we heard the shouts of the police ordering to be let into the house. Lindsey and I ran down the stairs, threw the door open, and stood back as six LAPD officers rushed past us with guns drawn and flashlight beams sweeping every corner of our large entryway.

As Lindsey hit the light switch, he was immediately ordered to drop the gun and identify himself as two of the officers pointed their weapons at him. In a heartbeat, the gun fell to the floor and was kicked away by a grim-faced cop. We were ordered to stay right where we were as they picked up the gun and ran toward the kitchen. The alarm company's officers arrived and within seconds our house was swarming with armed men searching every single room and corner of our two-story home.

We heard shouts coming from our backyard as the police gave chase to what we'd later learn was a man dressed in black. He got away by running through our back gate, onto the golf course directly behind our home. After thirty minutes, it was all over. The police found the window jimmied in the laundry room. God only knows what would have happened in the dark entry hall if a shot had been fired from the gun in Lindsey's hand.

Once again, help arrived just in time, and after it was finally over and all of the officers had left our home, Lindsey and I looked at each other and knew that we would never again feel safe in the house we had grown to love. Within two days, we'd put our home on the market and I was once again spending time looking at houses for us. Rentals this time—with the months of touring ahead, we didn't have time to look for a permanent home. We wanted a house that came stocked with dishes, furniture, and linens. And until we found one, we packed our suitcases and moved into the Century Plaza Hotel. I never again wanted to feel the terror and horror I felt as I walked down a dark hallway seeing only a dull silver gun glinting in Lindsey's hand.

15

STORMS

Within a week our realtor had found us the perfect house. It was on Coldwater Canyon and the owner was offering it to us completely furnished—down to the silverware. At a costly rent of $5,000 a month, it was a two-story house with a pool, a small gym, and three bedrooms. Bob would be moving in, of course. He'd become a permanent part of our household and both Lindsey and I wanted him with us.

There was only one problem. The band was leaving for Japan in two days and someone had to stay behind to move our clothes and personal items into the new house. There was also a multitude of business matters that needed to be handled in connection with selling our home in Hancock Park, and with Lindsey touring I was the only one who could do it. It was decided that I'd stay behind with Bob while Lindsey spent the next three weeks in Japan.

I missed him after he left, but I was so busy that the first five days seemed to fly by. On top of moving into our house, I was already being booked on interviews for Elite Modeling. I was scrambling to have pictures made for headshots and arranging my portfolio under their direction. I'd also been chosen to do a photo shoot for the Eagles songbook for *The Long Run* album. A photographer friend of mine, Jim Shea, would be shooting it and I was thrilled. I told myself that between the house, Elite, and the Eagles, I was not going to have one minute of free time to get too lonely. As it turned out, I needn't have worried.

On the sixth day of the tour the phone rang at 3 A.M. It was J.C., who told me that Lindsey hated being in Japan. The food sucked, as did the hotels, and worst of all, he had no weed to smoke. None. There were no drugs on this leg of the tour. Barely a month before, a humiliated Paul McCartney had been busted for trying to smuggle marijuana into Japan, making headlines across the world. In Japan it was a very serious offense to be caught with any kind of illegal substance, so it was too great a risk for Fleetwood Mac to take. But, like Lindsey, the other four were not pleased. All they had was warm sake and vodka tonics and that was not quite cutting it. Bottom line: Fleetwood Mac was not a happy group of campers, J.C. said.

"They're making my life a living hell, Carol. And Lindsey's totally miserable. You have to fly out tomorrow. I'm booking the ticket for you right now. I know you're busy there, but you *have to come*! I'm begging you. I need you to fly out and that's that," he finished in a pleading yet commanding tone.

Oh, ick. If everyone's at each other's throat, that's the last place I want to be. I hate Japan anyway. But if Lindsey needs me, I'll be on that plane, I said to myself as I listened to J.C. breathing heavily into the mouthpiece. With a sigh I told him that I'd pack first thing in the morning and asked him to get me an afternoon flight. I'd been to Japan before meeting Lindsey and I absolutely hated the two weeks I spent there on vacation. It was a wonderful place for many people, but personally I couldn't wait to get out of there. The most vivid memory I had of Japan was walking down the street in Tokyo and having multiple vendors offer me a fried sparrow on a stick. For a bird lover to see rows of tiny, crispy, *innocent* little birds being eaten like hot dogs was enough to make me ill.

I'd spoken with Lindsey on the phone during the past five days, and I already knew that he was unhappy, but I had no idea that things were as bad as J.C. was now saying. But, knowing the band the way I did, it was fairly obvious that in a week's time they'd be murderous—the lack of drugs and nothing whatsoever to make up for it would see to that. It was a tenuous balance within Fleetwood Mac at the best of times. I couldn't even imagine how bad it could be at the *worst* of times. And a drug-free tour in Japan would definitely, for Fleetwood Mac, qualify for one of the worst.

Ten minutes later, the phone rang again. It was Lindsey. J.C. had speed-dialed him to tell him that I was coming and he was ecstatic. He didn't want to ask me to come, he said, because he knew how busy I was with the house. But he was glad that I was on my way and he'd be at the airport to meet me in Tokyo. Two days later, after a twenty-hour flight, I was standing exhausted but happy by Lindsey's side once again. But at that night's show I found that not everyone was glad to have me back on the road.

Stevie seemed first shocked and then angry when I walked into the venue with Lindsey. Puzzled at first by her hostile attitude, I tried to rationalize that since her breakup with Mick, my new friendship with Sara—the woman who stole his heart away from her—was what had her upset with me. But I couldn't shake the feeling that there was more to it than that. Her reaction to me was exactly the same as when I first hit the road with Lindsey at the beginning of the *Rumours* tour. And it made me sad. *It's going to be a long two weeks,* I thought to myself with a sigh.

J.C. was right. Japan was a drag. The whole band was in a surly mood, bitching and moaning about no cocaine, no hamburgers, and just about everything to do with that leg of the tour. When a band's on the road, it's all about the hotel, room service, and, in Fleetwood Mac's case, the drugs. There's no time or energy for sightseeing, to do the things that other people do when they're in a new country. There was nothing to take Fleetwood Mac's mind off the hard work of touring. Japan was a flashback to Birmingham, England, during the *Rumours* tour, only there the audiences spoke English and responded to the band's concerts in a "normal" fashion: they yelled and screamed and applauded throughout the show.

In Japan the audiences sat quietly throughout the entire concert and then applauded politely at the end. It was like playing to a city of the dead, I told Lindsey. As I stood on stage and watched the kids sitting calmly in their seats, they barely even coughed during a song, much less showed excitement. That wasn't the Japanese way. We had no doubt that they were enjoying the show. It was just that they felt that it was rude to interrupt anyone—and screaming and dancing in the aisles was definitely considered rude. In Japan, politeness ruled. It wasn't that they didn't love the band; they respected them so much that they would rather commit *hara-kiri* than offend them.

The band appreciated this, but it didn't make for a very good time at the show. To make a bad situation worse, there was a documentary crew there filming the band both on and off stage, recording it all for posterity. And it was just totally embarrassing. Fleetwood Mac was so used to getting intense audience feedback that they were having a hard time playing when they got none at all. And with no drugs to give them fuel, it wasn't a pretty picture.

What was amazing in Japan was that in the airports and on the streets the band was treated as if they were royalty. We were followed everywhere by TV cameras, paparazzi, and hundreds of fans clamoring for autographs. So that appeased all five members of Fleetwood Mac quite a bit. Even so, everyone was relieved when it was time to leave Japan and go down under to Australia.

We landed in Perth on February 19. It was summer in Australia and everyone was thrilled to be in an English-speaking country. It just made everything easier. After Japan, Australia was like nirvana to us. The food was great, the hotels were plush, and the audience response was exactly like in America. The fans loved Fleetwood Mac and showed it by yelling and screaming hysterically from the moment they walked onto the stage until they left it. And the band was back in business with their party supplies. Everyone was happy and J.C. couldn't have been more relieved.

For the first eleven days things went smoothly. And then everything began to spin out of control as one thing after another turned a promising stay into a very ugly experience for both the band and myself. It was like a dark spell had been cast over the Australian leg of the tour. At first it seemed strangely funny. Then it turned into a nightmare.

Mick Fleetwood on the Australian Tusk *tour.*

First, the Melbourne police rousted Mick out of bed. They'd intercepted a small package of weed being delivered to one of Fleetwood Mac's roadies. They decided that Mick, perhaps because he had the same first name as the guy, was a heroin addict. They turned his room upside down looking for heroin and even examined his body for injection marks. Of course, they didn't find a thing, but it was disconcerting nonetheless. Mick took it in stride and managed to add the whole episode to his repertoire of sick jokes, regaling us all with the "life and death" horror of it.

But, underneath, I could see he was shaken. Who wouldn't be? It made the whole entourage nervous. But it didn't stop the partying—and that partying contributed to what happened next.

At the first of three shows in Melbourne, the band took the stage after indulging in a lot of pre-show "refreshments" of cocktails and blow. They still hadn't gotten over their deprivation in Japan and were spending every second making up for it. The band seemed to be having a great time on stage, going for it with their usual intensity when, for no reason whatsoev-

er, Lindsey lay down on his back in the middle of the stage and didn't get up. He hadn't collapsed. He didn't fall. He was just lying there flat on his back still playing like a demon—but doing it horizontally. I could see the other band members' faces fill first with concern, then confusion, and finally fury as he began writhing around like a maniac, refusing to get up even after Stevie stomped over and screamed at him.

He had a shit-eating grin on his face and as a reply to her angry remarks he used his feet to push himself around and around in a circle, never missing a note but nevertheless taking the coolness right out of Stevie's big showstopping rendition of "Rhiannon." And he stayed that way for three whole songs. Then he jumped back up and went back to playing as usual, obviously not giving a damn about the band's fury.

Lindsey and Stevie on the Tusk *tour.*

And it wasn't over yet. As soon as they took the stage again for their encore song, "Sisters of the Moon," he was at it again. Stevie's trademark entrance with robes flowing and a translucent shawl draped over her blonde hair was turned into a comic farce as Lindsey followed her every footstep with a shawl wrapped around *his* head. Looking like a demented Bedouin, he pranced around behind her, refusing to stand less than two feet away as she struggled to get through her song. The crew was sniggering and the audience was laughing, but Stevie wasn't. She was rigid with furious indignation. But what could she do? She made it through the song and abruptly walked off stage and didn't return. The show was over.

Not one band member talked to Lindsey backstage, but he didn't seem to care. He sipped his Myers's and Coke, partied on his own, and then we headed back to the hotel. There I spent another of my long nights watching over him as he sat propped up in bed, head on knees, rocking back and forth. I'd given him his Dilantin before the concert, but I was still worried and vigilant until finally, around 3 A.M., he slumped down and fell into a deep sleep. *He's OK now, so he'll be fine tomorrow. Just had a weird night, that's all . . . and God help me, I know it's awful but he was pretty funny tonight,* I thought just before sleep overtook me.

The next show passed without incident, and even though the band was still angry with him, Lindsey gave a solid performance and it seemed that the night before was a bizarre Fleetwood Mac aberration. But it wasn't. The last show in Melbourne would be more shocking than the first.

Just like the previous nights, the pre-show partying was twice what it was in the States. The consumption of alcohol and cocaine was way over the top, even for Fleetwood Mac. Despite this, the show was going great, and since Sara had arrived the day before, I was having a blast. Hopping on stage right before "World Turning," I stood

Lindsey on the Australian Tusk *tour.*

Photography © Ed Roach, roach-clips.com

Mick Fleetwood performing "World Turning."

quietly listening to the first half of the song. As Mick took center stage to do his wild-man act on the bongos I was turning to leave when suddenly a hand gripped my upper arm like a claw. Fingers dug into my arm and I was spun around and found myself inches from Stevie's hot, sweaty, and angry face.

Her fingers tightened like steel and as I tried to shake her off, pain shot down my arm like fire. Looking at her in confusion and shock, I could smell the alcohol on her breath as she started to scream at me that I was evil. Evil, evil, evil! She *hated* me, she said.

She screeched that she was never going to let Lindsey marry me. Because I was *evil!* I couldn't understand half of the things she was saying, but their meaning was clear enough. She hated me, hated that I was with Lindsey, and she'd see me in hell first before she "let" us marry.

While all this was happening the band was still playing. Stevie was supposed to be on stage singing, but instead she was spitting and screaming directly into my face. The others, naturally, knew that something was very wrong, but Stevie blocked me from their view. And because of this, they had no idea what was happening.

Suddenly J.C. came racing to my side and struggled to get Stevie to let go of me. With a last glare of fury at both of us, she wheeled around, almost falling before she regained her balance and stomped back on stage. J.C. helped me down the stairs and walked me to the dressing room. Even though he kept asking what had happened, I didn't trust myself to speak. I wanted to talk to Sara. Shaken and more than a little shocked, I quietly sat down next to her and told her what just happened. Looking at me in disbelief, she began to smile and within seconds we were both laughing hysterically. And we couldn't stop. With my arm still aching, it was the only reaction I'd allow myself. Even though I was laughing, I was on the verge of tears, but I refused to give in to them. I was too angry.

After the show Stevie once again left immediately and Lindsey was in high spirits, as was the rest of the band. They were pissed off about Stevie missing "World Turning," but attributed it to her overdoing it at the band's private pre-show partying. I didn't say a word to Lindsey about what had happened. I was torn between trying to keep peace among the band members and standing up for myself.

I'd risen above a lot of Stevie's slings and arrows since meeting Lindsey, but this time she'd stepped over the line and I didn't think I could let it go. But I was shell-shocked, upset, and tired, and I just wanted to go back to the hotel and go to sleep. *I'll think about it tomorrow, when my mind's clearer. I'll decide then if I'm going to tell Lindsey,* I promised myself as we finally left. Back at the hotel I went straight to bed while he worked on a new song. Within an hour I fell into a restless sleep.

The next morning Richard came to our room to smoke a joint with Lindsey before we left for the flight to Brisbane. I heard his voice in the outer room as I came out of the shower. Sitting back on my heels, I rubbed my sore arm, feeling angry and chagrined as I relived the past night's event. And I knew that I had to tell Lindsey. Because, as mad as I was, I didn't even trust myself to come face to face with Stevie on the plane. I needed him to tell me what to do. What happened to me was sordid and shocking—and I didn't intend to let it ever happen again. It was just too much.

Walking quietly into the living room of our suite, I sat down next to him. "I need to tell you something, Lindsey," I said in a low voice.

After taking one look at my face, both Richard and Lindsey stopped laughing and asked in unison, "What's wrong?"

I closed my eyes for a second, then told them everything that occurred between Stevie and me the night before. As I talked Lindsey's face went from concern to fury and then settled into grim determination. "*Fuck!* I fuckin' don't believe it!" he shouted.

Taking my hand, he told me to leave it to him—he was going to handle it. Richard's eyes were wide and his face solemn as he walked beside us out to our waiting limo. Both he and I knew that there was going to be trouble, no doubt about it.

Once on the plane, Lindsey made sure that I was comfortable and then walked like a panther back to Stevie, who was settling herself into a seat. He leaned over and talked to her for about two minutes and as I watched him walk away, I saw her stricken face and felt a sorrow that surprised me. I knew that I'd every right to feel furious, but knowing that didn't change the fact that I felt responsible for making her a target of Lindsey's anger. His wrath was no laughing matter and it was about to fall on Stevie. As he settled himself beside me he smiled grimly and told me that he and Stevie would have a private meeting once we got to our hotel in Brisbane. I nodded, then stared out of the window, trying to ignore the pangs of anxiety that were shooting through me. I really did like Stevie and this setback in our friendship truly upset me.

As soon as we reached the hotel Lindsey handed me our room key and told me he was going to see Stevie. I watched him follow her into an elevator and I took the next one alone up to our suite. Lighting a cigarette, I sat in the semi-dark room, waiting for his return. After an hour, a feeling of panic swept over me unlike any I'd felt before. And with the panic, nausea clenched my stomach and I couldn't seem to catch my breath. I stood up shakily, made my way to the bed, and lay down. I'd never felt anything like this before and it scared me. Trying to slow my breathing, I lay with eyes closed for what seemed like hours but was probably only fifteen minutes. And then the panic and nausea slowly gave way to exhaustion and weakness. I stared at the darkening sky outside my window, waiting for Lindsey—and my strength—to return.

I heard the door slam and within seconds Lindsey was sitting down next to me on the bed. Stroking my hair, he told me that everything was fine. He looked calm as he told me that he loved me and that when it was time for us to get married we would. And then he said that I'd see for myself at the show that night that I'd never have to worry about Stevie seeking retribution again.

I didn't ask any questions. I didn't really want to know what happened between them. But I was glad that it seemed to be resolved. I just wanted everything to be OK again. I didn't tell him that earlier I'd gotten sick out of the blue. We'd both been through enough for one day, and in two hours we had to leave for the show. This was one show I was not looking forward to, but I was going and that was that.

As soon as I walked into the dressing room Christie came running toward me. "Stevie wants to see you in the next room. Will you come, Carol?" the makeup artist asked in an urgent whisper. With a nod I followed her as Lindsey watched, a smile of satisfaction on his face.

Entering the makeup room, I stopped dead in my tracks as Stevie rushed toward me. Pulling up her shirt, she showed me her stomach, which was covered in ugly red blotches. She told me over and over again how sorry she was about what happened the night before as she pointed to her stomach as proof of how much she was suffering over it. "I broke out in hives! That's how upset I am, Carol! I don't remember much about last night, but I never meant to say those things and I'm really sorry. Don't be mad at me. OK?"

As she threw her arms around me I whispered that I was sorry too. "I just want us to be friends, Stevie," I said in a hushed voice. "I'm sorry that I had to tell Lindsey. I just didn't know what else to do." Seeing her poor stomach and the distress that was she going through, I knew that the few hours she'd spent with Lindsey that afternoon must have been intense. *The whole episode has been awful for both of us,* I said to myself miserably as I hugged her. *My head hurts and I don't think I can stand thinking about it any longer. Enough. This is dreadful and I hate it.* And I backed out of the room after giving Stevie one last hug.

Later that night during the show I was sitting with Sara backstage when Greg walked into the room. "Carol, I can't believe you're back here! Stevie just dedicated 'Landslide' to you!"

"She did?" I asked in surprise. As Greg nodded I groaned, "Sara! I probably just got my first and only dedication from Stevie on stage and I missed the whole thing! Don't tell her I missed it, Greg, OK?" A little confused, he left the room and I leaned back, closing my eyes as I thought, *I hope that's the end of it. I don't think I can take this drama any longer. Surely after tonight, everything that could happen has happened.*

STORMS

Two days later Lindsey and I sat at Brisbane Airport in a private room with the band. As glad as everyone was in the beginning to be out of Japan, the fact that we didn't have the Fleetwood Mac plane on this leg of the tour was now a source of much irritation to the band. Used to the luxury and privacy of their own jet, they were now quite pissed off about having to travel as "punters," and J.C. was once again the target of a lot of bitching and moaning about the hardship of flying commercial airlines.

But I wasn't complaining. Lindsey and I had just spent a very romantic night together and I sat contentedly in my chair watching him rummage through a carry-on bag. He was looking for an empty cassette to use to record a song idea that was going through his head. Holding up a tape with my name on it, he asked if he could have it. Assuming that it was one of the many assorted music tapes that I'd made at home upon which I'd recorded my favorite songs, I nodded and smiled as he sat down on the floor cross-legged and popped it into his cassette player.

He was humming as he pushed "record" and after less than a minute, he rewound the tape, put on a set of small headphones and pushed play. A minute passed, then another. He was lost in his own creative space, his fingers keeping time with the music. Suddenly, his hands froze. He looked confused, startled. His hands became fists and an empty look replaced his rapt expression. With a sense of foreboding, I reached out my hand to him. This morning's love was gone. He stared at me with accusing blue eyes that held only icy calculation. He ripped off the headset and threw it at me. "Put these on, now!" he commanded.

I put them on and heard Sara and me talking. It was one of my many "girlfriend" tapes that I'd made with Sara during the *Tusk* album. I was telling Sara about an incident on the road where one of J.C.'s paramours spilled a drink on my dress. Recounting the incident to her, I was saying what a great road manager and friend J.C. had been to me, that he always took care of me, and that I felt safe when he was around. He's a gentleman, I heard myself tell Sara earnestly. *Could this be why he's so angry? But there's nothing on that tape that should upset him! What is he hearing on that stupid tape? Oh my God, what did I say? Is he this angry because we're praising J.C.?* I wondered in disbelief.

I jerked the headset off and tried to explain to Lindsey that what he was listening to was just a silly "girlfriend" tape—and that when I said good things about J.C., it was all meant in the nicest way possible. But Lindsey wasn't hearing me. He put the headset back on and, as our flight was called and we walked onto the plane, continued to listen.

All through the two-hour flight, Lindsey listened to the tape. He sat stiffly in his seat, headphones clamped tightly on his head as he pushed play, rewind, play—over and over again. And he stared at me with eyes full of angry accusation. I knew that face. I'd told myself that I would never see it again. I knew that face and I was terrified of it. My mind raced back to the night of the Elvis Costello show and then leaped to what had happened at Christine's after my sleepover. Images of his face full of rage, hands reaching for my throat, a car screeching down a driveway, and handfuls of long blonde hair floating away in a bathtub tinted pink with blood. *No, it can't happen again, it can't . . . it won't, it won't . . .* I began to chant over and over as I clasped my hands tightly together to keep them from shaking.

A feeling of dread descended upon me, so powerful that it silenced my frantic internal dialogue. Like a mental anesthesia, this total absence of thought was calming. I looked past Lindsey to the small window, and saw the terminal growing larger and larger. I hadn't even felt the plane land.

In a little while, we would be alone at the hotel. The numb silence inside of me dissolved my fear and my jangled emotions. Most of all, it took away my confusion. What was there to be confused about? My path was clear. In a few moments I would walk off the plane with Lindsey, and whatever was going to happen would happen. Maybe someone in the band would step forward, take my hand, and shelter me from Lindsey's anger—for his face signaled his rage. If not, then I would hold on to what I'd always held on to: the knowledge that this was the man I loved and who loved me. That was all that mattered, wasn't it? It was all I had.

As the plane came to a stop, Lindsey stood up, his eyes never leaving my face. Within seconds, I felt the cold, hard grip of his fingers encircling my arm. Without a word, he pulled me into the aisle and shoved me toward the exit. When we stepped into the terminal, he wrapped his left arm around my shoulder and gripped me to him tightly.

As we walked through the terminal, the band members spoke to each other in hushed voices, as they watched Lindsey almost drag me. I was gripped so tightly to his side that I kept stumbling every few steps—and I would be jerked back upright and pushed forward—over and over again. I looked up as Lindsey roughly pushed the huge doors open to the sidewalk outside and saw Stevie staring at us with a shocked expression on her now white face. She looked into my eyes and took a few steps toward us, only to be pulled back by an equally white-faced wardrobe girl, Sharon Celani.

Lindsey came to a dead halt. J.C. was directing the band members to their individual Cadillac limousines, and I watched as Stevie climbed into the second car in line. I heard her call out J.C.'s name after she'd disappeared from view and he went rushing over to her limo. J.C. kept glancing nervously over his shoulder at us. He seemed to be arguing with Stevie.

Lindsey hugged me to his chest. He kept one hand secured to the back of my head as he shouted at J.C., "Damn it, J.C.! Which fucking car is mine?" There was no answer, and Lindsey muttered, "Fuck it, come on." He let go of my head, jerked me back around, and pulled me toward an empty car, a driver waiting patiently beside it.

"Mr. B.!" I heard J.C. shout. "Your luggage is in another limo! Stevie wants to talk to—"

His words were lost as Lindsey pushed me into the back seat and slammed the door. I pulled my legs up underneath me and tried to make myself as small as possible in the plush leather upholstery.

The driver climbed behind the wheel, powered down the glass partition separating the front seat from the luxurious rear passenger section, and nervously cleared his throat. "Uh, sir, I believe Mr. Courage wants me to wait—" the driver stammered.

"Fuck Mr. Courage!" Lindsey shot back. "*I'm* paying for this car! Take me to my fucking hotel! Now!"

The driver looked at Lindsey with a blank stare.

"Put the window back up!" Lindsey commanded. "I don't like being stared at!"

The driver quickly turned around and slipped on his sunglasses, offering a meek, "Yes, sir." Smoothly, he pulled away from the curb and pushed a button. The window hissed back up, hiding us from his view.

I quickly glanced at Lindsey and saw he had once again donned the headset. I leaned my head back, closed my eyes, and waited. The minutes passed. We sat, completely still. Only silence. Loud, loud, silence.

Suddenly desperate to see sunlight, I sat up straight and opened my eyes. Lindsey was staring out the window at the looming city of Melbourne, looking but not seeing. Only the movement of his hand betrayed the fact that he was not listening serenely to music. The hand that had been tapping out an unknown chorus of musical notes at the airport in Brisbane was now clenching and unclenching in his lap. I kept staring at his hand, as though I could will it to stop.

Our car pulled into a sweeping driveway and stopped in front of the Melbourne Hilton. Lindsey opened the car door and stepped out. I didn't want to move. He loomed over me. "Get out," he said softly.

I picked up my purse and climbed slowly out of the car. I saw J.C. entering the revolving door to the lobby, and I wanted to break into a run and throw myself into his arms. Lindsey caught hold of my wrist and held it firmly as we walked into the lobby. He left me at the elevator, muttering, "Don't move," and headed for the front desk. He walked up to J.C., looked him directly in the eye, and held out his hand for the room keys. J.C. handed him the envelope, dropped his gaze, and turned away.

Within two minutes, Lindsey inserted the key into the lock of our door, waited for me to enter, and then slammed it shut. The sound echoed in my head like a rifle shot. Lindsey grabbed my arm and threw me on the bed. "Get comfortable, 'angel'!" he intoned quietly. "Now that we're finally alone, we can listen to this together."

"Lindsey, don't," I begged as tears started to flow.

"SHUT UP!" he shouted as he slammed down the tape recorder and started to rewind the tape. "I want you to hear this with me. Together, baby, so we'll know what a bitch you are. That's what you are, isn't it? A little bitch that I can't so much as FUCKING TRUST!"

He paced across the room, his coldness replaced with anger so hot his eyes seemed to burn with it. I started to move away from him, to the far side of the bed, trying to put as much distance between us as possible. "Don't you fucking move!" he shouted. "I want you to sit close to me," he commanded in a seductive tone that was far more chilling than his explosive shouts. Moving quickly toward me, he grabbed me by the throat and started to squeeze as he whispered, "I want to look into that pretty face of yours and be close to you—just you and me, alone. No one to disturb us, interrupt us, while we listen. Ready?" Letting go, he picked up a lock of my hair and twisted it in his fingers, pulling it tight as I gasped for breath. "I asked you a question: *Are you ready?*"

I nodded, wiping the tears running down my face with the back of my wrist. He took a few steps to the cassette player and pushed the play button. He glided back and sat down next to me with a strange, fixed smile. We listened.

An eerie melody filled the room. Lindsey crooning a love song, low and wistful, then girlish laughter and the sound of two voices. I heard Sara giggling and saying, "Carol, tell me again what she said to you. I mean I can't believe she would dare speak to you after she'd spilled a drink on your dress! Start from the beginning."

I heard my voice answering, "OK. First of all, I couldn't believe it when we walked into the dressing room and I saw her hanging all over J.C. You know how cool he is, Sara. I mean, where would he pick up a groupie like that? [More laughter.] Don't say it . . . God, Sara, you should've seen that dress she had on. It was the worst!" I leaned back and closed my eyes as the tape continued. I heard two girls, laughing, acting deeply immature, talking about clothes, the crassness of a groupie, and our love and admiration of a gallant road manager.

I held my breath, waiting to hear whatever it was that I'd said on that tape that had transformed Lindsey from the warm man I knew and loved to this icy, black threat that was in front of me now. Lindsey jumped up off the bed, and I watched as he prowled across the room, running his fingers through his hair and cursing.

The two disembodied voices continued to reverberate throughout the room. I was now describing a new dress I'd bought, gushing about the design, the fabric, and color. The conversation was centered around fashion magazines, hairstyles, and what clothes we each had decided to take with us on the Australian tour. Nothing about secret crushes on other men. No complaints about my life or the love of my life, Lindsey Buckingham. No mention of Lindsey at all.

I tried to hear whatever it was on the tape that Lindsey seemed to be hearing. I was on emotional overload: exhausted, hurt, and over the edge. My mind raced, *Listen to it, Carol, listen. There's got to be something there. Something, anything that will explain why he's doing this. And if I can hear what's made him so angry then I can fix it—I can calm him down because I'm so scared and I don't know how to make it stop because I don't know why it started . . . what did I do? Was it my fault? Is this my fault? Lindsey loves me, I know he loves me and there's nothing on this tape that would make him do this. Lindsey, Lindsey, please . . .* As these thoughts ran through my mind, my body began to tremble, and I knew I was going to be sick.

I slid off the bed and staggered into the bathroom. Sinking to my knees, I began to throw up over and over again. The silent tears now gave way to sobs as I leaned my head against the cold tiles of the bathroom wall. I gave in to the numbness that crept over me.

Outside, I heard nothing. The tape had finished. Then laughter broke the stillness. Like a wounded animal, I shrank back against the wall. The murmur of words and then another laugh, and I realized that Lindsey was talking to someone on the phone. Without being aware of it, I'd gotten to my feet. Holding myself up with one hand against the wall, I took small steps toward the sound of his voice.

"Don't worry about it. I said she's not feeling well. Is he calling the airport? The earlier, the better. C'mon, J.C., what's the problem?"

Lindsey was sitting in a chair watching as I slowly made my way to the bed.

"Six A.M.? Good. Who's taking her? She doesn't need two bodyguards, J.C. Send Jet. Great. I don't want to think about the show right now. I'll call you tomorrow. Yeah, yeah. Bye."

So I was leaving. I sank down on the bed and felt the first flicker of hope as I watched Lindsey hang up the phone. Maybe it was over. Maybe I could just lie down now and close my eyes and wait to be sent away.

Still crying, I lowered my head to my knees. Within seconds, pain ripped through my scalp as Lindsey wrenched me to my feet by my hair.

"Are you trying to make me feel *sorry* for you?" he snarled as he half pushed and pulled me to the center of the room. I twisted myself out of his grasp and stumbled backward, speechless with shock.

"How *dare* you try to make me feel sorry for you!" A flash of movement, a fist to the side of my face, and the back of my head slammed into the wall. I crumpled to the floor.

"Get up."

Before I could answer, before I could think, before I could scream, he dragged me to my feet again.

Almost gently, Lindsey backed me up against the wall and held me by the throat. As his hands tightened, I could see the rage in his eyes and I knew that I was helpless. I could hear myself gasping, struggling for breath, but I felt so removed from it now. His face began to fade. And I must have been falling because the room was moving across my vision and then it stopped. There were no images now, only different shades of gray.

I didn't want to come back. I fought to keep the grayness around me. I didn't want to feel anymore, I didn't want to see anymore, I didn't want to try to understand anymore. I never knew before that I could feel so empty. The physical pain was intense—but it was the sensation of emptiness and helplessness that made me bring my hand to my mouth and bite down on it to keep from screaming. I was afraid to move, to make a sound, to do anything that would draw Lindsey back to me.

Deathly quiet enveloped the room, the quiet that you hear after thunder, as loud as the preceding explosion. Darkness was pressing in on me. I moved my head a little, just a little, desperate to see something familiar. I felt so lost as I slowly looked around the room. I didn't recognize anything. Not the chairs, the table, the carpet, the bed—the man on the bed. I didn't know the man on the bed. I could see the shape of his face through the shadows of the room and although it was Lindsey's face, that wasn't the Lindsey I knew. The tears started again, and I made no effort to stop them.

Slowly, I sat up. I looked at Lindsey and saw that he was watching me. Using the wall for support, I pulled myself to my feet and took faltering steps toward the bed.

Lindsey held my gaze for a few seconds and then turned over on his side. I climbed slowly onto the bed. Carefully lying down, I inched myself onto my back and stared at the ceiling. There would be no merciful sleep for me as I waited for the knock on the door. Pain and tears and a desperate sense of loss fought with my exhaustion to keep me awake, depriving me of even one small victory that day.

As dawn filled the room, I heard a knock, and I pushed myself off the bed to answer it. Jet was standing outside the door, waiting to guard me and take care of me. With one look at my face, he knew it was too late for that. His face froze with shock as he reached out to touch me.

I shook my head at him and stepped back. A small voice inside of me screamed, *Where were you when I needed you?* I cut the voice off with another shake of my head and pointed to my suitcase. It hadn't been moved from the spot where it was first placed by the bellman the night before. With his eyes still glued to my face, he picked it up and set it outside the door.

"Wait," I whispered, and shut the door, leaving him standing outside. Walking into the bathroom, I stared at myself in the mirror. There were two handprints on my neck. So perfectly formed, it looked as though an artist had pressed them onto my flesh in gray-blue paint. I looked away, knowing that if I gazed at those bruises a second longer I was in danger of losing the calm control that I was shielding myself with.

Mechanically, I splashed my face with water and turned to look for my carry-on bag. I reached into it and pulled out a long velvet scarf, carefully wrapping it around my neck. I didn't want anyone looking at me, talking to me, asking me questions. I didn't want to lie to anyone. I didn't want to bother anyone. There could be no explaining to strangers.

I picked up my carry-on, grabbed my purse from the floor, and paused briefly to take one last look at the man asleep on the bed then stepped out the door and closed it softly behind me.

A shocked and bewildered Jet escorted me through the airport as tears streamed down my face. On the plane I sat and quietly sobbed as the woman next to me stroked my hair, trying to console me. But I could find no consolation. I was utterly devastated.

Going straight home from the airport in L.A., I fell into a fitful sleep full of horrible images with a soundtrack of girlish voices laughing. At 4 A.M. the ringing of the phone woke me. It was Lindsey. He just wanted to make sure I was home safe, he said. He didn't mention the horrible fight. He told me that the band would be in Hawaii within a week's time and he wanted me to fly there to rejoin the tour. Exhausted, bewildered, but grateful that for now, at least, he seemed calm, I quietly told him, "Lindsey, we need to talk—"

Lindsey interrupted me, "There's nothing to talk about. Everything's fine. I want you to come to Hawaii, Carol, I miss you."

"Sure," I said softly and hung up the phone. Tears ran down my face as I tried desperately not to think about what had happened in a nondescript hotel room in Australia. And I tried to understand how without warning, Lindsey would become a dangerous stranger, but that afterward he would once again be the Lindsey I knew and loved—but refused to acknowledge that anything had ever happened. Did he really not remember? It made no sense, but yet, it was true.

STORMS

A part of my mind knew that I should pack my suitcase, move out before he got back, and never, ever see him again. But I felt so shell-shocked, so exhausted, and so overwhelmed that doing that seemed beyond me. And I still loved him. God, how I loved him. I didn't understand why this had happened—and I doubted that I ever would—but it didn't matter if I understood it. I just had to make it stop. For his sake, as well as mine. I knew that I hadn't done anything wrong to cause his rage, but at the same time I felt that it must be my fault for not knowing how to keep it from happening again. And I truly believed that if I tried hard enough, was smart enough, loved long enough—that I could save us both from whatever demons seemed to be following us. I knew that I had to try.

Four days later I received a phone call from Sara. Things were not good, she told me. As I listened in stunned disbelief she told me about what had just happened in Auckland, New Zealand. At a concert in front of thirty thousand people, Lindsey totally lost it on stage. The show was being simulcast over radio to all of New Zealand, which only added to the horror of what she was telling me. I sank down onto the floor as I listened to her story.

The band had only been playing for a little while, she said, when Lindsey suddenly pulled his jacket up over his head—once again mimicking Stevie and her shawl-draped stage persona. He followed her around in grotesque imitation, intentionally playing the wrong parts on his guitar song after song. And then, before anyone could even try to stop him, he started kicking out at her with his heavy cowboy boots, doing his best to land blows on her unprotected legs—and when he did, the kick seemed to stun her.

The audience was also stunned, Sara said. Stevie frantically tried to stay away from his steel-toed cowboy boots and the whole show fell apart. And it all happened in front of thirty thousand fans in the audience and untold thousands listening on their radios. Afterward, when the band headed back to the dressing room, Christine walked up to Lindsey and slapped him hard across the face as she screamed, "Don't you ever do that to us again, do you hear me? How dare you do that to the band and Stevie?" She then threw a drink in his face.

As I listened in shock I thought back to the fight Lindsey and I had that caused me to leave for home and I felt sick to my stomach. "He hasn't called me today, Sara. I don't know what to tell you. I don't know what's wrong. Tell Stevie how sorry I am that it happened, OK? I feel really, really awful that she had to go through that."

"She cried hysterically after the show. It was really bad. Carol, what happened between you and Lindsey the night before you left?" Sara asked softly.

"I don't want to talk about it, Sara. I just can't right now. But let J.C. know that I'm coming to Hawaii. Maybe once the band is back in the States everything will be back to the way it was before Australia. I don't know, Sara," I told her with a heartfelt sigh. "I'll see you real soon. Thanks for letting me know, honey. I'm going to call Lindsey. I need to make sure that he's all right."

As soon as I'd hung up the phone I went running for my *Tusk* road book and dialed Lindsey's room. He answered and in a subdued voice told me that he wasn't feeling well but that he couldn't wait to see me. He just wanted to go to sleep, he said. As we made small talk I kept waiting for him to bring up New Zealand, or what happened between us in Melbourne, but he didn't. So I told him that I loved him and hung up the phone. *I pray that I never, ever have to go to Australia again,* I thought to myself as I slowly walked upstairs to our bedroom. I loved the country when I first arrived. But now I knew that my last night in Australia would forever haunt my dreams—and Melbourne had now become my city of the damned.

Three days before I left for Hawaii I got a much-needed distraction. It was time for me to do the shoot for the Eagles songbook. Jim wanted to use me as the model for two songs, "Disco Strangler" and "King of Hollywood." The first shoot was done during the day in his studio and I got to dance all day long dressed in a gold Stephen Burrows cocktail dress as a leering "strangler" lurked in the background. That night we did the second shoot in the backyard of my home in Coldwater Canyon.

There was a Jacuzzi by the pool and with a sleazy-looking actor and Jim's girlfriend Karen as my fellow models, we took the pictures for "King of Hollywood." The shoot was a total success. I was already a friend of Jim's live-in girlfriend and we had a blast as we giggled and posed in the Jacuzzi as naive models falling under the spell of the sleazy character in the Eagles song. And it felt so good to laugh again.

Jim was happy with the shoot, as was I—until he told me what he assumed would be an amusing anecdote. Jim laughingly told me that one of Glenn Frey's friends had asked for my phone number from him—

and I gasped in horror. Glenn's band opened for a small part of the *Rumours* tour and one of his band members shadowed my every move on the road. And Lindsey was not pleased. It led to an apology from Glenn to me (even though it wasn't his fault) and I was more than relieved when his band's stint with the tour was over. With all that was happening in the unhappy world of Fleetwood Mac, all I needed was to start receiving phone calls from an obsessed male admirer. The very thought made my blood run cold.

When I landed in Oahu two days later, Lindsey was waiting for me at the airport. He looked wan and thin as he threw his arms around me. There was a haunted expression in his eyes now that wasn't there before Australia. It reminded me of a photograph I saw once of a soldier standing alone in the jungles of Vietnam, looking lost and at war with his own demons—demons that he never realized existed. And as I held Lindsey a wave of empathy and concern washed over me. And I knew that my appearance was the mirror image of his. For the first time in my life I was having horrible headaches that lasted for hours and nightmares that lasted all night. The Far East *Tusk* tour had taken its toll on both of us.

The band was playing three shows on Oahu, and then taking a month off before the next leg of the tour. I took a deep breath as I climbed out of the limo and headed toward the backstage dressing room. With all of the ugly, sordid events of Australia weighing heavily on everyone's shoulders, it was a tense and cold atmosphere that greeted me as I entered the room. The usual banter, ribald joking, and excitement was now replaced with uneasy glances, resentment, and a heavy silence as the five members of the band went about their pre-show rituals.

But you know what? For the first time since meeting Lindsey I really didn't give a damn about the intrigues and soap-opera dramas that were ebbing and surging around the backstage and its inhabitants. I'd had enough. It seemed almost childish and definitely self-indulgent of the band members to walk around with their alternating tragic, angry, and martyred expressions. *Why don't they just sit down and talk to each other?* I thought in frustration. *Why is everything always allowed to simmer and fester until the inevitable explosion? I understand why Stevie can't do it with Lindsey—but maybe if the rest of the band did that then none of this would have happened. I really believe that they thrive on it. Enough already.*

I had my own personal trauma to deal with and the usual Fleetwood Mac soap opera just couldn't compare with what I experienced in Australia during my fight with Lindsey in our hotel room. I just wanted to go home and put the past weeks behind me. And I was not alone.

Richard Dashut had quit. Those three shows in Hawaii would be his last on the *Tusk* tour. He was tired of touring, he told me. He needed a break and he didn't know when, if ever, he'd tour with the band again. Even though I was surprised and saddened to hear that Richard would no longer be on the road, I completely understood. Touring with Fleetwood Mac was insane at the best of times. It was hell on earth during the worst.

Despite the storm clouds hanging over all of us, the shows passed without incident. Everyone was just too tired and emotionally drained to do any more damage to the fragile ties that were keeping the band together. But in the middle of the grimness a little light shone—even if it was unintentional satire at my expense.

Backstage after the first show, I looked up in surprise as I heard Stevie calling my name as she beckoned me into the small makeup room. Surprised and curious, I followed her into the brightly lit room. Stevie threw her arms around me and gave me a brief hug and then stood with both of her hands resting on my shoulders. She told me that she wanted to talk to me about Lindsey and my relationship with him. *Please no,* I thought desperately. *I can't deal with another scene right now. I really can't.* I started to pull away from her but found that her slim fingers were holding me tightly. Trapped, I waited with resignation for whatever was coming.

I got a thirty-minute lecture about how to be the perfect woman for Lindsey. She told me that she was aware of how difficult it must be to live with him. She should know, she said. We both began laughing and I started to relax. She went on and on about how perfect Lindsey and I were for each other. After fifteen minutes she started talking about auras and visions and for the life of me I couldn't really make sense of what she was saying. I mean, Stevie's philosophy about "Life with Lindsey Buckingham" was so mystical and otherworldly that a mere mortal had no hope of understanding it.

After twenty-five minutes head was spinning. I knew that Lindsey must be wondering where I was, and just when I was about to make my excuses to Stevie and tell her thanks for the talk but I gotta go, I heard a voice behind me say, "OK. That's great. It's a wrap in here." Turning in shock, I saw that a camera crew had filmed the entire discussion. With my back to them, I had no idea they were there—but Stevie knew. As soon as they said, "It's a wrap," she smiled sweetly at me and swept out of the room.

Unh! I can't believe what just happened! She just used me for one of her "crystal vision" speeches and it's all on fucking tape! I can't friggin' believe it! How embarrassing is this? Oh my God. Grabbing the camera operator by the arm, I demanded an explanation. "It's for the documentary we started in Japan. I thought you knew we were taping! It's a great piece. I'm sure we'll use some of it. We'll send you a copy when it's finished."

"Don't bother. You might have Stevie's permission to use this, but you don't have mine. If you have a problem with that, take it up with Lindsey!" I said sharply. With a not too pleased nod the camera operator looked balefully at me as I stomped past him and went in search of Lindsey. After I told him what just happened, he laughed.

"It's just Stevie doing her high-priestess act, Carol. I'll tell the director to cut it. Too bad you had your back to the camera, though. It could have been your big break into the movies!" he sniggered. With a roll of my eyes, I followed him out to our waiting limo.

After the last show Richard was given a royal send-off—Fleetwood Mac style, of course. He was made to crawl and grovel through the debris of a huge cake to find a gold Rolex watch given as a parting gift by the band. Cream pies were thrown like confetti by the crew at each other, the band, and the inner circle before a cheering crowd of fans gathered in the backstage area.

But, despite the surface appearance of camaraderie and celebration, there was an underlying tension that showed in the subdued but still malevolent glances between Christine, Stevie, and Lindsey. And as soon as Richard found his watch the band members departed in their separate limos in an unseemly rush to be rid of each other. With half-hearted good-byes we scattered to the four winds to take our month off to recover from the Far East *Tusk* tour.

16

ENDLESS SUMMER

Over the next month Lindsey and I stayed in our new home on Coldwater Canyon, trying to leave the stress behind us and doing our best not to speak of the events in Australia, which wasn't hard. Lindsey refused to speak about what happened between us and honestly, I was afraid to insist. I told myself that we both needed to heal and that what was done was done. And I told myself that it couldn't possibly happen again.

We spent our days lying by the pool, going out to our favorite restaurants, and trying to keep to a "healthy" lifestyle. We didn't do blow, we had no all-night parties, and, most importantly, we had no contact whatsoever with the band. The only dark cloud hanging over us was the sales figures for *Tusk*.

They were very disappointing to Lindsey and it wasn't just the new direction of the album that had hurt sales. Warner Bros. broadcast the entire album on the radio a week before its release. Fans by the thousands taped the whole thing, thus avoiding having to spend hard-earned money on a double album. Bootlegs were already circulating across the country, and they were a lot cheaper than the $16.98 that the stores were asking.

My experience in bootleg records came in handy this month as I explained to Lindsey, over and over again, the realities of avid fans and collectors when it came to music: taping a radio broadcast of an unreleased album was a fan's fantasy, an artist's nightmare, and a record bootlegger's dream. There was little doubt that people were listening to the record. It was just that, thanks to the radio broadcast, they didn't have to pay for it.

But we both knew that the band members would blame Lindsey for the sales and not the preemptive radio broadcast that had cut deeply into those numbers. He was the easiest target. Unlike Lindsey, the band wasn't into the Clash and the Sex Pistols or finding a new direction in their music. They still didn't seem to get his new music at all. Even so, Lindsey stood by his creative decision to not do another *Rumours* album. And I was his most ardent supporter.

Two weeks before we left to go back out on the road, Lindsey asked me to design a new stage look for him for the rest of the tour. He was tired of the suit and wanted something completely different. I designed flowing, sheer loose shirts made from silk gauze with gold and silver threads and paste jewels glittering against their sheer fabrics. Once made, they resembled New Wave pirate shirts. I also chose heavy Chinese silk cloth embossed with dragons and symbols for three fitted blazer jackets in silver, blue, and red. He'd wear the shirts

Lindsey offering his idea for a new stage look.

and jackets with blue jeans. Armed with Lindsey's measurements, I took the designs and fabric to a seamstress and by the time we went on the road they were ready. And, just like the Armani suit, the new wardrobe rocked.

A day before we climbed on board the Fleetwood Mac jet we got the news that we had a buyer for our June Street house: Francis Ford Coppola. The director of *The Godfather* would be moving in as soon as it was out of escrow. Collapsing in hysterical laughter, Lindsey and I spent the day envisioning break-in scenarios where the hapless degenerates of Hollywood came face to face with Marlon Brando, Robert De Niro, and Al Pacino sipping coffee in our living room. And we knew that if that were to happen, Coppola could just turn off the alarm system permanently. Because nobody liked waking up with a decapitated horse's head under their bed covers, Coppola's offer on our house was one that we just couldn't refuse.

The U.S. tour was subdued but successful. The band and the inner circle were walking on eggshells around one another. None of us wanted a repeat of Australia. And slowly but surely the fractured relationships between band members were healing. If anything, the ugly scenes in Australia had shocked all of us into being on our best behavior. We were so polite and solicitous to one another that it was downright sickening. But still, it was a welcome change from the ugly tension and viciousness that had left all of us scarred from the last leg of the tour.

We left for Germany on May 25 and on the first day of June, the band headlined an outdoor show at Munich's Olympic Horse Riding Stadium. Playing before thirty thousand people in the huge, rainswept stadium was mind-blowing for the entire Fleetwood Mac family. Watching the vast and frenzied German audience made all of us realize just how loved the band's music had become. It was one thing to know the album sales and the chart numbers, but it was quite another to see with your own eyes thirty thousand young, hip *German* rockers singing along in English to "Go Your Own Way." And it was a pretty sensational kick-off for the European *Tusk* tour.

It was Mick and J.C.'s genius idea to have us travel by train through Germany and into France and Holland. At least it would have been a genius idea if not for one small macabre fact. The lounge car of our small private train once belonged to Adolf Hitler. When we first boarded we oohed and aahed over the luxurious velvet curtains and sofas, the gilded lighting fixtures and the gleaming wood interior of the perfectly preserved coach. Then

John McVie on the European Tusk *tour.*

we found out who the original owner was and we all felt like vomiting. It was totally sick and no one—not even the Third Reich collector maniac John McVie—could stand spending more than one minute within its walls. And it got worse.

The elderly and distinguished white-jacketed attendant on board was once the Führer's own servant. It was a little like being on a train from hell. Needless to say, we spent the entire time in the dining car and in our private tiny sleeping rooms, trying to avoid the train's ghastly lounge car and its polite but creepy manservant. We counted the minutes until we could get off and leave the Twilight Zone for our hotel in the cities scheduled on this leg of the tour.

Two days after Munich, on a hot and sunny day, Fleetwood Mac played before fifteen thousand American GIs on the U.S. Army base an hour outside of West Berlin. All of us had been looking forward to this show. The stage was gigantic and the band started playing before dusk in deference to the soldiers' early-morning wake-up time on the base. I was wearing a cropped white top and long, thin gauze skirt over knee-high boots, and under the klieg lights and the still-smothering heat of the waning sun, I was dying from the heat.

As I stood on the side of the stage I noticed that there were two huge fans set up behind the band to cool them down as they performed and I walked over to stand in front of one. The stage was so large that I assumed that I'd be barely noticeable as Fleetwood Mac swirled and performed in front of me. But I was wrong. As I stood there enjoying the wind on my back, flashbulbs started popping like mad and wolf whistles replaced the cheers that had only moments before been accompanying the band's set.

What the . . . ? What's going on? Did Stevie's top fall down or something? I thought in bewilderment. For there was no mistaking the soldiers' reaction—a male roar of approval for a skimpily clad female. Looking in confusion at Stevie still draped in her shawls, I gave a mental shrug and went back to listening to the music.

Suddenly I saw J.C. charging toward me. Laughing so hard that his face was crimson, he grabbed me by the arm and started pulling me frantically toward the side of the stage. "What are you doing, J.C.? Have you lost your mind?" I shouted as I tried to shake off his arm.

"Oh my God, Carol! You have to get off the stage right now!" he shouted back as he stood in front of me, blocking my view of the front of the stage. As the soldiers started booing he doubled over in hysterical guffaws.

"What's happening? I don't understand! What did I do?" I screamed as I peered over J.C.'s shoulders at the thousands of guys in the audience.

"Carol, you're standing in front of lights and a fan. Your skirt is see-through! You look stark naked up here except for your boots! It's like you're a *Playboy* pin-up! It's ruining the show—no one's paying any attention to the band! You gotta get off the stage right now! I'm not kidding, man. Oh my God!" J.C. gasped through his giggles.

Looking down at my skirt in horror, I clamped my hand over my mouth and screamed, "*Jesus,* J.C.! Get me *outta* here!" Grabbing his hand, we both took off running as the soldiers applauded and whistled. With the sound of laughter and cheers ringing behind me, I fled backstage with J.C.

Jeez, I thought as we scurried through the backstage halls, *I bet more pictures were taken of me than of the band tonight. It could have been worse, I guess. At least my T-shirt isn't see-through.* I felt like banging my head down on the nearest table as I meekly hid in the band's dressing room for the rest of the show. I'd be mercilessly teased for days about my unintentional burlesque performance in front of America's GIs. But at least I did my part by lifting the spirits of American soldiers.

The Third Reich train carried us to Cologne, where two shows were scheduled. At the first I watched the band's entire set standing below the stage. I was still chagrined about making a public spectacle of myself in front of the GIs and I paid penance by standing in the dark wings and watching from afar.

After the show our caravan of seven limousines pulled up in front of our hotel and came to a dead halt. There was nowhere to park—the whole front of the building was already lined with limos. We climbed awkwardly out into traffic as our angry driver cursed the other cars. It was normal for there to be a few other limos at any of the five-star hotels we stayed at on the road, but to see an endless line of long cars was definitely out of the ordinary. And as soon as we entered the lobby we found out whose they were.

Mick Jagger, with his entourage of about thirty people, was sitting in the opulent lobby. He was holding court seated alone on a gold velvet couch and he called out a welcome to us as we stood gaping at his unexpected presence. Gesturing royally for us to enter his abode, he started with a loud, "So sorry I missed your show, mates. Couldn't make it, I'm afraid . . . but have a quick drink with me."

Looking diminutive but every inch the rock star that he was, he held up a bottle of champagne and beckoned us to come closer. We did—or at least we tried to. His entourage, except for the empty space next to Jagger on his couch, took every available inch of seating space. As he sat waiting expectantly, it was immediately obvious that the only course of action was to pretty much line up like idiots and pay homage to him one at a time.

And, to Lindsey's dismay, this was exactly what everyone did. It was apparent that to the other four band members and our inner circle Jagger was well worth the wait in line. I saw Lindsey's face darken as first Christine, then Stevie, blushed and giggled in his presence. Each one sat beside him for five minutes and then stood up to let the next person sit down. While Jagger was sitting like the king of cool, offering a limp handshake to the other band members and basking in the attention, I swear I could almost see steam coming out of Lindsey's ears. He pulled me back and muttered that the whole scene was making him sick and he grabbed my arm as he headed to the bar. Once there, he knocked back two shots of Jack Daniel's and gave me an evil grin.

"Let's go pay homage to the king, shall we, Carol?" he slurred as he started walking back to the line of people still waiting for their turn to bow before the great Mick Jagger. Cutting into line in front of Curry, within minutes we were standing in front of the face with the sensual big lips and carefully coiffed hair that had graced a thousand magazine covers and sold millions of records.

Glancing up at Lindsey, I caught my breath as a sense of foreboding washed over me. He had the look on his face that my cat used to get right before he'd knock over the parakeet cage to try to catch and eat the poor fluttering birds as they spilled feathers and careened around our living room in Tulsa. *Uh-oh. This is not good. Please, Lord, don't let Lindsey loose on poor unsuspecting Jagger; he'll never know what hit him. Oh no, here we go,* I thought as I put a restraining hand on Lindsey's arm, but I knew it was no use. Once he got in the mood to knock someone off whatever pedestal they'd foolishly climbed onto in his presence, the result was usually quite unnerving. Add a couple of large shots of Jack Daniel's to Lindsey's sarcastic wit and there was no telling what could happen. I felt sorry for Jagger as Lindsey sat down quietly next to him. Holding my breath, I waited for the inevitable taunts to begin, for I was used to Lindsey's sarcasm and was almost always extremely entertained by it. But even I gasped in horror at what came out of his mouth.

Lindsey threw himself down onto the couch next to Mick and fixed him with a steely gaze. Jagger sat looking expectantly at him, waiting for a handshake or at least a nice "How do you do?" from Lindsey. He didn't get it. Lindsey waited a full thirty seconds and then proclaimed in a loud voice to Jagger, "I hear you'd like to suck Tom Petty's dick."

As Lindsey's words rang out into the lounge, a deathly silence fell over the lobby. Jagger's entourage and the Fleetwood Mac inner circle froze, staring in stunned disbelief. Mick's face turned bright red as his eyes rolled wildly in his head. He looked exactly like a trapped animal staring at his executioner.

"What did you say?" Jagger stammered.

"I read *Rolling Stone* a few weeks ago and you were going on and on about how much you liked Tom Petty, Mick. And that's what you said you liked to do, isn't it?" Lindsey said with a wicked smirk. As Jagger stuttered that what he meant was that he just liked Petty's music, Lindsey interrupted him to ask him the same question about doing the nasty with Tom, insisting that he was only repeating a direct quote from Jagger.

And I was dying. I was having a hard time trying to keep from bursting into hysterical laughter, but at the same time I was all too aware of the mutinous mutterings that were beginning to rumble all around us from Mick's loyal entourage. Looking desperately around for help, I saw J.C. getting off the elevator and ran to him. When I whispered into his ear what Lindsey just said to Jagger, he took one look at me and exploded into laughter.

"It's not funny, J.C.! You better help me get him away from Jagger or God only knows what's going to happen next!" I grabbed J.C. by the hand and we both rushed up to Lindsey, who now looked like a very evil cat who'd *killed* a parakeet and was chewing on its bones. J.C. and I started talking to Jagger in a stream of words: "It's nice to meet you . . . Gotta run . . . Gotta go . . . See ya!" We each took one of Lindsey's arms and pulled him away from the stunned and humiliated lead singer of the Rolling Stones.

Lindsey went willingly with us. His mission was done. He'd knocked Mick Jagger flat on his ass. It wasn't that Lindsey had any personal dislike of Mick. We both loved the Stones. He just hated pretentiousness. And I had to admit, the scene in the lounge when we first arrived was the epitome of vain posturing. Happy now that he'd dethroned the king of cool, Lindsey came quietly to our room with me and fell asleep as soon as his head hit the pillow. Giggling, I climbed into bed and did the same.

In the Sportshalle dressing room the next night, it was thirty minutes before showtime and J.C. was freaking out. No one knew where Mick Fleetwood was. He'd vanished. As he was usually the first to arrive at every single show, for him to be this late was enough to put him on a missing person's list at police headquarters. Frantic phone calls were going back and forth to the hotel and every member of the band and crew had been questioned over and over again about the last time he was present and accounted for.

J.C.'s face was blanched and pinched with the knowledge that all was not well in the land of Fleetwood Mac. The last reported sighting of Mick had been in Jagger's hotel suite and that was at 6 A.M. Nobody was answering the door and the hotel was refusing to forcibly enter the domain of the legendary Jagger to look for a missing drummer. Meanwhile the band was growing increasing irritated and worried.

Suddenly, like an apparition from hell, Mick appeared like a six-foot-six zombie in the doorway of the dressing room and, as one, we gasped. For as he stood there clutching the doorframe, not only did he have dark circles under eyes in a chalk-white face, he was wearing dirty jeans and a T-shirt that was *inside out*! Nobody had ever seen Mick dressed in anything that even sported a wrinkle, much less dirt. As soon as I saw that T-shirt I knew that we were in deep trouble. Mick's everyday sartorial splendor was his trademark. He wore a gold pocket watch in his tailor-made waistcoats even on a day off.

As Mick took a few halting steps into the room, J.C. grabbed his arm before he fell onto the floor like a giant tree. Moaning, Mick threw a hand over his mouth and we all knew that he was going to spew. With a strangled cry he wrenched himself from J.C.'s grasp and ran to a bathroom that was, thank God, just a few feet away. As we listened to him vomit violently into the toilet we stared at the bathroom in dismay.

No one said a word. We were all too shocked. J.C. walked grimly into the bathroom and walked back out looking as ill as Mick sounded. "Grab your purses and wallets and go straight to the limos. Mick's as sick as a dog—as you can hear. There's not gonna be a show tonight. I want the band out of here before we announce it. It's too dangerous to have any of you still in the hall when we tell the punters that the show's been cancelled.

Goddammit!" he screamed as he glared over his shoulder at Mick, who was still vomiting.

We all sprang into action, grabbing our bags and taking off at a run down the long hallway back to the loading dock where our cars were waiting. It was past showtime already and we could hear stomping and frenzied shouts coming from inside the theater. The crowd was growing impatient for Fleetwood Mac to take the stage and it was already turning ugly. And it was scary. Still dressed in their stage clothes, the band was grim-faced as we reached the limousines. Mick was half-walked, half-carried by two huge venue bodyguards and pushed none too gently into his car. The smell of vomit followed in his wake and I felt nauseous as the smell enveloped me.

There was a sense of fear and urgency in the air as we threw ourselves into the cars. I heard Stevie's wail of frustration as one of her shawls slipped off her shoulders and landed on the dirty ground. Greg grabbed it and threw the sparkling silk garment into the car, slamming the door behind her. Screaming, "Go, Go, Go!" at the chauffeurs, he stood with his arms crossed and a worried look on his face as we went speeding by him.

As we raced away I looked back over my shoulder to the still-full parking lot of the arena and worriedly asked Lindsey what he thought would happen when the cancellation was announced. He grabbed my hand and reassured me that it was going to be OK. "They'll reschedule the show," he said, but he was clearly angry and upset about having to disappoint over fifteen thousand fans. He was very quiet on the ride back to the hotel and paced the room for an hour waiting for J.C.'s phone call.

It wasn't good news. The fans rioted after the announcement. Chairs were thrown as fights broke out in an apparent rush for both the stage and the exit. And Fleetwood Mac would have to pay for the damages. Luckily none of the crew or fans were hurt and everyone got out—but it was an ugly scene. I knew that Mick was on *everyone's* shit list for his twenty-four-hour party with Mick Jagger. Lindsey and I both agreed that we were glad that Jagger was knocked off his pedestal the night before. But then again, he got his revenge. The band lost a show and their drummer his dignity—but it was only rock 'n' roll, as the Stones would say.

The rest of the tour through Europe seemed tame compared with Germany. The finale was six sold-out shows in Wembley Stadium in London. Like the Forum in L.A. and Madison Square Garden in New York, playing

Wembley was the epitome of success for a rock band. And Fleetwood Mac gave amazing performances at each of the shows.

But it wasn't the Fleetwood Mac shows that had Lindsey and I so excited about being in London. We were

Carol Ann and Lindsey playing Monopoly on a day off.

going to see the Clash play in a small hall on the outskirts of the city. This band had inspired Lindsey to walk down a new path with his music and both of us had memorized all the lyrics from their double album *London Calling*. We'd played it nonstop on this tour. So it was a nice change for Lindsey to be the one feeling the excitement of being a fan instead of the adored artist. And I was every bit as thrilled.

The concert was held in an old decrepit hall. Stark and dirty, it was absolutely perfect as a backdrop for the band. Dressed in ripped jeans and T-shirts, we managed to slip unnoticed into the upstairs balcony, Lindsey keeping his head down.

When the Clash took the stage, the punked-out audience went mad. The music hit us like a wall of unpolished sound and raw emotion. The acoustics and almost nonexistent mixing board erased the subtle nuances of the recorded versions, but still, it was the Clash, and that was all that mattered. They were the antithesis of Fleetwood Mac—gangling blue-collar boys singing rage-infused melodies. It was dripping with feeling and Lindsey listened in rapt attention as he downed pint after pint of beer.

Once the show was over I almost had to carry him out to the car. Thinking all my troubles were over as soon as Lindsey and I were seated in the limo, I settled in for a nice ride back to the hotel. Just as the car got on the freeway, Lindsey announced in a loud voice that he had to pee. Looking in dismay at the road, I could see that there were no exits in sight. None. "Lindsey, you can wait, right? I mean, there's nowhere the driver can pull over!"

With a shrug and shrill giggle Lindsey said, "Too bad"—he had to go and that was that. The driver was watching us in his rearview mirror with a stunned expression on his face as Lindsey started unzipping his jeans.

"Oh, hell no, Lindsey! You can't just pee in here!" I said as I, too, started to giggle hysterically. "Wait! Take off your boot! Use that!" By this time we were both laughing so hard that I was about to pee my own pants as I struggled to get Lindsey's cowboy boot off his foot. And within thirty seconds he was pissing away inside his boot as our driver looked on in horror.

We rode the rest of the way into London with the sound of urine sloshing around in a $600 Tony Lama cowboy boot. I think Joe Strummer would approve, I told Lindsey as we tossed it into the gutter before the scowling face of our driver. As he ambled through the plush lobby of our hotel Lindsey looked arrogant, drunk, and a bit lopsided. Actually, he looked like he belonged on stage with the Clash.

The band returned to the States for a four-week break. But when I got back, instead of a peaceful month off, I began to experience terrifying attacks of illness that struck me out of the blue. First I'd break out in a cold sweat, which would be quickly followed by nausea, chest pains, and room-spinning disorientation. When the room stopped whirling, a severe headache was the signal that, for the time being, all that was left was pain, and then the episode would be over. The attacks lasted for over an hour, leaving me so weak that I couldn't even walk across the room without Lindsey's help.

After a battery of blood tests, neurological MRIs, and electrocardiograms, the specialists could find no real cause for the attacks. Since leaving the road I hadn't touched cocaine and since I never drank alcohol, the doctors were completely baffled by my symptoms. But they had plenty of medications to treat them. I was given an arsenal of pain medication, heart medication, and antianxiety drugs. I had so many pills to take at specific times that I had to keep a time sheet in my purse to remind me when and how to take them all. And I hated it, but the attacks were so bad that I'd do anything to make them stop.

While both Lindsey and I were worried about my health, we were too busy to dwell on it. The band had the last leg of the *Tusk* tour yet to complete and I didn't have time to be sick. And I didn't want Lindsey to worry about me. So I started hiding my pain, my nausea, and my fear about what was happening to me. *He needs me to be strong for him. There's a lot of shows left to do and his health is what's important, not mine,* I told myself. I packed my medications along with my clothes and left with Lindsey for the summer *Tusk* tour.

It was the last six weeks of a grueling yearlong tour and everything had a sameness to it now. The cities went by in a blur of chaotic hotel rooms, limos, and sold-out shows. The fights between band members were repeats of

the ones that had gone before: the same words, same accusations, same anger, same everything. The drug and alcohol consumption had increased alarmingly, but everyone was so exhausted that no one even noticed. At this point, whatever it took to get the band and its inner circle through the days and nights of life on the road was done

Lindsey and Jeff Buckingham playing Risk on the road.

without thought or concern over anything as mundane as health or worry over being wasted in front of fans and reporters. We just didn't care.

To fill the boring hours, the Fleetwood Mac family entertained themselves with "all in the family" sex. There were so many "affairs" going on that I couldn't keep track of who was sleeping with whom. Curry was spending long nights "visiting" Stevie; Sharon Celani, Stevie's wardrobe girl, was ending her relationship with our latest security man, Jet, and beginning a new one with Lindsey's faithful roadie, Ray Lindsey; Christie, the makeup artist, not only had an on-again, off-again "friendship" with Curry but was falling in love with Greg; John McVie (who was still in the doghouse with his wife Julie after spending lovely evenings with one of the band's personal

Greg Thomason offering advice.

assistants at the beginning of the tour) was once again making cow eyes at the assistant. And Mick was prowling around *again*, having a mysterious "affair" with a woman no one had even seen but with whom he swore he was "in love." But at least this unknown woman wasn't a member of the Fleetwood Mac sixteen—and I gave him credit for that.

It had gotten so bad that people couldn't even be bothered to hide their sex toys. One morning I opened the door of our room to place our breakfast dishes outside and glanced down at the breakfast tray sitting on the floor next to mine. On it was a tall, thin cardboard box with a picture of a vibrator emblazoned on the side—and thrown on top of that was an empty battery package. Screaming with hysterical laughter, I rushed inside to drag Lindsey out into the hall for a look, and we both almost gagged as we realized that the room belonged to a member of our personal security who'd spent the night with one of Stevie's crew members. We were completely grossed out. It was the kind of information we didn't need. Lindsey and I didn't care what people did behind closed doors, but Jesus, don't leave your nasty, giant vibrator box *outside* the door of your boss's room. It was very trashy, very uncool, and very, very icky.

Not surprisingly, everyone's health was deteriorating rapidly. Mick was having severe problems with his hypoglycemia; extra doses of Dilantin were slipped to Lindsey during the performances to counteract any warning signs of another seizure; I was taking my prescription drugs precisely as ordered while chasing them with cocaine to offset the drowsiness they caused; and Christine, Stevie, and John were self-medicating with any and every available substance backstage. We were just trying to get through it at that point, trying to survive the last exhausting weeks in any way we could.

"Tell Your Story Walkin'" button.

If one thing summed up the summer tour for *Tusk* it was the badge-like buttons that J.C. had ordered for the band, inner circle, and crew. They read: "Tell Your Story Walkin'." It was exactly how we were feeling inside: "Get the fuck away from me. Don't talk to me, don't bother me, just get the hell away. I don't give a shit about what your 'story' was, will be, or is. Just leave me the fuck alone."

Already antiso-
cial before the tour,
we'd become isolation-
ists—and anyone not
inside the inner circle
was viewed at best with
distaste and boredom,
and at worst with hos-
tility bordering on hate.
During the *Rumours*
tour and the beginning
of this one Fleetwood
Mac would always stop
and sign autographs for
the fans. They'd always
smile even when they
felt like shit, always
do their best to answer
questions and pose for
pictures when they'd
rather be doing any-
thing but catering to

Show Schedule

Mon Aug	4	Lakeland, Florida (Rehearsal)
Tue	5	Lakeland, Florida
Wed	6	Miami, Florida
Thu	7	OFF
Fri	8	Atlanta, Georgia
Sat	9	OFF
Sun	10	OFF
Mon	11	Mobile, Alabama
Tue	12	Birmingham, Alabama
Wed	13	Baton Rouge, Louisiana
Thu	14	OFF
Fri	15	OFF
Sat	16	Dallas, Texas
Sun	17	San Antonio, Texas
Mon	18	Houston, Texas
Tue	19	OFF
Wed	20	OFF
Thu	21	Omaha, Nebraska
Fri	22	Oklahoma City, Oklahoma
Sat	23	Wichita, Kansas
Sun	24	Kansas City, Missouri
Mon	25	OFF
Tue	26	OFF
Wed	27	Las Cruces, New Mexico
Thu	28	Tucson, Arizona
Fri	29	Phoenix, Arizona
Sat	30	OFF
Sun	31	Los Angeles, California
Mon Sep	1	Los Angeles, California

END OF TUSK WORLD TOUR, 1979 - 1980

Summer Tusk *tour schedule.*

the public. And always, always, they tried to present a united front to
show that they were warm, friendly, and approachable.

But that was ancient history. For almost a year now photographers,
reporters, sycophants, and fans had surrounded us—and the family couldn't
bear another minute of it. We just wanted to be left the hell alone. We wanted the tour to be over. And finally we were down to the last two shows.

Fleetwood Mac checked into the L'Ermitage hotel in Beverly Hills for the
two-show finale of the *Tusk* tour at the world-famous Hollywood Bowl. J.C.
forbade any of us to go to our respective homes. Like a nanny with unruly
children under his supervision, he didn't trust us to run around loose in
L.A. He had a well-founded fear that if he let the band out of his sight, there
was a clear and present danger that one or all of them might go missing in
action and not make it to their own concerts. With a sigh of relief he got us

into our limos for the first night's show. After a year on the road Fleetwood Mac would end the tour under the starlight in their hometown.

As we climbed out of our long black car in the summer twilight I could see hundreds of fans lined up with their bodies and faces pressed against a six-foot chain-link fence that separated them from their idols.

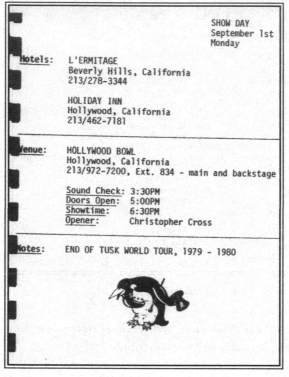

Day page from Tusk *tour schedule.*

SHOW DAY
September 1st
Monday

Hotels: L'ERMITAGE
             Beverly Hills, California
             213/278-3344

             HOLIDAY INN
             Hollywood, California
             213/462-7181

Venue: HOLLYWOOD BOWL
             Hollywood, California
             213/972-7200, Ext. 834 - main and backstage

             Sound Check: 3:30PM
             Doors Open: 5:00PM
             Showtime: 6:30PM
             Opener: Christopher Cross

Notes: END OF TUSK WORLD TOUR, 1979 - 1980

Lindsey laughed and waved, but the pleas for autographs went unheeded as we walked quickly toward J.C., who was beckoning us at the door of the backstage dressing rooms. Even though we weren't wearing our buttons that night, the urge to flee the sea of strange faces was ever-present as we stepped into the band's inner sanctum.

A few steps inside the door, J.C. handed each of us a vial of cocaine and explained that it was a "welcome to the end" gift. Beaming, he gestured to a large room at the end of the hall and told us that the party had started without us. As we walked in I saw the already-wasted and terminally handsome Dennis Wilson sitting on the floor talking earnestly to Gary Busey, a new addition to the band's celebrity friends. Gary had shot to fame with his amazing performance as Buddy Holly in the movie of the same name. With his caustic wit and good looks, he'd been welcomed with open arms into the band's exclusive circle. All of our friends were backstage—but no family members were. Tonight was for intense partying, and having parents present tended to put a damper on the festivities.

During the show Julie, Dennis, Gary, and I watched the band give one of the best performances of the tour. Stevie was bewitching, Lindsey was raging, Mick was insane, Christine and John were laughing—and the L.A. crowd went mad.

After their encore the band raced backstage and the party resumed. J.C. had hired a video cameraman to shoot footage not of the show, but of the band and inner circle celebrating Fleetwood Mac style with blow, vodka tonics, and Dom Pérignon flowing. The video was for our eyes only—a tape of the band doing lines of blow was not something they wanted leaked to the press. So far, there had been only rumors of the band's drug use and nobody wanted documented proof. But we did enjoy the idea of a personal "diary" for ourselves, and now we'd have one.

Tonight everyone was happy. And as vials and packets were passed around, crazed laughter and heart-to-heart, alcohol-induced maudlin speeches were flying fast and furious. Before we left the venue to continue the party at L'Ermitage, Lindsey, Mick, and I found ourselves in a small side room with Don Fox, one of the main promoters for the past year's tour. As the celebration continued in the next room Don told us that he had a bit of bad news.

"Let's have it," Mick said as we all took seats on a small couch and a couple of chairs and looked at Don expectantly. Looking a bit sheepish, Don told the three of us that it appeared that the *Tusk* tour had barely finished in the black. With a shrug he said that he couldn't really explain it, but the facts were the facts. Fleetwood Mac had toured for a year, grossed millions, and not turned a profit.

"You're kidding. Tell us you're kidding, Don," I said in a low voice, looking worriedly at Lindsey out of the corner of my eye. He was staring at Don with a blank look on his face. As Don assured all of us that he wasn't kidding, I waited for one of them to explode, or ask questions, or say something, anything, about the shocking piece of news that Don had just tossed out into the room as though he was informing us there was no room service back at the hotel.

But Mick and Lindsey didn't ask questions. They assured Don that it wasn't his fault and with a shrug got up from their seats and prepared to leave the room. I was stunned. First of all, I couldn't believe that it was true. Second, I couldn't for the life of me understand how two band members who'd just finished a yearlong tour could take news like this so calmly. But they did. They didn't seem to care! I kept my mouth shut. Who was I to call Don Fox on the carpet? It wasn't my place, or my responsibility, to make sense of the band's finances.

Maybe Mick and Lindsey are just too out of it right now to understand what Fox just told them. I'm sure that in a while it's going to hit them and then they're going to freak, I told myself as I took one last look at Don's relieved face as we left him standing alone in the small room. *I'd look relieved too, if I were Don. He just dodged a bullet in there—for now,* I thought. But I knew without a doubt that a bullet would be fired. And when it was, there was going to be blood. It just remained to be seen who was going to get shot.

Back at the hotel, the all-night party continued all over the building. We jumped from room to room reminiscing about the past year while each and every one of us ricocheted from tears to laughter to tears again. We were all semi-hysterical and very high and as dawn approached, the "transcending" showed no sign of slowing down. Around 4 A.M. I was invited to come up to Greg's room to have a toast with all of the security guys that were our own personal band of brothers on the road. I was greeted with more drugs, champagne, and speeches. After twenty minutes Dwayne threw his arm around my shoulder and told me how glad he was that I'd been "allowed" to come up and spend time with them.

"What are you talking about, Dwayne? I know that I don't get much chance to hang out with you guys on the road—you're always so busy when I'm around. But what do you mean by 'allowed'?"

"Oh shit, I'm going to get in trouble," Dwayne told me as Greg and Jet glared at him. "Fuck it. It's not that we were so 'busy' whenever you're around us, Carol. We're under strict orders to talk to you as little as possible. J.C. told us that Lindsey doesn't like it when we spend too much time around you. I thought you knew!"

Why am I surprised? I thought to myself. *I know that Lindsey watches over me, but this is so insulting. What does he think? I'm going to fall for one of the roadies? My God!* With a bright smile I changed the subject, but I no longer felt like celebrating. I could see the guys glancing at their watches and at one another. And in their eyes I saw a sense of fear that I recognized—fear of Lindsey's anger. Nobody wanted to be the target of Lindsey's fury—and this, I understood.

With a sigh, I told them they should run back downstairs and they left with an air of relief—and worry. They were afraid, I was sure, that I was going to confront Lindsey and J.C. about their "hands off" orders concerning me. But I wouldn't. I didn't want to cause problems for them or myself, and anyway, the tour was almost over. So what difference would it make now? Instead of going back to the party, I went straight to our room. I didn't feel in a party mood any longer. I felt humiliated and sad. I'd given Lindsey no reason not to trust me, and to find out that my friendships on the road were not only carefully watched but also dictated was more than I could deal with on this night.

Things were calmer backstage at the last concert of the tour. The band was eager to play but just as eager to finish. I watched them walk through the night and up metal stairs as J.C.'s voice cried out, "Ladies and gentlemen, please give a warm welcome to Fleetwood Mac!"

The smell of endless summer was in the air as I took my place by the side of the stage. Night-blooming jasmine competed with the pungent odors of cigarettes, joints, and burning electricity from massive banks of overhead lights and the ever-present hot power cables that propelled the sound of Fleetwood Mac's music into the open-air seating of the Hollywood Bowl.

I closed my eyes and let the music wash over me. When I closed my eyes it was easy to forget the bad memories of the past year. It was easy to forget the fights, the vicious words, and the ugly scenes of Australia. Easy to forget the venomous relationships between the band members and the seething anger that permeated the atmosphere backstage at the shows.

And it was easy to remember the smiles, the soft words, and the sarcastic jokes. Easy to remember nights spent in effortless camaraderie with those same band members singing in harmony to 1950s blues songs as dawn was breaking outside the closed curtains of a hotel room. Nights when a bond of love between them broke down the old anger of broken relationships and wrapped itself around all of us. And it was easy to remember that, in bad times and good, we were a family. And it seemed we always would be.

17

ANCIENT BATTLEGROUNDS

Three weeks later the band was gathered at Mick's home in Bel-Air. After a careful audit ordered by the band members' separate attorneys, it turned out that vast sums of money were missing and unaccounted for from the *Tusk* tour. The band had gathered in Mick's living room for a meeting accompanied by power lawyers and a new manager. Ugly words and accusations were flying through the air like heat-seeking missiles. And they were mainly directed at Mick Fleetwood. None of the other band members could understand how, after playing a solid eight months of shows and grossing millions, no one had made any money from the tour.

Sitting quietly in the dining room, I could hear Mick talking fast and low about vast expenditures on the road to cover the band's extravagant lifestyle while defending his 10 percent management fee. Everyone was upset. No one was listening to explanations. They didn't want to hear them. Because the bottom line, they said, was that even after documented expenses, the money that should be left over just wasn't there. And as "manager" of Fleetwood Mac, they were holding Mick responsible.

Irving Azoff, the power manager for the Eagles, was now representing Stevie. And he was ruthless as he took charge of the inquisition. He told Mick that there would be no in-house managing of his new client, Ms. Nicks. Nor would she be paying for office overhead, accounting fees, or *management* fees. And he made it clear that, in his eyes, Mick had done a horrific job of looking out for the band's best interests over the past two years. Mickey Shapiro, who represented Mick, Christine, and John, was caught between a rock and a hard place.

Two of his clients were as unhappy as Stevie and Lindsey, but at the same time he tried to defend Mick. There was little defense, though. Five-star hotels, grand pianos, and unlimited drugs seemed a flimsy excuse for the claimed expenditures of the tour. And if the band didn't spend the money, then where was it?

By the end of the meeting it was clear that from that point on Fleetwood Mac as an entity would be under the careful watch of a committee of separate lawyers, managers, and business managers. The bullet that I'd known would be fired on the night of the band's Hollywood Bowl show was loaded into the gun. And J.C. was the first person to be shot. The band's new overseers fired him immediately after the meeting.

After the lawyers left the house, Mick sat in the backyard. Visibly upset and shaken by the awful meeting, he seemed inconsolable as I watched the rest of the members of Fleetwood Mac sitting next to him trying to offer comfort. On the drive home Lindsey told me that nobody thought Mick stole money from the band. Everyone knew that Mick would never, ever do anything like that. But as band manager, he was the person to catch the fallout from the shocking fact that out of millions of dollars earned during the tour, none of it went into the band's pockets. The money was gone. It was an ugly mystery that would never be solved. For months there would be whispers of possible embezzlement by the various concert promoters and their underlings, but no actual investigation was ever launched. Fleetwood Mac was far more comfortable with gossip and innuendo than they were with cold hard facts. Besides, to have irrefutable proof that someone they knew and liked—or even loved—had stolen from them was too much for anyone to deal with.

Within a few weeks Mick took a bullet as well. He was fired as manager. From now on he'd just be the drummer in the band known as Fleetwood Mac. That was it. Nothing more. Financial and management control over the namesake band he'd started in the 1960s was gone forever. It was the end of an era.

The Fleetwood Mac family splintered almost immediately. Stevie, Lindsey, Christine, and Mick were all starting solo album projects. J.C. moved to Hawaii—hurt and angry after the brutal treatment that he'd been given at the hands of the new "management" team. John disappeared by slipping into the mists of the ocean, sailing away from home and the ugliness in L.A.

I was stunned over the loss of J.C. He'd been my friend and protector during the tours and I couldn't imagine not having him there the next

Lindsey in Hawaii.

Carol Ann in Hawaii.

time the band went on the road. But I didn't say a word. After what had happened in Australia, I knew better than to voice these sentiments to Lindsey. His shocking reaction to my praise of John Courage on my "girlfriend tape" had shown me that these were feelings I had to keep to myself.

Lindsey and I also left. We went to Hawaii for a month's stay at the Kahala Hilton. This time we rented a cottage right on the hotel's beach and spent the first three weeks baking in the sun, eating coconut cream pie, and sipping tropical drinks. Feeling restless, we decided to island-hop and pay a visit to John and Julie's wonderful little house in Maui. They had a houseguest I was anxious to see: Sara. Once there, we had a couple of all-nighters at the McVies', where Sara, Julie, and I spent hours talking about the two hottest gossip subjects: the breakup of Dennis Wilson and Christine, and "the Blob."

Christine had finally ended her almost three-year love affair with Dennis. Fed up with his drug and drinking binges, his womanizing, and his penchant for spending her money like water, she'd called their engagement off in December. Each of us had stories to tell about Dennis's bad behavior while he was living with Chris. How he'd used her credit card to buy designer clothes for teenage girls at Charles Galley and Maxfield Bleu, and the blatant affairs that he didn't even try to keep secret during the three years they were living together.

The crowning glory was, of course, the heart-shaped garden he ordered for Christine's backyard as a Valentine's Day surprise. It was huge and beautiful and cost thousands. This, too, he charged on one of Christine's cards. While we totally understood why Chris called off their engagement, we all agreed that it was a drag. Despite his reprehensible behavior, he was a total blast to hang out with and we were going to miss having him around. He was, after all, one of our "girlfriends."

The story about "the Blob" had all of us laughing so hard that we almost choked. Right before the end of the *Tusk* tour Sara packed her bags and left Mick over a ridiculous secret "affair" that he'd pursued throughout the entire tour. He'd called Sara from the road in August and told her that he'd fallen in love with a woman whom he'd never met but had been speaking to for months—the same woman that he'd bragged to us about on the road. He'd fallen in love with a voice over a telephone. *That explains why we never saw her,* I thought, as the riddle of Mick's "mystery woman" from the tour became crystal clear. To make a long story short, Sara told him to shove it and moved out of his house. Mick, in turn, hired a private detective to find his dream girl. And he did. She was hideously overweight, plain, and more than a little wacko.

Mortified, he'd been begging Sara to come home—but she wouldn't. Right after Lindsey and I left for L.A., Mick came on bended knee to Maui to get her back, and after putting him through hell she gave in and returned to his new home in Malibu. Christened "the Blue Whale," it would become my home away from home for the next three years.

Three months after the end of the *Tusk* tour, in January 1981, Lindsey, Bob, and I moved into our new home in one of the most exclusive areas in all of Los Angeles: Bel-Air. Our one-story home rested on a beautiful mountaintop and had a 180-degree view of the metropolis below. We'd had it extensively remodeled so that the once-conservative ranch-style house was now an eclectic mansion with glass walls.

Walls had been knocked down inside to create large and airy rooms. We'd had a "rain room" built as an extension to the kitchen. It was a huge glass dome built around a magnificent tree. Squares of glass were molded around its shape and water pipes were hidden within its branches. With a flip of a switch, gentle rain started to fall onto the glass like diamonds. Of course, the glass squares were always leaking, but nevertheless I loved to sit and look out at the newly planted "tropical forest" that surrounded the rain room. The Gothic furniture we bought for our June Street house was left in storage and we hired a new decorator named Murphy who had filled our home with wonderful white fabric couches, tapestries, and tables of green stone.

Everything in the house was the direct opposite of the dark wood and velvets of our last home and we loved it. A five-foot wooden replica of King Tut's sarcophagus that was a liquor cabinet had a place of honor in the huge living room—and I swore that Tut's Egyptian makeup resembled Lindsey's stage persona (a comparison that creeped him out).

Immediately upon moving in, Lindsey started construction on the garage. He turned it into a complete home recording studio, and once again he began to spend all of his time shut inside its doors. Just like at June Street, I began wandering through this house like a ghost as eerie, muffled music made its way down the halls. Music that would, eventually, become his first solo album, *Law and Order*.

Lindsey driving in Bel-Air.

So all was well in Bel-Air—until Lindsey received a series of phone calls demanding that he direct his attention to a new project: the next Fleetwood Mac album. The sunny atmosphere in our home darkened as he was forced to stop work on his solo album and begin composing songs for a record that he didn't have a lot of interest in making. A record that the press had predicted would never be made.

In March the *New York Post* ran a story under the headline, "Looks like the end of the line for Fleetwood Mac." The story quoted highly placed sources within the music industry that said that "there's big trouble among members of rock's hottest group and the band is swiftly headed for the rocks." Citing loss of income from the *Tusk* tour and creative differences as the root cause, the piece went on to say that the untimely breakup of Fleetwood Mac would cause shock waves throughout the music industry unlike any since the breakup of the Beatles.

After this story, small blurbs of speculation began to appear in music magazines and newspapers across the country hinting at the infighting, drugs, and personal problems within the world of Fleetwood Mac. *If only they knew how bad it really was—and is,* I thought as I kept track of the clippings that the band's publicist sent to our house on a regular basis. *But somehow Fleetwood Mac endures and it remains to be seen how rough it's going to be on all of us during this next record and tour. I'm almost afraid to think about it.* With a sigh I tossed the clippings into a pile and flipped the switch on the rain room to shut off the bad memories of the *Tusk* tour.

As time would prove, I had every reason to be worried. From the very first minute, the new album was like an albatross landing on a ship at sea. It was a bad omen that would make what had gone before in the lives of the Fleetwood Mac family pale in comparison. From that point on, all of our worlds would start to crumble into ruin.

This time the band insisted on doing an "updated" version of the musical sound of *Rumours.* Lindsey didn't fight them on it, but he wasn't happy. And his anger and frustration over having to quit work on his own record and start an album that he wasn't really into manifested itself in angry confrontations with me. Even though I understood that it wasn't me he was actually angry with, I couldn't help but be hurt and upset at outbursts that now seemed to occur on a weekly basis.

I did my best to let his anger roll over me and tried not to let him see my tears. *After all,* I told myself over and over, *they're just words. It's not like before, so it's not that bad.* But I cried as soon as he slammed the door and went back into his studio. Walking quietly into the rain room when I was once again alone, I stared through the artificial rain falling softly around me.

Within two months, Lindsey was finished with his songs for the band's next record. The sooner that record was completed, the sooner he could get back to work on his own material—and that was all that mattered, he told me. *And then everything will go back to being the way it was before he had to stop working on* Law and Order, *I whispered to myself. He'll be happy again, and we'll be happy again. It's just this stupid band record, that's all.* On May 1 we headed for France and Le Château, a studio located sixty miles outside of Paris, in Hérouville.

Because of Mick's tax situation, the rest of the band had agreed to record for a month in France. Mick had declared himself a resident of Monaco and had to prove to the IRS that he wasn't liable for American taxes on his income from the record. It was always confusing, to say the least, to try to make sense of Mick's financial ups and downs and by now no one even tried. After the debacle of his firing as band manager, everyone wanted to help him out to make up for hurting his feelings.

Lindsey entertains himself on the road.

And that was why we were stuck in an old château that was beautiful—but decidedly icky. It was a damp, moldy, spider-and-ant-infested building with almost no modern amenities. The bedrooms were small, the bathrooms even smaller, and to call the dormitory-style kitchen "rustic" was being kind. After American hotels with room service, it was a shock to have to pick dead flies out of the butter before we could spread it on our toast. Call us spoiled, and we surely were, but when you're among people trying to do something as intense as recording a new album, the luxuries of normal life just make everything a lot easier. But as with everything else connected to this album, "easy" just wasn't in the cards.

Lindsey and I gritted our teeth and tried to make the best of it. Some mornings we woke up in a bed full of ants and I went screaming for the insect repellant. Lindsey would shrug into yet another set of wrinkled clothes and head out to the separate building that housed the recording studio. The whole setup was like a scene from a Gothic horror story. All that was missing was a headless horseman wandering the halls.

To add to the rather ominous, supernatural feel of Le Château there were the very real, sinister fights that echoed from the recording studio into our rooms every night. The screams and curses of the band members fighting with one another sounded demonic within the walls of the dormitory. And I cringed at night as I listened to them. This time around I had no desire to even walk into their recording sessions. Being with the band during the daylight hours was bad enough already.

For the five members of Fleetwood Mac there was no such thing as "forgive and forget." As they had proved since the recording of *Rumours*, the album that documented the disintegration of their intimate relationships, they were quite capable of not only carrying ugly grudges but also savoring bloody retaliation. They were experts at pushing one another's buttons, experts at opening old wounds, and experts at carving new ones. And in France there was a lot of material for them to use against one another.

Mick had insisted on releasing *Fleetwood Mac Live*, a live double album that no one else in the band ever wanted to have on the market. Its poor sales figures were infuriating to a band that took great pride in protecting every aspect of Fleetwood Mac's artistic reputation. Since I'd been with Lindsey, I'd seen them turn down lucrative endorsing deals and veto crass advertising campaigns dreamed up by Warner Bros. for the sales of their records. And they had never, ever sold out for money. The live album was, in everyone's eyes but Mick's, a sellout. And they were very pissed about it.

From the moment we arrived, Lindsey's resentful anger, which began with the work on his songs for the band's new album, had turned into simmering rage. During band meetings he was being told that, unlike the *Tusk* album, each of his songs would have the entire band playing on them. In an effort to duplicate the success of *Rumours*, it had become a major issue. Mick apparently blamed Lindsey's "work methods" for the "unsuccessful" *Tusk*. Lindsey's songs on *Tusk* were, for the most part, entirely *solo* tracks that he recorded at home alone.

At Village Recorder his total control over every harmony and instrument riff on his songs that *did* include the band enraged the other four members of Fleetwood Mac. The fact that *Tusk* sold five million records notwithstanding, Mick believed that if the band had been allowed to participate as a *unit* on Lindsey's tracks, *Tusk* would have had much higher sales. But Lindsey hated being told what to do when it came to his music. And he was not shy about expressing himself.

The fact that Christine, Stevie, and Lindsey had to interrupt their solo projects to come all the way to Hérouville to record was another source of resentment. And, of course, it didn't help matters at all that Jimmy Iovine had shown up on the doorstep to "visit" Stevie.

He was a well-respected producer who was spending a lot of time whispering advice into Stevie's ear—advice that may or may not be greeted warmly by her fellow band members. And that was not the only thing he'd been whispering into her ear. Stevie and Jimmy were now lovers. And as I watched them together he seemed both Svengali and boyfriend to her.

Lindsey was not thrilled. It was certainly not the first time that Stevie had had a boyfriend by her side in the recording studio or on the road. During the *Tusk* recording sessions she was involved with Mick, and later, with the about-to-be-married second engineer—an affair that not only broke his heart but his abandoned fiancée's as well. On the road a series of handsome men were involved with her off and on. And understandably so—Stevie was beyond beautiful and her charisma was off the charts. But this was the first time that one of her boyfriends was also a well-respected record producer—a producer who was also in charge of her first solo record, *Bella Donna*. And it was causing professional tension within the band.

So mix all that together with "normal" band rivalries and the simmering old rage between them and it was a grim picture. The communal lunch and dinners were eaten in almost total silence by the band and their inner circle, who had accompanied them to France. Julie and I tried to keep up a light banter of safe subjects during our meals, but it was exhausting and after a while we gave it up. The wall of silent fury that surrounded and separated the band members was now so impenetrable that there was nothing any of us could do to break it down.

STORMS

It was misting outside on a late afternoon as I stood and looked out at the grounds surrounding Le Château. And in the distance I saw Christine, Stevie, and Lindsey walk out of the recording studio into the light rainfall. I watched through cold glass as all of them started walking in different directions, aimless yet purposeful in their strides, walking as far away from one another as they could get.

There was a feeling of a battleground in this place. And the figures outside the window seemed weary combatants who were still very much in the war, but who were now sick to death of the battle-scarred landscape around them; sick of the pain; sick of the wounds that never healed; sick of the things that were once so important and were now only dusty memories. As they walked with their heads bowed, they looked bone-weary from years of carrying the horrific weight of ancient hurts, vengeance, and vendettas.

As they turned and headed to the building in which I stood, I seemed to see a yearning in their downcast faces. A yearning to be set free from the ties that bound them together—their own brilliance and collective creative force. A force that had created Fleetwood Mac—a band that had now become a prison for the five souls who created it.

I felt a sense of overwhelming frustration and sadness as they disappeared from view. For me, it had been five years of watching people who once loved each other—and still did—suffer and endure while seemingly refusing to at least try to be healed of the pain and fury they felt in one another's presence. But at the same time I knew it wasn't their fault. This band had been caught in a vicious trap. The pain and rage of *Rumours* that catapulted them to superstardom was made from their personal heartbreak. And each heart could never heal as long as it was forced to live side by side with the person who made it bleed. There seemed to be nothing anyone could do to help the members of Fleetwood Mac. With a sigh I turned away from the window and smiled at Lindsey as he walked up behind me. My senseless chatter made him laugh—and in the atmosphere of Le Château that was indeed a victory.

After two weeks I decided that I needed to get away from the gloom of the place and I overnighted my headshots to seven modeling agencies in Paris. Even though I'd only be in France for a few more weeks, I was eager to see if my pictures were good enough to elicit a response from the world-famous agencies I'd chosen. They did. I got called for five interviews and I jumped up and down in excitement as the heavily accented voices on the phone asked me to visit their agencies.

As I made my announcement over lunch there was laughter and conversation around the table. Lindsey looked proud as everyone—even Stevie—congratulated me and before I knew it, it was all arranged. Wayne Cody, one of the band's most loved and trusted bodyguards, would be accompanying me on my trips, and he looked almost as excited as I was. He too wanted to spend a little time away from the Gothic château.

We had a blast for the three days we ran in and out of agencies. But it was the next-to-last interview on my list that sent us both hurrying back to the safety of Le Château.

The first three agencies accepted my pictures for "consideration" for beauty ads and sent me away with business cards and phone numbers. As we entered a beautiful agency I felt a sense of pride that they'd responded to my photos. That wouldn't last long. Within ten minutes of my "interview" I was asked to go into the next room and take off my clothes—to get shots for a "pictorial section" of a magazine. In other words: a centerfold.

"What?" I screamed. "I'm not taking my clothes off! What are you talking about? You want me to do a *centerfold?* What kind of agency is this?" I squeaked as I lost the battle to keep my composure.

"We're a French subsidiary of *Playboy* magazine—we publish French *Oui.* It's a younger, hipper version of *Playboy.* We like your pictures. You really should let us do a few shots," the agent continued in his now smarmy-sounding French accent.

"Oh my God. Thanks, but no thanks! Gotta go!" Blushing, I grabbed my portfolio off his desk and, taking Wayne by the hand, ran out of the office. Jumping into our limo, I started to laugh as I told him about my "job offer."

"Lindsey would fire my ass if he knew I'd let you go in there! Don't tell him you went there, OK, Carol? Oh my God! Don't tell him anything!" Wayne moaned. As I burst out laughing I told him that I'd try, but I knew that I had to tell Lindsey. It was just too embarrassingly funny to keep to myself. And in France opportunities to make him laugh were few and far between.

Fleetwood Mac's new album now had a name: *Mirage.* When Lindsey played me the tapes in Le Château's studio I knew it was going to sell. Although to me it didn't have the sparkle that made *Rumours* and *Tusk* creative jewels, it was a good album. And considering that they spent literally one month recording it, it was mind-blowing. All it needed were the final mixes, and those would be done in L.A. To celebrate, the band had invited two special guests to a small listening party at Le Château: John McEnroe and Vitas Gerulaitis, world-famous tennis pros competing for the 1981 Wimbledon Cup in London.

Everyone was excited to have them as guests for a day. And a typical Fleetwood Mac "transcending" party took place during their day-long visit. The band took turns playing table tennis with the two tennis greats and then kept them up all night in the studio playing the new (almost) finished album. Finally it was time to leave France and return to L.A. Time to go home to our new house and leave Le Château and the ugly coldness that was now the world of Fleetwood Mac. I was ready to go back to the warmth and happiness of my life before the pressures of creating *Mirage* took it away.

Christine and John McVie in Hérouville, France.

Mick and Dennis Dunstun in Hérouville, France.

But as the summer months passed, things didn't go back to the happy, carefree atmosphere in which we'd lived before the strain of working on the new album interrupted Lindsey's creative progress on his solo debut. The tension and grimness of France had followed us to L.A. and seemed to color all of our days in shades of gray.

Lindsey now had the added weight of trying to do the final mixes on the tracks from *Mirage* while spending every free hour on his own songs for *Law and Order*. While both projects were progressing well, the burden of work seemed almost too much for him to bear. New faint lines appeared around eyes that had a constant faraway stare. And his movements were stiff and angry, betraying emotions so complex that I felt helpless. I was chilled by the knowledge that there was little I could do to help ease his burden.

I tried to be cheerful and supportive while doing my best to once again resume the role of muse that served both of us so well during the making of *Tusk*, when his talent was taking him into unknown waters. But it was harder this time, because now there was a wall of anger that wasn't there before—and by now, I knew better than to take his angry outbursts lightly.

Stevie's *Bella Donna* had been released to rave reviews and this had added another dimension to Lindsey's internal battles. The creative rivalry between them was stronger than ever, and the success of her first solo album made him feel that he had even more to prove. And his angst made me feel as though I were constantly walking on eggshells, for a wrong word or comment would set off an explosion of anger against which I had no means of defense. Once again it was all about the music—and how could I fight something so abstract? How could I defend myself against the invisible force of creative frustration?

But just because it was invisible didn't mean that it wasn't destructive. Angry words and brooding silences filled the air of our Bel-Air mansion. I never knew before that it was possible to feel lonelier *with* Lindsey than without. But I knew now. And it left me with feelings of inadequacy and despair. Sometimes it felt like I was living with two different men who just happened to share the same face and body. One I knew and loved, the other was a frightening stranger. But I told myself that after both records were finished things would return to normal. Because if they didn't, I didn't think that I could bear it.

My terrifying attacks of illness came back with a vengeance as I struggled with the stress and anxiety that were now a part of my everyday existence. I took my medications religiously, but nothing seemed to stop the episodes that struck me out of the blue and left me sick, helpless, and scared. I returned to my neurologist and after more tests he called me into his office to deliver news that left me stunned. He explained to me that he felt my episodes were not linked to a physical disease or injury, but were instead triggered by psychological stress while I looked at him in dismay.

It was inconceivable to me that stress alone could cause the vomiting, chest pains, and room-spinning disorientation that had now become so violent that I was literally incapacitated when it happened. But if it was true, then it seemed that there was nothing I could do to make these episodes stop. I lived in a world where anxiety and chaos were considered normal. Fleetwood Mac's world and everything that came with it had been my environment since the day Lindsey and I fell in love, five long years before. Now one of the world's top neurologists was telling me that he believed my life by Lindsey's side was destroying my health.

Not willing to face what he was telling me, I desperately searched for a simpler, easier reason to blame for what was happening to me. "Is it because I did cocaine on the road, Dr. Weiss? Did that do something to damage me?" I asked in a small voice.

"Carol, it didn't do you any good, but that's not what's causing your illness. What you've been experiencing are known in the medical profession as 'panic attacks.' Yours are quite severe, as you already know. And they're caused by stress and pressure that is so intense that your subconscious is triggering these attacks as a warning to you. Panic attacks are the mind's way of letting a person know that things are too much for them. When they're as severe as yours are, then we have to find a way to help you deal with the root cause. And once we do, they'll stop. Is there something you're not telling me about your home life? Something other than your unorthodox lifestyle that could explain what's happening to you?"

I shook my head and lowered my eyes. No one knew how bad it could get behind the closed doors of my life at home. No one knew how Lindsey's anger burned and threatened to consume me with its intensity. I wouldn't talk about it. I couldn't talk about it. How could I explain something that I myself didn't understand? When the anger came, it was never because I'd done something to set it off; it seemed to come from out of nowhere and then afterward our lives would return to normal, as though nothing had happened. I'd learned to lock away these "bad memories" in a corner of my mind. I never, ever let myself think of them—much less talk to anyone about them. And, panic attacks or not, I had no intention of starting now.

Dr. Weiss told me that he'd arranged for one of his colleagues, a top psychiatrist, to oversee my treatment with him. This doctor had a lot of experience with people in the entertainment industry, he said. He felt that

I needed to talk to someone I could trust. Someone who would be bound by professional ethics not to disclose anything I might need to "talk about." And he told me he wanted to check me into a hospital for observation. A place that would take me away from my home environment and allow them to monitor my panic attacks. These were devastating to my physical health, he reiterated, and we had to find a way to make them stop.

As I listened to his words I didn't know if I should laugh or cry. It wasn't that I was taking anything he was saying lightly. On the contrary, I was scared and shocked by the diagnosis that he'd given me. But on the other hand, the sheer irony that it was I, of all the members of my Fleetwood Mac family, who was being told to see a psychiatrist and check into a hospital was so ludicrous that I was finding it hard to keep a straight face.

To say that the band members were eccentric was putting it mildly. The behavior I'd witnessed over the past five years made anything I'd ever done seem like a child misbehaving at Sunday school. The anger and vendettas among the band members made the Mafia look tame in comparison. Not to mention the incestuous relationships, drugs, drinking, and insane antics. Granted, I could be crazy, too—but my only vices were sarcasm, doing blow with the band, and a fondness for shopping. I could easily see that each and every member of the Fleetwood Mac family would benefit from a little therapy, but I was the only one being forced to seek medical help. Go figure.

If it weren't so depressing, I'd die laughing, I thought to myself. With a sigh I stood up and nodded my head. "Fine. You don't have to convince me, Dr. Weiss. I'll do whatever I need to do to stop my panic attacks."

Seeing the look of resignation on my face, he took both my hands in his. "You have to do this, honey. You're suffering physical pain and damage and it's got to stop. There's nothing to be afraid of. Ridge Hospital is more like a country club than a hospital. Just think of it as a vacation. OK? It's my job to take care of you. Trust me. Do you want me to call Lindsey for you and tell him what's going on?"

I nodded gratefully and gave him the private number that Lindsey and I used for each other and a handful of intimates. As I sat and listened to him talk to Lindsey, I stared off into the distance. After he hung up the phone he told me that Lindsey was upset and worried and that he was sending a limo to pick me up. Lindsey didn't want me to drive, and he'd told the doctor to make arrangements for me to check into the hospital in two days.

"It's settled then," I said resolutely as I got up to leave. "I'll see you at the hospital, Dr. Weiss."

As soon as I arrived home Lindsey came running to meet me. Speaking to me gently and lovingly, he took me inside and insisted on putting me to bed. His face was full of worry as he curled up next to me. And for the first time since he started working on *Mirage*, I felt that his focus had shifted back to the world outside his studio, back to the life that we shared together, and for the first time in months I felt protected, safe, and completely loved.

I checked into the exclusive Beverly Hills "retreat" known as Ridge Hospital. And I felt like I was on a solo vacation for a week. Lindsey visited me every day and was surprised to find that I was quite enjoying myself. It was completely relaxing and more like being at a spa than a hospital. During my daily sessions with my psychiatrist I only spoke in general terms of my life within the world of Fleetwood Mac. I wasn't ready or willing to talk about my personal life with Lindsey.

The rest of the time I hung out with my wealthy fellow patients. Compared with the people with whom I'd spent the past five years, they seemed both boring and normal. Best of all, I had no panic attacks or weird symptoms of any kind. I felt great and that was all that mattered. *It's time for me to go home*, I told myself as I packed my small suitcase the night before I was scheduled to leave. And I went to sleep with a smile on my face.

At dawn, heavy knocking on my bedroom door awakened me. Looking in confusion at the two detectives standing before me, my eyes traveled from their badges to their grim faces. I listened, stunned, as they told me that the hospital administrator was murdered in the dead of night: shot in the back in the hospital parking lot. I didn't see or hear anything, I told them. After they left I sunk down onto my bed and started to cry.

An image of the kindly, gray-haired gentleman who always had a smile on his face flashed through my mind and I couldn't believe that he was dead. I couldn't believe that anything so horrible could happen to someone that I knew. It was beyond my comprehension how someone could commit such a violent murder. I wanted to go home. Rushing to the phone, I called Lindsey and he arrived in twenty minutes flat.

I clung to his arm as we walked quickly to our car. I cried silently all the way home. And Lindsey looked as upset as I. It was an act of senseless violence and shocking reality that neither of us knew how to deal with. In comparison, my panic attacks and Lindsey's burden of musical work seemed very small indeed. I sent flowers to the hospital, and Lindsey swore that he'd never let me check into another one. It was too dangerous.

A few weeks later, we hired a woman to be our housekeeper. Her name was Desi Tobias—she was black, she was in her sixties, and she was one of the most wonderful people I had ever known. Her wisdom, humor, and infectious laughter brought a shining light into the house every week when she came to work—and within a few weeks, she'd become a surrogate mother to both Lindsey and me. And from that moment on, she was a member of our family.

Lindsey had a surprise for me. A month after I came home from the hospital he tossed a 45-rpm single into my lap and told me to listen to it and learn the lyrics.

"What for?" I asked as I picked up the record and peered at it. On the label was the title "It Was I" by a singing duo named Skip and Flip.

"We're going to sing a duet on this song. It's going on my album. So learn it fast, OK? We record in two days," he said with a grin.

"Oh my God! I can't sing, Lindsey! You're kidding, right? Tell me you're kidding!" I almost screamed as a picture of me behind a microphone made my blood run cold. "I'll sound like a little kid!"

Sitting on the floor next to me, he told me that he wanted me to be involved in his first solo album, and what better way than to sing a song with him? Before I totally freaked out he put the record on our player and turned up the volume. I heard a 1950s pop hit about two ex-lovers blaming each other for the breakup of their relationship. It was very catchy and I understood immediately why he liked it. Despite my pleas for him to find someone else to do it with him, he refused. I was going to sing it with him and that was that.

I was thrilled that he wanted me to do it, but at the same time I'd never, ever wanted to sing. I could carry a melody, but was I a *singer*? Hell no! But apparently that was beside the point. I was about to make my musical debut and there was nothing for it but to learn the words to the song that could make me a laughingstock in the world of Fleetwood Mac. Let's face it, to even try to follow in Stevie's musical footsteps was a ludicrous concept, and no one in her right mind would even try. So I didn't.

I just had fun with it, and with Lindsey by my side the song took on a feeling of teenage angst over the loss of a first love. And thanks to his genius, my harmony sounded childlike and unpretentious. Instead of being laughed at by the band, I received a bouquet of flowers from each and every one of them with notes of congratulations after the recording session—and Stevie's bouquet was the most beautiful of them all. When her flowers arrived, I cried. I had grown to love her as the years passed and it seemed that finally my wish for us to be friends had come to pass.

As I heard the songs on *Law and Order*, I was amazed at the mixture of satirical humor, darkness, and longing that Lindsey was conveying through his music. The first track, "Bwana," was a slightly sarcastic nod to Mick Fleetwood's solo record *The Visitor*, which he recorded in Africa. "Johnny Stew" was a tribute to our close friend John Stewart, of the famous Kingston Trio. Lindsey had learned to play guitar at the age of seven listening to John's Kingston Trio records and during *Tusk*, Lindsey helped produce Stewart's hit record *Bombs Away Dream Babies*.

As I sat and listened to the song I reminded Lindsey of the first time we met Stewart. Lindsey and I went shopping at a JC Penney department store,

Lindsey at Kingston Trio recording session.

bought a short-sleeved striped shirt, penny loafers, and rolled-up jeans for Lindsey. We then gleefully walked into a Kingston Trio recording session with Lindsey looking as though he'd stepped straight off one of the Kingston Trio album covers from the 1960s. It was a total blast and the three of us had been good friends ever since.

"September Song" and "A Satisfied Mind" were cover versions of poignant songs that were so beautiful that they made me want to cry. I threw my arms around him and told him that I loved his record—and that I was so happy that he'd made me a part of it. Within a few years, however, we'd both look back in disbelief as we realized that the song we recorded together for *Law and Order* was a premonition of the end of our relationship.

Law and Order was released in November, going to number thirty-two on the U.S. charts. The first single, "Trouble," hit number nine and, to my amazement, "It Was I" went to number two on the British charts. In the early fall we starred in a video together for "It Was I" and my contribution to the world as a "musician" was officially signed, sealed, and delivered.

While I now understood the thrill of actually recording a song and hearing it played over the radio, I knew that I never wanted to do it again. I was more than content to sit on the couch in the recording studio instead of behind a microphone. Even if I had the talent—which I didn't—I would never want to be a musician. After living among the members of Fleetwood Mac, I knew only too well how tortured a musician's life could be. And I couldn't imagine anyone with a shred of sanity who'd want to become one.

18

BOULEVARD OF BROKEN DREAMS

As hot Santa Ana winds howled outside the doors of the huge SIR sound-stage, the gala release party for the *Mirage* album raged inside. While songs from the band's new album blasted at earsplitting volume, two hundred music industry invitees drank champagne and glad-handed one another under flashing red and blue lights. As usual, the band and the inner circle were all gathered in close proximity to one another, almost as though there was an invisible rope separating us from the well-heeled guests who had come to party at Fleetwood Mac's celebration bash for the release of *Mirage*.

Miraculously, everyone behind our "invisible rope" seemed to be having a great time. Standing next to Sara, I watched a grinning and obviously thrilled Lindsey shouting into the ear of his Beach Boy hero Brian Wilson. Walking over to where they were standing, I got a shy smile from Brian as a reward.

Pulling me close, Lindsey closed his eyes as the opening chords of "Oh Diane" echoed around us. It sounded like a heartthrob hit from the 1950s—like a song James Dean would have loved. "I picture you wearing a gold lamé suit every time I hear this, Lindsey! Maybe that's what you should wear on the road for the tour!" I shouted into his ear, doing my best to sound earnest.

"Fuck that. Elvis had the corner on the gold lamé suits, Carol. You'll have to think of something a lot simpler for me to wear this time around. I don't give a shit about road wardrobe. I don't want to even have to think about my clothes on stage. I just want to be comfortable. I mean, who cares? Let Stevie have the glamour this time around. I don't need it."

Drawn by the sound of her name, Stevie materialized beside us, holding on to Jimmy Iovine's hand. It had been almost a year since I'd seen Stevie. The last time was the summer before at Le Château. It'd taken a full year for Richard and Lindsey to finish the mixes, overdubs, and then more remixes for the band's new album. It was August 1982 now, and I couldn't believe that time had gone by so quickly. Like the rest of the band, Stevie had been busy. Her solo record *Bella Donna* was released in July '81 and with three hit singles that had reached *Billboard*'s top ten, she and Jimmy Iovine had every reason to look happy.

Throwing her arms around me, Stevie asked if I was having a good time. Blinking in surprise at her unexpected show of affection, I smiled and nodded while hugging her back. "Hey! Congratulations on your album, Stevie. It's doing really well. I'm happy for you!" I yelled over the music. As she told me thanks, she looked expectantly at Lindsey, who was staring at her through narrowed eyes. With a groan, I poked him sharply in the ribs with my elbow as he rolled his eyes at me.

"Yeah, right. Congrats, Stevie. I really like your single 'Stop Draggin' My Heart Around,'" he said with a straight face. And I almost died. Ever since the release of Stevie's song, which was a duet on *Bella Donna* with Tom Petty, Lindsey had sneeringly referred to it as "Stop Draggin' My Career Around." It'd become a catchphrase between Richard and Lindsey, and while it was funny, I didn't think Stevie would appreciate it if she knew. But thankfully, Stevie took his compliment at face value and I breathed a sigh of relief. It had been such a great night so far that the last thing I wanted was for another band fight to break out in front of the movers and shakers of the music industry.

To my shock, Lindsey suddenly announced to Stevie and the rest of the band who had migrated toward us that he wanted everyone to come up to our house in Bel-Air as soon as the *Mirage* party wrapped up. I couldn't believe my ears! Lindsey had zealously protected his privacy at our home and, aside from Richard and Mick Fleetwood, absolutely none of the band members had set foot in our house, even though we'd been living there for over a year and a half.

It had been a difficult and lonely year and a half for me. Other than visits to Sara and Julie a few times each month, I'd been pretty much on my own for most of it, filling my days with shopping and reading while

trying to keep my panic attacks at bay. Lately I'd been feeling much better—Lindsey had been happier as the work on *Mirage* neared its end and
that, of course, had made life at home much more peaceful.

So I was thrilled when I heard his unexpected invitation to our friends.
About to rush to Sara's side, I stopped dead in my tracks as I heard Stevie
say, "Can I ride with you?" Startled, I looked quickly around me, so sure
was I that she must be speaking to someone other than me. But she wasn't.
She was standing expectantly in front of me waiting for my answer.

"You want to ride with me?" I asked incredulously.

With a laugh Stevie grabbed my arm and told me that she did. "Let
Lindsey and Jimmy ride together. I haven't seen you in ages, Carol, and I'm
dying to see your house. So let's get out of here, OK? Everyone else can follow us up when they're ready."

What the . . . ? I thought incredulously as I stood staring at her. *I don't
think Stevie and I have ever been in a car alone together! Actually, I don't think
we've ever been alone with each other for more than a few minutes. How weird is
that?* After hesitating for a few seconds I chided myself for being nervous.
With a mental shrug, I reminded myself that things were different now.
*Stevie's in love with Jimmy and she's happy. It's time that she and I got to know
each other better.*

After leaving a speechless Lindsey and Jimmy behind, Stevie and I
climbed into my BMW and headed toward Bel-Air. I rolled down the window, letting the desert winds blow our blonde hair into tangled snarls.
Stevie turned on the radio and with rock music blaring we sped down
Sunset Boulevard, laughing and talking about the party we'd just left.
Stevie asked me to pull over on a side street as she dug around in her purse.
Triumphantly, she held up a bottle of blow and handed it to me. As we both
dumped some onto the back of our wrists, she told me that it was the first
hit she'd had all night.

With a sigh she told me Jimmy didn't really like cocaine, so she tried not
to do it front of him. It drove her crazy in a way, she said. She wasn't used to
being told what she could and couldn't do, but at the same time she wanted
to please him. She looked at me earnestly and announced, "He's a lot like
Lindsey!" And I started to laugh.

"I know exactly what you mean," I said. "I've learned over the years
that anything and everything I do is watched—and if he's in a mood to

disapprove of something then I find out quickly, believe me. It doesn't matter if he does the same thing himself the very next day. Sometimes, I feel as though I need to ask permission for every move I make."

With a knowing smile she told me that it didn't sound like he'd changed a lot since they were together. "Don't you get tired of it?" she asked.

"Yep. But I love him, Stevie. It's hard sometimes, but we make it through, you know?" Unwilling to tell her *how* hard it could get, I changed the subject. "Stevie, thank you so much for your beautiful flowers. It made me really happy to get them. You know that I care about you a great deal, don't you?"

With a smile, Stevie answered, "I care about you too, Carol. I know it's been hard on both of us. But I hope that we can put all of that behind us. We're sisters. All of my girlfriends and I are 'sisters of the moon.' I've given every woman I love a little half moon necklace to wear—just like the one I'm wearing now! I'd give you one too, but it would drive Lindsey crazy and God knows you don't need that!"

"Thanks for the thought, Stevie. It means a lot to me!" I said as I reached over and gave her a hug. "How's Robin doing? Is she feeling any better at all?"

With a sigh, Stevie shook her head no. Robin shocked all of us almost two years before. She was deliriously happy being newly married to the love of her life, Kim Anderson, when she began to have a series of unexplained sore throats and fever. Concerned, but not worried, she'd gone to her doctor for a physical and had been given the worst news imaginable. She had leukemia. The diagnosis stunned all of us who loved her and completely devastated Stevie, her best friend.

"You know she's pregnant, don't you, Carol?" Stevie asked in a small voice. I nodded and sat quietly, aware that Stevie was struggling to keep her composure. In that moment, I would have given anything to help her deal with the pain of Robin's tragedy. Five months earlier, Sara told me of Robin's unexpected pregnancy. Against her doctor's wishes, she'd refused to terminate her pregnancy—a move that would have prolonged her life—and insisted on carrying her baby to term. Stevie's grief seemed to fill the car as she sat deathly still.

"She's so brave, Carol. I can't believe how brave she is! Having this baby has cut her life short by at least a year, but she's so selfless—she's a saint.

Robin's in the City of Hope Cancer Center and so far the pregnancy is going as well as can be expected. But you wouldn't recognize her if you saw her. The treatment is so harsh and she's so thin. I miss her all the time and I don't understand why this has happened to her."

As Stevie began to cry silent tears I reached over and took her into my arms. Soon we were both crying and as I tried to whisper soothing words to calm her, I knew that there was little I could do or say to ease her pain. There were no words that could make either of us feel better. As sad as I was over Robin, I couldn't even begin to imagine the grief that Stevie must have been feeling. How horrific it must be to watch a woman you loved like a sister dying of leukemia and know that there's nothing you can do for her. I'd only known Robin for six years and I both loved and respected her. Everyone did. But we all knew that whatever pain we were feeling over her tragedy paled in comparison to Stevie's. Wiping away her tears, she gave me a shaky smile and told me that she was OK for the time being. With a last hug I pulled back into traffic and headed up to Bel-Air.

Even though Stevie and I took our time going home, we were still the first to arrive. I showed her around the house and she freaked when she saw the rain room. She absolutely loved it. We turned the rain on, ran around lighting candles, and finished up just as the first cars began to pull through the gates to our estate. Standing on both sides of the large copper front doors, Stevie and I greeted our fellow Fleetwood Mac family members as they entered. Everyone looked shocked and bewildered that Stevie and I were so obviously having a great time together. Lindsey stopped dead in his tracks and stared as though he were having a hallucination. With a confused smile and a shrug, he told Mick that he felt like he was on acid as he looked at the two of us standing with our arms around each other.

"Well, Lindsey, you better get used to it. Carol and I have decided to hang out together every day. Wouldn't you like that?" Stevie said in a teasing voice. Making the sign of the cross, Lindsey backed away, dragging Mick with him. Soon our home was full of people and music started echoing over the built-in speakers that were hidden in the walls throughout the house. I couldn't believe what I was hearing. Lindsey was playing the live bootleg albums that I'd released before we met. Live music of the Stones and Beatles filled the rooms and everyone was complimenting me on what they were hearing.

Speechless at first, I soon found myself holding an audience as I explained the ins and out of the "live" bootleg record business in the early 1970s. It wasn't illegal, I explained. There were no laws covering "sound waves" recorded at a concert before 1976. I felt a sense of pride that I hadn't felt in a long time. The recordings were really good—and rare. And it'd been a long time since I'd been able to take credit for something I had achieved in the music business. My modeling was different. I was proud of my portfolio and the work that I'd done as a model. But to me, sitting in front of a camera had been a very passive achievement. My record business, on the other hand, gave me the opportunity to create something tangible—a product that gave people all over the world a lot of pleasure.

And for the first time in years I realized how much I'd missed that feeling of pride and accomplishment. But hearing my concert albums brought it all back. A longing to find another field where I could once again do something, once again *have* something all my own, swept over me. And I knew that somehow, someway, I was going to find it. *I'll talk to Lindsey about it after the tour—surely by now, it will be possible for me to have a career of my own. Modeling just isn't enough,* I told myself while trying not to think of his reaction years before when Bob Ezrin offered me a career on a silver platter.

In true Fleetwood Mac style the party went until almost sunrise. After everyone left, Lindsey and I sat out by our pool and watched the dawn break over Los Angeles. *It's the perfect end to a perfect evening. And maybe the beginning of a whole new world for me after the tour,* I thought happily as the dark night lightened around us.

The next day, Lindsey had a surprise for me. He walked into the bedroom holding a small gray and white kitten and I screamed in excitement when I saw it. I'd been begging for a kitten for years—my love of cats knew no bounds—but Lindsey had rightly believed that because we were on the road for such long periods of time, a cat just had to wait. And so when I saw what he was holding, I couldn't believe my eyes.

"I told Bob to find you a kitten, and he did. Do you like him?" he asked with a grin.

"Oh my God, I love him! I adore him! Thank you, Lindsey . . . you've made me so happy!" I gushed as I cradled the small, fat ball of fur in my arms. I sat the kitten down on the bed and took a good look at him.

"He's going to be *huge*, Lindsey. Look how big his ears are! He looks like Dr. Spock! What shall we name him?"

"He's your kitten, but I kinda like the name Eddie Clift," Lindsey answered.

"I love it! It's perfect! Are you sure you don't want to call him 'Charlton'?" I answered as I started to giggle.

With a groan, Lindsey shook his head, "I'd never do that to a defenseless animal. I don't want him to be a failure. Jesus, that book is unbelievable!"

Lindsey with our kitten Eddie Clift.

He was referring to a biography of Charlton Heston that I'd bought for him. Lindsey had read it three times. He said that to him, the story of Heston's life was a study in failure. Charlton Heston had made the wrong career choices over and over again and Lindsey was fascinated by Heston's mindset.

His other favorite book was a biography of Montgomery Clift. Clift, who changed his first name from Eddie to Montgomery for the stage, had been James Dean's idol—and his story was tragic. He was a brilliant actor who had seen his career and personal life go spiraling out of control after a horrific car crash that smashed every bone in his face. His addiction to painkillers and alcohol sent him into the sordid underbelly of Hollywood life and brought him to an early death. Lindsey loved the Clash song "The Right Profile" about Montgomery Clift and I'd given him three framed Montgomery Clift movie posters for his birthday—so naming our kitten after him was a no-brainer.

Two weeks later Lindsey and I were once again starting to pack for another tour. My movements were slow and sluggish. I hadn't been feeling well at all since the night of the *Mirage* listening party, and it worried me. I had an appointment to see Dr. Weiss in an hour and I gave up on the packing and threw on jeans and a shirt. Afterward I would wish I'd never gone.

Dr. Weiss didn't want me to go on the road. He was worried about my health and knew full well the extent of the partying that was the mainstay of each and every show. I'd told him all about it. Because if you couldn't tell your doctor the truth about what you'd been doing, then what was the point? I wasn't the only patient he had in the entertainment business so he wasn't exactly shocked, but he wanted to keep me a safe distance from life on the road until he'd had a chance to run more tests to see what was causing me to feel so ill. And reluctantly I'd agreed.

Standing in our driveway, I gave Lindsey one last kiss before he climbed into the waiting limo that would take him to the Fleetwood Mac jet. It felt strange to not be climbing in right behind him, but I'd be joining the band soon—after my tests were finished. As he promised me again that he'd call as soon as he got to the hotel, I nodded and told him not to worry.

"I'll be fine, Lindsey. I have little Eddie to keep me company. And anyway, Walter and Tom should be here any minute. So if I get sick, they'll be here for me. Just have fun—but not *too* much fun without me. I'll talk to you tonight, OK?" I said brightly, trying to hide my disappointment that I'd have to stay behind. I watched his car pull out of the driveway before walking slowly back into the house.

Walter Egan's band would be recording in Lindsey's studio while he was on tour, and I knew that I'd have little time to be lonely. I would have

preferred to be on my own, since I wasn't feeling well, but Lindsey had offered his studio to Walter's band at no cost. And I loved Walter. I'd been the model for the back of the record cover of his hit album *Magnet and Steel* and I got along well with the

Carol Ann and Annie McLoone, singer in Walter Egan's band, in Bel-Air.

rest of his band. *It's probably going to be quieter on the road than up here in Bel-Air once Walter's gang arrives,* I thought with a shake of my head.

A few nights later I decided to drive out to Mick's house in Malibu to spend the evening with Sara. She too had stayed behind but, unlike me, was used to it. I'd been by Lindsey's side on every single tour and it felt strange not to be with him at the beginning of this one. All in all, since I'd met him, I'd probably only missed three weeks out of the *Rumours* and *Tusk* tours combined. And I couldn't wait until I could join him.

As I drove down Pacific Coast Highway, I watched the waves crashing on the public beaches beneath weathered small houses with cozy lights burning softly against the black velvet of the ocean. As I neared Paradise Cove and its private beaches surrounding million-dollar mansions, I wondered why the million-dollar homes seemed so cold and lifeless compared with the beach houses a few miles down the road. Listening to Tom Petty sing "Luna" over the cassette player in my car, I felt peaceful, happy, and safe.

After an hour's drive I arrived at Mick's rather strange mansion known within the Fleetwood Mac family as "the Blue Whale." Sara and I stood under the small fake balcony in the living room looking up at the life-size dummy of a man hanging with a noose around his neck. No matter how many times I saw it, it always creeped me out and I couldn't understand how Sara could bear living with it. But it was just another sign of Mick's twisted humor. Even so, I told Sara that I couldn't bear being in the same room as the "hanging man" and with a laugh she pulled me by the hand to lead me to the large, homey kitchen.

But I didn't make it. Before I'd taken even three steps, everything went gray and then black as I felt myself falling. As from a great distance, I could hear Sara frantically calling my name, and then everything was still. Nausea and shades of misty light that formed into the face of Sara pulled me back from the darkness and I knew that I was lying on the floor—but I didn't know how I gotten there.

"Oh my God, you scared me, Carol!" Sara cried as I tried to focus on her face. "You fainted! Can you stand up?"

Shaken and still nauseous, I managed to get to my feet with Sara's help and make it to her bed. She rushed to the bathroom and brought back a cold washcloth for my face and slowly I began to feel better. I couldn't remember fainting since I was a little girl. *What happened?* I wondered as I clung to Sara with ice-cold hands. Sara insisted that I go first thing in the morning to see Mick's physician, Dr. Unger. "He's really good, Carol. All of us go to him. I know you're seeing a neurologist, but I want you to go to our doctor. Promise me. OK?"

With a nod I told her I would. Afraid to drive home, I spent the night there and then drove back into L.A. and Dr. Unger's office the next day. Dr. Unger was a handsome, friendly man who seemed to brighten the room as he walked into it. He would himself become something of a celebrity when he married the widow of Peter Sellers a few years after we met.

Greeting me warmly, he checked my vital signs and told me he wanted me to have an echocardiogram—a test that allowed him to see my heart beating on a monitor.

After the test Dr. Unger told me that I had a congenital heart defect: a mitral-valve prolapse. It was a defect in which one of the valves of your heart pumped harder than it should and it could easily be the reason I fainted. "You're just more sensitive to everything because of your heart condition. It's not fatal. You can live with it. But you have to take care of your health. Obviously, it makes you a little more delicate and you need to be aware of that."

Thanking him, I returned home in a daze, finding the house mercifully empty. Crawling into bed, I fell into a dreamless sleep and awoke feeling depressed and listless. I was already tired of dealing with the physical symptoms of my panic attacks, so the news of my heart defect had come as a real blow. I'd always considered myself a healthy person and I wasn't used to doctors and dire diagnoses. And I didn't want to get used to it. So I pushed away all thoughts of being "delicate" and got out bed determined to do something that would prove I wasn't.

Walter's band was playing in our garage studio, and after dressing quickly I crept down the hall away from them. I was sick of rocker boys and their crude jokes and dreams of musical fame. I needed a little time to myself. I needed to be alone. Walking into the rain room, I flipped on the switch and watched as the soft drops of water cascaded over the glass. *I know what I'll do! I'm going to redecorate this room! And I'll start by moving all the furniture around!* I said to myself as I surveyed the rain room.

As I pushed, pulled, and lifted the heavy chairs and tables I felt a sense of inner peace that one only gets from physical labor—and it was wonderful. But after two hours I began to have dull, aching pains in my lower back that became sharper and more defined as each minute passed. I stopped for a moment and sat down, certain that I'd just strained my back. Suddenly

I almost doubled over with the worst abdominal cramps I'd ever had. The pain was excruciating and I gasped as it washed over me in waves.

What's wrong with me? I thought worriedly as I curled into a ball and closed my eyes tight against the torturous cramping. I lay motionless for what felt like hours, the pain finally eased and I walked slowly back to my bedroom, locking the door behind me. *I'm fine,* I told myself. *I'm probably just getting my period. It's bad, but by morning I'll be OK.*

After a fitful night of pain I woke to find that I was bleeding heavily—more than I ever had during my normal periods. With shaking hands I called my gynecologist's office and explained to his nurse what was happening.

"Are you pregnant, Carol?" she asked quickly. I explained that I was on the Pill, so it didn't seem possible. With a crisp voice she told me that the doctor was out of the office for the day but to come in first thing in the morning. After phoning in pain medication, she ordered me to stay in bed until I could get into the office.

During my nightly phone conversation with Lindsey I didn't say anything about my "girl" problem. He'd been surprisingly uninterested when I told him of my heart defect the day before. And to tell the truth, it both hurt and surprised me. So I did my best to make sympathetic noises as he complained about being on the road and how bored he was. Because I was feeling unwell, I got off the phone as quickly as possible.

The next morning I slowly walked into the bathroom and stared at my reflection in the mirror. My face was so white it seemed translucent in the early morning light, and the skin around my hollowed eyes looked bruised with purple shadows. Wincing in pain as I slowly stepped into the shower, I felt almost otherworldly as I struggled to keep my balance. Slipping into a dress, I inched my way down the hall and out to my car. I was feeling so faint that it took all my energy and concentration not to crash my car on the long drive to Dr. Jackson's office.

As I walked through the doors of his suite his nurse took one look at me and rushed out from behind her reception desk. Slipping her strong arm around my waist, she almost lifted me off my feet as she rushed me back to an inner room. "The doctor will be right here. Just lie down now, I'll be right back," she said in an urgent tone as she gently helped me lie down on the examining table.

Within minutes Dr. Jackson walked in and immediately started barking orders to two nurses hovering just outside the door. After a half-hour of blood samples and examinations, Dr. Jackson brushed my long, sweat-soaked hair off my forehead as he sat on a chair beside me. "Carol. You're hemorrhaging. You've had a miscarriage and you've lost a lot of blood. We need to get you checked into the hospital as soon as possible. I'm sorry, hon."

"What? But how is that possible? I didn't even know I was pregnant, Dr. Jackson! I had a period last month. I can't be pregnant!" I said as I began to cry. And then I told him about the heavy lifting I'd done two nights before. "I'm to blame, aren't I? That's what caused me to miscarry?"

In a soft voice Dr. Jackson explained to me that while he doubted it, there was no way to know. He thought the pregnancy was already in trouble. My light period the month before was breakthrough bleeding and the fainting spell was another indication that something was amiss. He believed I was two months along before I began to hemorrhage. I needed surgery, he explained, after telling me to check into Cedars-Sinai Hospital first thing in the morning for a D&C procedure. With condolences and words of warning about the trauma my body had been through, he sent me home.

Leaving my car behind, I climbed into a cab and closed my eyes for the entire ride home. I tried not to think about what I'd just been told. I tried not to think about the baby I hadn't known I was carrying. I tried not to think about what might have been. But all my thoughts seemed dark and empty and it felt as though I could barely breathe.

As I walked into the house I could hear Walter and the laughter of his band echoing down the hallway from the studio and I knew that I couldn't bear it. Calling Bob's name, I walked into his bedroom and looked at him numbly as he smiled at me. "Bob, I'm ill. I have to go to the hospital tomorrow. I want you to ask Walter and his band to leave. I'll let you know when they can come back."

Before he could ask any questions, I said softly, "Look, Bob, I've had a miscarriage. I don't want anyone in the house right now but you and me. Don't tell them anything. Just say that I'm sick. I'm going to call Lindsey and then I need you to drive me to the hospital in the morning. Can you do all of that for me?"

He mumbled that he could and I walked slowly to my bedroom and once again locked myself in. I could hear Walter's loud words of protest quickly grow quiet as Bob explained the situation, but it seemed so unimportant to me if they were angry or upset over having their recording sessions cut short. Curling up on the bed, I listened as car doors slammed outside in our driveway and then I reached for the phone. I had to tell Lindsey.

I don't know what I expected Lindsey's reaction to be. Shock perhaps, or sadness, or at the very least, concern over my health. But I got none of these reactions. Instead, I had to endure a ten-minute tirade of accusations about how I was hiding a pregnancy from him. And to Lindsey that seemed the ultimate betrayal. I explained over and over again that I hadn't known that I was pregnant, but he didn't want to hear it. He wasn't listening to anything I said.

There were no words of consolation, none of concern. He was angry. Enraged. And it made no sense at all to me. I was in pain, I was hemorrhaging, and I couldn't understand his fury. And for the first time in our relationship I realized that I didn't want to understand it. He seemed a stranger to me and already in shock over the loss of a child I hadn't known that I was carrying, I hung up the phone, silencing the screaming voice on the other end. As the phone immediately began to ring I unplugged it from the wall, climbed under the covers, and cried myself to sleep.

As they prepared me for surgery the next morning, I told myself that things couldn't get any worse. But I was wrong. The anesthesiologist couldn't find any veins for the injections I needed to have. They'd almost collapsed from my heavy loss of blood and after twenty minutes I was hysterical from not only the painful probing needles and the sheer horror of the miscarriage but also Lindsey's rage from the day before. As his ugly words echoed in my mind I seemed to see a baby's face that had Lindsey's eyes and my blonde hair, and I felt as though I were in the middle of a living nightmare.

Dr. Jackson came rushing to my side and with soothing words and gentle hands somehow injected me and I mercifully succumbed to blackness. When I awakened, the first thing I saw was Sara's anxious face bending over me. I tried to smile, but I couldn't. I was too weak to make the effort. Sara sat by my side, holding my hand, as I seemed to drift under the heavy pain medication. I didn't feel any pain. I didn't feel much of anything.

As if from far away, I heard the phone ringing and as Sara held it up to my ear I heard Lindsey's voice asking how I was feeling. "I don't know," I said in a whisper. He told me that he was flying home for me and that I should come directly to L'Ermitage as soon as I left the hospital. The band would join us in a few days, he said, and I would then accompany Lindsey for the rest of the tour. "Sure. Whatever. I have to go now. I don't feel very well." Handing the phone back to Sara, I turned over on my side and closed my eyes. I could hear her speaking to him softly, but I didn't listen. I just wasn't interested.

The next day, as Bob waited for me in the hospital corridor, I pulled my clothes on slowly. Just as I was ready to leave the room, the phone once again rang. It was Lindsey. He sounded terrible. He hasn't had much sleep, he said. Could I ask my doctor for something to help him rest? As I listened incredulously to him telling me how sick he felt, it was like he'd forgotten that he was talking to me in a hospital room—the morning after I'd had surgery after losing his child. Forgive my skepticism, but it seemed hard for me to believe that his lack of sleep was caused by worry over me. "I'll ask the doctor," I told him, and then hung up the phone.

After we arrived in Bel-Air, I called Dr. Jackson and asked for sleeping pills. Knowing what a hard time I'd had, he was only too happy to oblige. After showering and packing a small overnight bag, I grabbed Lindsey's birthday present before I left the house. About a month before, I'd taken the three snapshots that Lindsey had of his father and had them blown up and beautifully framed as a surprise for his birthday. I'd also made framed copies for his two brothers. I'd been so shocked months earlier when Lindsey confided that those three snapshots were about the only good pictures he had of his father. And I'd wanted to preserve them for both him and his family.

Even though I was under strict orders not to drive, I knew I needed to be alone before I faced Lindsey. Firmly refusing Bob's offer to drive me to the pharmacy and the hotel, I climbed into my car, picked up Lindsey's pills, and went straight to L'Ermitage. As soon as I entered our suite Lindsey wrapped his arms around me and told me how much he'd missed me. Handing him the pills and brightly wrapped gift, I tried to smile as I murmured that I loved him too and walked into the bathroom, closing the door behind me. Closing my eyes, I sank down onto the floor, putting off the "reunion" that only a few days before I'd looked forward to so eagerly.

I felt angry, betrayed, and, most of all, heartbroken. Angry over his furious reaction to the news of my miscarriage; betrayed that he would think

I would ever try to hide a pregnancy from him; and heartbroken because he'd shown so little concern about my health and the pain I'd endured both physically and mentally over the loss of our child. And worst of all, devastated that he seemed to care so little that our baby would never be born.

As I heard him call my name I got up and slowly walked into the bedroom. Sitting in the middle of the bed, he was staring at my birthday gift of pictures with tears in his eyes. He thanked me profusely as he pulled me down on the bed beside him. He made no mention of my miscarriage. Not a word. He went on and on about what a drag the road had been without me and how glad he was that I'd now be joining him for the tour. He loved the pictures of his father, he told me, and was overwhelmed by them. He didn't seem to notice that I was barely speaking. Which was just as well, because right then I had nothing to say to him.

But like so many times before, all thoughts of myself disappeared as I looked into his pale, overwrought face and all my instincts told me that he needed me to take care of *him*. And I did. I put him to bed, watched as he washed down his sleeping pills, and then curled up beside him. With superhuman effort I buried my pain and hurt feelings and fell asleep repeating a now-familiar mantra: *It's not his fault. It's just the pressure he's under that's making him behave in a way that I cannot understand. He swears that he loves me and I want to believe him.*

We left the next day to join the band in Houston, Texas. As we arrived backstage at the amphitheater it was immediately apparent that this tour was nothing like the *Rumours* or *Tusk* tours. Everyone in the band just seemed to be going through the motions as they got dressed and sat through the ten-minute countdown. Even though drugs and alcohol were being consumed like water, they seemed to have little effect on lifting anyone's spirits or changing their apathetic moods.

The band was bored—and they'd only been touring two weeks. The electricity in the air that was always present before a concert was gone. And no one seemed to care. After giving a performance that would have seemed barely adequate by the standards set during the *Tusk* tour, the band had little to say about it after the show. There was no discussion of what went wrong, or right. Everyone headed for the drinks table, picked up powder-filled bottle caps, and changed into their street clothes to head back to the hotel.

And this would set the tone for the rest of the *Mirage* tour. With the exception of Mick and John, nobody wanted to be on the road. And slowly but surely the fights and ugliness that were present at Le Château once again

Lindsey on the road during the Mirage *tour.*

became commonplace whenever the band was together—and all of us were suffering from it. By Halloween, Stevie, Lindsey, and Christine had told John and Mick that after next month's U.S. tour dates were completed the *Mirage* tour was over.

There would be no European or Far East tour. With *Mirage* at number one for two straight months, the band was over it. They wanted to pursue their solo projects. They wanted a long break from Fleetwood Mac— and they couldn't give a damn about record sales, fans, and the future of

the band that had made them superstars. For now, the party was over. And just when it seemed things couldn't get any worse on the road, they did.

On October 12, I answered the phone in our hotel suite and heard Stevie's tearful voice on the other end of the line asking for Lindsey. She haltingly told me that she was sorry about my miscarriage and as my voice caught in my throat, I thanked her as she broke down into sobs. Biting my lip, I worriedly handed Lindsey the phone. Watching his face, I knew with a sinking feeling that it was the bad news that we'd all been expecting: after giving premature birth to a beautiful baby boy six days before, Robin had died last night at City of Hope.

I could hear Stevie's sobs reverberating from the receiver as I slowly sank to the floor. Laying my head on my knees, I cried for Robin and her motherless child. It felt as though everything that was once so beautiful and sparkling behind the golden curtain of fame that surrounded Fleetwood Mac's world was crumbling into desolation and ruin. The curtain remained, but the inhabitants it shielded were no longer protected from the ravages of life.

19

IT ALL GOES INSANE

The years 1983 and '84 were when it all went wrong. When a fortune was lost. When the world fell apart. When another life was taken. When it all went insane. And for a few of us, they would be years in which we left it all behind and tried to find a way out of the darkness that had settled over the kingdom of Fleetwood Mac.

It was late afternoon when we got the phone call. After over seven years by Lindsey's side I didn't think anything could shock me any more. But I was wrong. This call not only horrified the two of us, but also sent every single member of the band and the inner circle reeling in stunned disbelief.

Stevie Nicks was married. In a small, sparsely attended ceremony on a Malibu beach, she had exchanged marriage vows with Kim Anderson, the widowed husband of her best friend, Robin. I don't think anyone believed that Stevie was in love with Kim. Everyone understood that she did, however, want Robin's baby. But the question we all kept asking ourselves was how, in the name of God, could she rationalize marrying her best friend's husband only two months after Robin's tragic death?

Even though incestuous relationships were a way of life within Fleetwood Mac's world, this morbid marriage was beyond the pale. But when I thought of the inconsolable grief Stevie had shared with me in my car on the night of the *Mirage* listening party, I could only speculate that it was this grief that was responsible for a type of temporary insanity where the only end result would be disaster. That speculation came true when, just three months later, she filed for divorce. From that point on, not only would she not talk about baby Matthew or Kim, she barely even acknowledged that the marriage happened.

The shock of Stevie's marriage and quickie divorce faded quickly, as all things seemed to do in Fleetwood Mac land. In a world where bizarreness, backstabbing, bad relationships, stupid behavior, and insanity were the rule instead of the exception, a tasteless marriage only held our attention for so long. Soon it was business as usual for everyone.

Stevie went right back to work on her second solo record, *Wild Heart*. Mick set out on an embarrassing fiasco of a tour with his new band, Mick Fleetwood's Zoo, to support an unsuccessful follow-up solo album to his first effort, *The Visitor*. Traveling by bus and playing to audiences in almost empty clubs, they met with dismal failure. Afterward Mick fell deeper into a lifestyle of all-night drug binges at his home, which was becoming a refuge for anyone and everyone who wanted a place to party or crash. Christine escaped to England to finish her solo record, and John once again disappeared into the Pacific Ocean in his boat.

In Bel-Air, Lindsey was busy at work on a project that was, for him, just an amusing distraction before he began work on his second solo album.

Harold Ramis, the famous director of Bill Murray's *Caddyshack*, had asked Lindsey to write two songs for his new movie, *National Lampoon's Vacation*, starring Chevy Chase. Arriving on our doorstep with his wife and very young daughter, he convinced Lindsey to venture into movie soundtracks.

The visit from Harold Ramis had given me an idea. I hadn't forgotten my longing and desire on the night of the *Mirage* listening party to find an outlet for myself that would, hopefully, lead to a career. If anything, it now seemed more important than ever. Since my miscarriage it felt as though something had emotionally shifted inside of me. Before I lost the

Carol Ann in Lindsey's Bel-Air studio.

baby I'd completely devoted myself to Lindsey and his career, believing that my role in our relationship was ultimately as his future wife and the mother of his children. And before my miscarriage, even my longings for a career came second to that. Looking back over the years I'd been by his side, I did this willingly. Nothing was more important than the future we would have together—despite all the bad and frightening incidents of irrational anger.

Things had changed for me now, however. It was like I'd woken up from a dream. A dream that I would love to hold on to, but after his reaction to the loss of our child, a dream that I now knew was one I might not want. And yes, it scared me to even think of my relationship with Lindsey in such a cold, brutally honest way. Even if a part of me still wanted to go back to playing the part of his fiancée who never questioned and only obeyed, I knew that I couldn't go back. And I knew that I didn't want to.

Without discussing it with Lindsey, I called Bjorn and asked him to recommend an acting teacher for me. I'd always been curious about acting and it seemed the next logical step to take after modeling. I had no idea if I had any acting talent—or if I even wanted to be an actor. I only knew that I wanted to find out. More importantly, I knew that I wanted to do something just for myself. I spent long hours talking to Desi about it, and with her encouragement, I went for it.

Within a week I was taking private lessons from a wonderful old gentleman with an impeccable resume—and I loved it. It felt wonderful to have something completely different to be excited about. Even if, in the scheme of things, an acting class might not mean a lot to most people, to me it did. Unlike modeling, learning the basics of acting was a challenge, and that was why I was enjoying it so much. Talent or no talent, it felt great to try my hand at something that took both skill and creativity. For three weeks I'd been enjoying every second of it. And for the first time in years my every waking moment wasn't focused on Lindsey's career and the world of Fleetwood Mac.

Lindsey had become silent and withdrawn as my enthusiasm for my classes spilled over into our dinner conversations and the breaks he took from the studio. But I was so caught up in my newfound passion that I failed to read these warning signs. Warning signs that I'd seen before during the years I'd spent with him. Warning signs that always, always predicted an explosion of unfocused anger; anger that was just as devastating whether he was sober or not; anger that seemed to need no reason or incident to set it off. All I had were the warning signs, which were like the quiet before a storm. And even though I'd learned there was nothing I could do to prevent it from happening, I always tried to do whatever I could to lessen the impact when his rage exploded.

Entering the house after my afternoon class, I saw Lindsey's silhouette in the doorway of our living room. I walked toward his shadowy form, my words of greeting fading as I looked into his eyes, which flashed with intense emotion as he stared at my happy face. With a sneer he said, "Welcome home," as he walked purposefully toward me.

No, no, no! It's not going to happen again. It can't. It won't. This is just a bad dream. It's not really happening! a voice screamed inside my head. But it was happening. He lunged for me and wrapped his hands around my throat, and I began to fight back. I somehow twisted myself out of his grip and stumbled backward, almost falling as my back hit the doorframe of the open front door. Turning quickly, I ran for my car. Throwing myself inside, I hit the locks as I started to sob. With harsh, unintelligible words screaming behind me, my hands shook as I fumbled the keys into the ignition and floored the gas, almost hitting a tree by our driveway.

Without looking back I swung the car around and drove recklessly back out through our gates. Glancing in my rearview mirror, I saw Lindsey standing in the middle of the street, unrelieved anger making his face almost unrecognizable. I drove as fast as I dared, and only let myself slow down when I hit Sunset Boulevard, knowing that for now, at least, I'd managed to escape from Lindsey's fury.

With tears streaming down my face I drove straight to the Century Plaza Hotel in Century City. At the front desk, the smile from the friendly desk manager faded as he saw my face. He knew me well. I'd come here at least five times over the past few years when a fight with Lindsey had turned from bad to horrific. With a look of concern he asked me if I was all right and if he could do anything to help. Shaking my head, I stammered that I just needed a room. He gently patted my hand as he gave me a room key and I managed to make it all the way up to my suite before I collapsed in tears.

I knew that Lindsey would eventually come for me. He knew where I went for refuge after a fight. It might be tomorrow, or the day after that. And when he did, he'd no longer be angry. And we wouldn't speak of why I was at the hotel—only that it was time for me to come home. And for a few months everything would once again be calm.

In the beginning, after the first few horrific rages, I'd told myself that it would never happen again. And I would blame myself for what happened while vowing to do everything within my power to be the perfect girlfriend. Months passed in which Lindsey and I were completely happy—months when I felt so loved that it was easy for me to believe that the ugliness was behind us.

But that belief had finally been shattered that day. I now knew that nothing I seemed to do—or not do—made a difference. And facing up to that was not only painful, it was absolutely devastating. A day that began so full of light and happiness had turned black. And my heart was breaking.

Two days later Lindsey knocked on the door and calmly, lovingly escorted me home. This time, however, it was harder for me to smile. It was harder for me to go about the pretence that my home life was fine. I returned to days spent in a house that felt deserted. The only evidence that I wasn't alone was the constant muffled sound of music coming from Lindsey's garage studio. As I drifted through rooms filled with tapestries and porcelain vases the only proof that I was actually there was my transparent reflection in the glass walls of our home.

On the surface, I was living the fantasy life of most young women. I was in the company of a musical genius. I had material wealth beyond my wildest dreams. My consort was a member of rock 'n' roll's royalty: a poetic, exquisitely tortured romantic. But behind the iron gates, where photographers and reporters never ventured, I felt desperate, alone, and empty. And I needed to do something—anything—to keep from falling apart.

I'd found out the truth about fame. I'd learned that for Fleetwood Mac and their inner circle, it came with a heavy price. And to me, the biggest cost of all was the suffocating isolation that it imposed. The only people we could trust were those within our own small circle of friends. In seven years, I could count only two people outside of the inner circle as my friends—Bjorn and Desi. And they both had such busy lives that I was lucky to have contact with either of them on a weekly basis. I'd made friends easily my entire life, but those days were long gone.

Now any new "friend" was suspect, because how could you ever know if they cared about you or just wanted a door into the life that you were leading? You couldn't. Every single member of the inner circle had found out the hard way that 99 percent of the people who tried to befriend us were only there because of who we were with, not who we were ourselves. And it hurt—a lot. For the five band members of Fleetwood Mac, the price they paid for that fame was well worth it. For their wives, fiancées, and boy-friends, it became a quarantine. No one from the outside world could be let in. And you couldn't get out.

So as Lindsey worked in the studio fourteen hours a day, I turned to the only person who I felt could help me escape my isolation at home: Sara. I began to spend a few days a week in Malibu, where I escaped the loneli-ness of Bel-Air. It was a stark contrast to the lonely, quiet days that I'd been accustomed to at my home.

Being at the Blue Whale was no different from being on the road. There was a nonstop party atmosphere twenty-four hours a day. We all had our drugs of choice. Mine was cocaine; Sara, Stevie, and Christine did blow and drank alcohol; and the men snorted, smoked weed, and drank. We didn't see it as debauchery, it was just our reality. It had been since the day I entered the world of Fleetwood Mac and nothing had changed except that it had become a thousand times more intense.

Sara and I spent hours by the pool watching the crazed antics of Richard Dashut, Dave Mason, and Billy Burnette, son of Rocky Burnette, a famous musician and friend of Elvis Presley in the 1950s. As we tossed a vial of blow back and forth between us, we talked, laughed, and sometimes cried. I'd finally told Sara everything about my relationship with Lindsey. She knew the dark secrets about the fights that I'd tried to keep hidden from the rest of the inner circle. And I, in turn, heard about her troubles: mainly that Mick was quickly sinking into financial quicksand.

On this day Sara was recounting horror stories of bounced checks and declined credit cards all over Malibu. Embarrassing moments at supermar-kets and restaurants were so numerous that she was now on a cash-only basis with all of them. She was worried, but hopeful that everything would turn out fine. I murmured reassuring words as I watched Mick stumbling by the pool, a tray of cocaine in hand. As he sat down on a chair opposite us and offered us the tray, I was struck again by how much I adored Mick. He was a naughty child in a man's body and it was impossible to imagine that anything bad could ever happen to him.

But it did. In less than a year's time Mick would be forced to declare bank-ruptcy. He'd managed to blow through an estimated $8 million and would lose his house, cars, recording equipment, and, temporarily, Sara. She didn't leave because of the bankruptcy—she left because she'd finally reached a point where she had to get away from the madness and chaos that surrounded her. But she'd return and eventually marry Mick in 1988—with me by her side—and remain his wife until Mick's playboy ways forced her to file for divorce. And through it all she and I would remain best friends.

As the summer passed, I continued with my acting classes and Lindsey stayed holed up in the studio. Having finished two songs for *Vacation*, he was now in the beginning phase of recording his second solo album. The only time I saw him was a few minutes each morning and late at night. Unlike *Law and Order*, where he was free and open with the music he was recording, this time he had become a recluse in the studio. No one was welcomed in, not even me. It wasn't that I was banned from entering, it was just that when I did, he seemed frustrated and angry that I'd bothered him, so after a while, I stopped walking through the studio door. He seemed glad that I was spending time with Sara as often as I could instead of being isolated in our house. Once or twice a month he drove with me to Malibu and we stayed until dawn, partying together at the Blue Whale. And these nights I treasured, for without them I would barely be able to spend time with him at all.

In August, Lindsey did a music video for his *Vacation* soundtrack song "Holiday Road" and I was incredibly excited. It was a chance for me to be on another shoot. After being on the set for Fleetwood Mac's music video of the track "Gypsy," I'd been enthralled not by what was happening in front of the cameras but what was happening behind them. While the Fleetwood Mac family sat in their dressing rooms, I'd been out on the soundstage inspecting the makeup and wardrobe trailers and talking to the crew, trying to learn as much as I could about everything that was happening around me.

On the set for "Holiday Road," I stood and watched the video crew go about their jobs as they made what was essentially a mini-movie. The director, Mark Resycka, was warm and friendly. He spent the entire day giving me a play-by-play of everything that went into making a music video. As I listened and learned I discovered an element of the film industry that was so appealing and refreshing that it blew my mind: no one in the large crew behind the camera was starstruck. It didn't matter who the band was or how famous they might be: in the eyes of the director and crew, the band and/or actors were just another tool to use to create a piece of art.

Whether the shoot was for Fleetwood Mac or a movie starring Al Pacino, it was the piece of film that was the star, not the talent. And by the end of the day I knew that I'd found an industry that was perfectly suited for me. I felt at home standing behind the camera. I felt comfortable talking to the director and producer—and I knew that this was where I wanted to be. This was the career that I'd been looking for. As I watched the costume designer working in her wardrobe trailer I realized that I could do her job—and I'd be good at it. And the best part of it was I would need to prove my worth as myself, not as Lindsey Buckingham's girlfriend. To Mark and his crew, Fleetwood Mac was just a great band: nothing less, nothing more. The power of Fleetwood Mac, Mark told me, had no bearing on whether I could succeed in the film industry.

But he wanted me to try. While Lindsey performed, Mark and his wife Mary encouraged me to visit their production offices. They offered to help me learn firsthand the ins and outs of the movie business. And over the next months I visited often. While Lindsey worked in his Bel-Air studio, I drove to Hollywood and spent hours at Pendulum Productions. With Mary, I stood on the set of "Dancin' with Myself," watching Billy Idol perform as Mark sat in the director's chair; I stood behind the monitor as he directed AC/DC, Quiet Riot, Journey, and Lionel Richie. And before I knew it, I was learning just about everything I needed to know to work as a costume designer. It was a career that would not only prove to be successful beyond my wildest dreams, it would also be my salvation.

At night before we went to bed I talked to Lindsey about what I was learning from Mark and Mary, my excitement dulling my senses to the ever-increasing tension that played across his features each and every time I chattered on. At first his facial expressions were those of a man indulging a child in her fantasy. He listened with an air of not-so-amused tolerance as I recounted my adventures and what I was learning about the film industry. But as the weeks passed, that tolerance changed from indifference to cold cynicism. Cutting remarks and impatient glances were his response whenever I spoke of my hopes for a career in costume design, and I knew that either he didn't think I was capable of achieving it, or he hated the idea of it.

And I realized that it would be a long time, if ever, before Lindsey reconciled himself to the fact that I needed more in my life. That I needed interests other than being a supportive girlfriend—a girlfriend whose world revolved just around him and Fleetwood Mac. But a stubborn voice inside my head refused to accept what my heart already knew—that anything that seemed to draw my attention away from life in the world of Fleetwood Mac was unacceptable to Lindsey.

I told myself that he'd accept it—as soon as he saw that there was no threat to our relationship. With another Fleetwood Mac album or tour not even on the schedule for the next few years, why couldn't I finally have a career of my own? Why couldn't I also have a creative outlet that was as important to me as Lindsey's music was to him? Even if I didn't understand why, I would soon suffer the consequences of asking for it.

It was Thanksgiving morning. While other Americans were celebrating with their families, I was grabbing handfuls of clothes and throwing them into my suitcase. With shaking hands and a splitting headache, I eased it closed. I needed to get out of the house before Lindsey woke up. The night before at a club it had happened again. One moment we were having a good time listening to Walter Egan's band play, and then—just like at the Elvis Costello show—Lindsey had become quiet, seething with fury. All night he'd been laughing and talking and then, over the space of ten minutes, his expression had grown dark and he'd exploded.

Lindsey hadn't screamed at me—instead he'd whispered taunting words as he wrapped his hands around my throat. And somehow, that made it all the more surreal, all the more terrifying, and as it was happening, time slowed down. The noise from the stage and the surrounding crowd of people faded into the background. All that I was aware of was the whisper of Lindsey's voice in my ear and the pressure of his fingers on my neck. Instinct kicked in and I desperately tried to stop what was happening by using the only weapon that I had—my voice. I began to speak softly and reasonably to the man who had his hands around my throat. Answering his taunts with calm measured words declaring my love for him while denying all accusations of infidelity. I had never been unfaithful to him, I whispered truthfully, and I never would be. As I talked, I could feel the pressure of his fingers lessening as he listened. I knew that somehow I had to get through to the Lindsey inside the stranger next to me. The Lindsey who loved me—the Lindsey who would, I still felt, be horrified about what was happening. For I held firm to my belief that there were two Lindseys— one who loved me and one who despised me. If I could get through to *my* Lindsey, then I could make this stop. In the back of my mind, a voice was pleading, *Scream, Carol, scream . . . get help . . .* but I wouldn't listen. There were record executives in the audience and close friends, and I knew that if I screamed for help, the news and gossip of what had happened would spread like wildfire—maybe even to the press. And I was so used to protecting Lindsey and Fleetwood Mac that the thought of doing anything that would bring that kind of attention to us was repellent to me. I knew that it made no sense, but I just couldn't do it.

Instead, I focused on the pitch of his voice, not the words, and I struggled to show no fear, no anger, and I whispered only calm, calm words of love and reassurance, changing only my tone to match the pressure of his fingers. After what seemed an eternity, his hands fell away and I was able to lean back. He stared at me—as though surprised to see that I was free— and with a snarl, he curled his hand into a fist and hit me in the face.

I didn't feel any pain as my head whipped back from the force of the blow. Too stunned perhaps—or just too shocked. There was a voice in my head that keep repeating, *Get up, get away—move slowly—get away . . .* and without breaking eye contact with him, I did just that. Aware that any sudden movement might make him lunge for me, I carefully stood up, unhooked my purse from the back of my chair, and started to back away.

As I turned to make my escape, Christie Thomason grabbed my shoulder. "I was watching you and Lindsey, Carol. He must love you so much. He was holding you so tight as he whispered into your ear that I wondered how you could breathe!" And then she stopped speaking as she stared at my face. "Your lip is bleeding, Carol. What did you do?"

I looked at her and tried to smile as I wiped my lip with the back of my hand. My mind reeled at her words. *She didn't see that he had his hands around my throat! No one in here knows what happened! I'm glad, I'm glad . . .* I thought as I struggled to keep my voice steady. "I'm fine, Christie, but I just . . . I have to go. Make sure Lindsey gets home OK, will you? Tell Greg that

I had to leave and you guys get him home. I can't stay." And I spun on my heel and ran from the club, leaving Lindsey behind.

But once I'd climbed behind the wheel of my car, I knew that I couldn't go straight home. I could barely turn my head without excruciating pain shooting down my spine. I was dizzy and the left side of my face was aching. As tears streamed down my face, I started the car and drove slowly to the hospital down the street from the office of Lindsey's business managers: Century City Hospital.

Once there, I walked numbly into the empty emergency room and asked for a doctor. As the nurse asked probing questions about how I was injured, I felt something give way inside. I just couldn't do it any longer—I just wasn't strong enough at that moment to carry this horrible secret any longer. So there in that antiseptic white room, I started to talk. I felt so alone, so hopeless, and she was a shoulder to lean on. So I told the nurse that my boyfriend, Lindsey Buckingham, had hurt me. It was the first time that I'd told anyone, other than Sara Fleetwood, and the enormity of what I was doing threatened to overwhelm me and I began to sob. Whispering words of sympathy, she placed ice on my bruised face, wiped away my tears, and then walked me down to be X-rayed.

Fifteen minutes later, an elderly doctor entered the room and with a minimum of words, he placed a neck brace around my throat and wrote prescriptions for pain medication. As he handed them to me, he looked straight into my eyes for the first time.

"The nurse reported to me that you received these injuries from your boyfriend. Your neck is badly sprained. There might even be some torn ligaments judging from the amount of pain that you're in. And I can see bruising on your throat. Miss Harris, if you hadn't been honest about how this happened to you, I wouldn't have felt that I could say this to you. But I want to tell you something and I hope that you'll hear my words and think long and hard about it. And what I want to say is this: I see a lot of women come in here with injuries done to them by their husbands or boyfriends and they always go back to their men. And then I've seen a few of the same women come in again—and it's too late for me to help them. They leave here in a body bag. It's not going to stop, Miss Harris. It's going to get worse. I know that you think you love him and that you can stop it, but I honestly doubt if you can. This is very serious, and you need to protect yourself. You need to leave him. Just think about it, OK?"

I stared at this doctor who looked like someone's kindly grandfather. He had just said things to me that left me feeling even more shell-shocked than I already was. I could only nod my head and whisper, "Thank you, doctor," as he squeezed my hand. No one had ever spoken to me like that. I'd never allowed myself to believe that things could get any worse than they already were during our fights, but his words rang true—and even though I couldn't deal with it right that minute, I knew that I would never be able to forget what he'd said to me.

And now, the next morning, I could still hear the doctor's earnest words reverberating in my mind. I shook them out of my head as I latched my suitcase. I needed to think for the moment and my only thought now was to get as far away from Lindsey as possible. I was headed to the airport. I wanted and needed my family.

Walking as quietly as possible, I slipped out of the front door and struggled to carry my heavy suitcase down to the large wooden gates guarding our estate and the cab that waited on the other side. Two hours later I was at LAX, waiting to board a plane that would take me to Tulsa and my six sisters. They didn't know that I was coming. I hadn't had time to call. But I knew that I'd be welcomed with tenderness and love. And right now I needed both desperately.

It was dark, cold, and raining in Tulsa as I pulled out of the terminal in my small rental car. It was after midnight, and the roads were almost deserted. I'd had to wait for hours at LAX before I could get a flight out and I was totally spent. After phoning my sister Tommie from the airport, I'd insisted on driving myself to her home.

"I'll be fine, Tommie. I'll drive slowly. I just need you right now. I'll explain when I get there," I said through my tears. Just the sound of her voice had been enough to break down the thin wall of control that I'd managed to maintain all through the flight. And I knew that once I saw her I'd more than likely fall to pieces. I had no more courage left. I was tired of trying to be strong. All I wanted was to have someone take care of me . . . and, for a little while, forget that I had to make the hardest decision of my life: was I going to leave Lindsey?

STORMS

After the bright lights of L.A. I'd forgotten how black and desolate the streets of Tulsa could be in a bad rainstorm. As howling winds made my small car shudder, I leaned forward behind the wheel, trying desperately to see the highway through the heavy downpour. Warm lights spilling through windows of snug houses seemed to mock me as I drove by them. I turned my tear-streaked face away and tried not to think of my own home in Bel-Air.

The rain and wind pounding against the windshield unwillingly brought back memories of another rainy day seven years before. My mind flashed back to Producer's Workshop and the image of Mick Fleetwood dropping sheets of glass in the parking lot for the background on "Gold Dust Woman." The shards of breaking glass against wet pavement lent an eerie sound quality that was brilliant. The stark contrast between that happy day before *Rumours* hit the airwaves and this one was so shocking that I began to sob.

A chill went through me as the song played in my head. It was a song about digging your grave with a silver spoon; about heartless lovers shattering your illusions of love and tauntingly asking if you can pick up the pieces and go home. Was I the pale shadow of a woman facing the darkness? In my heart, I knew I was.

Twenty minutes later I was climbing a long stretch of hill into my sister's suburban neighborhood. It was pitch black, and as I eased to a stop at the stop sign I breathed a sigh of relief that I was less than a mile away from Tommie's house. The rain was coming down harder now, slashing against the car as though heaven itself had unleashed its fury. All I could think about was pulling into my sister's driveway and feeling her arms around me. I'd cried myself out on the long drive to her home and now I was numb.

In life there are moments when one can look back and clearly see when one decision—one seemingly meaningless act—changed your destiny. For no apparent reason, I glanced down at my lap and realized that my seatbelt was undone. Reaching down, I clasped it shut, feeling foolish about doing so when I was only minutes away from my destination. Turning right, I hit the gas on the two-lane blacktop, thinking of nothing but seeing my sister's face after a hellish day. Within seconds I realized that something was terribly wrong. I was no longer on the paved road. Instead, I was somehow on the flooded grass embankment next to it. And I knew I was going to crash.

I saw a huge tree haloed straight ahead in the glare of my headlights and as I desperately hit the brakes nothing happened. Instead of slowing down, my car accelerated, hydroplaning on the rain-soaked grass. As the tree rushed toward me I felt not panic but a sense of inner peace, for there were no decisions to be made. My fate was sealed. Whether I survived or not was in God's hands. As my car hit the tree with a loud crash of twisting metal and breaking glass, time stood still. Thrown forward with a force unlike any I'd ever felt, my head hit the dashboard as I heard a scream and with a surreal feeling I knew the voice was mine.

And then silence. Stunned, I sat in the wreckage of my small car, listening to the storm raging outside. I didn't know if I was hurt. I couldn't feel anything. I stared at the shattered windshield, knowing that if not for my seatbelt I would have been flung through it. Terror washed over me. I pushed hard on the driver's door and clumsily climbed out of the car, shivering in the cold and wet as I looked up and down the road for headlights. There was only darkness. No sign of life anywhere. I managed to walk a few steps and then doubled over as nausea coursed through me.

Nobody's coming, a small voice said in my mind as fear threatened to send me into hysterics. Suddenly it was replaced by a stronger voice of reassuring reason. *You're going to be fine. Just get back in the car. You need to get your purse and try to walk to Tommie's. You can make it to Tommie's, but you need to do it now. You need to get out of the storm.*

Without hesitating I climbed back into the wreckage and closed the door against the rain. The contents of my purse were spilled everywhere and in a daze I looked for my wallet and phone book. Encumbered by my neck brace, I slowly and painfully searched the floor of the car. Finding them under the seat, I clutched them to me as though they could pull me back to reality and wake me from a bad dream. Pushing on the door to once again climb outside, I struggled with the handle. It wouldn't open. I sat back and looked at the passenger door, only a few feet away. I started to crawl over to it clumsily but stopped as sharp pain pierced my palm. A shard of shattered glass was sticking out from it and I cried out as I wrenched it free. Wary of the climb now, I renewed my efforts on the driver's door and finally managed to wrench it open, leaving smears of blood on the handle.

STORMS

Grateful to be outside, I pulled my overcoat around me and started walking. Twenty minutes later I pounded on Tommie's door and fell into her arms, incoherently trying to explain about the car crash through my tears. After putting me to bed and bandaging my hand, she drove to the accident site with my brother-in-law. I could hear them talking worriedly in the living room as I drifted off to sleep, exhausted.

The next day I learned that my rental car was totaled. It wasn't a surprise. What was, however, is that if I hadn't hit the tree head-on, then my car would have continued for another three feet. And those three feet would have taken me over the edge of a fifty-foot cement drop-off into an empty reservoir below. I would have died. And even more chilling, if I had gone out the passenger side door, I could have stepped over the edge in the darkness and fallen to my death.

It was too much for me to take in. But as the days passed I tried to come to terms with the miracle of my survival: my inexplicable fastening of my seat belt and the old tree that had not taken but saved my life. I'd escaped death at least twice in one night and what was I going to do about it? What was I going to do with the miracle of my second chance?

Lindsey's persistent phone calls over the past week for me to come home had become so urgent that I knew I had to go back. He seemed badly shaken over the accident and wanted me home. So I left despite my family's objections. I'd told my sisters about my life now in Fleetwood Mac's world: about the drugs, the lifestyle, Lindsey's frightening anger, the aching loneliness, and my desire for a career of my own. I couldn't bring myself to tell them about what the kindly doctor had said to me. I couldn't bear to think about it, much less repeat those words out loud. But even without telling them this dire warning, they wanted me to stay in Tulsa, safe and sound, until I made life decisions that were, in their view, cut and dried. They thought that I needed to leave Lindsey, or at least ask for a separation. And I knew they were right—but I loved him. So for me, it wasn't so cut and dried.

If I separated from Lindsey and it became permanent, I would also be saying goodbye to my Fleetwood Mac family—at least for a good long while. I readily admitted that as a family we were incredibly dysfunctional, but I had grown to love each and every member of the band and the inner circle that surrounded them. And unlike Stevie, whose breakup with Lindsey had resulted in constant contact for almost eight years now, I wasn't in his band.

I realized, of course, that this was the kind of pain that every person must go through in the event of a "divorce," but it filled me with a sense of loss and incredible sadness. My time spent with these brilliant, creative people had been some of the happiest of my life—and also some of the worst.

Upon my return Lindsey welcomed me with open arms. No mention was made of the reason why I'd left for Tulsa. It was like it had always been after he flew into a rage at me—only this time I no longer believed that it would never happen again. I knew that the doctor at Century City Hospital was right. I knew that it would happen again—maybe next month or six months later, but it would happen—and knowing that, believing that, was worse than anything I had gone through so far. Because how insane is it when you have to leave the man you love because you can no longer deal with the fear?

Worried about my soft-tissue back injuries from the car accident, Lindsey hovered over me, bringing back memories of Paris, when I'd been

Lindsey in Bel-Air.

so ill with pneumonia. And it felt so good to once again be the center of his loving attention that it was easy to forget how upset I'd been when my car went off the road—and I was too exhausted, weak, and injured to deal with the reason I'd been there in the first place.

Over the next two weeks, I grew weaker as the pain increased in my back. Finally, my doctor insisted that I spend at least a week in the hospital where I could have complete bed rest, intravenous painkillers, and intense physical therapy. Five days before Christmas, I was admitted into Cedars-Sinai Hospital in West Hollywood. Lindsey didn't want me to check in. He wanted me to go with him to Palo Alto to spend the holidays with his family. My doctor was shocked that I would even consider a trip, so despite Lindsey's insistence I did what I knew I had to do. I went to the hospital.

Hours after I checked in, Lindsey left for Northern California. I felt a bit sorry for myself, but I completely understood his wish to not disappoint his mother and brothers. *No one wants to spend Christmas in a hospital room,* I told myself, as I stared out the window wishing I were anywhere but there.

The days passed tediously, but I got much needed rest and on Christmas Eve, I called Sara. She, too, was spending the holidays alone. Mick had left for England to spend Christmas with his daughters and Jenny, and she was feeling as forlorn and lonely as I. We talked for hours and at precisely midnight, Sara opened her Christmas present from Mick. With the crinkle and rip of wrapping paper, we made countless guesses over what could possibly be inside the large box that he'd left for her.

"It's from Maxfield Bleu!" Sara laughed breathlessly. "I know that's your favorite store now, Carol, and I love their clothes too! I hope it's something by Armani!"

"Open it, Sara! I'm dying to find out what it is. I'm already jealous!" I said as I laughed with her.

"It's a . . . it's a blue something . . . a blue . . . what the hell?"

I heard a clunk of the phone and the sounds of a box being dropped onto the floor. I could here a faint "Oh my God, are you kidding me?" as I shouted, "Pick up the phone! What is it?"

Sara's stunned voice answered, "Well, it's a dress, Carol. It's a friggin' *huge, huge, ugly dress!*"

"What do you mean, *huge?*" I asked, thinking that perhaps the dress was long, or had lots of fabric to it.

"I mean it's a *giant* dress! It's got to be at least a size twelve and I wear a four! You could get three of me into it, and it's the ugliest dress I've ever seen. I'm not kidding. I didn't even know that Maxfield's carried anything this ugly!" And we both began to laugh and we couldn't stop. We laughed until we choked and I had to drop the phone myself for a drink of water.

"What was he thinking? Did he mean for this icky dress to go to his sister Sally or something? I mean, *jeez,* you'd think he'd at least know my size by now, Carol. Dammit!" Sara screeched.

"Well at least you got a present, Sara!" I said and we both began to giggle all over again. Sara was well aware of the fact that I never, ever got a Christmas present from Lindsey. Lindsey hated to shop for gifts. It just wasn't something he enjoyed and as a result, I'd gotten used to never having a Christmas present from him. He was incredibly generous to me all year long and was always happy to send me off shopping. But if I wanted a Christmas present, I had to go buy it for myself. Sometimes I *would* buy a dress or a pair of shoes. But most years, I just forgot about it.

Lindsey and I always bought gifts for everyone else and I would get one for him, for I loved to buy him presents. I didn't have a problem spending hours inside stores because like a lot of women, I loved to shop. I would spend weeks and sometimes even months planning his birthday and Christmas gifts—and to me, that was more fun than getting anything from him. The year before, I'd shopped for hours in art galleries, and I'd found the perfect gift: a piece of art that was composed of three different photographs of Elvis encased in one beautiful, stark frame. It had a piece of chicken wire under glass across all three eight by ten rare photos and the effect was incredible. He'd loved it. This year, I'd not been able to do anything and it made me sad.

"Well, at least you'll never have to open a big box and find the world's ugliest blue dress inside of it, Carol . . . Mick must have been so high when he bought it that he was hallucinating or something. Or did he get me mixed up with someone else? Maybe this is for the Blob! I bet it is!" Sara squealed, and we were hysterical as we remembered Mick's embarrassing phone love affair with the very large, strange woman. By 2 A.M., we were still giggling and gossiping and the night nurse had to make me hang up the phone. I needed my rest, she said primly. With a heartfelt "Merry Christmas," Sara and I finally said goodbye. It had turned into a great Christmas Eve for both of us after all.

On December 28, I was finally discharged and I gratefully went home. Lindsey arrived late in the afternoon and found me propped up on the living room couch. He'd had a nice Christmas, he told me, talking happily about his young nieces Amy and Laura as he showed me the children's books that they each had given him as presents. He handed me the books and I flipped on the TV as Lindsey flopped down beside me on the couch. The news was on and a cold wind seemed to blow through the room as we struggled to comprehend what was playing out before our eyes on television. There were pictures of a small yacht anchored in Marina Del Rey and a bodybag lying on the wooden boards of a pier. We listened in horror to the newscaster's voice.

"The body of Dennis Wilson has been found minutes ago after a search by the Coast Guard. Reports are coming in that Wilson was reported missing by friends after diving off a boat during a party. He has apparently drowned. Dennis Wilson is dead at the age of thirty-six."

As pictures flashed of Dennis playing with the Beach Boys, Dennis surfing and laughing, I started to sob. *"No, Lindsey! No! Not Dennis! It's not Dennis!* There's a mistake! They've made a mistake, please, please, *please . . ."* Crying hysterically, I struggled to stand as Lindsey held me tightly. His face was white with shock as he murmured sympathetic words to calm me. Together we tried to understand and accept what we now knew was true: Dennis was gone. Forever.

Ed Roach and Dennis Wilson.

In the days that followed we learned that Dennis had been partying for three days straight—something he'd done many times before on the road with us. Only this time the people he chose to hang out with didn't watch over him as the Fleetwood Mac family always did. They either didn't understand or didn't care that Dennis needed special attention when he was that out of control.

We always kept an eye on him. We never left him alone when we knew he was having one of his "parties," because we knew he was like a child and a danger to himself—at risk of overdosing or just doing something stupid. Like diving off a boat for a swim and hitting his head on a rock, knocking himself unconscious. I could not accept or believe that the people who were supposedly his friends didn't even notice he was missing for quite a while. And when they did it was too late. And I truly believe that if one of us had been there, then maybe Dennis would not have drowned. We might have gotten to him in time. And I know that I'll never get over his death.

Photography © Ed Roach, roach-clips.com

As Lindsey spent more and more time in the studio working on his album, tension once again saturated the atmosphere of our house. The success of Stevie's *Bella Donna* had fueled Lindsey's already cutthroat competitive battle with her and it now seemed to be all-out war. I'd never seen him push himself so hard, and I'd never seen him work with this level of feverish intensity. Whenever we were together—on the rare occasions that he ventured out of the garage studio—his eyes seemed to spark and flash with his internal struggles with his own creativity. He'd entered into another world where nothing mattered except for the music. And, for the first time, he was unwilling to let me hear any of it.

He did, however, ask for my help with the lyrics to songs that I'd never heard. With a smile I told him that I'd do my best. Not being a poet myself, I turned to the professionals. I pored over poetry books, copying passages that seemed to create imagery that I felt might be perfect for Lindsey's songs—whatever they might be. As I turned my selections over to him, he seemed both happy and pleased as he disappeared back into the studio, taking my pages with him.

On a day when rain was softly falling outside I walked into Lindsey's studio and asked him plaintively if he could stop recording for a little while. Could he come outside with me and play in the rain? I told him that I missed him and needed to spend time with him. And as I stood looking like a child in a raincoat that hung down to my feet, he gently took my face in his hands and kissed me softly. "I can't, Carol. I have to work on a song."

As I nodded and walked out the door into the rain I glanced over my shoulder and saw him staring at me with a look that seemed to speak volumes. It was a look of regret and longing in the eyes of a face filled with feverish passion for something that was much more important to him than me: *the*

Lindsey in Bel-Air.

music. And as I walked down the beautiful streets surrounding our estate, I felt in my heart that there would never come a time when I—or any woman—would be more important to Lindsey than that. And while I'd always accepted and understood that truth, it was becoming harder and harder to live with.

I walked through the mist, thinking about the man inside the studio. I remembered his smile on the day that we met—the blue of his eyes when he looked into mine, and the passion between us that remained strong as ever. I remembered the laughter as we held hands in countless dressing rooms, breathless with the intoxication of a sold-out concert and the wild nights of crazed fans, cocaine, and limousines that went with each and every show. And I thought about the dark days when his face flickered with self-doubt over music that was playing nonstop through a mind that seemed to never have one second without its drumbeat coursing through it. And I knew that to be with a man like this for almost eight years had been a gift. And to survive it had been a miracle.

It had been the hardest thing I'd ever done in my life. I'd had to learn how to deal with a tortured genius, a spoiled rock star, a man who could be so gentle at one moment and a frightening stranger the next. And for the first time I admitted to myself that, knowing what I did now, I should have turned away the day we met. But I didn't know. So on that cold, rainy day in November 1976 we looked at each other and didn't look away for eight years.

Eight years of living in the world of Fleetwood Mac. Eight years of amazing memories of laughter, music, and adventure. Eight years of friendships with people who were brilliant, loving, funny, and complete originals. And eight years in which I'd seen gold and glittering rooms serving as a backdrop to ugly, unforgivable acts of people who were trapped inside a world of which they'd dreamed—only to find themselves imprisoned by their own superstardom. We were all changed now. We were all suffering. I doubted that any one of us could have honestly said that we were happy. And though I knew the reasons why, I refused to accept the fact that there was nothing any of us could do about it. But I knew that I wanted to be happy again. No matter what it took, I wanted to be happy.

I knew that life changed everyone. But life with a superstar band changed people in ways that anyone on the outside couldn't even begin to understand. It had changed me—and I knew that I didn't like who I was any longer. Before I entered the world of Fleetwood Mac on Lindsey's arm, I was both proud and sure of myself—but not any longer. The only time that I felt good about myself as a person was when I was at a production company learning about the film industry. And I wanted to be the Carol Ann I once was. I needed to find her. But could I do that if I stayed by Lindsey's side? I realized there was a chance that Lindsey wouldn't like me if I changed, but it was a risk that I had to take.

As tears spilled down my already rain-streaked face I knew that I had to ask Lindsey for a separation. So many things had made me come to this decision: the deaths of people I loved; my miscarriage and Lindsey's reaction to it; the career that I was longing for but Lindsey didn't support; my own miraculous escape from death in Tulsa and the knowledge that I'd been given another chance to change my life.

And most of all, the realization that no matter what I did or didn't do, no matter how hard I tried or how long I waited, the anger inside of Lindsey that could manifest itself in ways that left me terrified had only grown worse over time. And I didn't know if I had the strength or the courage to withstand much more. I still loved him. And I believed that he loved me. But I now had to face the fact that maybe that wasn't enough to save us from everything that had gone wrong. I needed time on my own to decide what I needed to do.

Over the next few months Lindsey and I spent hours talking about a trial separation. Talks full of tears, love, and pain that hurt so much that sometimes I felt I could barely breathe. But finally it was settled. At my insistence, his business managers had drawn up a prenuptial agreement between us. I didn't want Lindsey's money. I signed papers that gave me $2,000 a month for rent and groceries for a period of three years—and signed away my rights to the fortune that I could most likely have had as his "unofficial" common-law wife in the event of a permanent breakup.

I had a lawyer—legally I had to be represented before signing the agreement—who advised me of what I was signing away. Because we'd lived together for almost eight years, I had established all of the prerequisites for a strong "palimony" case. I could have taken him to court if I'd wanted a large settlement of cash. And I undoubtedly would have won, according to my attorney. I'd lived for Lindsey night and day for almost eight years—made homes for him, took care of him, and actively participated in helping to further his career. But the thought of all that ugliness if I followed my attorney's advice and sued made me feel sick. I also knew something that my lawyer didn't—that Lindsey could be a very scary person when he was angry, and it just wasn't worth it. Besides, everyone that I knew had a lot of money and they weren't happy. I just didn't want it.

I'd never been with Lindsey because of what he was or how much money he had. I was with him because we loved each other and it was important to me that everyone knew this. That Lindsey knew this. Lindsey and his business managers were understandably surprised and pleased at my decision—and the inner circle was shocked. But to me it was all about my dignity, proving my integrity, and protecting myself. I knew that I'd done the right thing.

I found a house on Benedict Canyon, fifteen minutes' drive away from Bel-Air. Lindsey didn't want me far away, he said. And even after I'd "moved in," I spent the next four months in Bel-Air, only going to my newly rented house to grab clothes. Even though officially I had the space and independence I needed, my reality was that Lindsey never wanted me to spend a night away from our home. And I didn't. Because I, too, was finding it hard to walk away and do what I knew I needed to do: have time away from Lindsey.

But that was all about to change. Lindsey had to make an unexpected trip to Europe for three weeks. He asked me to go with him, and even though I didn't really want to go, I packed my clothes. An hour before we departed for the airport Lindsey paced while I searched for my passport. I couldn't find it. It seemed that fate had stepped in to separate us for at least three weeks and there was nothing to be done about it. As the limo pulled out of our driveway I got into my car and drove to Benedict Canyon to spend my first night in my house. As the wind blew through my hair from the open car window, I felt a sense of excitement and freedom. For the first time in years, I was truly on my own.

During the days and weeks that Lindsey was gone, I spent time with Mark and Mary learning more about the film industry, and I continued with my acting classes. I was in my coach's regular class now, sharing the stage with about a dozen other actors. And I loved it. As I was leaving class one night Mr. Richards called me back inside.

"Carol, I have to tell you something. I think it's important. When I first met you, you never looked me in the eye. You walked with your head down, never smiling, never laughing. In the past few weeks you're like a different person! You're bright and cheerful and I just wanted to tell you that whatever's happened to change you, you have to keep it up. You can't go back to being the way you were. I've been worried about you since the day we met, but now I hope that I no longer have to be."

I listened to him, stunned at what he was telling me. I never realized that I walked with my head down. I never realized that I rarely smiled or laughed. *My God, was it possible? Had I been that unhappy? Had I been so lost?* I understood about the panic attacks, but this I couldn't understand. And I didn't want to believe it, but something inside of me knew that it was true. A lost passport gave me the opportunity to be outside the world of Fleetwood Mac and live a "normal" life for a few brief weeks, and in that short time I'd quickly become a different person. And I knew that until I found out why, I couldn't go back to Bel-Air or Lindsey.

Four days later the phone rang. It was Lindsey. I'd spent the past days waiting for this phone call. I'd planned exactly what I wanted to say. But when I heard his voice all of my carefully planned words seemed convoluted and ridiculous. So, in a small voice, I talked to him from my heart. I told him that I couldn't see him for a while. I didn't know for how long. I explained how upset I'd been over what my acting coach had said to me. "I love you, Lindsey, but spending time on my own seems to be good for me. I need to do this for myself—and for you. There's a lot I still need to figure out, and until I do, I can't come home."

I knew that he understood what I was talking about: the miscarriage, the decadence of our lifestyle, and the fights. I just couldn't deal with the fights any longer. He listened silently as I spoke. In a broken voice I finished by saying, "I know I might lose you but I have to take care of me right now, Lindsey. I'll call you when I feel ready to come home. I love you, and I hope that you'll wait, but if you can't, I understand." I could tell that he was crying and I knew that both our hearts were breaking. But I couldn't do anything but pray that in the end, if we were meant to be together, then I would ultimately return to Bel-Air and a new life with Lindsey Buckingham.

I didn't see Lindsey over the next several months. I led a quiet life, coming and going from visits to video sets and my acting classes. At the beginning of July I returned home to my house on Benedict and found a cassette propped up against my front door. It was Lindsey's new album. With a sense of excitement I rushed inside and opened the cellophane wrapping. I gasped in surprise when I saw the dedication "This album is for Carol Ann" on the liner notes. With trembling hands I put it into my cassette player and sat on the floor to listen. As one song after another blasted through my living room, I sat stunned.

Every single song on his album, except one, was about our relationship. Songs that were so full of vindictive rage, blame, love, and longing that by the end of the record I felt heartbroken, shattered, and enraged. The songs painted a picture of our relationship that was so inaccurate and so unfair that I was stunned. His anger was obvious. His unwillingness to even mention how his unfocused fury against me was the main reason I'd left seemed both cowardly and indefensible.

Half of the songs were of love and longing. And these I understood, for I felt the same as he in spite of the problems we had together. But the vitriolic blame and slanted truths of the rest of them were of such magnitude that I started throwing things against the wall in fury. I felt violated. The lyrics on "Bang the Drum" were taken from our last phone conversation when I told him that I couldn't see him for a while because of my shock, dismay, and fear over what my acting coach had said to me. "Play in the Rain" not only quoted my exact words the day I asked him to spend time with me, but also recounted how lonely he knew I felt. "I Must Go" made it seem as if I were the only person in the world of Fleetwood Mac who touched cocaine. In this song, he told the world that I left in the morning and that I didn't come back, which left him all alone. Over and over again he sang that I needed to leave the "little drug" alone.

As I listened to this song I thought about the days that I'd left him in the morning and hadn't returned until night: days that I'd spent at the production company learning about the film industry, and other days when I'd gone to a hotel room to literally hide from him after an explosion of anger forced me to. Yet, to the world—and our friends—I would be the one who was to blame for the end of our relationship. I'd told only Sara the truth about it. In the lyrics on this record (as in real life) no mention was made of his explosive rage or the fact that I had tried so hard to stay in spite of it. And no mention was made that when I did cocaine I did it with the rest of the Fleetwood Mac family—and Lindsey himself. Although weed was his drug of choice, he snorted cocaine on and off the road, in the recording studio, and at almost all of the Fleetwood Mac gatherings just like every other member of the band and the inner circle. After listening to the cassette, it was obvious to me that Lindsey's fury over the fact that I'd left him had been poured into his music. And the truth behind the music was of little importance.

But after the first rush of anger my mind knew what my heart didn't want to accept. Lindsey was not a man who ever took no for an answer. Not from Stevie, not from the band, and certainly not from the woman he loved. The separation I'd asked for and the reasons I'd given to him he'd taken like a slap in the face. He was angry. And *Go Insane* was a message to me. He loved me—but I'd better do what he told me to. He was the one with the power. He was the one who got to call the shots, no matter what I might have needed or wanted.

But one thing he didn't seem or want to understand was this: I had a little power of my own. I could decide who I spent the rest of my life with—and as of that moment, no matter how much I still loved him, I could never forgive or forget this ultimate insult. He'd lost me. *Go Insane* was the epitaph for our relationship.

As the weeks passed my phone seemed to ring at all hours of the day and night. It was Lindsey, leaving messages for me to please call, please see him—but I just couldn't. Most of his calls I never returned. When I did pick up at the sound of his voice it was to tell him that he'd hurt me more than words could express and I was not ready to talk about us. I was just too hurt. The chain which had kept us together was now broken. "The Chain" and its lyrics that had long symbolized everlasting unity to us all now spoke to me in an entirely new way.

> *Down comes the night*
> *Run in the shadows*
> *Damn your love*
> *Damn your lies*

STORMS

❧

In August a reporter from *Rolling Stone* phoned. They were doing a four-page feature titled "Lindsey Buckingham: Lonely Guy." It was about Lindsey's *Go Insane* album and our breakup. The reporter kept trying to goad me into telling "my side" of the story of why Lindsey and I split, but I wouldn't. I wasn't willing to disclose the intimate details of the real reasons I left: the truth behind our fights and my unhappiness with the life I'd found myself living.

As a joke, I told him that I still liked cocaine, and then quickly told him that I no longer did it. I didn't expound upon it—in my naivete I assumed that I didn't need to. I hadn't done cocaine in months. It had been hard at first to stop doing something that had, during my years with Fleetwood Mac, become such a "normal" part of my existence. With the help of my therapist, I now realized how self-destructive I'd become. It was much easier to do a line with Sara when I was feeling upset or depressed than to let myself feel the pain of what was behind it. Cocaine made me feel better—it made me forget just how much I hurt inside and I'd never realized before that I had to feel the pain or I could never move on or heal. Through therapy, I was being given the tools to leave it behind—and work was a very important part of my healing.

In my new world, none of my industry friends used cocaine—5 A.M. call times and sixteen-hour shoots made it very difficult to party and still be successful as a member of a video crew. And, like them, I wanted to be successful very, very badly. With this as yet another motivation, I'd been determined to remain completely sober. I now understood the insidious danger of it and I was determined to do my best to leave it behind.

But of course, when the article came out, the reporter wrote that I said I still loved it without bothering to print that I *also* said that I no longer used it. I shook my head wearily as I read it. In the next issue of *Rolling Stone* there were five letters to the editors where the public wrote that they didn't understand how any woman could live with anyone with as big an ego as Lindsey's—and I couldn't believe it. What did the world expect from a rock star? Of course he had an ego—he deserved to—and his accomplishments spoke for themselves. I sighed as I thought to myself, *I guess Lindsey's not too thrilled with this interview either.*

The last letter made me cringe—it was from a woman who said that she would *love* to be Lindsey's girlfriend and suggestively said that maybe she could show him just how much sometime. *OK, that's a bit creepy,* I thought as I gazed at the magazine, *now he's going to get stalked!*

I went on with the new life I'd started to build for myself, spending time now as a wardrobe assistant to one of my new friends. And I found the work both grueling and exhilarating. Three months after starting as her assistant, I was ready to become a costume designer with an assistant of my own. The music video shoots that I was hired for were more stressful and more exciting than anything I'd ever known. And with the support of the new friends I was making in the "real world," the aching loneliness I felt whenever I thought of Lindsey became tolerable.

For there were nights, nights when I ached for him so much that I actually doubled over in pain. Nights when I cried so hard and so long that the dawn would creep over the hillside accompanied by my sobs. But no matter how much pain I was in, how much I wanted to go home to Lindsey, I knew that I couldn't. I saw clearly now what I would be returning to: a life where betrayal was as commonplace as that day's joint, line of cocaine, or vodka tonic. A life where the love between the members of Fleetwood Mac had become simmering rage and that rage tainted everything and everyone around it. The love was still there, but oh, it had been so long since they'd shown it—and I wondered if they would ever show it again.

I believed for so many years that the love I shared with Lindsey would survive anything and everything within the world of Fleetwood Mac. But now I knew that that only happened in fairy tales. And while Fleetwood Mac had indeed created its own fantasy existence, it was no longer one in which I wished to live. I made a choice. I didn't want to live in a kingdom where the inhabitants were unhappy and lonely. That world had numbed us all to the fact that beneath the fame and despite the wealth, we would never be happy unless somehow our own value as people could be based on more than record sales and the designer clothes we wore.

Almost a year from the time of my phone call to Lindsey telling him that I wouldn't be coming home, he arrived unannounced at my door. There was a white Porsche sitting in the driveway and he told me he'd rented it just for this "special" day. There was something he wanted to ask me, he said, and gestured for me to get into the car. Without saying anything,

I climbed inside. I knew that Lindsey was now living with another woman, and I, in turn, had been dating an art director.

So I was stunned when he took my hand and once again asked me to marry him. He told me that he loved me and that he wanted to produce an album where I would be the artist and he my producer. That way, he said, I'd have my own money and everything in our world would be perfect. I closed my eyes for a second and remembered the last time he'd proposed to me so many years before. I remembered my joy and excitement—and I remembered how as the years passed and the fights between us shattered me time and time again, I kept putting off our wedding until finally neither of us spoke of it. I sat silent as I listened to his new plans, and when he was done speaking I gave him my answer: no.

"It's too late, Lindsey. I have a new life now and I'm happy." Seeing the hurt look on his face, I gently continued, "I'm not a singer. I'm a costume designer and I'm really good at my job. Lindsey, I'll always love and care for you, but I can't go back to living in a world where nothing matters but music. It was so bad at the end—you weren't happy and neither was I—and I can't go back to that, baby. I'm sorry, Lindsey."

I kissed him one last time before I climbed out of the car and walked through the fading daylight to the shadowy entrance of my home. As I opened the door and stepped inside, I knew I was walking away from Fleetwood Mac and Lindsey forever. And I knew that I'd made the right decision.

Nine years before, a young girl had fallen in love with a man who turned out to be a prince in the kingdom of Fleetwood Mac. Overnight her life had been transformed. She'd lived in Lear jets, five-star hotels, and mansions. She had material wealth beyond her wildest dreams. But unlike the fairy tales of her childhood, it was a world where love could not triumph over darkness. And in the end that girl felt lost, lonely, and afraid. In real life, sometimes the girl doesn't marry the prince. Sometimes she walks away from the castle and off into the sunset alone . . . finding true happiness in the real world beyond.

EPILOGUE

Three years later, in 1987, I was sitting on an airplane reading a copy of *Rolling Stone* when I came across a review of *Tango in the Night*, Lindsey's fifth album with Fleetwood Mac. In it they spoke at length about Lindsey's songs "Caroline" and "Tango in the Night." The reviewer wrote that these two songs were about a past love and were brilliant, angry, and poignant. I knew, of course, that both songs were written about and to me. But it would take me months to find the courage to listen to them. And when I did I was struck by the anger and longing in Lindsey's song "Caroline," as well as the love expressed for me in "Tango in the Night," from a man who had once been the center of my universe. And I cried. For the love I'd shared with Lindsey came back to me with the force and fury of a hurricane. I knew then that Lindsey's voice would always speak to me through his songs.

Today his voice no longer has the power to haunt me, but it always, always makes me stop and remember.

I went on to have a successful career as a costume designer. I designed the wardrobe for the music videos of Billy Idol, Mötley Crüe, Ben E. King, Jon Bon Jovi, Slaughter, James Brown, KISS, Queensryche, and Guns N' Roses' debut videos "Welcome to the Jungle" and "Sweet Child of Mine"—along with 150 other artists. And, to make the circle complete, I was booked for the pick-up shots for Fleetwood Mac's "Little Lies."

By that time, I was so busy that sometimes I would be shooting two videos on the same day—and because of this, I was on another set when Lindsey shot his segments. Which was how I wanted it. It was still a bit soon for me to take any encounters with him lightly, and I'm sure that he felt the same way. I did, however, arrive in time to spend hours with John McVie and Mick—and it was both sad and wonderful to be with them again. As the years passed, I would spend time with every member of Fleetwood Mac at weddings, baby showers, and chance encounters.

STORMS

In the early 1990s, I was reunited with my daughter and I learned that her adoptive parents had kept their promises to me. My daughter was not only highly educated, she was beautiful, funny, and one of the sweetest women you could hope to meet. It was one of the happiest days of my life when I once again was able to put my arms around her and tell her that I loved her. A short time later, I attended her wedding.

In 1993 I saw Lindsey at the funeral of our beloved housekeeper Desi. We'd lost her to a sudden heart attack and both Lindsey and I were devastated. I sat next to him at the memorial service and he held me close as I sobbed. The very last thing that he said to me before I walked out of the church with Sara Fleetwood was, "You still have the most fragile feel to your shoulders of anyone I've ever met." We stood and looked at each other, faces wet with tears, and we smiled.

And then we walked away—back to our separate lives.

INDEX

Buckingham, work, 173
Harris, boredom, 212
Studio D, 163, 178
  recording, 191
Village Voice (newspaper), negative *Rumours* review,
  37–38
Visitor, The (album), 325, 344
vodka, odor (permeation), 199
Vogue (magazine), 144–145, 219

W

Warner Brothers
  executives, phone calls, 143
  money men (executives), 42
  presence, 215
  Rumours release (February 1977), 40
"Watching the Detectives," 184
Weiss, Dr. (neurologist), 320–323
  worries, 333–334
Welch, Bob (introduction, Wong arrangement). *See*
  Fleetwood Mac
"Welcome to the end" gift. *See* Courage
"Welcome to the Jungle" (video), 372
Wembly Stadium (London), *Tusk* performance,
  298–299
West Berlin, *Tusk* performance, 293
"What Makes You Think You're the One" (recording),
  159
"What You Won't Do for Love," 173
White House, visit, 182
Wild Heart (album), 344
Williams, Dr. (specialist), 115–117
Wilson, Brian, 221
  genius, 58
  party, appearance, 232

Wilson, Carl, 221
Wilson, Dennis
  Bad Boy of Summer, 202
  breakup. *See* McVie
  clothes, purchase. *See* Charles Galley; Maxfield Bleu
  death, report, 360–361
  distraction, 216
  introduction, 202–203
  lies, 233–235
    impact. *See* McVie
  McVie
    anger, 220
    infatuation, 203–204
    love, 215–216
  stories. *See* Harris; Recor
  unconsciousness, 258
Wimbledon Cup (1981), competition, 319
Woman Most Likely to Uncover Hidden Motives, vote,
  16
Wong, Judy (secretary)
  dress, loan, 92
  introduction, 14
  knowledge, 63
"World Turning," Melbourne performance, 272–274

Y

"You Make Loving Fun," 11
  rehearsal, 27
  San Francisco performance, 45

Z

Zoo. *See* Mick Fleetwood's Zoo